MYTH
AMERICA

MYTH
AMERICA

Volume I

Edited with an Introduction by
Patrick Gerster
and
Nicholas Cords
Century College

BRANDYWINE PRESS • St. James, New York

ISBN 1-881-089-37-1

1st Printing 1997

Telephone Orders: 1-800-345-1776

Printed in the United States of America

But how do they spend their time, think you?
Faith, in imagining and framing fictions to
themselves of things never done nor never likely
to be done, in believing these their fictions, and
in following these beliefs. This is the reason why
they . . . hate to be interrupted in their airy
castle-buildings.

Joseph Hall,
The Discovery of the New World (1605)

In the beginning all the world was America.

John Locke

The past is never dead. It's not even past.

William Faulkner

Contents

III

Myths of Nationalism and Jacksonian Democracy   **85**

IV

Myths of Sectionalism, Slavery, and Expansionism   **149**

V

Myths of the Civil War and Reconstruction   195

Preface

The selected historical myths discussed and analyzed in *Myth America* can best be understood as a series of *false beliefs* about America's past. They are false beliefs, however, that have been accepted as true and acted upon as real, and in that acting they have acquired truth. Therefore, myths remain both true and false simultaneously. In fact, the making of myths is a process by which a culture structures its world and perpetuates its grandest dreams.

The idea for *Myth America* grew out of our own teaching experiences. In continuously dealing with students who for the most part were beginning their collegiate study of American history, we found that a thematic approach to the nation's past was stimulating. The theme of myth as threads within the diverse tapestry of cultural experience proved to be especially engaging.

While offering a strong foundation of classic historical writing and interpretation, *Myth America* includes numerous fresh selections on the Pilgrims, the nature of the Revolution, popular participation in the Revolutionary War, native Americans, the Founding Fathers, Spain and the California missions, the Louisiana Purchase, Confederate women, Robert E. Lee, the Gettysburg Address, and rape in the antebellum and postbellum South. We have been guided in our final selections by a desire to offer articles that voice our mythic theme in a scholarly and provocative way: articles that offer students readability and current interest without sacrificing the demands of thorough historical scholarship. We occasionally refer to historiography, for historians function as the culture's preeminent storytellers and so maintain their seemingly contradictory roles of mythmakers and myth-debunkers.

PATRICK GERSTER
NICHOLAS CORDS

To Carole and Maggie

Acknowledgments

As the past itself is a collaborative enterprise, so too is this book. We think the mythic theme applies across the entire landscape of American history, and we gratefully acknowledge those whose efforts came in various ways to be reflected in the final product. Our greatest thanks must be extended to our professional colleagues; their many years of scholarly effort comprise the very heart of this work. Without their passion to explain and interpret the past, their intellectual skills, their narrative talents, this book would not have been possible. Students have helped us both to hone our ideas and to gauge better the critical reception of individual selections. Ms. Patricia Loving of our college library staff abetted computer searches of interpretive literature. Our families have granted us both support and a sounding board for the joys and problems that cumulatively accrue to such a project. The publishing support system of Brandywine Press, and especially the aid and encouragement of David Burner and Thomas R. West, both as historical colleagues and as editors, were indispensable to bringing our ideas through their editorial journey from mind to printed page. To all of these we offer thanks.

PATRICK GERSTER
NICHOLAS CORDS

Introduction:
Myth and History

"Human Being is a featherless, storytelling animal. . . . We tell stories—myths— about who we are, where we come from, where we are going and how we should live. And the myths we tell become who we are and what we believe—as individuals, families, and cultures."[1]

In *Myth America: A Historical Anthology,* we address these questions: What is myth? What is myth's relationship to history? Why study American history by means of myth?

Myth and history came to life together. In preliterate societies, a sense of origins and traditions was preserved in cultural memory through stories told by elders whose task it was to be custodians of the past. While not always—or even often— factually accurate renditions of the culture's past, myths were able to provide a sense of cultural continuity. Myths have been the traditional stories a culture tells itself about itself.

Today the fashion regarding myth is to associate it with the ancient world—as Greek myths, for example, tell fantastic tales of gods and heroes and collective cultural accomplishments. Also dating from classical times is the common historical usage of *myth* as a pejorative term, a synonym for "lie," "fabrication," or "false belief." Plato declares myths to be "sublime lies," little more than silly beliefs on false parade. Aristotle, on the other hand, describes myths as a treasury of cultural stories about the past that provide meaning and hold together a diverse people. Since Greek times, then, the understanding and use of myth have been ambivalent. Myth may be dismissed as a mutation of historical fact, more false than true, or respected as allegorical, discussing cultural values under images containing a special brand of truth. The use of the term *myth* in American historical studies mirrors this ambivalence with which Western culture has long contended. The term *myth*, as presented in this set of readings, is employed in both ways.

"A historical myth," wrote the American historian Thomas A. Bailey over two decades ago, "is . . . an account or belief which is demonstrably untrue in whole or substantial part."[2] Some scholars are determined to isolate and debunk what they regard as erroneous belief and misguided scholarship. The goal of historical study, as they would have it, is to record history as clean, unadorned fact. The historian must stand as a transparent witness to the occurrences of the past. The truth, if diligently sought and recorded, will out.

An opposite perception of myth has an illustration in Henry Nash Smith's famous study *Virgin Land: The American West as Symbol and Myth*. For Smith, a cultural or social myth, even while often factually false, needs to be sympathetically reckoned with, for it contains an internal treasure—a culture's ideological foundations. Myth, says Smith, is "an intellectual construction that fuses concept and emotion into an image."[3] Myth is, so to speak, a mental movie, with accompanying script, that Americans carry around in their heads regarding their heritage and sense of special destiny. When sensitively deconstructed, myths can be shown to embody American culture's basic beliefs and highest aspirations—honesty, unpretentiousness, optimism, tolerance, hard work, sympathy for the underdog, dedication to perfectionism, an abiding concern for the general well-being, and a special esteem for freedom. The American past is therefore scarcely a dead past. It continues to live within us. Myth lays claim to preserving, repeating, and defending the treasury of wisdom our forebears entrusted to us.

At times both senses of myth are present; on occasion they become nearly indistinguishable. The University of Chicago historian William H. McNeill observes that "myth and history are close kin inasmuch as both explain how things got to be the way they are by telling some sort of story."[4] In the Italian and Spanish languages, for example, the words *history* and *story* are interchangeable. Historians are essentially the storytellers of the tribe, functioning as purveyors of cultural stories. In this sense, historians are mythmakers. And they must be so. Being human, they reflect their personal backgrounds, their times, their methodologies, their current interests including biases and prejudices, and sometimes even their whims. All historical interpretation is both time-bound and ideological—such is the nature of what has been called "the politics of interpretation." Historians, moreover, constantly revise one another's work and sometimes even their own. This process of mythmaking by professional historians—myths as a critical by-product of what historians do—receives major emphasis in this book.

In addition to formal, academic presentation of American history, an assemblage of assumptions, some of them competing, forms a sense of the past. These, too, structure and sustain the illusions and traditional stories—the myths—about America's past. Television and film, two of American culture's favorite media, especially transmit to eager audiences images and re-creations of the past in appealing sight and sound, most often with an eye to drama rather than research and scholarly validity. Historical novels, poetry, political rhetoric, children's literature, paintings, ballads, oral traditions, folklore, political cartoons, tourist shrines, and culturally induced sexist and racist stereotypes contribute in their own ways to our collective impression of the past. In the aggregate they probably represent as consistent and enduring a fund of historical information as is learned in more formal educational settings. As Americans internalize cultural tradition, they fashion a colorful mental mosaic of their history. In acting as if the myths are true, Americans make them true. Policies—even laws—are based on them. The making of myths is a process by which a culture perpetuates its grandest illusions even as it gives substance, order, and stability to its world. The mathematician and philosopher Alfred North Whitehead told a Virginia audience over half a century ago:

The art of a free society consists first in the maintenance of the symbolic code; and secondly in a fearlessness of revision, to secure that the code serves those purposes which satisfy an enlightened reason. Those societies which cannot combine reverence to their symbols with freedom of revision, must ultimately decay either from anarchy, or from the slow atrophy of a life stifled by useless shadows.[5]

Seeking to offer cautionary comment as to American culture's many "useless shadows" while still cultivating a decent respect for "the symbolic code," *Myth America* offers much fresh material that illuminates both. Together with classic essays, readings from scholarship of the 1990s and 1980s add to the master narrative of American history. It is hoped that this selective study of myth and the American experience will launch the reader on an especially rewarding journey through America's storied mythic past.

Notes

1. Sam Keen, "Personal Myths Guide Daily Life: The Stories We Live By," *Psychology Today*, 23 (December 1989), p. 44.
2. Thomas A. Bailey, "The Mythmakers of American History," *The Journal of American History*, 55 (June 1968), p. 5.
3. Henry Nash Smith, *Virgin Land: The American West as Symbol and Myth* (New York, 1950), p. v.
4. William H. McNeill, "Mythistory, or Truth, Myth, History, and Historians," *The American Historical Review*, 91 (February 1986), p. 1.
5. Alfred North Whitehead, *Symbolism: Its Meaning and Effect* (New York, 1959), p. 88.

Credits

MYTH
AMERICA

I

Myths of Early America

The early history of America reflects a European sensibility that for centuries had been nurtured by mythical dreams of a New World. Particularly, the discovery of the New World in the midst of the European Renaissance fed the fiction of America as an Earthly Paradise. A great variety of European explorers, popular writers, mapmakers, conquistadors, and settlers entertained extravagant visions of America as a place of ease and abundance or a continent of epic adventure and unlimited opportunity for economic, religious, or political change and renewal. In America, Europeans could reinvent themselves.

Within this utopian and mythical milieu occurred the discoveries of Christopher Columbus and the explorers who followed him. For the Spaniards in his wake, the sixteenth century—their years of encounter with the mythical Americas—became rather instant legend known to posterity as the *Siglo de Oro*, the century of gold. It was to them their grandest era, an age of explosive confidence, heroic stature, and intoxicating romance. Mythical images and utopian dreams strongly influenced the New World ventures of the French as well. Fantasy and reality merged under French colonial control of northern America to fashion a richly imagined locale of cultural dreams wherein Noble Savages and thoughts of empire could cohabit and flourish.

With this utopian spirit as its creed Englishmen launched their first permanent engagements with the New World. According to some reports, Sir Humphrey Gilbert just prior to his demise in 1583 somewhere in the North Atlantic was sitting on the deck of his ship reading a copy of Sir Thomas More's *Utopia*. Whether he was reading *Utopia* or, as some suggest, the Bible, or whether the account is sheer fabrication, the point is that Gilbert, roughhewn as he may have been, was representative of the breed of Englishmen who early dreamed of New World possibilities and then attempted to realize them. Many of this group, including Gilbert, the Hakluyts, and Sir Walter Raleigh, indeed had read *Utopia*, published in Latin in 1516 and rendered into English in 1551: they were generally well-educated, as well as being soldiers and courtiers (and, in the younger Hakluyt's case, clergyman and publicist). These men reflected the sensibilities of the English Renaissance, one of the most stimulating, productive, and expansive eras in all English history—the age of Jonson, Marlowe, Shakespeare, Byrd, Morley, and Bacon. Thomas More, a precursor of the English Renaissance, is supposed to have been sufficiently influenced by some of Amerigo Vespucci's crewmen to set his *Utopia* somewhere in the New World.

As so often in mythic renderings of history, the myth represented not only sentiment remaking fact but a sense of the truth. For both the presence of the New World and its interchanges with the Old wrought magic, an immense expansion in the possibilities of each, along with a mythic imagination that in time worked new political and material reality upon the globe.

Pocahontas: Myth of the Noble Savage. *(Courtesy, Library of Congress)*

The Pilgrims: Mythic Symbols. *(Courtesy, Library of Congress)*

O Strange New World

Howard Mumford Jones

America, Howard Mumford Jones, late professor of English at Harvard University, shows, was first an idea in the mind of Europe that conditioned the response of its early explorers and settlers. America represented a variety of sometimes contradictory things. It was the mystery of life, the possibility of freedom, wealth, and happiness, and the image of the Noble Savage—elements that eventually became the "American dream." But the new Western Hemisphere was also primitive and dangerous, full of cannibals, pagan lust, and unpredictable natural fury. Most of all, Europeans visualized a land of exploitable wealth, and that vision awakened everything vicious and predatory in the European nature while restraints of civilization might be left on the other shore of the Atlantic. Jones would have us remember this part of the American heritage that we prefer to forget.

Europe saw in the New World both its hopes and its fears; the continents were an uncharted region on which Europe could map its own ambivalent character. The haunting dreams that Jones relates became the American reality as Europeans realized their visions and imposed age-old patterns upon it. This land received the impress of Europe, and fulfilled the prophecy of the Shakespearean quotation from which Jones derives his title: "O Strange New World that Never Yet Was Young."

The belief in riches and perfection beyond the sunset is very old in Europe, a natural development, so to speak, among the cultures of the landlocked Mediterranean, whence the only sea route that leads at once everywhere and nowhere is through the Straits of Gibraltar. The sunset marks the end of day, and symbolically, the end of life; wherefore Homer's Elysian Fields lie vaguely in that direction, and Hesiod's Hesperides more decisively so. The Greek dramatists occasionally hint at a western paradise of some sort either for men or for their ghosts, and in Plutarch's life of Sertorius we read of Spanish sailors who had been to the Islands of the Blest. Seneca in a famous passage prophesied that mankind would one day discover a distant Western World. Moreover, Avalon was sometimes located westward, and so, for that matter, was Lyonesse—names that connote eternal spring, eternal peace, or eternal plenty. Indeed, as late as World War I the dying soldier "went west"

as the heroes of Homer had done. These places are not on the maps, though there were some who identified the Fortunate Isles with the Canaries when the latter were discovered in the twelfth century and rediscovered in the fourteenth.

But there were other legends long before Columbus. Notably in the sixteenth century, when the expansion of empires westward made the assertion of precedent claims, however shadowy, a useful legal fiction, men remembered the belief that the New World had been populated, or discovered, or settled, by a second Adam and Eve and their descendants (the problem of the origin of the American Indians is still troublesome), or by the Egyptians, the Tartars, the Canaanites, the Chinese, the Celts, the Norse, the Arabs, the Venetians, the Portuguese, or the Danes (under the leadership of a Polish pilot). Aside from that of the brothers Zeno, who came from Venice, the most substantial claim is clearly that of the Norse, since there is good evidence that Leif, son of Eric the Red, sailed to the New World in the year 1000, thus inaugurating a small succession of voyages of discovery that reached as far south as Cape Cod or Martha's Vineyard. An important element in the Norse accounts, as in that of the Zeno brothers, is the principle of plenitude. Thus in 1007 Karlsefne came to Markland, where he found plenty of wood and wild animals, and to Vinland, where the low ground was covered with wild wheat and the rising ground with grapes. Let us add the more improbable tale of Madoc, Prince of Wales, with whose voyage Hakluyt opens the "American" section of his great collection. Madoc reached a fertile and beautiful land in 1170—"Whereupon it is manifest that the countrey was by Britaines discovered, long before Columbus led any Spanyards thither."

The Atlantic hid in its misty vastness many wonderful islands, and these island images, compounded of wonder, terror, wealth, religious perfection, communism, utopianism, or political power, conditioned the European image of America. They floated on the maps of the Ocean Sea like quicksilver globules, now here, now there, now nowhere at all, some of them remaining on British Admiralty charts into the nineteenth century. Beyond them, westward was Asia or Eden or the Earthly Paradise, unless *they* were Asia or Paradise. The most famous of these islands is undoubtedly Atlantis, the legend of which we owe to Plato, and the locus of which has challenged the imagination of American writers as different as Ignatius Donnelly, the author of *Caesar's Column*, and Edwin Björkman, the translator of Strindberg. . . .

Mingled with this shadowy geography were other charming dreams. One, much debated by a growing minority of learned men, was that the shortest way to the fabulous East was to sail westward and be plunged into riches. The other important ideas implicit in some of these island stories are that life is prolonged, or men are happier, or one is nearer God somewhere in the Ocean Sea or on its distant borders. The cardinal Pierre d'Ailly, whose book Columbus took as his master text in geography, quoted with approval the opinion of the ancients that toward the south, where the days and nights are each six months long, people live who are so happy they never die except when, bored with life, they end it by throwing themselves from some high cliff into the sea—a notion he twice presents. The excellent cardinal also seriously inclines to an Earthly Paradise on or near

the Fortunate Isles by reason of the fertility of the soil, the excellence of the sun, and the benevolent influence of the stars—an idea so attractive that Columbus seriously presented it to "the most exalted monarchs in Christendom" when he wrote them from the island of Hispaniola during his third voyage. He informed Ferdinand and Isabella that the earth is shaped like a pear with a bump on top resembling a nipple; that, though he doubts the Earthly Paradise is in the form of a rugged mountain, it is certainly high up; and that, granted no one can go there except by the permission of God, yet a gradual ascent up the waters flowing from it seemed to some degree possible. He had been off the mouth of the Orinoco, though he did not know it, and he wrote: "I have never read or heard of so great a quantity of fresh water so coming into and near the salt. And the very mild climate also supports this view, and if it does not come from there, from paradise, it seems to be still a greater marvel, for I do not believe that there is known in the world a river so great and so deep." Thither, then, "where I believe in my soul that the earthly paradise is situated," he intends that three ships "well stocked with provisions" shall go to make "further investigation." In the Earthly Paradise is the Tree of Life, and from it issues a fountain, and from the fountain flow four of the chief rivers of this world—and the Orinoco was obviously one of them. . . .

Other examples of the components of this image of the Golden Age can be found in books about the New World by Oviedo, Acosta, Thevet, Garcilaso de la Vega, Hakluyt, Purchas, and others. Some projects then undertaken read so like fairy tales we wonder how sensible men could seriously propose to carry them out. Such, for instance, was the search by Ponce de León in Florida (or "Bimini" or both) for the Fountain of Youth. But Leonardo Olschki hunts out pictures of such a fountain in late medieval art and reproduces an Italian miniature of the fifteenth century depicting the fountain (inevitably in a *hortus inclusus*), and Peter Martyr devotes a lengthy digression to the possibility of its existence. Among the ancients, Martyr quotes Aristotle, Pliny, Homer, and the legend of Medea and Aeson, just as he appeals to the way of the eagle, the snake, the deer, the raven, and the crow to support so fascinating an idea: "If, therefore, all these things are true; if Nature, that astonishing creatrix, graciously shows herself so munificent and powerful towards the dumb animals . . .

how should it be astonishing for her to create and nourish in her bounteous breast similar phenomena in a superior order?" In the tradition of other enchanted lands, Ponce de León thought Florida an island, naming it, as all the world knows, for the Easter of the Flowers. Herrera tells us there was not a river, brook, lake, or puddle in which the Spaniards did not hopefully bathe. Half a century later Fontaneda was still looking for the waters of rejuvenescence.

The fairy-tale aspect of Ponce de León's search suggests what is true: that, particularly in the Iberian peninsula (but also in Italy and elsewhere), where the New World was concerned, men's imagination was conditioned by the elements of chivalric romance.... It should not be hard for us, who accustom our eyes to spacemen and the odd beings we imagine we shall find on the moon or Mars, to understand the age of Ferdinand and Isabella and that of Charles V in this respect. If Astolfo, Rinaldo, and others in the Italian chivalric romances vanquish thousands, defeat Satan, and deal chivalrously with a paynim prince, the conquistadors did precisely the same thing. It was impossible to number the Indian warriors; Christian knights are therefore described as vanquishing multitudes in the West Indies, in Mexico, or in Peru, and Satan flees from them.

Such, then, are some of the principal elements in the image of the New World formed by Europe at the end of the fifteenth century as enriched by the sixteenth. First, the component of wonder, incarnated, as it were, in the concept of islands where men do not die unless they want to, where it is always summer, where food is plentiful, and where nobody works. Then to a weary Europe came news that seemed to say the Earthly Paradise, Arcadia, or the Golden Age was practicable and could actually be found. These idyllic promises were crossed by tales of derring-do, and the New World image absorbed as well the enchanted fairyland of chivalric romance. Finally, precisely as the chivalric imagination of the South had possessed itself of the new image, so the pictorial imagination of the Mediterranean Renaissance turned naked Indians into gods and goddesses, warriors and nymphs, and what had risen out of a dream of antiquity became a mode of picturing actuality.

In the doctrine of Bishop Berkeley that the course of empire must move westward, in that of Whitman defining America as an athletic democracy which proclaims

I see not America only, not only Liberty's nation but other nations preparing,

in Lowell's exclamation about the brave new world that never yet was young, in the doctrine of progressive democracy and, for that matter, of an economy of abundance, in the dream of millions of emigrants that life is "better" in the New World, we find continuing echoes of these Arcadian preludes. Alas that the coin had baser metal in it! Alas that the Golden Age turned almost immediately into the age of gold! To the concept of Arcadia in reverse it is now necessary to turn.

*   *   *

The concept that the New World is the peculiar abode of felicity lingered for centuries in the European imagination and, like the youth of America, is one of its oldest traditions. Virginia, wrote Michael Drayton in his famous poem of 1606, is earth's "onely paradise," and Goethe not long before his death declared: *"Amerika, du hast es besser/Als unser Continent, das Alte."* As for France, the studies of Gilbert Chinard have shown the connection between America and an exotic dream of difference and perfection. The vitality of the idea runs so deep and long, the traditional image can be adapted to humor, so that William Byrd's satirical "Journey to the Land of Eden" in 1733 and Martin Chuzzlewit's unfortunate real-estate speculation in the fever-ridden Eden of Dickens' novel are proof of the vigor of a concept that has a thousand aspects, some of which I shall examine in other connections. But the coin, to change the figure, has another side....

The association of the New World with unlimited riches is a commonplace in the history of ideas, but until one realizes how immediate, coarse, and brutal was the response of European greed to the prospect of boundless wealth, one cannot understand how quickly the radiant image became crossed with streaks of night. It may indeed be true that mere greed for gold will not suffice to explain the superhuman exploits of the conquerors, but it is also true that superhuman exploits would not have been undertaken without the dream of reward. The economic theory of the Renaissance could not think of wealth except in terms of a cash nexus binding man to man, a theory the more persuasive as rulers beheld the wealth of the Indies turning Charles V into the master of Europe and doing mysterious things to prices. Gold, pearls, and precious stones were tangible, were concrete evidence of success, were proof that the New World was, if not the kingdom of Prester John, the empire of the Great Khan, or Asia heavy with the wealth of Ormuz and of Ind, then next door to it, or a passage toward it, or, better still a richer and more wonderful land. The lust for gold conquered morality, judgment, humanitarianism, and religion. To watch the banausic greed for it corrupt idealism is like watching the inevitable march of a Greek tragedy.

Columbus, his associates, his crew, and his rivals were convinced that gold was at hand, or concealed, or in the next island. They could not conceive that the indifference of the Indians to what the Europeans thought of as tangible wealth was anything less than cunning or treachery. In the interior, says the admiral in his first letter, there are mines of metals—though he never saw them. The evidence? In exchange for a European strap a sailor received gold to the weight of two and a half *castellanos* (46 decigrams). When Columbus returned on his second voyage, the Indians continued to barter casual gold for straps, beads, pins, fragments of dishes, and plates, and Indian kings who sought him out wore facial masks of beaten gold and gold ornaments in their ears and nostrils. The Indian chief Guacamari, suspected of responsibility for the murder of Columbus's original colony on Hispaniola, tried to placate the admiral with a gift of eight and a half marks of gold, five or six hundred stones of various colors, and a cap with a jewel that the Indian seemed to value highly. Then as later, alas! the real source of gold was somewhere else—in this case in an island called Cayre, where there is much gold and "they go there with nails and tools to build their canoes, and . . . bring away as much gold as they please." An expedition to "Cibao" "found gold in more than fifty streams and rivers," "so many rivers, so filled with gold, that all of those who saw it and collected it, merely with their hands as specimens, came back so very delighted . . . that I feel diffidence in repeating what they say."

By the third voyage the inevitable had happened: the thirst for gold had led to the enslavement of the Indians and to double-dealing among the whites, as, for example, Bobadilla, who stole all of Columbus's gold without measuring it or weighing it, once he had the Columbus family in chains. The Lord comforted the admiral, however, by sending him a vision of the Nativity during the night at Veragua on his fourth voyage, showing that gold is everywhere, and an Indian took him up to a hilltop and explained that gold was all around him so that he saw "greater evidence of gold on the first two days than in Española [Hispaniola] in four years." Perhaps uneasily conscious that gold and Christianity do not always mix, Columbus appealed to the great example of Solomon: "Gold is most excellent. Gold constitutes treasure, and he who possesses it may do what he will in the world, and may so attain as to bring souls to Paradise."

The Indians, as Peter Martyr observed, "know no difference between *meum* and *tuum*," but they learned to their sorrow that the white man's insatiable greed for property produced not happiness but treachery, enslavement, starvation, and death. The search for wealth became an obsession among the Europeans, sending Ponce de León, Hernando de Soto, Cabeça de Vaca, and scores of others on fruitless errands and often to miserable ends. Nothing is more characteristic than that Cabeça de Vaca, after his incredible sufferings in the New World, would neither affirm nor deny that there was gold in "Florida," an ambiguity that led many Spaniards to sell their possessions in order to join the ill-fated expedition of De Soto. Gold, it was thought, was everywhere. Fool's gold was solemnly loaded on Elizabethan ships and as solemnly assayed by London mineralogists—fool's gold or something like it. In the bleak Far North in 1577 Frobisher's historian, Dionysius Settle, could find no hurtful creeping beast "except some Spiders (which as many affirme, are signes of great store of gold)." As usual the natives made "signes of certaine people" living somewhere else "that weare bright plates of gold in their foreheads, and other places of their bodies." The mariners brought back some black stone. "And it fortuned a gentlewoman one of the adventurers wives to have a piece thereof, which by chance she threw and burned in the fire, so long, that at the length being taken forth, and quenched in a little vinegar, it glistered with a bright marquesset of golde. Whereupon the matter being called in some question, it was brought to certaine Goldfiners in London to make assay thereof, who gave out that it held golde, and that very richly for the quantity." Naturally the goldfiners "sought secretly to have a lease at her Majesties hands of those places, whereby to injoy the masse of so great a publike profit unto their owne private gaines."

Sir Humphrey Gilbert was so certain he would discover a gold mine in Newfoundland that he promised to ask no man for a penny toward financing his next expedition; and Sir George Peckham's "True Report" lists as probable products of the same territory gold, silver, copper, lead, tin, turquoise, ruby, pearl, marble, jasper, and crystal. Hariot in his *Briefe and True Report* on Raleigh's ill-fated colony tells of a man who gathered five thousand pearls from the Indians, "which for their likenesse and uniformity in roundnesse, orientnesse, and pidenesse of many colors, with equality in greatnesse, were very faire and rare: and had therefore beene presented to her Majesty," but "through extremity of a storme," they were lost "in coming away from the countrey."

Laudonnière reported "good quantitie of Gold and Silver" among the savages of Florida, who "say that in the Mountaines of Appalatcy there are Mines of Copper, which I thinke to be Golde." Perhaps more momentous than even this delusive idea is the effect of lust for wealth upon European conduct in Florida:

> Golde and silver they [the Indians] want not: for at the Frenchmens first coming thither they had the same offered them for little or nothing, for they received for a hatchet two pound weight of golde, because they knew not the estimation thereof: but the souldiers being greedy of the same, did take it from them, giving them nothing for it: the which they perceiving, that both the Frenchmen did greatly esteeme it, and also did rigorously deale with them, by taking the same away from them, at last would not be knowen they had any more, neither durst they weare the same for feare of being taken away.

More commonly Indians were enslaved, tortured, or killed if they would not reveal the existence of gold they knew nothing about in fact.

These instances, though they illustrate the fixed idea of Renaissance man that gold, silver, precious stones, and pearls were easily to be found anywhere from the Arctic Circle to the Straits of Magellan, are not prerogative instances; for these we must turn to the incredible history of the Spaniards in Mexico and Peru. The pages of Prescott narrate a tale of gold and greed, blood and bravery, treachery and daring made so familiar by the literary skill of a great romantic historian, one need here merely recall a few familiar episodes. On receiving the first embassy from Montezuma, which brought, among other gifts, a wicker basket filled with gold ornaments, Cortés sent back a gilt helmet, asking that it be filled with gold, and told the ambassadors the Spaniards were troubled with a disease of the heart, for which gold was a specific remedy—one of the great ironical statements in the history of the New World. A second embassy brought Aztec "armor" embossed with gold, birds and animals in gold and silver, two circular plates, one of silver, one of gold, as large as carriage wheels, and much else. Far from placating the Spaniards, these gifts inflamed their cupidity, and the fateful invasion pushed forward. After they had entered Tenochtitlán the Spaniards broke into Montezuma's private treasury, a large hall filled with riches that included ingots of gold and silver and many precious jewels. Montezuma sought vainly to ransom himself and his empire by causing three great heaps of gold and golden objects to be piled before his conquerors, heaps so big that even after three days they were not turned into ingots. The predictable consequences followed: the common soldiers, charging their leaders with bad faith, came near mutiny over the division of the spoils, Montezuma was eventually killed, and his successor, Cuauhtémoc [Guatemozin], last of the Aztecs, refusing under torture to tell where there was more treasure except that it had been thrown into the water, was judicially murdered by the Spaniards. The reconquest of the city and the failure to uncover more treasure stirred up the soldiers once more.

> The first ebullition of triumph was succeeded in the army by very different feelings, as they beheld the scanty spoil gleaned from the conquered city, and as they brooded over the inadequate compensation they were to receive for all their toils and sufferings. . . . Some murmured audibly against the general, and others against Guatemozin, who, they said, could reveal, if he chose, the place where the treasures were secreted. The white walls of the barracks were covered with epigrams and pasquinades levelled at Cortés, whom they accused of taking "one fifth of the booty as commander-in-chief, and another fifth as king."

Gómara reports a sentence worthy of an ancient Roman uttered by Cuauhtémoc while under torture, when a weaker victim complained: "And do you think I, then, am taking my pleasure in my bath?" Whatever the truth of the charges against Cortés, when he married upon his return to Spain, he gave his bride five invaluable emeralds cut by Aztec workmen, a gift that excited the greed and envy of the Queen of Spain. It is all like the curse of the Rhinegold.

The story of the conquest of Peru repeats in more lurid colors the story of the conquest of Mexico. The greed of Pizarro and his men was excited by glimpses of wealth caught on the coastal land, in Peru they seized the Inca Atahuallpa by treachery and simultaneously massacred some thousands of his attendants, the Inca, like Montezuma, sought to ransom himself and his people by filling a hall with gold, roving bands of Spaniards despoiled the Inca temples of their golden ornaments, the Inca was judicially murdered by the conqueror, civil war and conspiracy became commonplace, cruelty grew to be the daily experience of both Indian and Spaniard, and Pizarro and his attendants were eventually assassinated by Juan de Herrada and his followers. The epigraph from Lope de Vega's *El Nuevo Mundo* affixed by Prescott to the title page of the *History of the Conquest of Peru* could not be more ironically appropriate:

> *So color de religión*
> *Van a buscar plata y oro*
> *Del encubierto tesoro*

The massacre of Atahuallpa's attendants followed upon the exclamation of a Christian priest to Pizarro: "Do you not see, that, while we stand here wasting our breath in talking with this dog, full of pride as he is, the fields are filling with Indians? Set on, at once; I absolve you."

One final document, too important as literature to be omitted, and we shall be done with this nightmare. This is Raleigh's *Discovery of Guiana* (1595), which, better than anything else in Elizabethan literature, represents the shimmering mirage of gold and glory through which the sixteenth century saw the New World. The fact that Raleigh is interested in making out the best possible case for himself increases our sense that gold was the obsession of the age. He actually found none, nor did a subsequent expedition, but he saw some of the "kind of white stone (wherein gold ingendred)" in "divers hils and rocks in every part of Guiana, wherein we travelled." He reported that "al the rocks, mountains, al stones in ye plaines, woods, & by the rivers side are in effect throughshining, and seem marvelous rich" and were probably "El madre del oro" or at least "the scum of gold.". . .

Alas! Raleigh had more influence upon literature than upon kings: within ten years he was a prisoner in the Tower, a final expedition proved a complete fiasco, and on October 29, 1618, he was beheaded. Fantastic as the dream of El Dorado may seem, let us not forget that in 1577 Sir Francis Drake, putting in at a Pacific coast port called Tarapaze, found on the seashore a sleeping Spaniard "who had lying by him 13. barres of silver, which weighed 4000. ducats Spanish; we tooke the silver, and left the man."

The consequences of this *idée fixe* were of first importance in altering the picture of an Earthly Paradise. Though it was not the sole cause, the hunt for gold was one of the principal causes for the enslavement of the Indians. On Hispaniola, for example, by the end of the fifteenth century anarchy was more common than order. The Indians, when they rebelled against their conquerors, were condemned to pay tribute in gold, and when they were unable to find gold they were condemned to slavery—unless, indeed, slavery had been a prior punishment for rebellion. The *hidalgo* was supposed to fight and govern, not to labor; wherefore the Indians had to labor for him, and their women serve as his harem. As the Indian was himself unaccustomed to toil, notably toil in the mines, the population rapidly declined. European madness led to suicide, to aborticide, to infanticide; and since, unfortunately for the subjugated race, the white man brought his own diseases with him, sickness took off thousands. The population of Hispaniola has been estimated at a million in 1492; even if the figure is far too high, it is appalling to learn that the number of Indians living on that unhappy island had dropped to 14,000 by 1509. The Spanish court did what it could at long range to alleviate the lot of the Indians, and the great propaganda campaign of Montesinos and Las Casas finally ended the concept that the Indian was a natural slave. But the damage had been done.

Bloodshed, cruelty, and abuse could not last forever. The Anglo-Saxons remained alone in thinking that the only good Indian is a dead Indian, since the Spanish, the Portuguese, and the French, once the period of slaughter had waned, altered their philosophy and incorporated the Indians into their colonial cultures in greater or less degree. . . .

*   *   *

If the discoverers, in Peter Martyr's words, "ruined and exhausted themselves by their own folly and civil strife, failing absolutely to rise to the greatness expected of men who accomplish such wonderful things"—a judgment at once understandable and premature—the natives of the New World proved to be something less than pastoral inhabitants of an Earthly Paradise. The contrast between the two sides of the shield was sometimes merely puzzling and sometimes horrifying. When Verrazano made his voyage along the Atlantic seaboard in 1524 he found the Indians of the Carolina coast friendly and good-looking. They showed, he said, "the greatest delight on beholding us, wondering at our dress, countenances, and complexion"; they were "of good proportions, of middle stature, a little above our own, broad across the breast, strong in the arms and well formed in the legs and other parts of the body." They lived in a plentiful and lovely country where "the air is salubrious, pure and temperate, and free from the extremes of both hot and cold" and the sea is "calm, not boisterous, and its waves are gentle." But when he got to Cape Cod or its vicinity all was changed. The vegetation was "indicative of a cold climate," and the people were "entirely different from the others we had seen . . . so rude and barbarous that we were unable by any signs we could make, to hold communication with them." Clad in skins, living by hunting and fishing, and raising no crops, the Indians were hostile. "No regard was paid to our courtesies; when we had nothing left to exchange with them, the men at our departure made the most brutal signs of disdain and contempt possible." And when the expedition tried to enter the interior, the Indians shot the white man with arrows and raised the most horrible cries.

But this contrast was comparatively mild. The Europeans also discovered cannibals. In the West Indies Columbus's men came across "a great quantity of men's bones and skulls hung up about the houses like vessels to hold things" and reported bestial habits of the Caribs that were far, far different from the bookish theories Montaigne was to build on the cannibals. The Caribs raid other islands and treat their captives

> with a cruelty which appears to be incredible, for they eat the male children whom they have from [captive women] and only rear those whom they have from their own women. As for the men whom they are able to take, they bring such as are alive to their houses to cut up for meat, and those who are dead they eat at once. They say that the flesh of a man is so good that

there is nothing like it in the world, and it certainly seems to be so for, from the bones which we found in their houses, they had gnawed everything that could be gnawed, so that nothing was left on them except what was too tough to be eaten. In one house there was a neck of a man found cooking in a pot. . . .

Equally appalling was human sacrifice; for example, that practiced by the Aztecs. There are many accounts, one of the most graphic being that by Gómara in his *Historia General de las Indias* (1552), which, despite attempts to suppress it, was widely disseminated in Spanish, Italian, French, and English, especially Part II, the *Conquista de México*, translated into English by Thomas Nichols as *The Conquest of the West India* (1578). The Nichols translation carries an even more authentic repulsion than does the Spanish original. Elizabethans read of the great temple in Tenochtitlán with its two great altars, its twin hideous idols, its gutters of blood; and of

> other darke houses full of idols, greate & small wrought of sundry mettals, they are all bathed and washed with bloud, and so shewe very blacke through theyr dayly sprinklyng and anoynting them with the same, when any man is sacrificed: yea and the walles are an inche thicke with bloud, and the grounde is a foote thicke of bloud, so that there is a divelish stench. The Priests or Ministers goe dayly into those Oratories, and suffer none others but great personages to enter in. Yea and when any such goeth in, they are bounde to offer some man to be sacrificed, that those bloudy hangmen and ministers of the Divell may washe their handes in bloud of those so sacrificed, and to sprinkle their house therewith.

The priest bound the victim face upward on a large sacrificial stone with convenient runnels, opened his living breast with a flint knife, tore out the heart, and, offering it to the idol, smeared the god with fresh blood. "This done, they pluckt of the skinnes of a certeine number of them, the which skinnes so many auntient persons put incontinent upon their naked bodies, al fresh & bloudy, as they wer fleane from the deade carcasses. . . . In *Mexico* the king him selfe did put on one of these skinnes, being of a principall captive, and daunced among the other disguised persons, to exalte and honor the feast." I spare the reader other gory details but I must add that according to Gómara and Bernal Díaz del Castillo the victim was then cut up and eaten. . . .

The conflict of cultures was inevitable. When the white man tried to kidnap the Indian with the intent either of exhibiting him as a trophy, learning his language, or turning him into an interpreter, the Indian naturally grew suspicious and retaliated with whatever weapons he could command. When the Indian first roasted and ate a captured white man in order to acquire his knowledge or for ritualistic purposes sensible enough to the aborigine, the white man interpreted the act as the quintessence of diabolism. Against the superior military power and technological skill of the Europeans, the Indian could oppose only cunning and his knowledge of the land. Renaissance man—and this is particularly true of the Renaissance Englishman—found it difficult to understand how human beings (if they were human) could live without visible government, religion, or morality, and he therefore tended to assume that Indian culture, like all the rest of the world, was somehow organized under a king or an emperor with whom one could deal legally in matters of war and peace and the sale of land. Obviously the Indian had no concept of what to the Europeans were the elements of civil society; and he could fight the white man only by what the white man thought of as the basest treachery. The Machiavellian qualities in the European power struggle in some degree prepared the discoverers and the early colonists for some amount of bad faith, but not for the Indian usage of bad faith. Neither party to a treaty could understand what the word meant to the other. . . .

The Spaniards, working their way through difficult terrain, had to kidnap Indians for guides, the Indians retaliated by ambushing and assassinating the Spaniards, and the Spaniards countered on occasion by cutting off the hands and noses of Indians and sending them back to their village as a warning. In the Pequot War of 1637, the burning and massacre of some hundreds of Indian men, women, and children trapped in the "fort" at Mystic, Connecticut—a massacre that continued until the English "grew weary"—drew no reproof from contemporary chroniclers but was on the contrary regarded as a signal proof of divine intervention. "The Lord," wrote Edward Johnson in his *Wonder-Working Providence* (1653), the first published history of Massachusetts, "was pleased to assist his people in this warre, and deliver them out of the Indians hands." As for the famous King Philip's War, which lasted two years, cost the lives of one-tenth of the adult males in the Massachusetts Bay Colony, and exposed two-thirds of the towns and villages to Indian raids, the contest was illustrated on the side of the Indians by the raping and scalping of women, the cutting off of fingers and feet of men, the skinning of white captives, the ripping open of the bellies of pregnant women, the cutting off of the penises of the males, and the wearing of the fingers of white men as bracelets or necklaces. Naturally the whites retaliated. When King Philip was finally shot, his head and hands were cut off and his body was quartered and hung on four trees. "The Providence of God wonderfully appeared" in this, wrote "R. H." in *The Warr in New-England Visibly Ended* (1677).

The discovery that the Earthly Paradise was inhabited by the offspring of Satan compelled Europeans to choose between two alternatives, neither of which proved successful. Either you converted the Indians into children of Christ or you exterminated them in a holy war. The Mediterranean peoples made more progress in converting the children of Satan, the British in exterminating them. The long history of American injustice to the red man springs from a profound and brutal misunderstanding that passed into literary tradition, for, as Roy Harvey Pearce has shown, the so-called Indian captivity narratives understandably passed from fact to fiction. They became exercises in emotion, not historical records. The Indian long remained a figure of terror, a child of hell. . . . The Indian was not sentimentalized until he became relatively harmless. For most of North America throughout most of its history the Indian has been, like the rattlesnake, the alligator, and poison ivy, an inexplicable curse on Utopia. His tawny presence darkened the landscape, and his war whoop chilled the blood.

Colonial America Without the Indians

James Axtell

For many centuries before the arrival of Europeans native Americans enjoyed a civilized presence in North America. Yet only recently has American society become sufficiently aware of their omission from American history. The tendency habitually has been to regard them as a kind of historical antiquity—as "Vanishing Americans." Understanding seldom transcended the duality of Bloodthirsty Savage and Noble Red Man. As a result, American Indians have often been the victims of both neglect and distortion. James Axtell— William R. Kenan, Jr., Professor of Humanities at the College of William and Mary—here creatively corrects the historical record. Apparently agreeing with the belief that one grand mythology deserves another, Axtell contemplates early American history totally without an Indian presence and Indian contributions. He thus jars the reader's historical sensibility toward an appreciation of Indians as principal determinants of American history.

[The Historian of the West] Bernard DeVoto lambasted students of American history, especially the academic kind, for having made "shockingly little effort to understand the life, the societies, the cultures, the thinking, and the feeling of Indians, and disastrously little effort to understand how all these affected white men and their societies. . . . Most American history," he chided, "has been written as if history were a function solely of white culture—in spite of the fact that till well into the nineteenth century the Indians were one of the principal determinants of historical events."

Three decades later, it behooves us to ask whether we should be tarred with the same brush. Have we done any more or any better to understand the American natives and especially to integrate them into the main course of American history, not as an exotic if melancholy footnote but as one of its principal *determinants*? In answer to the first part of the question, it can be argued that the history of

America's Indian peoples has grown tremendously in volume and sophistication since 1952, thanks less to traditional American historians than to historically minded ethnologists and those hybrid progeny of history and anthropology known as ethnohistorians. As for the second part, it must be confessed that the current generation, no less than DeVoto's, has made "disastrously little effort to understand how [the Indians] affected white men and their societies."

Where historians have not deigned to tread, others have rushed in. Since the last quarter of the nineteenth century, several articles and chapters have treated "The Contributions of the American Indian to Civilization" or "Americanizing the White Man." But most of them are either derivative, unhistorical, or downright foolish. They all suffer from at least one of four major problems. First, with one antiquated exception, they take as their subject all of American history and culture, with no differentiation of sections, classes, demography, or chronology. Second,

"Indian" culture is similarly overgeneralized; no allowance is made for tribal, culture area, or chronological differences. Third, they focus on isolated *materials* and *traits* rather than on cultural *complexes* (how they were used, perceived, and adapted by the colonists). And, finally, the conclusions of some and the implications of all lack common sense. To suggest, even indirectly, that "what is distinctive about America is Indian, through and through" or that Americans are simply Europeans with "Indian souls" is blithely to ignore the "wholly other" nature of English colonial society—its aggressive capitalism; exploitative attitudes toward natural resources; social hierarchy; nuclear kinship system; religious intolerance; literacy and print communications; linear sense of time; imperialism based on conquest; superiority complex based on religion, technology, social evolution and, ultimately, race; and desire to replicate the major features of the mother society as completely and quickly as possible.

One predictable reaction to the well-meaning fatuity of such efforts to plug the Indian into American culture (if not history) was that of Wilbur Zelinsky, who surveyed *The Cultural Geography of the United States* in 1973. After scanning the colonial period, Zelinsky concluded that "the sum of the lasting aboriginal contribution to the North American extension of British culture was distinctly meager.... Had the European colonists found an utterly unpopulated continent, contemporary American life would not have differed in any major respect from its actual pattern."

Who's right—DeVoto or Zelinsky? Were the Indians a temporary and irrelevant backdrop to the realization of Anglo-American destiny or were they "one of the principal determinants" of American history? The answer is not without importance. If Professor Zelinsky is correct, colonial history can remain a monochromatic study of Puritan preaching, merchant adventure, and imperial legislation; and textbook publishers can—when the political "heat" from the Indian Movement cools—cut the now-mandatory opening chapter on America's "prehistory" and adventitious references to the familiar cast of kamikaze warriors, noble collaborators, and patriot chiefs.

In a brief essay it is impossible to describe all the ways in which the Indians determined American history in the colonial period. However, it might be possible to suggest the outlines of such a description by following Professor Zelinsky's lead and imagining what early American history might have looked like in the utter *absence* of Indians in the New World. This kind of counterfactual discussion has its pitfalls as history, but for heuristic purposes it has few rivals if handled with care. When the main issue is the indispensability or irrelevance of a people to a complex course of historical events, the shortest way to resolve it is to reconstruct those events without the disputed variable. "Had the European colonists found an utterly unpopulated continent," we should ask, "would colonial American life have differed in any major respect from its actual pattern?"

To begin at the beginning, in the period of European discovery and exploration, we can say with confidence that if Columbus had not discovered *los Indios* (and they him), the history of Spanish America would have been extremely short and uneventful. Since Columbus was looking for the Far East, not America or its native inhabitants, he personally would have not been surprised to find no Indians in the Caribbean—the new continent was surprise enough. But he would have been disappointed, not only because the islands of the Orient were known to be inhabited but also because there would have been little or no reason to spend time exploring and settling the New World in lieu of his larger goal. America would have been regarded simply as a huge impediment to his holy plan to mount an old-fashioned crusade to liberate Jerusalem with profits derived from his short-cut to Cathay.

If the Caribbean and Central and South America had been unpopulated, the placer mines of the islands and the deep mines of gold and silver on the mainland in all likelihood would not have been discovered and certainly not exploited quickly without Indian knowledge and labor. It is simply inconceivable that the Spanish would have stumbled on the silver deposits of Potosí or Zacatecas if the Incas and Aztecs had not set Spanish mouths to watering with their sumptuous gold jewelry and ornaments. Indeed, without the attraction of that enormous wealth to be commandeered from the natives, it is likely that the Spanish would not have colonized New Spain at all except with a few supply bases from which to continue the search for the Southwest Passage.

It is equally possible that without the immediate booty of Indian gold and silver, the Spanish would have dismissed Columbus as a crackbrained Italian after one voyage and redirected their economic energies eastward in the wake of the Portuguese, toward the certifiable wealth of Africa, India, and the East Indies. Eventually, sugarcane might have induced the Iberians to colonize their American discoveries, as it did the Cape Verdes, Madeiras, and Canaries, but black laborers would have had to be imported to mount production. Without Indian labor and discovery, however, saltwater pearls and the bright red dye made from the cochineal beetle—the second largest export in the colonial period—would not have contributed to Spain's bulging balance sheets, with all that meant for the political and economic history of Europe in the sixteenth and early seventeenth century.

Perhaps most important, without the millions of Native Americans who inhabited New Spain, our textbooks would be silent on the Spanish conquest—no "Black Legend," no Cortés or Montezuma, no brown-robed friars baptizing thousands daily or ferreting out "idolatry" with whip and fagot, no legalized plunder under the encomienda system, no cruelty to those who extracted the mines' treasures and rebuilt Spanish cities on the rubble of their own, no mastiffs mangling runaways. And without the fabulous lure of Aztec gold and Incan silver bound for Seville on the annual bullion fleets, it is difficult to imagine Spain's European rivals beating an ocean path to America to establish colonies of their own, certainly not as early as they did.

Take the French, for example. The teeming cod on the Grand Banks off Newfoundland would have drawn and supported a small seasonal population of fishermen, as it did early in the sixteenth century. But without the Indian presence, that would have been the extent of French colonial penetration. Verrazano's 1524 reconnaissance of the Atlantic seaboard would have been an even bigger bust than it was, having found no promising Northwest Passage to the Orient; and Jacques Cartier probably would have made two voyages at most, the second to explore the St. Lawrence far enough to learn that *La Chine* did not lie on the western end of Montreal Island. He would have reported to Francis I that "the land God gave to Cain" had no redeeming features whatever, such as the greasy furs of Indian fishermen and the promise of gold and diamonds in the fabled Kingdom of the Saguenay, of which the Indians seemed to speak with such conviction.

If by chance Champlain had renewed the French search for the Northwest Passage in the seventeenth century, he quickly would have lost his backers without the lure of an established fur trade with the natives of Acadia and Canada, who hunted, processed, and transported the pelts in native-designed, -built, and -manned canoes or on native snowshoes and toboggans. And without the "pagan" souls of the Indians as a goad and challenge, the French religious orders, male and female, would not have cast their lot with Champlain and the trading companies that governed and settled New France before 1663. Without the Indian fur trade, in short, no seigneuries would have been granted along the St. Lawrence, no *habitants, engagés* or "King's girls" shipped out to Canada. Quebec and Montreal would not have been founded even as crude *comptoirs*, and no Jesuit missionaries would have craved martyrdom at an Iroquois stake. Needless to say, no "French and Indian" wars would mar our textbooks with their ethnocentric denomination. North America would belong solely to settlements of English farmers. For without the Indians and their fur trade, the Swedish and the Dutch would have followed the French lead by staying home or turning to the East for economic inspiration.

Without the lure of American gold and the Elizabethan contest with Spain that grew partly from its advent, the English, too, probably would have financed fewer ocean searches for the Northwest Passage. Unless Indian chamberpots were thought to have been made of gold, far fewer gentle-born investors and low-born sailors would have risked their lives and fortunes on the coasts of America. Unless the Spanish had reaped fabulous riches from the natives and then subjected the latter to cruel and unnatural bondage, Sir Walter Raleigh would not have sponsored his voyages of liberation to Guiana and "Virginia." If the Spanish flotillas had not sailed regularly through the Straits of Florida, English privateers would not have preyed on the West Indies nor captured the booty that helped to launch permanent colonies in Ireland and North America. Arthur Barlowe's 1584 voyage to North Carolina would probably not have been followed up so soon without the discovery of friendly natives capable of securing a fledgling colony from Spanish incursions. If settlers had come the following year, fewer need have been soldiers, they need not have been deposited on Roanoke Island for security reasons, and they probably would never have been lost without an Armada scare to detain supplies or the freelance privateering of rescuers.

Sooner or later, the English would have established colonies in America to provide a safety valve for the felt pressures of population growth and economic reorganization and as a sanctuary for religious dissenters. But without the Indians, our textbooks would assume a very different appearance in the chapters beyond the first; and the first, of course, would not be about the Indian "prehistory" of the continent but a much truncated treatment of exploration that barely mentioned the Spanish, Portuguese, French, Swedish, and Dutch.

Once English settlement was under way, the absence of native villages, tribes, and war parties would have altered rather drastically the timing and chronology of American history. In general, events would have accelerated because in reality the Indian presence acted as a major check on colonial development. Without a native barrier (which in the colonial period was much more daunting than the Appalachians), the most significant drag on colonial enterprise would have been the lack of Indian labor in a few minor economies, such as the domestic economy of southern New England (supplied by Indian captives in the Pequot and King Philip's wars) and the whale fisheries of Cape Cod, Long Island, and Nantucket. Indians were not crucial to wheat farming, lumbering, or rice and tobacco culture and would not have been missed by English entrepreneurs.

Without Indians to contest the land, English colonists would have encountered no opposition to their choice of prime locations for settlement except from English competitors. They would not have had to challenge Indian farmers for the fertile river valleys and coastal plains the natives had cultivated for centuries. Without potential Indian or European enemies, sites could have been located almost entirely for economic rather than military considerations, thus removing Jamestown, Plymouth, and St. Mary's City from the litany of American place-names. Boston, New York, Philadelphia, and Charleston would probably have developed where they are, either because Indian opposition to their founding was minimal or because they were situated for optimal access to inland markets and Atlantic shipping lanes.

In an empty land, English leaders would also have had fewer strategic and ideological reasons for communal settlements of the classic New England type. Without the military and moral threat of Indian war parties, on the one hand, and the puzzling seduction of native life, on the other, English colonists would have had to be persuaded by other arguments to cast their lots together. One predictable result is that New England "Puritans" would have become unbridled "Yankees" even faster than they did, and other colonies would have spread across the American map with equal speed. In other words, by 1776, Anglo-American farmers in large numbers would have spilled over the Appalachians, headed toward their "Manifest Destiny" in the West. Without Indians, Frenchmen, or Spaniards in the Mississippi Valley and beyond to stop them, only the technology of transportation, the supply of investment capital, and the organization of markets en route would have regulated the speed of their advance.

Another consequence of an Indian-less America would be that we could not speak with any accuracy of "the American frontier" because there would be no people on the other side; only where two peoples and cultures intersect do we have a bona fide frontier. The movement of one people into uninhabited land is merely *exploration* or *settlement*, and does not constitute a frontier situation. In fact, without viable Indian societies, colonial America would more nearly resemble Frederick Jackson Turner's famous frontier in which Indians are treated more like geographical features than sociological teachers. In Turner's scenario, the European dandy fresh from his railroad car is "Americanized" less by contact with palpably attractive human societies than by the "wilderness" or Nature itself. Moreover, the distinctively "American" character traits in Turner's catalogue produced by living on the fore edge of westering "civilization" would have been exaggerated by the existence of *truly* limitless cheap land and much less control from the Old World and the eastern "Establishment."

Not only would Turner's mythopoeic frontier really have existed in a non-Indian America, but three other common misunderstandings in our teaching of colonial history would have been realities. First, America would indeed have been a "virgin land," a barren "wilderness" that was not home or well-known to perhaps 4 million native people north of Mexico. If those people had not existed, we would not have to explain their catastrophic decline—by as much as 90 percent—through epidemics of imported diseases, warfare, injustice, and forced migrations—the "widowing" of the once-virgin land.

Second, colonial history would be confined to the political boundaries of the future United States, much like the weather map on the six o'clock news. Without Indians, we could continue to ignore French Canada and Louisiana, the Spanish Southwest, the Russian Northwest (which would not exist without the Indian seal trade), and the borderless histories of Indian-white contact that determined so much of the shape and texture of colonial life.

And third, we would not have to step up from the largely black-and-white pageant of American history we are offered in our textbooks and courses to a richer polychromatic treatment if the Indians had no role in the past. We would not have to pay lip service to the roll call of exclusively male Indian leaders who have been squeezed into the corners of our histories by modern American Indian activists. Still less would we have to try to integrate into our texts an understanding of the various native peoples who were here first, remained against staggering odds, and are still here to mold our collective past and future.

To get a sharper perspective on an Indian-free scenario of colonial history, we should increase our focal magnification and analyze briefly four distinguishable yet obviously related aspects of colonial life—economics, religion, politics, and acculturation.

If Professor Zelinsky's thesis has any merits at all, they lie on the economic side of the ledger. The economy of Anglo-America without the Indians would have resembled in general outline the historical economy but with several significant exceptions. Farming would certainly have been the mainstay of colonial life, whether for family subsistence or for capitalist marketing and accumulation. But the initial task of establishing farms would have required far more grubbing and clearing without the meadows and "park-like" woods produced by seasonal Indian burning, and especially without the cleared expanses of Indian cornfields and village sites. Many colonists found that they could acquire cleared Indian lands with a few fathoms of trading cloth, some unfenced cows, or a well-aimed barrel of buckshot.

A more serious deficiency would have been the absence of maize or Indian corn, the staple crop grown by the colonists throughout the colonial period to feed their families and sometimes to fatten their livestock for export. If Indians had not adapted

wild Mexican corn to the colder, moist climates of North America and developed the agricultural techniques of hilling, fertilizing by annual burning, and co-planting with nitrogen-fixing beans to reduce soil depletion, the colonists would have lacked a secure livelihood in both the long and the short run, particularly in the early years before traditional European cereal crops could be adapted to the American climate and soils. Even if traditional crops could have been transplanted with ease, colonial productivity would not have benefited from the efficiency and labor savings of native techniques, which were found taught by Indian prisoners (as at Jamestown) or by allies such as Squanto at Plymouth. So central was maize to the colonial economy that it is possible that its absence would have acted as a severe brake on westward settlement, thereby counteracting to some degree the magnetic pull of free land.

The colonial economy would also have been affected by the lack of Indian trade, the profits from which were used to fuel the nascent economies of several colonies, including Massachusetts, Rhode Island, New York, Pennsylvania, Virginia, and South Carolina. Without early fortunes made from Indian furs, some of the "first families" of America—the Byrds, Penns, Logans, Winthrops, Schuylers—would not have been launched so solidly or so soon in shipping, slaves, rice, tobacco, or real estate. Nor would the mature economies of a few major colonies have rested on the fur trade well into the eighteenth century. New York's and Pennsylvania's balance of payments with the mother country would have been badly skewed if Indian-generated furs had not accounted for 30–50 percent of their annual exports between 1700 and 1750. By the same token, a substantial portion of English exports to the colonies would not have been sent to colonial traders for Indian customers, whose historical appetites for English cloth and West Indian rum were appreciated even by those who realized that furs accounted for only 0.5 percent of England's colonial imports, far behind tobacco and sugar.

The lack of Indians and Indian property rights in America would have further complicated the colonial economy by greatly narrowing another classic American road to wealth. If the new land had been literally inexhaustible and "dirt cheap," the range of legal and extralegal means to acquire relatively scarce land for hoarding and speculation would have been markedly reduced. Within the unknown connes of the royal response to a huge, open continent, very man, great and small, would have been for imself. If the law condoned or fostered the selective ggrandizement of colonial elites, as it tended to do istorically, unfavored farmers and entrepreneurs ould simply move out of the effective jurisdiction of ie government or find more congenial leaders to do neir bidding. The proliferation of new colonies seek-ag economic and political "independence" from the tyranny" of the Eastern Establishment would have een one certain result.

Finally, America without Indians would entail ie rewriting of the history of black slavery in the olonies. It is likely that, in the absence of Indians, the olonial demand for and use of African slaves would ave begun earlier and accelerated faster. For al-nough the historical natives were found to be poor vorkers and poorer slaves, the discovery took some me. Not only would the rapid westward spread of ettlements have called for black labor, perhaps more f it indentured, but the rice and tobacco plantations f the Southeast probably would have been larger nan they were historically, if scarce land and high rices had not restricted them. In a virgin-land econ-my, agricultural entrepreneurs who wanted to in-rease their acreage could easily buy out their smaller eighbors, who lacked no access to new lands in the vest. Of course, greater numbers of black laborers vould have been needed to do the work because vhite indentured servants would have been ex-remely hard to get when so much land and oppor-unity beckoned over the horizon. By the same token, ne slaves themselves would have been harder to eep to the task without surrounding tribes of Indi-ns who could be taught to fear and hate the African trangers and to serve the English planters as slave-atchers.

While most colonists came to the New World to etter their material condition, not a few came to meliorate the spiritual condition of the "godless" latives. Without the challenge of native "paganism" n America, the charters of most English colonies vould have been frankly materialistic documents vith pride of motive going to the extension of His (or ler) Majesty's Eminent Domain. Thus American his-ory would have lost much of its distinctively evan-,elical tone, though few of its millenarian, utopian trains. Without the long, frustrated history of Chris-ian missions to the Indians, we would lack a sensi-ive barometer of the cultural values that the European colonists sought to transplant in the New World and one source of denominational competi-tion in the eighteenth century.

Without Indian targets and foils, the colonists even of New England might not have retained their "Chosen People" conceit so long or so obdurately. On the other hand, without the steady native re-minder of their evangelical mission in America, the colonists' early descent into ecclesiastical "tribalism" and spiritual exclusiveness might have accelerated with time. The jeremiads of New England would certainly have been less shrill in the absence of the Pequot War and King Philip's War, when the hostile natives seemed to be scourges sent by God to punish a sinful people. Without the military and psychologi-cal threat of Indians within and without New En-gland's borders, the colonial fear of limitless and unpredictable social behavior would have been re-duced, thereby diminishing the harsh treatment of religious deviants such as Roger Williams, Anne Hutchinson, Quakers, and the Salem witches. Fi-nally, the French "Catholic menace" to the north would have been no threat to English Protestant sensibilities without hundreds of Indian converts, led by "deviously" effective Jesuit missionaries, ring-ing New England's borders. The French secular clergy who would have ministered to the handful of fishermen and farmers in Canada would have had no interest whatever in converting heretics hundreds of miles away and no extra manpower to attempt it.

The appearance of the "French menace" intro-duces the political realm of colonial life, which also would take on a new complexion in the absence of American natives. Even if the French had settled the St. Lawrence Valley without a sustaining Indian fur trade, the proliferating English population and Euro-pean power politics would have made short work of the tiny Canadian population, now bereft of Indian allies and converts in the thousands. In all likelihood, we would write about only one short intercolonial war, beginning much earlier than 1689. Perhaps the Kirkes would never have given Quebec back to the French in 1632. Without the Catholic Indian *reserves* of Lorette, Caughnawaga, and St. François, Canada would quickly have become English, at least as far north as arable land and lumber-rich forests ex-tended.

Without a formidable French and Indian threat, early Americans would not have developed—in conjunction with their conceit as God's "Chosen

People"—such a pronounced "garrison mentality" as innocent and holy victims of heavily armed satanic forces. If the English had not been virtually surrounded by French-allied Indian nations and an arc of French trading forts and villages from Louisiana to Maine, the Anglo-American tendencies toward persecuted isolationism would have been greatly sublimated.

As the colonies matured, the absence of an Indian military threat would have greatly lightened the taxpayers' burden for colonial defense, thereby placing much less strain on the political relations between governors and representative assemblies. Indeed, the assemblies would not have risen to political parity with the royal administrators in the absence of financial crises generated by war debts and defense needs. Intercolonial cooperation would have been even less conspicuous than it was historically. Royal forces would not have been called in during the eighteenth century to bolster sagging colonial defenses, and no imperial debts would have been incurred which the colonies would be asked to help amortize. Consequently, the colonies would have had few grievances against the mother country serious enough to ignite an American Revolution, at least not in 1776. And without the concentration of Indian allies on the British side, the colonists might have achieved independence sooner than they did.

Another reason why the colonists would probably not have been ready for revolution in 1776 is that, without the steady impress of Indian culture, they would not have been or felt sufficiently "Americanized" to stand before the world as an independent nation. Without Indian societies to form our colonial frontiers, Anglo-American culture would have been transformed only by internal developments and the evolving influence of the mother country and of the black and other ethnic groups that shared the New World with the English. Black culture probably would have done the most to change the shape and texture of colonial life, especially in the South. But English masters saw little reason to emulate their black slaves in any positive way, to make any *adaptive* changes in their own cultural practices or attitudes to accommodate perceived superiorities in black culture. English colonial culture changed in response to the imported Africans largely in *reaction* to their oppositional being, and pervasive and often virulent racism was the primary result. Other changes followed, of course, from the adoption of staple econo-

mies largely but not necessarily dependent on black labor.

English reactions to the Indians, on the other hand, were far more mixed; the "savages" were noble as well as ignoble, depending on English needs and circumstances. Particularly on the frontier, colonists were not afraid or loath to borrow and adapt pieces of native culture if they found them advantageous or necessary for beating the American environment or besting the Indians in the contest for the continent. Contrary to metropolitan colonial opinion, this cultural exchange did not turn the frontiersmen into Indians. Indian means were simply borrowed and adapted to English ends. The frontiersmen did not regard themselves as Indians nor did they appreciably alter their basic attitudes toward the native means they employed. But they also knew that their American encounters with the Indians made them very different from their English cousins at home.

While the colonists borrowed consciously and directly from Indian culture only on the frontier, English colonial culture as a whole received a substantial but indirect impress from the Indians by being forced to confront the novel "otherness" of native culture and to cope with its unpredictability, pride, and retaliatory violence. Having the Indians as sometime adversaries and full-time contraries helped not only to reinforce the continuity of vital English traits and institutions but to Americanize all levels of colonial society more fully than the material adaptations of the frontiersmen. These *reactive* changes were, in large measure, responsible for transforming colonial Englishmen into native Americans in feeling, allegiance, and identity, a change without which, John Adams reminded us, the American Revolution would have been impossible. The whole colonial experience of trying to solve a related series of "Indian problems" had much to do with giving the colonists an identity indissolubly linked to America and their apprenticeship in political and military cooperation.

What are some of these changes that would *not* have taken place in colonial culture had the continent been devoid of Indians? The adaptive changes are the easiest to describe. Without native precedent, the names of twenty-eight states and myriad other place-names would carry a greater load of Anglophonic freight. The euphonious Shenandoah and Monongahela might well be known as the St. George and the

Dudley rivers. We might still be searching for suitable names for the *moose, skunk,* and *raccoon,* the *muskelunge* and *quahog,* the *hickory* tree and marshy *muskeg.* It would be impossible, no doubt, to find *moccasins* in an L. L. Bean catalogue, or canned *succotash* in the supermarket. We would never refer to our children playfully as *papooses* or to political bigshots as *mugwumps.* Southerners could not start their day with *hominy* grits.

Without Indian guides to the New World, the English colonists upon arrival would have lacked temporary housing in bark-covered wigwams and longhouses. Not only would their diet have depended largely on imported foods, but their techniques for hunting American game and fowl and coping in the woods would have been decidedly meager. Without native medicines, many colonists would have perished and the *U.S. Pharmacopeia* would be short some 170 entries. Without Indian snowshoes and toboggans, winter hunting and travel would have been sharply curtailed. Without the lightweight bark canoe, northern colonists would have penetrated the country on foot, and not in comfortable moccasins and Indian leggings. English hunters probably would have careened around the woods in gaudy colors and torn English garments much longer, oblivious that the unsmoked glint of their musket barrels frightened the game. One can only imagine what Virginia's patriotic rifle companies would have worn in 1775 as an alternative to moccasins, leggings, fringed hunting shirts, scalping knives, and tomahawks.

Without native opponents and instructors in the art of guerrilla warfare, the colonists would have fought their American wars—primarily with the British—in traditional military style. In fact, without the constant need to suppress hostile natives and aggressive Europeans, they might have lost most of their martial spirit and prowess, making their victory in the now-postponed Revolution less than certain. Beating the British regulars at their own game without some of the stratagems and equipment gained from the Indians would have been nearly impossible, particularly when the British in the eighteenth century had gained experience in counterinsurgent warfare in Scotland and on the Continent.

Although the absence of adaptive changes such as these would have done much to maintain the Anglicized tone and texture of colonial life, the absence of Indians would have preserved a number of more fundamental cultural values that were altered historically. The generalized European fear of barbarism that worried colonial planners and leaders would have dissipated without the Indian embodiment of the "heathenism" that seemed so contagious to English frontiersmen or the greater danger of Englishmen converting to an Indian way of life in captivity or, worse still, voluntarily as "apostates" and "renegades." Without the seduction of an alternative life-style within easy reach, hundreds of colonists would not have become "white Indians."

Second, and more generally, the English definition of themselves in America would have lacked a crucial point of reference because the Indians would no longer symbolize the "savage" baseness that would dominate human nature if man did not— paradoxically—"reduce" it to "civility" through government, religion, and the capitalist work ethic. Only imported Africans, not American natives, could have shown "civilized men [what] they were not and must not be." Because the historical settlers were "especially inclined to discover attributes in savages which they found first but could not speak of in themselves," they defined themselves "less by the vitality of their affirmations than by the violence of their abjurations." While all peoples to some extent define themselves by contrast with other peoples, the English colonists forged their particular American identity more on an Indian anvil than upon other European colonists or Africans. If America had been vacant upon discovery, the Anglo-American character would have been very different from that which we inherited.

For the whole spectrum of colonial society, urban and rural, the Indians as cultural contraries were not as frustrating, alarming, or influential as the Indian enemy. As masters of an unconventional warfare of terror, they seared the collective memory, imagination, and even subconscious of the colonists, leaving a deep but blurred intaglio of fear and envy, hatred and respect. Having the American natives as frequent and deadly adversaries—and even as allies—did more not to "Indianize" but to "Americanize" the English colonists than any other human factor and had two contradictory results. When native warfare frustrated and humbled the English military machine, its successes cast into serious doubt the colonists' sense of superiority, especially when the only resource seemed to be the hiring of equally "savage" mercenaries. At the same time, victorious Indians seemed so insufferably insolent—a projection of the Christians' original sin—that the colonists redoubled their efforts to claim divine grace and achieve spiritual and social regeneration through violence. One of the pathetic ironies of early America is that in attempting to exterminate the wounding pride of their Indian enemies the colonists inflated their own pride to sinful proportions.

The Indians' brand of guerrilla warfare, which involved the "indiscriminate slaughter of all ranks, ages and sexes," torture, and captivity for adoption, gave rise to several colonial reactions. The first reaction to the offensive war of the natives (which was in reality retaliation for previous wrongs, real or perceived) was a well-founded increase in fear and paranoia. The second reaction, as we have already suggested, was the development of a defensive "garrison mentality," which in turn reinforced the colonists' sense of being a chosen if momentarily abandoned people. And the colonists' third response to being forced to confront such an enemy was that they were frequently torn from their own "civilized" moorings and swept into the kind of "savage" conduct they deplored in their enemies, motivated conspicuously by cold-blooded vengeance. Without Indian enemies, it is doubtful if the colonists would have fallen to the slaughter and torture of military prisoners, including women and children, taken scalps from friends and enemies to collect government bounties, encouraged the Spanish-style use of dogs, or made boot tops and tobacco pouches from the skins of fallen foes. It is a certainty that non-Indian enemies would not have been the target of frequent if unrealized campaigns of literal genocide; it is difficult to imagine English settlers coining an aphorism to the effect that "the only good Dutchman is a dead one."

It is both fitting and ironic that the symbol chosen by Revolutionary cartoonists to represent the American colonies was the Indian, whose love of liberty and fierce independence had done so much to Americanize the shape and content of English colonial culture. It is fitting because the Indians, by their long and determined opposition, helped to meld thirteen disparate colonies into one (albeit fragile) nation, different from England largely by virtue of having shared that common history of conflict on and over Indian soil. It is ironic because after nearly two centuries of trying to take the Indians' lives and lands, the colonists appropriated not only the native identity but the very characteristics that thwarted the colonists' ultimate arrogations.

If such a scenario seems plausible, we should be able to agree with DeVoto that, without the Indians, America would not be America as we know it. The sooner we acknowledge that fact, the sooner we can get down to the serious business of assessing the Indians' decisive place in American history.

Slavery and the Meaning of America

David Brion Davis

Early American history reflects a European opinion that for centuries had been nurtured by mythic predispositions toward a New World. It was under their spell and mythic atmosphere that the transoceanic expeditions and geographic discoveries of Christopher Columbus and others took place. Born in the romantic dreams of Europeans, reared in a tradition of glory and heroism, America soon became a land at ease with myth and legend. Contemporaneous with these visions of America were the beginnings of what a later scholar would see as the core of an American dilemma—black slavery. According to David Brion Davis of Yale University, the simultaneous development of utopianism and slavery has given the nation a paradoxical heritage. The presence of slavery in the "promised land" of the New World suggests important questions about the meaning of America.

From the time of first discoveries Europeans had projected ancient visions of liberation and perfection into the vacant spaces of the New World. Explorers approached the uncharted coasts with vague preconceptions of mythical Atlantis, Antillia, and the Saint Brendan Isles. The naked savages, living in apparent freedom and innocence, awakened memories of terrestrial paradise and the Golden Age described by the ancients. Even the practical-minded Columbus fell under the spell of the gentle natives on the Gulf of Paria, who wore golden ornaments and lived in a land of lush vegetation and delicious fruits. He concluded in August, 1498, that he had arrived on the "nipple" of the earth, which reached closer to Heaven than the rest of the globe, and that the original Garden of Eden was nearby. Seventeen years later, when Sir Thomas More began writing *Utopia*, he naturally chose the Western Hemisphere as his setting.

Columbus's successors pursued elusive visions of golden cities and fountains of youth; their narratives revived and nourished the utopian dreams of Europe. From antiquity Western thought had been predisposed to look to nature for the universal norms of human life. Since "nature" carried connotations of origin and birth as well as of intrinsic character, philosophers often associated valid norms with what was original in man's primeval state. They contrasted the restraints, prejudices, and corrupting tastes of civilized life with either a former age of virtue or a simpler, more primitive state of society. Many of the explorers and early commentators on America drew upon this philosophic tradition; in the New World they found an Elysium to serve as a standard for criticizing the perverted manners of Europe. Catholic missionaries, being dedicated to ideals of renunciation and asceticism, saw much to admire in the simple contentment of the Indians, whose mode of living seemed to resemble that of the first Christians. As Gilbert Chinard has pointed out, the *voyageurs* and Jesuit priests who compared the evils of Europe with the freedom, equality, and felicitous life of the American savages, contributed unwittingly to the revolutionary philosophy of the eighteenth century.

Some writers, to be sure, described the Indians as inferior degenerates or as Satan's children, and presented a contrary image of America as an insalubrious desert. Antonello Gerbi has documented the long dispute over the nature of the New World— "mondo nascente o neonato, mondo deserto e misero." Howard Mumford Jones has recently shown that America was conceived at once as an idyllic Arcadia and as a land of cannibalism, torture, and brutality, where extremities of human greed and cruelty were matched by the unexpected terrors and monstrosities of the wilderness. But in Hebrew and Christian thought the idea of wilderness had long been linked with rebirth and fulfillment. After being delivered from slavery in Egypt, the children of Israel had crossed the Red Sea and had wandered in the wilderness for forty years before finding the Promised Land. The desert was a place of refuge and purification, of suffering and perseverance; and no matter what hardships it offered, there was the assurance that a fertile paradise would ultimately emerge from its desolate wastes. Thanks to the researches of George H. Williams, we know what an important part such imagery played in Christian ideas of redemption. The wilderness might be thought of as a purely spiritual state, or as the abode of monks, hermits, or persecuted sects. But early American colonists could hardly escape the symbolic implications of a baptismal crossing of the Atlantic, or of dwelling in a land which could be seen as either desert or primeval garden. The New World, like the wilderness in both the Old and New Testaments, was a place of extraordinary temptation, obligation, and promise.

While a growing literature celebrated America as a symbol of nature, free from the avarice, luxury, and materialism of Europe, promoters and colonizers saw the virgin land as a place for solving problems and satisfying desires. This was true of the conquistadores who tried to recreate the age of chivalric romance; it was true of the Jesuits who followed Manuel da Nóbrega to Brazil, determined to purify morals and spread the faith; it was true of the English Puritans who sought to build a New Jerusalem as a model of piety for the rest of the world; it was true of the drifters and ne'er-do-wells, the bankrupts and sleazy gentlemen, who fluttered to the New World like moths drawn to a light. In America things would be better, for America was the Promised Land. It could be said, of course, that America was an asylum for scoundrels, adventurers, and religious fanatics. But in time much of the magic of the virgin continent seemed to rub off on its conquerors. French humanitarians, for example, found it easy to shift their enthusiasm from noble savage to peace-loving Quaker. In Saint-John de Crèvecoeur's *Letters from an American Farmer* we see perhaps the clearest picture of the American idyll, a skillful weaving together of primitivist, pastoral, and democratic themes, the portrayal of a land in which individual opportunity and social progress are somehow merged with the simple, self-denying virtues of Seneca and Vergil.

This long tradition, based on a mixture of Biblical and classical sources, helped to shape the American's image of himself as the new Adam of the West, a being unencumbered by the fears and superstitions of a moldering civilization, a wise innocent dwelling in a terrestrial paradise. He was at once the Happy Husbandman, content to enjoy the serene blessings of a simple, rural life, and an adventurous pioneer, expansive and supremely confident of his ability to improve the world. Such an image contained an intrinsic contradiction which contributed to severe tensions in the face of rapid social and economic change. But if Americans were often inclined to see Satan fast at work corrupting their new Eden, this only enhanced the moral importance of their mission. And by the time of the Revolution many European liberals looked to America as the hope of mankind, for it was there that institutions seemed most clearly modeled on nature's simple plan. By reconciling nature and human progress, the newly independent states appeared to have fulfilled the ancient dream of a more perfect society.

. . . Yet slavery had been linked from the very beginning with what Edmundo O'Gorman had called "the invention of America." The African voyages promoted by Prince Henry of Portugal prepared the way for the first crossing of the Atlantic; and when Columbus arrived in Lisbon in 1477 the trade in Negro slaves was a flourishing enterprise. The same Columbus who identified the Gulf of Paria as the gateway to the Garden of Eden had no compunction about sending hundreds of Indians to be sold in the slave marts of Seville, although some two hundred died on the first voyage and had to be thrown into the sea. It was thus the discoverer of America who initiated the transatlantic slave trade, which moved originally from west to east.

It was soon apparent, however, as the Spanish came close to exterminating the native inhabitants of Hispaniola, that successful colonization would require a fresh supply of laborers. Negro slaves arrived in the New World at least as early as 1502, and by 1513 the sale of licenses for importing Negroes was a source of profit for the Spanish government. Following the Guinea current and trade winds, Portuguese ships provided the colonists with a mounting supply of slaves, but seldom with enough to meet the insatiable demand. As Negro labor became indispensable for Spanish and then Portuguese colonization, European traders and African chieftains slowly built a vast commerical system which brought a profound transformation in African culture and stunted the growth of other commerce between Europe and the Dark Continent.

For three centuries the principal maritime powers competed with one another in the lucrative slave trade, and carried at least fifteen million Africans to the New World. Historians have long been inclined to regard this vast movement of population as an unfortunate but relatively minor incident in American history. Interest in national and sectional history has often obscured the significance of Negro slavery in the overall development of the Americas. But if the institution was of little economic importance in Massachusetts or Nova Scotia, it nevertheless extended from Rio de la Plata to the Saint Lawrence, and was the basic system of labor in the colonies most valued by Europe. In the most profitable colonies Negro slaves were employed in mines and in clearing virgin land, or on the great plantations which provided Europe with sugar, rice, tobacco, cotton, and indigo. The northern colonies that were unsuited for the production of staple crops became dependent, early in their history, on supplying the slave colonies with goods and provisions of various kinds. As a stimulus to shipbuilding, insurance, investment, and banking, the slave trade expanded employment in a diversity of occupations and encouraged the growth of seaports on both sides of the Atlantic. Africa became a prized market for iron, textiles, firearms, rum, and brandy. Investments in the triangular trade brought dazzling rewards, since profits could be made in exporting consumer goods to Africa, in selling slaves to planters, and especially in transporting sugar and other staples to Europe. By the 1760s a large number of the wealthy merchants in Britain and France were connected in some way with the West Indian trade; and capital accumulated from investment in slaves and their produce helped to finance the building of canals, factories, and railroads. Even after the United States had achieved independence and a more diversified economy, her principal export was slave-grown cotton, which was the chief raw material for the industrial revolution.

Without exaggerating the economic significance of Negro slavery, we may safely conclude that it played a major role in the early development of the New World and in the growth of commercial capitalism. Given the lack of an alternative labor supply, it is difficult to see how European nations could have settled America and exploited its resources without the aid of African slaves. Yet slavery had always been more than an economic institution; in Western culture it had long represented the ultimate limit of dehumanization, of treating and regarding a man as a thing. How was one to reconcile the brute fact that slavery was an intrinsic part of the American experience with the image of the New World as uncorrupted nature, as a source of redemption from the burdens of history, as a paradise which promised fulfillment of man's highest aspirations? . . .

The European thinkers . . . had somewhat ambivalent views on the moral influence of the New World. George Bancroft, the most popular and nationalistic of early American historians, had not the slightest doubt that the influence had been all for the good. Limiting himself to the area included in the United States, he set out to explain how in only two centuries the happiest and most enlightened civilization in history had arisen from the wilderness to become a model for the rest of the world. But when he grappled with the problem of slavery—how it was related to the American mission, whether it was integral to American development, and whether its extension to the New World was a retrogression from the course of progress—he resorted to a curious mixture of assumptions which reflected inconsistencies prevalent in American thought from late colonial times to the twentieth century.

As a loyal Democrat and patriotic American,

writing at a time when his party supported the expansion of slave territory, Bancroft went out of his way to emphasize the antiquity and universality of an institution which, one might conclude, was not so "peculiar" after all. . . . He found no continuing contest between liberty and bondage in the ancient world: "In every Grecian republic, slavery was an indispensable element." Nor was the practice wholly incompatible with virtue and religion, for "the light that broke from Sinai scattered the corrupting illusions of polytheism: but slavery planted itself even in the promised land, on the banks of Siloa, near the oracles of God." It was true that the extreme harshness of the Roman slave law had hastened the Empire's fall; but Bancroft's picture of the ancient world suggested that slavery might be planted in other promised lands without blighting their mission.

He adopted, however, the conventional view of Christianity slowly sapping the foundations of bondage in Europe. If slavery had not detracted from the splendor of Grecian republics, it was still incompatible with human progress, and would have disappeared entirely among civilized nations had not an outside force intervened. In Bancroft's eyes this outside force was not America, but the continuing wars between Islam and Christianity, which had nourished bigotry and revenge. Angered by the raids of Saracen corsairs, Christians had felt justified in capturing any Moor they could lay hands upon, and they had classified all Africans as Moors. In any event, the Negroes themselves had always accepted slavery, and when the Portuguese had commenced trading along the western coast of Africa, they had simply appropriated a commercial system which the Moors of the north had established centuries before. Bancroft admitted that the Portuguese were guilty of "mercantile cupidity," but in a certain sense it was Africa that had corrupted Europe.

The Spanish, who had also been brutalized by wars with the Moslems, had endeavored to enslave the Indians, or, as Bancroft called them, the "freemen of the wilderness." Even Columbus had participated in this unnatural act, though such a lapse was presumably redeemed by his contribution to the advance of liberty; and, as Washington Irving had said, "the customs of the times . . . must be pleaded in his apology." Slavery, however, was totally alien to American soil, and in order to rivet the system on their colonies, the Spanish had been forced to import a more docile and submissive race. The significant

point about Bancroft's interpretation is that he considered slavery basically extraneous to the New World and contrary to the natural development of Europe. It was thus a kind of abnormal excrescence which had been fastened on America by Europeans whose avarice and brutality had been stimulated by their contact with Africa.

When Bancroft turned to the founding of the North American colonies, he underscored the fundamental conflict between slavery and the very meaning of the New World. "While Virginia," he wrote, "by the concession of a republican government, was constituted the asylum of liberty, by one of the strange contradictions in human affairs, it became the abode of hereditary bondsmen." Monarchy, aristocracy, and priestcraft had no motive to cross the Atlantic—"Nothing came from Europe but a free people. The people, separating itself from all other elements of previous civilization; the people, self-confiding and industrious; the people, wise by all traditions that favored popular happiness—the people alone broke away from European influence, and in the New World laid the foundations of our republic." As part of this classic picture of American innocence and separateness, Bancroft stressed the original and deep antipathy that the people felt for slavery. His argument that slavery was essentially foreign to America appeared to stumble a bit when, discussing South Carolina, he seemed to adopt Montesquieu's belief in the primacy of climate; he even asserted that the contrast between Carolina and New York was due to climate and not to the superior humanity of the original Dutch colonists. Yet he thought that the people and legislation of every colony had favored freedom, and that Massachusetts, especially, had opposed the introduction of slaves from the beginning. In Rhode Island, if Providence and Warwick had failed to enforce their law of 1652 against slavery, "the principle lived among the people."

How, then, could one account for the survival and growth of an institution so repugnant to the desires of a free people? Bancroft's answer was one which Americans had long resorted to; it was founded on a sharp moral distinction between the original cause of American slavery—the selfish greed of European merchants and governments— and the conditions which led to its perpetuation. If the type of servitude fastened on America had been the same as that which Europeans had long endured, the problem would soon have been solved "by the benevolent spirit of colonial legislation." But from the beginning, America had been plagued with racial incompatibility: "The negro race, from the first, was regarded with disgust, and its union with the whites forbidden under ignominious penalties."

Thus racial dissimilarity could be offered as an excuse for laws and practices which simply made the best of an unfortunate situation. And when Bancroft took a larger perspective, he had to admit that America's burden was not, after all, without its rewards. In his native continent the African would have remained in "unproductive servitude"; in America at least his labor contributed greatly to the wealth of nations. Adopting for the moment one of the favorite theories of Southern apologists, Bancroft concluded that "in the midst of the horrors of slavery and the slave trade, the masters had, in part at least, performed the office of advancing and civilizing the negro."

While Bancroft saw a basic contradiction between slavery and America's mission, he resolved the dilemma in a manner that was apparently satisfactory to most of his countrymen. The institution was alien to the true nature of the New World; it had been imposed on the people against their will, and the guilt thus fell upon an already guilt-sickened Europe. Yet in a larger view, even slavery appeared as part of the providential plan for the redemption of the human race. In Bancroft's eyes the first ship that brought Negroes to America was a "sure pledge" that in due time ships from the New World would carry the blessings of Christianity to Africa. Even selfishness and injustice had a role to play in the historical unfolding of truth and liberty. Americans could comfort themselves with the thought that Negro slavery, a vestige of Old World corruption, was only a temporary irritant which would gradually disappear under the beneficent pressure of democratic institutions. The history of the slavery controversy in the United States well testifies that Bancroft was not alone in this optimistic belief.

We have suggested that Negro slavery, a product of innumerable decisions of self-interest made by traders and princes in Europe and Africa, was an intrinsic part of American development from the first discoveries. The evolution of the institution was also coeval with the creation of the idea of America as a new beginning, a land of promise where men's hopes and aspirations would find fulfillment. The dreams and ideals embodied in various images of the New World would not necessarily conflict with the enslavement of a foreign people unless there were already tensions over slavery in the system of values which Europeans applied to America. That there were such tensions remains to be shown. For the moment it will suffice if we note that the problem of slavery in the New World could be conceptualized as part of a general conflict between ideals and reality in the course of human history. Thus the Abbé Raynal hinted that the discrepancy between natural law and colonial slavery was so great that revolution might be necessary to bring the ideal and reality of America into harmony. For Henri Wallon and Auguste Comte, America itself was something of an anomaly, since it represented a disturbing retrogression from the course of historical progress. Yet Wallon's faith in the power of Christianity and Comte's confidence in the inexorable laws of history led them to expect the imminent triumph of freedom. To some extent all three of these thinkers associated the paradox of modern slavery with America itself, but to George Bancroft servitude was fundamentally extrinsic to the New World, whose very meaning lay in the emancipation of mankind. Although Bancroft recognized that the Negro had played a vital part in the founding of certain colonies, he felt that slavery was so contrary to America's destiny that it would evaporate from the sheer heat of triumphant democracy.

The Mythic Puritan

Carl N. Degler

Few groups in history have suffered more from a bad press than have the seventeenth-century Puritans of the Massachusetts Bay Colony. The word *Puritan* immediately evokes images of a dour and drab society populated by prigs. This popular image of the Puritans as premature Victorians needs readjustment. Carl Degler, Emeritus Professor of History at Stanford, challenges many of the stock notions so long associated with Puritan New England. He concludes that the Puritans were both more humane and more complex than formerly imagined.

To most Americans—and to most Europeans, for that matter—the core of the Puritan social heritage has been summed up in Macaulay's well-known witticism that the Puritans prohibited bearbaiting not because of torture to the bear, but because of the pleasure it afforded the spectators. And as late as 1925, H. L. Mencken defined Puritanism as "the haunting fear that someone, somewhere, may be happy." Before this chapter is out, much will be said about the somber and even grim nature of the Puritan view of life, but quips like those of Macaulay and Mencken distort rather than illumine the essential character of the Puritans. Simply because the word "Puritan" has become encrusted with a good many barnacles, it is worthwhile to try to scrape them off if we wish to gain an understanding of the Puritan heritage. Though this process is essentially a negative one, sometimes it is clarifying to set forth what an influence is *not* as well as what it is.

Fundamental to any appreciation of the Puritan mind on matters of pleasure must be the recognition that the typical, godly Puritan was a worker in the world. Puritanism, like Protestantism in general, resolutely and definitely rejected the ascetic and monastic ideals of medieval Catholicism. Pleasures of the body were not to be eschewed by the Puritan, for, as Calvin reasoned, God "intended to provide not only for our necessity, but likewise for our pleasure and delight." It is obvious, he wrote in his famous *Institutes*, that "the Lord hath endowed flowers with such beauty . . . with such sweetness of smell" in order to impress our senses; therefore, to enjoy them is not contrary to God's intentions. "In a word," he concluded, "hath He not made many things worthy of our estimation independent of any necessary use?"

It was against excess of enjoyment that the Puritans cautioned and legislated. "The wine is from God," Increase Mather warned, "but the Drunkard is from the Devil." The Cambridge Platform of the Church of 1680 prohibited games of cards or dice because of the amount of time they consumed and the encouragement they offered to idleness, but the ministers of Boston in 1699 found no difficulty in condoning public lotteries. They were like a public tax, the ministers said, since they took only what the "government might have demanded, with a more *general imposition* . . . and it employes for the *welfare* of the publick, all that is raised by the *lottery*." Though Cotton Mather at the end of the century condemned mixed dancing, he did not object to dancing as such; and his grandfather, John Cotton, at the beginning saw little to object to in dancing between the sexes so long as it did not become lascivious. It was this same John Cotton, incidentally, who successfully contended against Roger Williams' argument that women should wear veils in church.

In matters of dress, it is true that the Massachusetts colony endeavored to restrict the wearing of "some new and immodest fashions" that were coming in from England, but often these efforts were rustrated by the pillars of the church themselves. Winthrop reported in his *History*, for example, that though the General Court instructed the elders of the various churches to reduce the ostentation in dress by "urging it upon the consciences of their people," little change was effected, "for divers of the elders' wives, etc., were in some measure partners in this general disorder."

We also know now that Puritan dress—not that made "historical" by Saint-Gaudens' celebrated statue—was the opposite of severe, being rather in the English Renaissance style. Most restrictions on dress which were imposed were for purposes of class differentiation rather than for ascetic reasons. Thus long hair was acceptable on an upper-class Puritan like Cromwell or Winthrop, but it was a sign of vanity on the head of a person of lower social status. In 1651 the legislature of Massachusetts called attention to that "excess in Apparell" which has "crept in upon us, and especially amongst people of mean condition, to the dishonor of God, the scandall of our profession, the consumption of Estates, and altogether unsuitable to our poverty." The law declared "our utter detestation and dislike, that men or women of mean condition, should take upon them the garb of Gentlemen, by wearing Gold or Silver Lace, or Buttons, or Points at their knees, or to walk in great Boots; or Women of the same rank to wear Silk or Tiffany hoods, or Scarfes, which tho allowable to persons of great Estates, or more liberal education, is intolerable in people of low conditions." By implication, this law affords a clear description of what the well-dressed Puritan of good estate would wear.

If the Puritans are to be saved from the canard of severity of dress, it is also worth while to soften the charge that they were opposed to music and art. It is perfectly true that the Puritans insisted that organs be removed from the churches and that in England some church organs were smashed by zealots. But it was not music or organs as such which they opposed, only music in the meetinghouse. Well-known American and English Puritans, like Samuel Sewell, John Milton, and Cromwell, were sincere lovers of music. Moreover, it should be remembered that it was under Puritan rule that opera was introduced into England—and without protest, either. The first English dramatic production entirely in music—*The Siege of Rhodes*—was presented in 1656, four years before the Restoration. Just before the end of Puritan rule, John Evelyn noted in his diary that he went "to see a

new opera, after the Italian way, in recitative music and scenes. . . ." Furthermore, as Percy Scholes points out, in all the voluminous contemporary literature attacking the Puritans for every conceivable narrow-mindedness, none asserts that they opposed music, so long as it was performed outside the church.

The weight of the evidence is much the same in the realm of art. Though King Charles' art collection was dispersed by the incoming Commonwealth, it is significant that Cromwell and other Puritans bought several of the items. We also know that the Protector's garden at Hampton Court was beautified by nude statues. Furthermore, it is now possible to say that the Puritan closing of the theaters was as much a matter of objection to their degenerate lewdness by the 1640's as an objection to the drama as such. As far as American Puritans are concerned, it is not possible to say very much about their interest in art since there was so little in the seventeenth century. At least it can be said that the Puritans, unlike the Quakers, had no objection to portrait painting.

Some modern writers have professed to find in Puritanism, particularly the New England brand, evidence of sexual repression and inhibition. Though it would certainly be false to suggest that the Puritans did not subscribe to the canon of simple chastity, it is equally erroneous to think that their sexual lives were crabbed or that sex was abhorrent to them. Marriage to the Puritan was something more than an alternative to "burning," as the Pauline doctrine of the Catholic Church would have it. Marriage was enjoined upon the righteous Christian; celibacy was not a sign of merit. With unconcealed disapprobation, John Cotton told a recently married couple the story of a pair "who immediately upon marriage, without ever approaching the *Nuptial* Bed," agreed to live apart from the rest of the world, "and afterwards from one another, too. . . ." But, Cotton advised, such behavior was "no other than an effort of blind zeal, for they are the dictates of a blind mind they follow therein and not of the Holy Spirit which saith, *It is not good that man should be alone*." Cotton set himself against not only Catholic asceticism but also the view that women were the "unclean vessel," the tempters of men. Women, rather than being "a necessary Evil are a necessary Good," he wrote. "Without them there is no comfortable Living for Man. . . ."

Because, as another divine said, "the Use of the Marriage Bed" is "founded in man's Nature," the realistic Puritans required that married men unaccompanied by wives should leave the colony or bring their wives over forthwith. The Puritan settlements encouraged marriages satisfactory to the participants by permitting divorces for those whose spouses were impotent, too long absent, or cruel. Indeed, the divorce laws of New England were the easiest in Christendom at a time when the eloquence of a Milton was unable to loosen the bonds of matrimony in England.

Samuel Eliot Morison in his history of Harvard has collected a number of examples of the healthy interest of Puritan boys in the opposite sex. Commonplace books, for example, indicate that Herrick's poem beginning "Gather ye rosebuds while ye may" and amorous lines from Shakespeare, as well as more erotic and even scatological verse, were esteemed by young Puritan men. For a gentleman to present his affianced with a pair of garters, one letter of a Harvard graduate tells us, was considered neither immoral nor improper.

It is also difficult to reconcile the usual view of the stuffiness of Puritans with the literally hundreds of confessions to premarital sexual relations in the extant church records. It should be understood, moreover, that these confessions were made by the saints or saints-to-be, not by the unregenerate. That the common practice of the congregation was to accept such sinners into church membership without further punishment is in itself revealing. The civil law, it is true, punished such transgressions when detected among the regenerate or among the non-church members, but this was also true of contemporary non-Puritan Virginia. "It will be seen," writes historian Philip A. Bruce regarding Virginia, "from the various instances given relating to the profanation of Sunday, drunkenness, swearing, defamation, and sexual immorality, that, not only were the grand juries and vestries extremely vigilant in reporting these offenses, but the courts were equally prompt in inflicting punishment; and that the penalty ranged from a heavy fine to a shameful exposure in the stocks . . . and from such an exposure to a very severe flogging at the county whipping post." In short, strict moral surveillance by the public authorities was a seventeenth-century rather than a Puritan attitude.

Relations between the sexes in Puritan society were often much more loving and tender than the mythmakers would have us believe. Since it was the Puritan view that marriage was eminently desirable in the sight of God and man, it is not difficult to find evidence of deep and abiding love between a husband and wife. John Cotton, it is true, sometimes used the Biblical phrase "comfortable yoke mate" in addressing his wife, but other Puritan husbands come closer to our romantic conventions. Certainly John Winthrop's letters to his beloved Margaret indicate the depth of attachment of which the good Puritan was capable. "My good wife . . . My sweet wife," he called her. Anticipating his return home, he writes, "So . . . we shall now enjoy each other again as we desire. . . . It is now bed time; but I must lie alone; therefore I make less haste. Yet I must kiss my sweet wife; and so, with my blessing to our children I commend thee to the grace and blessing of the Lord and rest. . . ."

Anne Bradstreet wrote a number of poems devoted to her love for her husband in which the sentiments and figures are distinctly romantic.

> To my Dear and loving Husband
> I prize thy love more than whole Mines of gold
> Or all the riches that the East doth hold.
> My love is such that Rivers cannot quench,
> Nor aught but love from thee give recompense.

In another poem her spouse is apostrophized as

> My head, my heart, mine Eyes, my life, nay more
> My joy, my Magazine of earthly store

and she asks:

> If two be one, as surely thou and I,
> How stayest thou there, whilst I at Ipswich lye?

Addressing John as "my most sweet Husband," Margaret Winthrop perhaps epitomized the Puritan marital ideal when she wrote, "I have many reasons to make me love thee, whereof I will name two: First, because thou lovest God and, secondly, because thou lovest me. If these two were wanting," she added, "all the rest would be eclipsed."

It would be a mistake, however, to try to make these serious, dedicated men and women into rakes of the Renaissance. They were sober if human folk, deeply concerned about their ultimate salvation and intent upon living up to God's commands as they understood them, despite their acknowledgment of complete depravity and unworthiness. "God sent you not into this world as a Play-House, but as a Work-House," one minister told his congregation. To the Puritan this was a world drenched in evil, and, because it truly is, they were essentially realistic in their judgments. Because the Puritan expected nothing, Perry Miller has remarked, a disillusioned one was almost impossible to find. This is probably an exaggeration, for they were also human beings; when the Commonwealth fell, it was a Puritan, after all, who said, "God has spit in our faces." But Professor Miller's generalization has much truth in it. Only a man convinced of the inevitable and eternal character of evil could fight it so hard and so unceasingly.

The Puritan at his best, Ralph Barton Perry has said, was a "moral athlete." More than most men, the Puritan strove with himself and with his fellow man to attain a moral standard higher than was rightfully to be expected of so depraved a creature. Hence the diaries and autobiographies of Puritans are filled with the most torturous probing of the soul and inward seeking. Convinced of the utter desirability of salvation on the one hand, and equally cognizant of the total depravity of man's nature on the other, the Puritan was caught in an impossible dilemma which permitted him no rest short of the grave. Yet with such a spring coiled within him, the Puritan drove himself and his society to tremendous heights of achievement both material and spiritual.

Such intense concern for the actualization of the will of God had a less pleasant side to it, also. If the belief that "I am my brother's keeper" is the breeding ground of heightened social conscience and expresses itself in the reform movements so indigenous to Boston and its environs, it also could and did lead to self-righteousness, intolerance and narrow-mindedness, as exemplified in another product of Boston: Anthony Comstock. But this fruit of the loins of Puritanism is less typical of the earthy seventeenth-century New Englander than H. L. Mencken would have us think. The Sabbatarian, antiliquor, and antisex attitudes usually attributed to the Puritans are a nineteenth-century addition to the much more moderate and essentially wholesome view of life's evils held by the early settlers of New England.

To realize how different Puritans could be, one needs only to contrast Roger Williams and his unwearying opponent John Cotton. But despite the range of differences among Puritans, they all were linked by at least one characteristic. That was their belief in themselves, in their morality and in their mission to the world. For this reason, Puritanism was intellectual and social dynamite in the seventeenth century; its power could behead kings, overthrow governments, defy tyrants, and disrupt churches.

The Reformation laid an awesome burden on the souls of those who broke with the Roman Church. Proclaiming the priesthood of all believers, Protestantism made each man's relationship to God his own terrifying responsibility. No one else could save him; therefore no one must presume to try. More concerned about his salvation than about any mundane matter, the Puritan was compelled, for the sake of his immortal soul, to be a fearless individualist.

It was the force of this conviction which produced the Great Migration of 1630–40 and made Massachusetts a flourishing colony in the span of a decade. It was also, ironically, the force which impelled Roger Williams to threaten the very legal and social foundations of the Puritan Commonwealth in Massachusetts because he thought the oligarchy wrong and himself right. And so it would always be. For try as the rulers of Massachusetts might to make men conform to their dogma, their own rebellious example always stood as a guide to those who felt the truth was being denied. Such individualism, we would call it today, was flesh and bone of the religion which the Puritans passed on. Though the theocracy soon withered and died, its harsh voice softened down to the balmy breath of Unitarianism, the belief in self and the dogged resistance to suppression or untruth which Puritanism taught never died. Insofar as Americans today can be said to be individualistic, it is to the Puritan heritage that we must look for one of the principal sources.

In his ceaseless striving for signs of salvation and knowledge of God's intentions for man, the Puritan placed great reliance upon the human intellect, even though for him, as for all Christians, faith was the bedrock of his belief. "Faith doth not relinquish or cast out reason," wrote the American Puritan Samuel Willard, "for there is nothing in Religion contrary to it, tho' there are many things that do transcend and must captivate it." Richard Baxter, the English Puritan, insisted that *the most Religious*, are the most truly, and *nobly rational.*" Religion and reason were complementary to the Puritan, not antithetical as they were to many evangelical sects of the time.

Always the mere emotion of religion was to be controlled by reason. Because of this, the university-trained Puritan clergy prided themselves on the lucidity and rationality of their sermons. Almost rigorously their sermons followed the logical sequence of "doctrine," "reasons," and "uses." Conscientiously they shunned the meandering and rhetorical flourishes so beloved by Laudian preachers like John Donne, and in the process facilitated the taking of notes by their eager listeners. One of the unforgivable crimes of Mistress Anne Hutchinson was her assertion that one could "feel" one's salvation, that one was "filled with God" after conversion, that it was unnecessary, in order to be saved, to be learned in the Bible or in the Puritan writers. It was not that the Puritans were cold to the Word—far from it. A saint was required to testify to an intense religious experience—almost by definition emotional in character—before he could attain full membership in the Church. But it was always important to the Puritans that mere emotion—whether it be the anarchistic activities of the Anabaptists or the quaking of the Friends—should not be mistaken for righteousness or proper religious conduct. Here, as in so many things, the Puritans attempted to walk the middle path—in this instance, between the excessive legalism and formalism of the Catholics and Episcopalians and the flaming, intuitive evangelism of the Baptists and Quakers.

Convinced of reason's great worth, it was natural that the Puritans should also value education. "Ignorance is the mother (not of Devotion but) of Heresy," one Puritan divine declared. And a remarkably well-educated ministry testified to the Puritan belief that learning and scholarship were necessary for a proper understanding of the Word of God. More than a hundred graduates of Cambridge and Oxford Universities settled in New England before 1640, most of them ministers. At the same date not five men in all of Virginia could lay claim to such an educational background. Since Cambridge University, situated on the edge of Puritan East Anglia, supplied most of the graduates in America, it was natural that Newtown, the site of New England's own college, would soon be renamed in honor of the Alma Mater. "After God had carried us safe to New-England," said a well-known tract, some of its words now immortalized in metal in Harvard Yard, "one of the next things we longed and looked after, was to advance learning, and perpetuate it to posterity; dreading to leave an illiterate ministry to the churches, when the present ministers shall lie in the dust." "The College," founded in 1636, soon to be named Harvard, was destined to remain the only institution of higher learning in America during almost all the years of the seventeenth century. Though it attracted students from as far away as Virginia, it remained, as it began,

the fountainhead of Puritan learning in the New World.

Doubt as one may Samuel Eliot Morison's claims for the secular origins of Harvard, his evidence of the typically Renaissance secular education which was available at the Puritan college in New England is both impressive and convincing. The Latin and Greek secular writers of antiquity dominated the curriculum, for this was a liberal arts training such as the leaders had received at Cambridge in England. To the Puritans the education of ministers could be nothing less than the best learning of the day. So important did education at Harvard seem to the [colonies in Connecticut] in 1644 that the legislature ordered each town to appoint two men to be responsible for the collection of contributions from each family for "the maynetaunce of scolars at Cambridge. . . ."

If there was to be a college, preparatory schools had to be provided for the training of those who were expected to enter the university. Furthermore, in a society dedicated to the reading of the Bible, elementary education was indispensable. "It being one chief project of that old deluder Satan to keep men from the knowledge of the Scriptures" began the first school laws of Massachusetts (1647) and Connecticut (1650). But the Puritans supported education for secular as well as religious reasons. The Massachusetts Code of 1648, for instance, required children to be taught to read inasmuch "as the good education of children is of singular behoof and benefit to any Commonwealth."

The early New England school laws provided that each town of fifty families or more was to hire a teacher for the instruction of its young; towns of one hundred families or more were also directed to provide grammar schools, "the master thereof being able to instruct youths so far as they may be fitted for the University." Though parents were not obliged to send their children to these schools, if they did not they were required to teach their children to read. From the evidence of court cases and the high level of literacy in seventeenth-century New England, it would appear that these first attempts at public-supported and public-controlled education were both enforced and fruitful.

No other colony in the seventeenth century imposed such a high educational standard upon its simple farming people as the Puritans did. It is true, of course, that Old England in this period could boast of grammar schools, some of which were free. But primary schools were almost nonexistent there, and toward the end of the seventeenth century the free schools in England became increasingly tuition schools. Moreover, it was not until well into the nineteenth century that the English government did anything to support schools. Primary and secondary education in England, in contrast with the New England example, was a private or church affair.

Unlike the Puritans, the Quakers exhibited little impulse toward popular education in the seventeenth and early eighteenth centuries. Because of their accent on the Inner Light and the doctrine of universal salvation, the religious motivation of the Puritans for learning was wanting. Furthermore, the Quakers did not look to education, as such, with the same reverence as the Puritans. William Penn, for example, advised his children that "reading many books is but a taking off the mind too much from meditation." No Puritan would have said that.

Virginia in the seventeenth century, it should be said, was also interested in education. Several times in the course of the century, plans were well advanced for establishing a university in the colony. Free schools also existed in Virginia during the seventeenth century, though the lack of village communities made them inaccessible for any great numbers of children. But, in contrast with New England, there were no publicly supported schools in Virginia; the funds for the field schools of Virginia, like those for free schools in contemporary England, came from private or ecclesiastical endowment. Nor was Virginia able to bring its several plans for a college into reality until William and Mary was founded at the very end of the century.

Though the line which runs from the early New England schools to the distinctly American system of free public schools today is not always progressively upward or uniformly clear, the connection is undeniable. The Puritan innovation of public support and control on a local level was the American prototype of a proper system of popular education.

American higher education in particular owes much to religion, for out of the various churches' concern for their faiths sprang a number of colleges, after the example of the Puritans' founding of Harvard. At the time of the Revolution, there were eight colleges besides Harvard in the English colonies, of which all but one were founded under the auspices of a church. William and Mary (1693) and King's

College, later Columbia (1754), were the work of the Episcopalians; Yale (1701) and Dartmouth (1769) were set up by Congregationalists not comforted by Harvard; the College of New Jersey, later Princeton (1747), was founded by the Presbyterians; Queens College, later Rutgers (1766), by the Dutch Reformed Church; the College of Rhode Island, later Brown (1764), by the Baptists. Only the Academy of Philadelphia, later the University of Pennsylvania (1749), was secular in origin.

The overwhelming importance of the churches in the expansion of American higher education during the colonial period set a pattern which continued well into the nineteenth century and to a limited extent is still followed. Well-known colleges like Oberlin, Wesleyan, Haverford, Wittenberg, Moravian, Muhlenberg, and Notre Dame were all founded by churches in the years before the Civil War. By providing a large number of colleges (recall that England did not enjoy a third university until the nineteenth century), the religious impulses and diversity of the American people very early encouraged that peculiarly American faith in the efficacy and desirability of education for all.

When dwelling on the seminal qualities of the seventeenth century, it is tempting to locate the source of the later American doctrine of the separation of Church and State and religious freedom in the writings of Roger Williams and in the practices of provinces like New York, Maryland and Pennsylvania. Actually, however, such a line of development is illusory. At the time of the Revolution all the colonies, including Rhode Island, imposed restrictions and disabilities upon some sects, thus practicing at best only a limited form of toleration, not freedom of religion—much less separation of Church and State. Moreover, Roger Williams' cogent and prophetic arguments in behalf of religious freedom were forgotten in the eighteenth century; they could not exert any influence on those who finally worked out the doctrine of religious freedom enshrined in the national Constitution. In any case, it would have been exceedingly difficult for Williams to have spoken to Jefferson and the other Virginians who fought for religious freedom. To Williams the Puritan, the great justification for freedom of religion was the preservation of the purity of the Church; to the deistic Virginians, the important goal was the removal of a religious threat to the purity and freedom of the State.

The Pilgrims and the Mythic Maypole of Merry Mount

John Demos

The Pilgrims were not the Puritans. They were separatist—outside the Church of England. This small, struggling, generally poor group has exerted an influence on American history and its mythology far in excess of what might seem warranted. The myth-laden litany includes the desperate and heroic settlement at Cape Cod; early lifesaving aid from the Indians Samoset, Squanto, and Massasoit; the first written political covenant in America, the Mayflower Compact; the first Thanksgiving; the triangle of John Alden, Priscilla Mullins, and Miles Standish. It tells also of the Pilgrim battle with Thomas Morton's sinful town of Merry Mount, some forty miles northward. Here, the Yale historian John Demos, a leading social historian of colonial America, develops this story of Gomorrah in the wilderness. After the obligatory verbal and written remonstrances, military action set out to break up the revelry; Morton was arrested and exiled. No evidence is extant concerning how long Miles Standish and his troops observed the young Indian and white revelers before destroying the eighty-foot maypole, that dreaded Bachinalian icon, dripping with pagan symbolism. After recounting Morton's subsequent efforts against the Pilgrim and Puritan leadership, and his ultimate failure and demise, Professor Demos observes that Merry Mount might not have caused such a fuss had it occurred anywhere else in colonial America. In his book *New English Canaan*, Morton outlined an alternative vision for America—calling for respect for Indians and the environment. Can fun-seeking rascals be visionaries? Why not?

TIME: Summer, 1628. PLACE: Merry Mount, a small coastal settlement on the edge of the Massachusetts wilderness. "Pilgrim" Plymouth lies somewhat to the south; "Puritan" Boston will not be founded for another two years. ACTION: A group of young revelers, Englishmen and Indians together, dance around a lofty maypole. There is food and drink aplenty; jollity reigns. Caught in the spirit of the moment, the revelers do not sense an alien presence in the forest nearby. Then a band of Pilgrim foot soldiers bursts onto the scene. The dancing stops. The maypole comes down. Merry Mount will be merry no more.

Thus, the scenario above is a familiar set piece from the lore of early American history. But the script can be shaded in various ways. In one version this is a story of God-fearing pioneers clearing out a nest of wickedness. In another it is a tale of bigots and busybodies aroused to action against the innocent pleasures of simple country people. In still others, the elements are blended in more complicated ways. Indeed, Merry Mount figures in various guises in the work of Washington Irving, Nathaniel Hawthorne, Henry Wadsworth Longfellow, Stephen Vincent Benét, and Robert Lowell.

Like all such set pieces, this one has its cast of stick-figure characters. The principals are Miles Standish, captain of the Pilgrim band, and Thomas Morton, chief of the Merry Mount revelers. Standish, of course, is a folklore perennial, known to generations of schoolchildren from his own time to ours. But who was Morton? "A lord of misrule and riot and sin," writes Longfellow (taking his cue from William Bradford). "A merry man . . . [who] liked a merry frolic . . . [and] said 'Those long-nosed Pilgrims give an honest heart the colic,' " counters Benét (following Hawthorne and Morton himself). In fact there is a real historical personage buried somewhere in these contradictions—a man whose life can still speak to us across the centuries.

Almost nothing is known of his origins. An educated guess has him born about the year 1580, somewhere in the English "West country." He claimed for himself the status of a "gentleman" and the training of an attorney. Certainly he practiced law in the environs of London. His first definite appearance in any records still extant came with a series of legal proceedings that began about 1618; he was representing a certain widow Miller in a struggle with her eldest son for control of family properties. In 1621 Morton married his client and became himself a principal in the Millers' court case. The upshot, however, was a complete victory for the son, and a magistrate's complaint that Morton had "sold all [his wife's] goods, even to her wearing apparel, and is fled."

With this Morton then recedes into obscurity, emerging a couple of years later on the shores of New England. He belonged now to a shipload of would-be colonists led by a trader and sea captain named Wollaston. A landing was made near the site of the present-day town of Quincy, Massachusetts, and before long the group had erected a modest settlement there. The following spring, however, Captain Wollaston decamped to Virginia, taking most of the erstwhile settlers with him. Perhaps no more than a dozen remained—among whom Morton became de facto leader.

* * *

This settlement was the germ of the place that Morton would soon christen Ma-re Mount—and that others would know as Merry Mount. It was, in fact,

less a full-fledged community than a simple trading station, one of several such scattered around the perimeter of Massachusetts Bay. The goal was a share in the fur trade with local Indians, and there are reasons to think it was rapidly achieved.

Much of what we know about all this comes from an oddly engaging book written by Thomas Morton some years after Merry Mount's demise. Entitled *New English Canaan*, this work mixes propaganda, self-promotion, travel notes, and literary effect in roughly equal proportions. Long sections detail the manifold "commodities" of wilderness New England. ("The Otter . . . hath a furre so black as jett, and is a furre of very highe price. . . . Ducks, there are of three kindes . . . very fatt and dainty flesh. . . . Oakes are there of two sorts, white and redd . . . and they are found to be a tymber, that is more tough than the oak of England.") Indeed, this catalog of commodities reveals a commercial ambition extending well beyond the matter of furs. Morton conjures up visions of trade with far-off partners: barrel staves, for example, will make a "prime commodity" in the Canary Islands, while codfish will prove "better than the golden mines of the Spanish Indies; for without dried Codd the Spaniard, Portingal, and Italian, would not be able to vittel of a shipp for the Sea. . . ."

However, Morton's attraction to New England was not only by way of material gain. Indeed, the special charm of *New English Canaan* lies in its warm sensitivity to nature as such. The book abounds with small, sharp descriptions of animal biology and behavior: the flying squirrel "with bat like winges, which hee spreads when hee jumpes from tree to tree," the rattlesnake's tail "which soundeth (when it is in motion,) like pease in a bladder," the beaver's way of drawing logs "with the help of other beavers (which held by each others tayles like a teeme of horses). . . ." One feels in all this an ease, a quiet confidence, a kind of concert between the man and his surroundings. Occasionally Morton's tone becomes downright playful. "Turkies," he writes, have "divers times in great flocks . . . sallied by our doores; and then a gunne (being commonly in a redinesse,) salutes them with such a courtesie, as makes them take a turne in the Cooke roome. They daunce by the doore so well."

At some points the warmth of Morton's feelings overwhelms his powers of observation—and strains his reader's credulity. New England, he tells us, seems a "paradice" of "goodly groves of trees; dainty fine round rising hillucks: delicate faire large plaines; sweete cristall fountaines; and cleare running streames. . . ." Its very atmosphere is of such "excellency" that sickness has scarcely been known there; what is more, "divers arematicall herbes, and plants . . . with their vapors perfume the aire. . . ." The winds are "not so violent as in England," the rains "more moderate," the climate "a golden meane betwixt . . . the hote and cold. . . ." Take it altogether, and "in mine eie, t'was Natures Master-peece," Morton concludes. "If this Land be not rich, then is the whole world poore."

* * *

Furthermore, the riches of the land are matched by the gifts and virtues of its native people. Morton describes at length the ingenuity of the Indians in practical things like house construction, garment-making, hunting, and fishing, their "Subtilety" in personal relations, their hardihood in the face of adversity, even their "admirable perfection, in the use of the sences." But what he most admires is their moral character. Notwithstanding their ignorance of religion—and Morton says he would be "more willing to beleeve that the Elephants . . . doe worship the moone" than that Indians "have [any] kinde of worship"—their conduct is in many ways exemplary. They are honest, direct, generous to a fault. They especially discountenance lying and thievery. They share with one another the necessities of life: thus "Platoes Commonwealth is so much practiced by these people." They value "usefull things," not "baubles." In sum, "According to humane reason guided onely by the light of nature, these people leades the more happy and freer life, being voyde of care, which torments the mindes of so many Christians. . . ."

This rosy estimate was based on a prolonged, and apparently quite close, acquaintance. "I have seene," "I have observed," "I have known them": so speaks the first-person voice of authenticity. Indeed, *New English Canaan* offers many glimpses of Morton's life among the Indians. One man "who had lived in my howse before hee had taken a wife" asked Morton to board his young son (that the boy should "thereby . . . become an Englishman . . ."). Another was wont to join Morton in deer hunting. Yet another had guided him to significant points in the countryside, such as the sites of duels with "the trees marked for a memoriall of the Combat. . . ."

Of course it was trade—the buying and selling of "commodities"—that formed the basis for these shared experiences with Indians. And just here Merry Mount differed sharply from its better-known neighbor "plantations." At Plymouth, at Boston, and later at Hartford, New Haven, Providence, and elsewhere, the aim was to establish permanent communities based on a principle of *self*-provision. In these other places trade was secondary to agriculture and artisanship. In a sense these communities looked in on themselves, while Merry Mount faced out toward the wilderness. It is no accident, therefore, that Thomas Morton has more to tell us of New England and its original inhabitants than William Bradford, John Winthrop, and other resident-authors of the time.

But for all that, it was Plymouth and Boston that controlled the future; and it was Plymouth and Boston that would snuff out Merry Mount within a few years. The events that led to this are still not fully clear, but the notorious maypole surely played its part. In the spring of 1627, according to Morton, the Merry Mount group "did devise amongst themselves" a plan for "Revels, & merriment after the old English custome. . . ." A maypole was indeed constructed from "a goodly pine tree of 80. foote longe," and fitted out with ribbons, garlands of flowers, and a "peare of buckshorns" nailed to the top. Large quantities of food and drink were laid by; "drumes, gunnes, pistols, and other fitting instruments" were brought in to provide a satisfactory clamor. Indians arrived to watch—and, no doubt, to participate. The party continued for days. Morton mentions in particular "a merry song . . . sung with a Corus" while "they performed in a daunce, hand in hand about the Maypole. . . ." The words, presumably, conveyed the spirit of the whole occasion:

> Drinke and be merry, merry, merry boyes,
> Let all your delight be in Hymens joyes,
> Io! to Hymen now the day is come,
> About the merry Maypole take a Roome.
>
> Make greene garlons, bring bottles out;
> And fill sweet Nectar, freely about,
> Uncover thy head, and feare no harme,
> For hers good liquor to keepe it warme. . . .
>
> Give to the Nymphe thats free from scorne,
> No Irish; stuff nor Scotch over worne,
> Lasses in beaver coats come away,
> Yee shall be welcome to us night and day.

In due course news of the Merry Mount revels reached Plymouth, some forty miles to the south, and provoked a predictable outrage. In Bradford's eyes it was all a matter of "scandall" and "lasciviousness," something that recalled the "beastly practices of ye madd Bacchinalians!" (The maypole he branded an outright "idol.") But it was another year before he and his Plymouth colleagues could find sufficient pretext to intervene.

In fact, there was more than a maypole to worry the "precise Seperatists" (as Morton called them). The fur trade at Merry Mount was flourishing; increasingly, Bradford charged, its basis was guns and liquor. With firearms in the hands of the Indians, Englishmen all over Massachusetts would be endangered. Morton seems not to have denied the accusation, though he did deny trading in liquors. Finally, in the spring of 1628, the Plymouth leaders joined with representatives of the smaller settlements along the coast to plan a concerted response. They elected, first, to "write to him [Morton] and in a friendly & neighborly way to admonish him to forbear those courses." But when he "scorned all advice," they felt obliged to proceed to stronger measures.

*   *   *

Miles Standish and his band of soldiers set out for Merry Mount in early June, with orders to apprehend "this wicked man." But Morton proved to be absent—visiting, it seemed, at a neighboring settlement. They followed him and made their arrest, only to lose him again in a midnight escape. Morton then made his way back to Merry Mount with Standish in hot pursuit. And there a second arrest was made. This time they made it stick. Captors and captive marched away to Plymouth, from where Morton was "sent to England a prisoner." The sequence is fully detailed—with mixed bitterness and hilarity—in the concluding section of *New English Canaan*.

The ostensible charge against Morton was that he traded firearms to Indians—a practice forbidden, so the Plymouth leadership claimed, by royal proclamation. But behind this lay deeper worries. There was the maypole and the explicit affront it gave to Pilgrim sensibilities. There was the prospect that Merry Mount would become a magnet to evildoers—a place where runaway servants, "discontents," and "all ye scume of ye countrie . . . would flock" without regard for law or duty. And there was a darker threat implicit in Morton's close ties to the land and its "savage" people. "Lasses in beaver coats come away,/yee shall be welcome to us night and day," the Maypole revelers had sung. How revolting, how horrifying to right-thinking Englishmen! Merry Mount had realized their worst fears of the wilderness—the crumbling of civilized ways and a reversion to savagery.

There is no record of Morton's arrival in England, but evidently he did not stand trial. He seems, instead, to have remained free to pursue his own interests—and to subvert those of his Plymouth adversaries. He began at this time a lasting alliance with Sir Ferdinando Gorges, an English courtier with strong claims of his own to land in New England. Henceforth Morton, Gorges, and various associates would work almost continuously to undermine the legal foundations of the Puritan colonies.

Surprisingly Morton managed to recross the ocean to New England, barely a year from the time of his departure in chains. Indeed, his first stop was at Plymouth—"in the very faces" of Bradford and company, he wrote, and "to their terrible amazement to see him at liberty." A few weeks later he was back in his house by the bay. The maypole was gone—destroyed the preceding autumn by the Massachusetts magistrate John Endicott. And the name Merry Mount had been changed to Mount Dagon. But otherwise the little settlement remained intact. Morton resumed his Indian trade—more quietly this time.

Meanwhile a new shadow began to loom from the north. Endicott had been the leader of a small advance guard, and in 1630 the Puritan migration to Massachusetts began in earnest. This group, though not "separatist" (that is, cut off from the English mother church) like the Plymouth settlers, would be no less hostile to Morton and his irreverent ways. In fact, the former scenario soon repeated itself: confrontation, arrest, banishment to England. The charge was "a multitude of complaints were received" for harm done by him to both the English and the Indians; but more than that, the Puritan leadership wanted him out of the way. The court directed that all his goods be confiscated and his house burned to the ground. The order was carried out as the prisoner watched from the deck of the ship that would once more carry him overseas.

Through the next dozen years the trail of Thomas Morton can be followed only intermittently. His tracks appear most often in the records of various courts and commissions—the scene of his efforts to undo the "Kingdome of the Seperatists" (and his other New England adversaries) behind their backs.

For this he was able to call on his skills as a lawyer—and as a writer. *New English Canaan* was composed sometime between 1632 and 1635, largely for political reasons. Morton's glowing picture of New England and its "commodities" was meant to heighten royal interest there, while his account of Puritan misgovernment would presumably arouse royal indignation. The issue of the colonial charters did, in fact, reach the highest levels of Court administration, and at least twice revocation seemed near. But the outbreak of the English Civil War, in 1642, removed any realistic chance of turning official attention toward such remote problems.

There was, however, one route left to try: Morton could go back to his beloved "Canaan" to assert his claims in person. And by this time his claims had become very large indeed. With patents and commissions variously obtained he hoped to prove ownership of vast tracts in Maine, in Connecticut, in the Narragansett country of Rhode Island, and on Martha's Vineyard.

So it was that, in autumn 1643, he went westward across the Atlantic for the third and final time. As before, he landed at Plymouth; as before, he was greeted with much doubt and suspicion but was allowed to stay through the winter. Spring found him on the move through the wilderness, in pursuit of his ever-receding goals. Far from becoming a rich landowner at last, he "lived meanly" (so said his old Pilgrim antagonists) and "could not procure the least respect" from anyone. His land claims came to nothing.

*   *   *

Again the long arm of Puritan law caught up with him. Arrested in Massachusetts in September 1644, he was accused of having made "complaint against us" to the royal privy council. Why this should have been accounted a crime is far from clear, but in any case Morton could scarcely deny it. (A related accusation, that he had "set forth a book against us," could not be proved, since there was no copy of *New English Canaan* at hand.) The magistrates sent to England for "further evidence," while the defendant languished in a Boston jail. There he remained for almost a year—"laid in Irons," he complained, "to the decaying of his Limbs." Eventually the court released him ("being old and crazy") with a view to enabling him "to go out of the jurisdiction." And go he did—to a tiny fishing station in non-Puritan Maine. There he lived, Winthrop tells us, "poor and despised, [and] died within two years after."

It is fitting that what little we know of Morton's death should come from John Winthrop. For Morton's *life* would scarcely have been known to us but for the Puritans. Had he chosen to settle in Virginia or Maryland or New York, had he traded there with Indians, and raised a maypole, and led a springtime revel "after the old English custome," he would have gone unrecorded and unremembered. If he is in our history books today, and even in our folklore, it is because the Puritans put him there.

The Merry Mount–Puritan contrast is, in fact, still instructive. The Puritans' encounter with presettlement New England went all one way: in their own terms, the Indians had to be "civilized" (or eradicated), the "howling wilderness" had to be progressively transformed into a "pleasant garden." The sheer force of it all was and remains, impressive. Here is a prototype of much that came later in American history: the conquest of frontiers and their native populations, the massive development of environmental bounty, the whole "go-ahead spirit."

But Morton shows us another way—what might have been but wasn't. A willingness to bend to the wilderness, to learn from it, to enjoy its beauty (as well as its abundant "commodities"); an appreciation for the strange ways of a "savage" people; an instinct for compromise between human need and environmental constraint—if there is any enduring message from Morton and Merry Mount, that is it. On our shrinking planet of the late twentieth century, it sounds almost modern—and not a little appealing.

The Virginia Gentry and the Democratic Myth

D. Alan Williams

One tempting conclusion about early American history is that democracy had been widespread during the colonial period, particularly in the eighteenth century. Applied to Virginia, this belief holds that a political minority, the gentry, had to defer to the wishes of the majority—the owners of small and middle-sized farms. D. Alan Williams, professor of history at the University of Virginia, demonstrates here that it was in fact the landed gentry—a tight-knit group—that dominated Virginia's political, economic, and social life, with the support and good wishes of the lesser groups. The gentry controlled and filled important positions of power. The "people" could only vote for members of the House of Burgesses, and even then their choices came from among the privileged classes.

Colonial Virginia invariably provides the model for the typical southern colony—an aristocratic, staple-producing, agrarian society, divided geographically, economically, and socially into a coastal tidewater and an upcountry piedmont and valley. Originally conceived as a home for free laborers, craftsmen, and small farmers, Virginia by the eighteenth century exploited slave labor, nearly destroyed its yeoman farmer class, and turned over its government to a planter gentry. Land ownership was a prerequisite for voting and essential for political advancement and social prestige, and though many were landowners, government remained a monopoly of the wealthy and wellborn. The Anglican church was more firmly established in law than New England Congregationalism. All political officials were appointed, except members of the House of Burgesses. In sum, Virginia possessed most of the classic ingredients for social and political conflict.

Yet, in fact, sectional and social controversy were at a minimum in eighteenth-century Virginia. Some historians have even proclaimed the colony a democratic society with power in the hands of the people rather than the gentry. They have duly noted the presence of such Virginia revolutionaries, republi-cans, and libertarians as George Washington, Patrick Henry, George Mason, Thomas Jefferson, and James Madison. Indeed, they have seen in Virginia's golden age (1720–70) the symbol of the ideal agrarian society whose monuments have been preserved in Williamsburg, Mount Vernon, Monticello, and the great James River plantations.

Clearly, Virginia presents us with contradictions. How do we explain them? Are historical appearances deceiving? Or is it a matter of semantics? Does government led by the wealthy necessarily mean aristocracy? Does democracy exist just because a majority of the populace has the right to vote?

Essentially, seventeenth-century Virginia society was a small-farmer society. Although some large landholders existed, most settlers themselves cultivated the fields with the aid of an occasional indentured servant. Even the large farmers were self-made men who had attained their positions by hard work. Small farmer and large planter sat together on the county courts, the vestries, and in the assembly. Class distinctions were blurred in a society made up entirely of struggling farmers, most of whom found life crude and precarious.

Three major developments between 1660 and

37

1720 changed the kind of society and government Virginia would have: (1) establishment of the English imperial system, (2) Bacon's Rebellion, (3) introduction of slavery and the large plantation.

The great test of whether Virginia would manage her own affairs came between 1660 and 1720. From the collapse of the London Company until the restoration of Charles II in 1660, Virginia, an isolated and insignificant royal colony, had been virtually free from English control. After 1660, the English formulated a uniform policy for their expanding empire. Political economists, royal officials, merchants, and parliamentary leaders were confident they could construct a thoroughly planned and integrated economy by fitting all parts into the whole and enforcing mercantilistic principles through the navigation acts. The Crown would manage the operation. Charles II and James II appointed governors loyal to them, and issued orders making the royal colonies responsive to their wishes. No longer could Virginia act without recourse to the motherland; the colony must fit the pattern.

In Virginia, it fell to popular Governor William Berkeley (1642–52, 1660–77) to reconstitute royal government after the Civil War and to enforce imperial policies with which he frequently disagreed. These were years of poverty, turmoil, and upheaval. The navigation acts, naval wars with the Dutch, and overproduction almost ruined the tobacco trade and plunged Virginia into a prolonged depression. King Charles not only granted the Carolinas, the Jerseys, and Pennsylvania to his favorites, but also gave away valuable Virginia lands. All colonists suffered, but none more than the small farmers and the older colonial leaders. The result was Bacon's Rebellion.

Bacon's Rebellion of 1676 has been called the forerunner of the American Revolution, a class war between small farmers and planter aristocrats, a struggle for self-government against a despotic governor, and a typical encounter between irresponsible frontiersmen and ill-treated Indians. Some have contended that the revolutionary generation, eager to find precedents for its own rebellion, created a myth out of a minor incident little different from numerous rural disturbances in North Carolina, New Jersey, Maryland, and in England itself.

An Indian war was the immediate cause of the rebellion. The obvious sources of upheaval were economic—depression, high taxes, war, and the destruction of the Dutch tobacco trade by the navigation acts.

The underlying source was social—the old leaders' loss of status to new migrants coming into the colony after 1650.

For several years, both large landholders and small farmers had been gradually moving westward in search of rich tobacco land. They paid scant attention to Indian treaty rights or possible reprisals. Although settlement had reached only fifty miles beyond Jamestown and had barely penetrated inland from the rivers, incidents along the frontier mounted, with both whites and Indians committing raids and atrocities. The frontiersmen were no more restrained than the half-savage Indians. Though undeclared war raged, by early 1676 Governor Berkeley vacillated. He feared to touch off a general Indian war, which would bring needless bloodshed, as in King Philip's War in New England, and would upset the Indian trade that several of his friends were engaged in. The harassed settlers, some large landholders among them, rallied behind Nathaniel Bacon, a financially embarrassed young councilor whose overseer had been killed by roving Indians. Against Berkeley's express orders, Bacon attacked and slaughtered two tribes allied with Virginia. He contended that they were hostile Indians, but some cynics noted that these same Indians also held choice lands and large caches of furs. The governor promptly proclaimed the attackers in rebellion.

Bacon's forces, fully aroused and armed, turned from Indian problems to redress their political grievances, thereby revealing the social facet of the conflict. During the English Civil War, Virginians had had a taste of the independent local government they long savored. In the early part of the war, Berkeley set up efficient county and parish governments. After Cromwell triumphed in England, he abolished royal government in the colony and replaced Berkeley with powerless governors elected by the assembly. In the absence of effective central leadership, county justices of the peace, parish vestrymen, and local burgesses became Virginia's political leaders.

However, when the Restoration came in 1660, Berkeley regained his office and attempted to reestablish the central government in Jamestown. In the spirit of Stuart politics, he appointed favorites to the county courts and supported local cliques, which established property qualifications for voting and replaced popularly elected vestries with self-perpetuating vestries.

Berkeley consolidated his position by keeping

the same loyal assembly in session for fifteen years. To the chagrin of the early colonial leaders, his favorites were new men who had come to Virginia during and after the civil war. They were frequently well trained, and had political and economic connections in England. Bacon's chief lieutenants were older, established planters, disgruntled at losing their former power and prestige. These frustrated colonists seized on the unsettled Indian conditions to voice political protests. At a hastily called assembly in June, 1676, they passed laws, "democratical" in nature, aimed at breaking the power of Berkeley's county oligarchies and reasserting the position of the old settlers. What ultimately was intended is unknown. Bacon died; the rebellion collapsed; and Berkeley, going berserk, executed twenty men in what was the only political blood purge in American history.

Bacon's Rebellion produced no great Virginia victory over royal authority. Crown restraints in Virginia and other colonies grew greater in the 1680's. Governor Thomas Lord Culpeper (1677–83) and Lord Howard of Effingham (1684–88) both were selected representatives of Stuart imperial policies. Lord Howard, in particular, was a persistent, obedient servant of the Stuarts, a confirmed believer in the divine right of kings, and completely unsympathetic toward representative government. The assembly, he asserted, should meet only when called by the king, should consider business previously approved by the Crown, and should execute only those laws that had been scrutinized by royal attorneys. Had such a policy been carried out, colonial self-government would have been squelched. But this did not happen, because bitter opponents of the 1670's joined forces to isolate and neutralize the governors, thereby depriving them of the loyalty of a proroyalist political faction in Virginia.

The Stuart threat to representative government ended with the Glorious Revolution of 1688. Englishmen thrust James II from the throne and called William and Mary to be their monarchs. This bloodless coup brought significant changes to Virginia. Howard left the colony, and his able successors, if they did not always appreciate the assembly, respected its right to speak for the colony and relied heavily on it for direction. The Virginia Assembly, sensitive to the growing powers of Parliament, sought the same for itself. From stubbornly resisting direct royal influence in the 1680's, Virginia after 1690 waged a subdued, unspectacular, and highly effective campaign to neutralize the governor's influence in domestic politics. By 1720, the campaign had succeeded.

Social and economic changes understandably paralleled and interacted with political change. By the early eighteenth century, the Indian threat had vanished, expansion without fear was possible, altered marketing conditions in Europe created new demands, and English and Scottish merchants turned to the Virginia market with new vigor. The colony was looked on as an economically underdeveloped area in need of credit. British merchants who controlled the tobacco trades extended credit with reasonable assurance of recovering their investment. Most of this credit went to the larger planters and their friends, who, in turn, acquired more land, expanded operations, upgraded their standard of living, and built the great plantations for which the colony became known.

The slave was the decisive difference between mid-seventeenth-century and mid-eighteenth-century Virginia. Before 1680, slavery on a large scale was rare, but it was commonplace thereafter. Slavery and mass-production methods characterized the tobacco plantation economy after 1720. Virginians condoned slavery as an established fact, though few defended it. The real sufferers, they thought, were not the slaves but the small planter and yeoman farmers who worked the fields with their families and with an occasional indentured servant. The yeoman might draw some satisfaction from knowing that the slave was permanently tied to the bottom rung of the social scale, but he also knew that his position was not much higher because of that same slave. While the small planter might buy a few slaves, he lacked the resources to match his more affluent neighbors, and he lost economic power and social position to the growing number of large slaveholding, landed gentry.

One major change came after 1720, when thousands of Scots-Irish and German immigrants pushed down from Pennsylvania into the fertile Shenandoah Valley and into the western piedmont. Socially and religiously, these new settlers differed from those to the east. They were Presbyterians, Lutherans, Quakers, and German pietists—all dissenters from the established Church of England. Highly individualistic, they were alien to eastern traditions. Tobacco was not their king, since it could not be grown in the hilly backcountry. Yet, there was no sectionalism in colonial Virginia, no regulator uprisings similar to those of the Carolinas, no Paxton boys marching on Williamsburg as they did on Philadelphia, no tenant riots like those in New York and New Jersey. Unlike the Carolina frontier, the Virginia frontier was an overlay of new immigrants and old Virginians. At the same time that Germans and Scots-Irish were drifting south into the valley, settlers from eastern Virginia were moving west onto the piedmont, and speculators were making bold plans to sell their western lands. Acting with dispatch, the Virginia General Assembly wisely established counties and extended representation to the new areas, leaving the settlers with none of the complaints about governmental inequities that upset inhabitants in the Carolinas and Pennsylvania. In an earlier day, the influx of dissenters might have caused serious problems, but religious fanaticism (never strong in Virginia) was on the wane by the eighteenth century, and toleration was on the rise. Some dissenters were harassed, but most were left free to worship as they pleased, provided they paid their tithes to the Anglican church. Moreover, the colony's political leaders were also its leading land speculators. To sell land, they had to have settlers; to get settlers, they had to provide attractions. Their attractions were cheap land, available government, religious toleration, and a minimum of interference by spiritual and secular authorities. Most immigrants wanted no more than that. There was no sectionalism, for there were no sectional grievances. Sectionalism as a divisive force was not apparent until after the Revolution.

The golden age of the Virginia plantation society ran from about 1720 to the eve of the Revolution. The populace—free and slave, native and immigrant—doubled, tripled, and then quadrupled in number. Tobacco was king, land was wealth. With the widest coastal plain in the colonies and fertile valleys just beyond the first mountain ridge, Virginians, unlike South Carolinians, had little difficulty in acquiring land. Dominating this society were the planter gentry—the first aristocracy of the rural south, the counterparts of Charleston's planter-merchants, the equals of Philadelphia and Boston merchants.

The first planter gentry of Virginia had been a score or so of men, primarily members of the council—the Carters, Randolphs, Byrds, Lees, Custises, Pages, and Ludwells—whose families in Virginia had found positions denied them in England, and who had risen to the top through shrewd business practices and the accumulation of vast tracts of land. They had helped carve a civilization out of the wilderness with little help from the Crown; consequently, they often thought royal governors were interlopers gathering spoils after the labor had been done. By intermarriage, they had created a tight coterie of leaders that no governor could break. Sensitive to insult and quick to anger, they zealously guarded their interests through the distribution of Crown land, a function of the council. Generous in parceling land to themselves and their friends, they were equally generous in granting the king's land to all Virginians.

By the mid-eighteenth century, as the colony grew and tobacco trading flourished, the number of affluent planter families reached several hundred. The council could no longer contain all the gentry families. Many burgesses not only were as wealthy as councilors but also were their social equals. As the lower house gained ascendancy over the upper house, the new generation of Randolphs, Harrisons, Lees, and Pages preferred to sit in the House of Burgesses alongside other rising gentry. No longer did small planters gain election to this "tobacco club." Neither did small farmers serve as justices or vestrymen, for offices at all levels were taken up by the gentry and their sons. Distinctions between classes, blurred in the seventeenth century, were much clearer in the eighteenth.

Even though well-defined class lines existed in colonial Virginia, government by the gentry was not necessarily detrimental to the popular interests or so difficult to perform objectively as it would be in a more diverse and complex social order. First, the common bond of land and farming gave the large and small cultivators similar economic interests and made the society homogeneous, at least east of the Blue Ridge Mountains. Second, the lesser farmer naturally elected his more affluent neighbors to the House of Burgesses, since the poorly run plantation was no recommendation for a public office whose main trust was promoting agricultural prosperity. Third, the hard-working small farmers lacked the time to serve in political offices. Finally, since social mobility was fairly fluid in a fast-growing society, the independent farmers and small shareholders saw no reason to oust or destroy the larger planters. They wanted to join them.

The liberal humanism of the planter gentry did much to assure the people that they had little to fear from planter leadership. The gentry willingly served in government because they believed in noblesse oblige—with power and privilege went responsibility. Honor, duty, and devotion to class interest had called them to office, and they took the call seriously. Not without a certain amount of condescension, they thought that government would be run by those less qualified if they refused to serve. They alone had the time, the financial resources, and the education necessary for public office. Moreover, they were the social leaders, and were therefore expected to set an example in manners and morals, to uphold the church, to be generous with benevolences, to serve the government with enlightened self-interest, and in general to be paragons of duty and dignity.

Not surprisingly, they enjoyed the prestige that came with office. To be in a position of authority, to control government, to enact laws, to have the power of life and death over men are intangibles for which there can be no financial compensation. Not that such compensations were omitted from the scheme of things. The real advantage of political service to most officeholders came from the opportunity to acquire land and to extend their business acquaintances. It would not be remiss to say that the gentry had a split personality—one side governed by duty, the other side by lust for land. Perhaps this is what is meant by "enlightened self-interest."

Trained for public duties on their self-contained plantations, the gentry brought to office well-developed talents and tastes for wielding power. Though they remembered their own interests, they nevertheless believed that they were bound to respect and protect those of others. They held that sovereignty was vested in the people, who delegated certain powers to government. They extolled republicanism and willingly enfranchised the people. Their humanism was a product of experience, common sense, and the common law. Liberal humanism not only seemed the right and just attitude; equally important, it worked. Of course, the Virginia gentry were in a position to be charitable. They trusted the people because the people trusted them. One may speculate whether their view of individual liberties would have been so liberal had Virginia been less homogeneous in character or had the lower classes challenged their leadership.

The small farmers and slaveholders had one protection against gentry oligarchy: they were in the majority and they had the right to vote. True, they elected only the burgesses, but that single choice was an important guarantee of their rights, since the House of Burgesses was the strongest political body in Virginia. Thomas Jefferson once remarked that the election process itself tended to eliminate class conflicts and extremism; the aristocrat with no concern for the small farmer was not apt to be elected, and the man who demagogically courted the popular vote was ostracized by the gentry. Therefore, the House of Burgesses became, at the same time, the center of planter rule and of popular government. It operated as a restraint on oligarchy.

Recently, historians Robert and B. Kathryn Brown have gone one step further and argued that Virginia, like Massachusetts, was a democratic society. Economic, social, and political opportunity, they say, existed for all. Far from the gentry's dominating the society, while the small- and middle-sized farmers and slaveholders deferred to their judgment, the reverse was actually the case. Since the gentry were in a minority, they had to defer to the wishes of the majority—the small landholders—if they wanted to retain the reins of office. So say the Browns.

A comparison of the relative positions of the small landowners in the seventeenth and eighteenth centuries shows that without doubt they had immeasurably improved their economic lot at the same time they were being socially outstripped by their more affluent neighbors. Politically, they shifted from holders of office to a check on officeholders.

Yet, was this democracy? What good, indeed, was majority vote when the majority had so little to vote for? Choosing a burgess to sit at the occasional meetings of the General Assembly in Williamsburg was not nearly so important as having a voice in county affairs, where most matters affecting small farmers were decided. Could a society be democratic when every single official except one was appointed by self-perpetuating justices, vestrymen, councilors, and the royal governor, none of whom was responsible to the electorate? Could it be democratic when only men of means held office and when advancement seemed more dependent on wealth and birth than on talent? To a large extent, the small farmers were effectively separated from the power structure, with little means of uniting in a rural society.

The gentry, a minority, were a group of like-minded men working in close alliance, careful not to disturb the social equilibrium. When they contested each other for a seat in the assembly, they offered the electorate only a choice between planter A and planter B, between Tweedledum and Tweedledee. They were the perfect example of what has been consistently true in American society: a cohesive minority dominating an amorphous majority. Perhaps the question that ought to be asked about this planter gentry government is not whether it was democratic but whether it was effective. William Penn once wrote, "Governments depend on men rather than men upon governments, let them be good and government cannot be bad." If this is the primary question, then must not one say that the planter gentry, with their own type of consensus politics, provided eighteenth-century Virginia with enlightened and dynamic leadership?

Or is the half-century of the golden age a period too short to judge the gentry society? After the Revolution, Virginia declined as the soil lost its richness, tobacco lacked foreign markets, and the younger generations moved west and south to more promising opportunities. When the planter aristocracy ceased to be infused and refreshed with the rising gentry, it became inert, lacking in insight, inbred, and distrustful of progress elsewhere. In the place of a masculine Washington or a visionary Jefferson, nineteenth-century leadership could offer as its spokesmen only an effete Edmund Randolph and a myopic John Tyler. Equally significant, the lower class, having deferred so long to the excellent leadership of the eighteenth century, could not recapture what it had let atrophy—its political consciousness.

II

Myths of the Revolutionary Era

Political institutions, religious organizations, and cultural groups invariably shape an identity by way of a myth of origins. Such creation myths always tell of a special moment in the remotely remembered past, a dream time, in the beginning, or once upon a time, when the people or the tribe first came to be. Since the Revolution marks the origins of American political culture, that era especially has symbolically functioned in this mythic way, as the touchstone of the nation's collective identity. It was the time of heroes, the historically consequential moment of sacred time, the classical age of cultural invention and creation whence the country's shared sense of tradition and destiny ultimately derive. It is a story eloquent and compelling in its simplicity.

The historian and later United States senator, Alan Simpson, however, has counseled students of the nation's past to be aware of what he calls the "special character of American history"—its "deceptive resemblance to a short story with a simple plot." Especially when we read history backward, and assign to the past a drama, destiny, or inevitability it never enjoyed, seductive simplicity has a way of overriding the inherent complexity of the historical record. The nation's history is far too often simply portrayed as an extension of its assumed mythic origins—American history rendered as the unfolding of the meaning of the Revolution.

The Revolution and its heritage have at various times served to justify the designs of social and political movements from the radical left to the reactionary right. Both black nationalists and the Daughters of the American Revolution have found the Revolution natively American. Historians, however, have taken matters far beyond merely questioning the historical accuracy of Paul Revere's ride or the revered story of Washington crossing the Delaware. Myths reside here, but they ultimately are of little import in and of themselves. The need is to reexamine critical elements of the traditional tale: the standard emphasis on the assumed heroism of the revolutionary leadership; the myth that assumes a unity of sentiment in support of the revolutionary cause; the quite different stories regarding the revolution as seen from the vantage point of native Americans; the glorification of the Founding Fathers and the related mythology of "constitutional intent"; and the little examined role of women in the Revolution. The selections that follow seek to present significant challenge to simple renderings of the American tradition.

Revolutionary Heroine: The "Savage" Murder of Jane McCrea. *(Courtesy, Library of Congress)*

National Origins. *(Courtesy, Library of Congress)*

Daughters of the American Revolution. *(Courtesy, Library of Congress)*

Washington Crossing the Delaware. *(Courtesy, Library of Congress)*

The Radicalism of the American Revolution

Gordon S. Wood

To examine the causes, nature, and results of the American Revolution is critical to the understanding not only of that subject, but of all subsequent American history. It is axiomatic that historians reflect their times as well as their own personal interests; thus it should surprise no one that the Revolution has been interpreted in a variety of ways. Some sensed the hand of God guiding the patriots to victory. Others have argued that the event is most properly viewed as occurring within the expanding and financially-troubled British empire. The Revolution's nature has also variously been presented as intellectual, economic, or social. The conflict involved a class struggle, best seen from the bottom up. The list goes on. In this article Gordon S. Wood, professor of history at Brown University, argues that the American Revolution was radical in nature. Not only was it radical in its almost total transformation of the nation as a whole, it was the most radical and far-reaching event in all American history. Accepting eighteenth-century terms that saw society as political and hierarchal, Wood charts a mercurial liberalizing course through roughly fifty years, beginning in 1760, from monarchy to republicanism to democracy. A concomitant development reflected a new and vital emergent commercialism that, like democracy, came to pervade the land. Time was when students of American history viewed the Revolutionary Era as a struggle between Hamiltonian commercialism and Jeffersonian democracy. Professor Wood has demonstrated that, no doubt unbeknown to the protagonists, these two elements were "advancing independently along somewhat parallel lines."

We Americans like to think of our revolution as not being radical; indeed, most of the time we consider it downright conservative. It certainly does not appear to resemble the revolutions of other nations in which people were killed, property was destroyed, and everything was turned upside down. The American revolutionary leaders do not fit our conventional image of revolutionaries—angry, passionate, reckless, maybe even bloodthirsty for the sake of a cause. We can think of Robespierre, Lenin, and Mao Zedong as revolutionaries, but not George Washington, Thomas Jefferson, and John Adams. They seem too stuffy, too solemn, too cautious, too much the gentle-men. We cannot quite conceive of revolutionaries in powdered hair and knee breeches. The American revolutionaries seem to belong in drawing rooms or legislative halls, not in cellars or in the streets. They made speeches, not bombs; they wrote learned pamphlets, not manifestos. They were not abstract theorists and they were not social levelers. They did not kill one another; they did not devour themselves. There was no reign of terror in the American Revolution and no resultant dictator—no Cromwell, no Bonaparte. The American Revolution does not seem to have the same kinds of causes—the social wrongs, the class conflict, the impoverishment, the grossly inequitable distributions of wealth—that presumably lie behind other revolutions. There were no peasant uprisings, no jacqueries, no burning of châteaux, no storming of prisons.

Of course, there have been many historians—Progressive or neo-Progressive historians, as they have been called—who have sought, as Hannah Arendt put it, "to interpret the American Revolution in the light of the French Revolution," and to look for the same kinds of internal violence, class conflict, and social deprivation that presumably lay behind the French Revolution and other modern revolutions. Since the beginning of the twentieth century these Progressive historians have formulated various social interpretations of the American Revolution essentially designed to show that the Revolution, in Carl Becker's famous words, was not only about "home rule" but also about "who was to rule at home." They have tried to describe the Revolution essentially as a social struggle by deprived and underprivileged groups against entrenched elites. But, it has been correctly pointed out, despite an extraordinary amount of research and writing during a good part of this century, the purposes of these Progressive and neo-Progressive historians—"to portray the origins and goals of the Revolution as in some significant measure expressions of a peculiar economic malaise or of the social protests and aspirations of an impoverished or threatened mass population—have not been fulfilled." They have not been fulfilled because the social conditions that generically are supposed to lie behind all revolutions—poverty and economic deprivation—were not present in colonial America. There should no longer be any doubt about it: the white American colonists were not an oppressed people; they had no crushing imperial chains to throw off. In fact, the colonists knew they were freer, more equal, more prosperous, and less burdened with cumbersome feudal and monarchical restraints than any other part of mankind in the eighteenth century. Such a situation, however, does not mean that colonial society was not susceptible to revolution.

Precisely because the impulses to revolution in eighteenth-century America bear little or no resemblance to the impulses that presumably account for modern social protests and revolutions, we have tended to think of the American Revolution as having no social character, as having virtually nothing to do with the society, as having no social causes and

no social consequences. It has therefore often been considered to be essentially an intellectual event, a constitutional defense of American rights against British encroachments ("no taxation without representation"), undertaken not to change the existing structure of society but to preserve it. For some historians the Revolution seems to be little more than a colonial rebellion or a war for independence. Even when we have recognized the radicalism of the Revolution, we admit only a political not a social radicalism. The revolutionary leaders, it is said, were peculiar "eighteenth-century radicals concerned, like the eighteenth-century British radicals, not with the need to recast the social order nor with the problems of the economic inequality and the injustices of stratified societies but with the need to purify a corrupt constitution and fight off the apparent growth of prerogative power." Consequently, we have generally described the Revolution as an unusually conservative affair, concerned almost exclusively with politics and constitutional rights, and, in comparison with the social radicalism of the other great revolutions of history, hardly a revolution at all.

If we measure the radicalism of revolutions by the degree of social misery or economic deprivation suffered, or by the number of people killed or manor houses burned, then this conventional emphasis on the conservatism of the American Revolution becomes true enough. But if we measure the radicalism by the amount of social change that actually took place—by transformations in the relationships that bound people to each other—then the American Revolution was not conservative at all; on the contrary: it was as radical and as revolutionary as any in history. Of course, the American Revolution was very different from other revolutions. But it was no less radical and no less social for being different. In fact, it was one of the greatest revolutions the world has known, a momentous upheaval that not only fundamentally altered the character of American society but decisively affected the course of subsequent history.

It was as radical and social as any revolution in history, but it was radical and social in a very special eighteenth-century sense. No doubt many of the concerns and much of the language of that premodern, pre-Marxian eighteenth century were almost entirely political. That was because most people in that very different distant world could not as yet conceive of society apart from government. The social distinctions and economic deprivations that we today think of as the consequence of class divisions, business exploitation, or various isms—capitalism, racism, etc.—were in the eighteenth century usually thought to be caused by the abuses of government. Social honors, social distinctions, perquisites of office, business contracts, privileges and monopolies, even excessive property and wealth of various sorts—all social evils and social deprivations—in fact seemed to flow from connections to government, in the end from connections to monarchical authority. So that when Anglo-American radicals talked in what seems to be only political terms—purifying a corrupt constitution, eliminating courtiers, fighting off crown power, and, most important, becoming republicans—they nevertheless had a decidedly social message. In our eyes the American revolutionaries appear to be absorbed in changing only their governments, not their society. But in destroying monarchy and establishing republics they were changing their society as well as their governments, and they knew it. Only they did not know—they could scarcely have imagined—how much of their society they would change. J. Franklin Jameson, who more than two generations ago described the Revolution as a social movement only to be roundly criticized by a succeeding generation of historians, was at least right about one thing: "the stream of revolution, once started, could not be confined within narrow banks, but spread abroad upon the land."

By the time the Revolution had run its course in the early nineteenth century, American society had been radically and thoroughly transformed. One class did not overthrow another; the poor did not supplant the rich. But social relationships—the way people were connected one to another—were changed, and decisively so. By the early years of the nineteenth century the Revolution had created a society fundamentally different from the colonial society of the eighteenth century. It was in fact a new society unlike any that had ever existed anywhere in the world.

Of course, there were complexities and variations in early American society and culture—local, regional, sectional, ethnic, and class differences that historians are uncovering every day—that make difficult any generalizations about Americans as a whole. This study is written in spite of these complexities and variations, not in ignorance of them. There is a time for understanding the particular, and

there is a time for understanding the whole. Not only is it important that we periodically attempt to bring the many monographic studies of eighteenth-century America together to see the patterns they compose, but it is essential that we do so—if we are to extend our still meager understanding of an event as significant as the American Revolution.

That revolution did more than legally create the United States; it transformed American society. Because the story of America has turned out the way it has, because the United States in the twentieth century has become the great power that it is, it is difficult, if not impossible, to appreciate and recover fully the insignificant and puny origins of the country. In 1760 America was only a collection of disparate colonies huddled along a narrow strip of the Atlantic coast—economically underdeveloped outposts existing on the very edges of the civilized world. The less than two million monarchical subjects who lived in these colonies still took for granted that society was and ought to be a hierarchy of ranks and degrees of dependency and that most people were bound together by personal ties of one sort or another. Yet scarcely fifty years later these insignificant borderland provinces had become a giant, almost continent-wide republic of nearly ten million egalitarian-minded bustling citizens who not only had thrust themselves into the vanguard of history but had fundamentally altered their society and their social relationships. Far from remaining monarchical, hierarchy-ridden subjects on the margin of civilization, Americans had become, almost overnight, the most liberal, the most democratic, the most commercially minded, and the most modern people in the world.

And this astonishing transformation took place without industrialization, without urbanization, without railroads, without the aid of any of the great forces we usually invoke to explain "modernization." It was the Revolution that was crucial to this transformation. It was the Revolution, more than any other single event, that made America into the most liberal, democratic, and modern nation in the world.

Of course some nations of Western Europe likewise experienced great social transformations and "democratic revolutions" in these same years. The American Revolution was not unique; it was only different. Because of this shared Western-wide experience in democratization, it has been argued by more than one historian that the broader social transformation that carried Americans from one century nd one kind of society to another was "inevitable" nd "would have been completed with or without ne American Revolution." Therefore, this broader ocial revolution should not be confused with the American Revolution. America, it is said, would ave emerged into the modern world as a liberal, emocratic, and capitalistic society even without the evolution. One could, of course, say the same thing bout the relationship between the French Revolution and the emergence of France in the nineteenth entury as a liberal, democratic, and capitalistic society; and indeed, much of the current revisionist historical writing on the French Revolution is based on ust such a distinction. But in America, no more than n France, that was not the way it happened: the American Revolution and the social transformation of America between 1760 and the early years of the nineteenth century were inextricably bound together. Perhaps the social transformation would have happened "in any case," but we will never know. It was in fact linked to the Revolution; they occurred together. The American Revolution was integral to the changes occurring in American society, politics, and culture at the end of the eighteenth century.

These changes were radical, and they were extensive. To focus, as we are today apt to do, on what the Revolution did not accomplish—highlighting and lamenting its failure to abolish slavery and change fundamentally the lot of women—is to miss the great significance of what it did accomplish; indeed, the Revolution made possible the anti-slavery and women's rights movements of the nineteenth century and in fact all our current egalitarian thinking. The Revolution not only radically changed the personal and social relationships of people, including the position of women, but also destroyed aristocracy as it had been understood in the Western world for at least two millennia. The Revolution brought respectability and even dominance to ordinary people long held in contempt and gave dignity to their menial labor in a manner unprecedented in history and to a degree not equaled elsewhere in the world. The Revolution did not just eliminate monarchy and create republics; it actually reconstituted what Americans meant by public or state power and brought about an entirely new kind of popular politics and a new kind of democratic officeholder. The Revolution not only changed the culture of Americans—making over their art, architecture, and iconography—but even altered their understanding of history, knowledge, and truth. Most important, it made the interests and prosperity of ordinary people—their pursuits of happiness—the goal of society and government. The Revolution did not merely create a political and legal environment conducive to economic expansion; it also released powerful popular entrepreneurial and commercial energies that few realized existed and transformed the economic landscape of the country. In short, the Revolution was the most radical and most far-reaching event in American history.

George III: The Myth of a Tyrannical King

Darrett B. Rutman

The name of George III of England and the word *tyranny* were once synonymous in the American mind. Representative of those who have contributed to the rehabilitation of his tarnished image is Darrett B. Rutman of the University of Florida. One of the leading scholars of colonial America, Professor Rutman here speaks of the seminal importance of Thomas Paine in redirecting the colonists' revolutionary sentiment from Parliament to King. Before the appearance of Paine's pamphlet *Common Sense* in January 1776, Rutman argues, the colonists had sustained their loyalty to the Crown and sought not independence but "home rule under the king" and a redress of grievances from the British Parliament.

What the colonists considered an effort to change the governance of the empire by depriving their little parliaments of the exclusive right to legislate in local affairs—an effort increasingly discerned as a conspiracy of tyrants against man's innate liberty—had led to open war. Through all of this, however, the colonists had remained loyal subjects of George III. Stamp distributors, customs commissioners, lobsterbacks, the intolerable acts—all symbolized a confrontation with Parliament and ministers, not king. Indeed, during the early years of argument, the king's governors were obeyed, even to the extent of the Virginians going unrepresented in the Stamp Act Congress because their governor dissolved the House of Burgesses just as it was about to name representatives. As late as 1775 the same crowd which "huzzahed" for George Washington as he crossed Manhattan Island on his way to take command of the colonial forces around Boston rushed to the Battery to "huzzah" for a newly-arrived royal governor. Anglicans in the colonies prayed for the health of the king in conformity with the Book of Common Prayer, while in the taverns men drank the health of George and wished him the best of fortune.

> This bumper I crown for our sovereign's health,
> And this for Britannia's glory and wealth.

So went the last verse of "The Liberty Song," almost the national anthem of pre-independence days. Petitions and remonstrances directed to the king professed in all sincerity the loyalty of the colonists. And as the confrontation with Parliament and the king's ministers continued in time, as the colonists came to the position of denying Parliament any authority whatsoever over them, the king, to an ever increasing extent, symbolized the colonists' attachment to an empire which they had not yet considered leaving. "Allegiance to Parliament?" the Second Continental Congress asked rhetorically in 1775; "we never owed—we never owned it. Allegiance to our king? Our words have ever avowed it—our conduct has ever been consistent with it."

Allegiance could be stretched so far, however, before it would break. And colonial allegiance to king and empire was brought almost to the breaking point by Lexington and Concord. In New York and Georgia, militiamen seized control of the ports; in Williamsburg, militiamen (including students at William and Mary College) patrolled the streets to prevent the royal governor from seizing the arms in the public magazine. Extra-legal governments began making their appearance, in some cases extensions of the committees of correspondence, more usually the old lower houses of the legislatures sitting independently of the governor and council. Thus in Virginia, when the governor attempted to stop certain activities of the House of Burgesses by dissolving the House as had been done in Stamp Act days, the House, rather than meekly obeying him, trooped across the street to a tavern and went about its business, subsequently setting itself up as a supreme Virginia Convention. Soon after the governor fled to the safety of a British warship. By December 1775, royal governments had been swept away in all but New Jersey, although the proprietary governments of Pennsylvania and Maryland remained. By July 1776 these too were gone.

On an inter-colonial level, the Second Continental Congress met in May 1775 to remain in session throughout the remainder of the controversy and through the war years ahead. The delegates from the various colonies to the Congress immediately accepted the war situation which existed. In June an organization for war was created, the Congress assuming control of the forces besieging Boston and appointing Virginia's George Washington to command. To pay for the war effort, the Congress authorized the issuance of two million dollars in paper money. In July a "Declaration of the Reasons for Taking up Arms" was issued.

Yet war and independence were not synonymous, a fact which the members of the Congress pressed in their "Declaration." Their quarrel was still with corrupt ministers and a Parliament which had sought "all the easy emoluments of statutable plunder" by undertaking "to give and grant our money without our consent, though we have ever exercised an exclusive right to dispose of our own property." They were resisting only the "intemperate rage for unlimited domination" on the part of ministers and Parliament. This had led to war, but for their part military activities would cease "when hostilities shall cease on the part of the aggressors, and all danger of their being renewed shall be removed." They were

not seeking to break with their "friends and fellow subjects in any part of the empire." "We assure them that we mean not to dissolve that union which has so long and so happily subsisted between us, and which we sincerely wish to see restored." In a petition to the king approved at the same time—the so-called "Olive Branch Petition"—their loyalty to George III was expressed in fervent terms, and that good monarch was humbly requested to intercede for them with Parliament and the ministry to obtain a repeal of the intolerable acts, the withdrawal of the troops, and a renunciation of Parliament's assertion of authority over the colonies. Some objected to what seemed a craven appeal. Massachusetts' John Adams, a delegate to the Congress, considered that the outbreak of war signified the end of such petitions and denounced the Olive Branch as putting "a silly cast on all our doings." But undoubtedly it represented the feelings of most of the colonial leaders. They were fighting to preserve their liberty within the empire as it had been prior to 1763 and as they had come to define it formally during the long controversy: Home rule under the king.

For over a year the Continental Congress remained in this anomalous position of leading a fight against the king's troops for liberty under the king. In July 1775, the Congress hinted at the possibility of looking for foreign aid against the king's army and shortly after set up a five-man "Committee of Secret Correspondence" for the purpose of corresponding with "friends in Great Britain, Ireland, and other parts of the world"—the last phrase ominously portending the future alliance with France. War supplies were purchased abroad and a navy provided under Commodore Esek Hopkins. To the north, Fort Ticonderoga was taken by "rebels" commanded by Ethan Allen and Benedict Arnold; the Battle of Bunker Hill (more accurately Breed's Hill) was fought June 17, 1775 and the siege of Boston went on; an unsuccessful march on Canada was set underway. All in the name of the king.

But the king would not accept the role assigned him by the colonists. He would not be their father and protector. Firm in his support of Parliament and his ministers, he curtly rejected the Olive Branch Petition in August 1775. Subsequently he proclaimed that the Americans were in a state of rebellion to his person.

In the situation the position of the colonists was somewhat unique and certainly difficult. The king was the only link to England and empire which they were prepared by this time to admit, yet the king refused to serve as such a link. As a consequence this last link had to be severed.

It was not easy to do. The colonial leaders were Englishmen. Their professions of loyalty to the monarch were and had always been sincere. If they discerned—and wrote of—a conspiracy to tyrannize in London, the king was no part of it, only his ministers and the Parliament they dominated. Moreover, the king over the years of argument had always been well presented. There was, in effect, little if any animosity toward him.

Still, the last link was severed. Gradually the person of the king began losing some of the sanctity attached to him. The action of the monarch in bluntly and personally refusing the Olive Branch tarnished his reputation, as did the hiring of German mercenary soldiers for the war in America. The various actions of royal officials "in the name of the king" rubbed off on the monarch—Falmouth, Maine, shelled; Norfolk, Virginia, shelled and burned. Then, in January 1776, an outright attack on the king appeared, the first of importance since the start of the troubles. This was *Common Sense,* a little pamphlet by Thomas Paine, an English radical newly arrived in Philadelphia.

Here the very institution of monarchy was attacked, and the English monarchy in particular:

> Government by kings was first introduced into the world by the heathens, from whom the children of Israel copied the custom. It was the most prosperous invention the devil ever set on foot for the promotion of idolatry. The heathens paid divine honors to their deceased kings, and the Christian world has improved on the plan by doing the same to their living ones. How impious is the title of sacred majesty applied to a worm, who in the midst of his splendor is crumbling into dust!

> England since the conquest hath known some few good monarchs but groaned beneath a much larger number of bad ones; yet no man in his senses can say that their claim under William the Conqueror is a very honorable one. A French bastard landing with an armed banditti and establishing himself king of England against the consent of the natives is in plain terms a very paltry rascally original. It certainly hath no divinity in it.

> In England a king hath little more to do than to make war and give away places, which in plain terms is to impoverish the nation and set it together by the ears. A pretty business indeed for a man to be allowed eight hundred thousand sterling a year for and worshipped into the bargain! Of more worth is one honest man to society, and in the sight of God, than all the crowned ruffians that ever lived.

> But the king, you'll say, has a negative in England; the people there can make no laws without his consent. In point of right and good order, it is something very ridiculous that a youth of twenty-one (which hath often happened) shall say to several millions of people older and wiser than himself, 'I forbid this or that act of yours to be law.'

George III himself was castigated as "the royal brute." Aristocracy was castigated for its continual exploitation of the people for the support of luxuries. All the difficulties of the last years were laid not merely to Parliament or the ministers, but to the king as the very leader of their conspiracy against liberty and the thought of reconciliation under the king was dismissed as ridiculous. Independence and a republican government were, to Paine, the common sense solution to the preservation of liberty in America. Sold in record numbers, passed from hand to hand and from tavern to tavern, the pamphlet was vital in creating a tyrant of George III.

The Myth of Popular Participation in the Revolutionary War

James Kirby Martin

On the eve of the conflict with England, the great majority of Americans could justly be described as reluctant revolutionaries. Most simply sought their rights as Englishmen. By most estimates fully one-third of colonial society harbored loyalist sentiments and thought revolution ill-advised. These Loyalists or Tories—those who remained faithful to England and King and to a British America under the Crown—represent the forgotten Americans of the Revolutionary Era. At one point, in fact, history textbooks that told their story were banned from public schools.

Here James Kirby Martin of the University of Houston alludes to the Loyalists and casts by extension a special light on the "sunshine patriots" who also were none too passionate in systematically supporting the Revolution. Indeed so shaky was popular support for fighting that indenturerd servants, African Americans (both slave and free), and women (Margaret "Dirty Kate" Corbin, for one) were mustered into service. Professor Martin accords special attention to the case of Benedict Arnold—ultimately a "loyalist," judged by history as a "traitor." Arnold's behavior at least in some measure, was due to the noticeable lack of public support for the War for Independence. History is particularly harsh with losers. It tends to recall mainly the triumphs and achievements of the victors—and even then often gets the story wrong. Such is the case with the myth of the citizen-soldiers of the American Revolution.

In December 1776, a grim-faced George Washington wondered how much longer the Revolution could last. Since late August the Continental army units under his command had suffered a series of devastating reverses as the British under General William Howe kept coming after his poorly-trained, ill-disciplined troops in the vicinity of New York City. In November, Washington led his force in a desperate flight across New Jersey. He hoped to get across the Delaware River before his army disintegrated completely. Once in eastern Pennsylvania, he would gather together whatever rebel units were still active and attempt some offensive operation, however reckless, to roll back the minions of Howe before everything was lost. "I think the game is pretty near up," Washington wrote on December 18, as he considered various options. "No man," he concluded, "ever had a greater choice of difficulties and less means to extricate himself from them." Had the commander spelled out his problems, the lack of popular support and participation would have headed his list.

Back in the autumn of 1774 at the time of the First Continental Congress, virtually everyone in His Majesty's thirteen colonies had shown genuine concern about protecting and defending American liberties. Patriot leaders at the First Congress still hoped to settle differences with the British parent nation over matters of taxes, representation, and other issues bearing on Colonial rights. Knowing reconciliation might fail, however, they called upon militia companies to muster together and train rigorously, in case defensive warfare against the King's redcoats proved necessary.

Every propertied white adult male, according to the colonists' militia system of defense, had an obligation to bear arms in resisting any threat to home, family, and community. Such military service was synonymous with public virtue, or the willingness to set aside one's personal interests in serving the greater good of the whole community. Above all else, in theory at least, the virtuous citizen-soldier was to do everything possible, including making the ultimate sacrifice of life itself, to preserve the community's best welfare.

Patriot leaders assumed that at the first danger, propertied white males would rush to arms. That fateful moment came on April 19, 1775, when patriot Minute Men and British regulars fired the shots heard round the world at Lexington, Concord, and the road leading back to Boston, Massachusetts. By nightfall, the British had suffered 273 casualties, as compared to 95 for the colonists.

Born on that day was a myth of the Revolutionary citizen-soldier who, when justly grieved and roused to action, not only came forth but also stayed out for the eight-year fight until American liberties and independence were permanently in hand. Certainly the rush to arms on the day of Lexington and Concord—and immediately thereafter—was astounding. Within two weeks as many as 15,000 New Englanders had gathered outside Boston, effectively entrapping General Thomas Gage's 4,000 redcoats in that port city. In March 1776, the British finally abandoned Boston, and all the while the myth of the patriot citizen-soldier kept growing. A Philadelphian aptly summarized these impressions when he wrote of the "Rage Militaire," or what might be called "a passion for arms" that "has taken possession of the whole Continent." Explained one rebel enthusiast, "Our Troops are animated with the love of freedom—We confess that they have not the Advantages arising from Experience and Discipline. But Facts have shown, that native Courage warmed with Pa-

triotism, is sufficient to counterbalance these Advantages."

Pretty words, however, could only cover up reality for so long. During the summer of 1775, the Second Continental Congress "adopted" the patriot soldiery outside Boston as its Continental army. Then Washington, once in overall command, tried to instill discipline, which he called "the soul of the army" that "makes small numbers formidable; procures success to the weak and esteem to all." The citizen-soldiers resisted; they had already proved they could stand up to the British; furthermore, they had begun to find camp life boring; and a few had succumbed to the terrible diseases that infested eighteenth-century military camps. Hundreds of citizen-soldiers decided not to re-enlist for the 1776 campaign; appeals from recruiters to these "guardians of liberty" to "persevere" in resisting the imperial tyrant did not move them. They went home instead.

In 1776, Washington had to build a new army from virtual scratch. The commander stressed the need for rigorous training and discipline, and he drew up plans for a force of 75,000 to include thousands who would accept long-term service—three years or the duration of the war. The army Washington had on hand in August 1776, however, was a pale comparison of the ideal. On paper he had 28,000 troops, but when the British launched their imposing onslaught in the vicinity of New York City that month only 19,000 were present and fit for duty. Many of Washington's troops were untrained militiamen, and his force as a whole was hardly prepared to stand up against the massed firepower and gleaming bayonets of William Howe's 30,000 highly-disciplined soldiers, a portion of whom were Hessians.

Washington's soldiers did not always fight poorly, but retreat was their lot. As they scampered across New Jersey in November, they received virtually no assistance from local militia units. Thomas Paine railed in his first *Crisis* paper against "the summer soldier and the sunshine patriot" who would not rally to the cause in so critical an hour. "These are the times that try men's souls," he wrote plaintively. "Tyranny, like hell, is not easily conquered; yet we have the consolation with us, that the harder the conflict, the more glorious the triumph." The virtuous, propertied citizen-soldier of myth-made America understood what Paine meant, but the *rage militaire* was over. Keeping the Revolution alive would henceforth depend on other kinds of persons stepping forth to assume the primary burden of personal self-sacrifice in the Revolution's service.

In December 1776, Washington knew how grave a problem he had in the matter of popular support and participation. He did not yet have a solution as he rallied together slightly more than 6,000 troops, including local militia. On Christmas evening some 2,400 made it across the icy Delaware River and caught 1,500 Hessians off guard at the advance British outpost at Trenton. Two-thirds of these Hessians became American prisoners, and a week later Washington drove off an enemy relief column a few miles north at Princeton. The stunned British soon pulled their Jersey outposts back toward their main base in New York City.

Washington's triumphs at Trenton and Princeton, accomplished by a mere handful of patriot troops, proved that the American cause was not yet moribund. The two turnabout victories, however, did not generate significant new popular support. Leaders in Congress hoped that vigorous recruiting would help fill the army's ranks, but these efforts proved how few people were willing to sign on for the long-term fight. In May 1777, as the campaign season was about to commence, Washington, having camped that winter in the vicinity of Morristown, New Jersey, had only 10,003 troops on his muster rolls (7,363 actually present and fit for duty). He also had promises from Jersey militia units about coming to his aid, should General Howe venture forth with a sizable force from New York City. Given the faint-hearted performance of Jersey militiamen the previous November, the commander knew better than to rely on them for vital support.

The concerns of Washington and other patriot leaders about flagging or nonexistent popular support received confirmation that spring when a British and loyalist force of 2,000 troops under William Tryon, the former royal governor of New York, invaded western Connecticut. Tryon landed his troops on April 25 and marched thirty miles inland with the intention of destroying Danbury, a rebel supply depot. Tryon and his raiders met with no Lexington and Concord. Not until after leveling Danbury did they have much to contend with. By that time, Continental army general Benedict Arnold, then visiting his home in New Haven, was working with other leaders in trying to rally to arms a populace if not frightened at least apathetic. Arnold's hastily-assembled following did inflict some modest wounds on Tryon's col-

umn before it left the state, but the unwillingness of so many alleged patriots to defend their own communities was an embarrassment at best.

The American cause limped along after 1776, not because of so much personal sacrifice as national myth would have us think but because of so little. Washington proved adept at working with what few resources he had. He believed, for instance, that the Revolution could claim to exist only so long as some form of a respectable Continental force, however small, was in the field. Congress and the states agreed, and they sought to enlist every "able-bodied and effective" person who would agree to long-term service.

Washington and other leaders had a sense of the population base from which they could hope to recruit soldiers. In 1775, about 2.5 million people were resident in the thirteen rebellious colonies. Eliminating the unfree (about 450,000 slaves and indentured servants) and those individuals who maintained their allegiance to the British Crown (perhaps as many as 500,000), the available pool of free white adult males between the ages of 16 and 50 was close to 350,000, based on the assumption that white males in this age group represented 1 out of every 4 to 5 persons resident in the colonies. As such, Washington could have had a substantial force of 30,000 for each campaign had 1 out of just under 12 adult white males enlisted for long-term service. At no time after 1776 did the Continental army come close to having that many long-termers in its ranks.

Propertied, middle-class civilians showed their lack of resolve in various ways, perhaps most visibly when states attempted to draft people into the army's ranks. They had the right, if threatened by conscription, to hire substitutes. In April 1777, for example, seventeen-year-old Joseph Plumb Martin of Connecticut agreed to serve in the Continental army for the duration of the war as a substitute for some local gentlemen being threatened by the draft. Wrote Martin in later years, "the men gave me what they agreed to; I forgot the sum. . . . They were now freed from any further trouble, at least for the present, and I had become the scapegoat for them" in serving the cause of liberty.

Like Martin, hundreds of poorer young white males with few economic prospects were among those who were willing to try long-term Continental service—in return for enlistment bounties, promises of regular pay, decent food and clothing, and free land, if the rebels somehow prevailed, at war's end. Lacking property to defend, poorer civilians had little incentive to serve and possibly sacrifice their lives in return for vague promises of gaining access to free land—and a minimal propertied stake in society—at war's end. Some, however, found enlistment promises and long-term service more enticing than merely subsisting as farm hands or day laborers, if and when they could find work.

Still, the numbers of struggling white males who came forward were not very substantial, and Washington might not have been able to keep an army in the field had he not had other groups to draw upon, among them indentured servants and slaves. By the end of 1777 northern states had declared African-Americans, both slave and free, eligible for Continental service. Among the southern states, Virginia and Maryland began to allow masters to send forward slaves as their substitutes, which caused one Continental general to ask sardonically why some "Sons of Freedom" were so anxious "to trust their all to be defended by slaves."

Poorer women likewise performed valuable Continental service, normally in return for "half rations." Their duties ranged from nursing the sick and wounded to scavenging fresh battlefields for weaponry and clothing. (These Continental women in the ranks should not be confused with camp followers—those who traveled along with husbands and lovers or made livings for themselves as prostitutes.) Once in a while Continental women engaged in combat. Margaret "Dirty Kate" Corbin was such a person. When her husband, a cannoneer, was shot dead in trying to defend Fort Washington in November 1776, Kate replaced him. She helped the crew keep the cannon firing until she sustained a serious wound, but Kate survived and was able to tell her story after the war.

By drawing upon unfree persons and women, Congress and the states expanded significantly the population base from which to draw potential long-termers. As time passed, these numbers came to include troublesome loyalists, whom local authorities made choose between hanging and serving in the Continental army, and even common thieves and criminals. Certainly, too, an important source of Continental troop strength came from Irish and Hessian soldiers who either deserted British units or were captured and given a choice between Continental service and confinement as prisoners of war.

The story of General John Burgoyne's army is illustrative. After two heated battles when patriot forces captured Burgoyne's force north of Albany at Saratoga in October 1777, the question was what to do with nearly 5,000 enemy troops. Some were Hessian mercenaries, whom greedy leaders from various German principalities had dragooned into the King's service in return for lucrative bounty payments. Congress and Washington finally decided to march Burgoyne's army south from New England to interior Virginia, where the troops could build huts for themselves and sit out the remainder of the war.

As this force trudged toward Virginia, state recruiters desperately trying to fill Continental troop quotas kept besetting Burgoyne's soldiers and imploring them to consider joining the American cause—and the army. Promises of free land especially appealed to the Irish and Hessian troops, who had virtually no prospect of ever gaining title to farmland back home. Some signed on and performed well in the Continental ranks.

One distinguishing characteristic of Washington's Continentals after 1776 was that they were almost invariably from straitened economic and social circumstances. Another was that they grew increasingly restive about lack of pay, food, and clothing. Some 11,000 of them entered the Valley Forge winter encampment in December 1777. Nearly 2,000 were shoeless. Food and clothing supply systems were breaking down, and even before the New Year some could be heard chanting, "No bread, no soldier!" Many deserted, and by springtime about 2,500 had died from exposure to the elements, malnutrition, and disease. The suffering at Valley Forge was not something the general populace shared, as is too often implied in patriotic myth. That burden fell on a few thousand valiant souls, and the reason they experienced such distress was that civilian patriots, although aware of the army's plight, did not seem to care. Far too often for too many "sunshine" patriots during the Revolutionary War, the definition of public virtue was to let others do the sacrificing from which they might hope to derive some benefit.

The soldiers who survived the Valley Forge winter did not easily forget the public neglect. In early 1779, two Connecticut regiments nearly mutinied over deplorable living conditions, and in May 1780, after another horrible winter, virtually the whole Connecticut Continental line threatened to resign unless its members started to receive adequate pro-visions. In January 1781, the Pennsylvania line did just that and began marching for home. When offi-cials promised better treatment, some returned to camp, but others had endured enough. They pre-ferred to re-enter civilian life, no matter how bleak their prospects for making decent wages.

So much disharmony in the ranks worried Wash-ington greatly. When the New Jersey line, seeing the success of its Pennsylvania brethren, also rose up and gained concessions in January 1781, the commander in chief decided he had to act. "Unless this dangerous spirit can be suppressed by force," he fumed, "there is an end to all subordination in the Army, and indeed to the Army itself." He ordered the summary execution of rank-and-file leaders among the Jersey-ites who had stirred up the mutiny. Two soldiers soon died by firing squad.

Washington's harsh action reflected on much more than his desire for discipline and obedience among the soldiery. His major concern remained the survival of the cause of liberty, which he still believed could not endure without some semblance of an organized army in the field. Reasserting control over the angry soldiery, he felt, was the only way to pull that army and the Revolution back from the brink of collapse, especially since any significant depletion of troops would have reduced the army to something much weaker than the shell of a respectable martial force.

After 1778, Washington lacked the troop strength to make serious plans for offensive opera-tions, particularly in trying to dislodge the British from their main base in and around New York City. Despite so much recruiting and dragooning among the poor, the unfree, and various other groups, most notably captured Hessian and Irish troops, the ranks remained too thin to accomplish much more than maintaining an appearance of organized rebel resis-tance. Rarely did the commander have more than 10,000 troops present and fit for duty, and sometimes that number was hardly above 5,000, such as dur-ing the time of the Pennsylvania and New Jersey mutinies.

The inadequacy of popular support and partici-pation continuously bothered Washington and his key officers. One of the army's most talented gener-als, Benedict Arnold, spoke out about popular indif-ference just before returning his allegiance to the British in September 1780. He "lamented that our army is permitted to starve in a land of plenty." Even though Americans have become accustomed to dis-missing Arnold as a greedy turncoat, his critique was nonetheless of value. He did not see how the Ameri-can people could ever achieve a stable republican polity with so few willing to serve the community's greater good. British allegiance thus seemed a safer haven to the thoroughly disillusioned Arnold, as it did for thousands of other loyalists.

In the end, Washington, Congress, and the states never resolved their manpower problem. No resur-gence of the *rage militaire* took place, not even in the wake of well-attended public ceremonies denounc-ing Arnold's treason. Castigating Arnold, who had given so much to the cause, may have absolved the guilt of patriots who had offered so little of them-selves over the years. After all, no matter how feeble their own records of service, they had not publicly renounced the cause of liberty.

Two elements above all else saved Britain's North American colonists from experiencing failure in their Revolution. One was that hardy band of down and outers who not only signed on but stayed out for the long-term fight. Some did not survive, and others gave up and deserted, but enough of them endured to allow Continental forces to maintain a continuing presence in the field. The other was in-valuable assistance from such traditional British ene-mies as France and Spain. In the case of France, the infusion of thousands of soldiers as well as naval forces made up for Washington's ongoing troop defi-cits and resulted in combined operations that made possible the critical victory at Yorktown in October 1781.

Still, once the war was over and Washington's long-termers had dispersed to the wind, patriot civil-ians, some of whom had performed occasional mili-tia service, began reclaiming the Revolution as their own—as if the outpouring of truly virtuous citizen-soldiers at Lexington and Concord had characterized the whole wartime experience. Many modern histo-rians have preferred this interpretation, and some have even made the myth of sustained popular par-ticipation their core precept in arguing that the Revo-lution represented the first of the modern wars of liberation in which the people rose up in one unified body to break forever the enslaving chains of mon-archism.

Private Joseph Plumb Martin, who was there for the long-term fight, knew better. He composed his highly engaging memoirs in part because he was troubled by commentators who were claiming that "the Revolutionary army was needless; that the militia were competent for all that the crisis required." Martin does not deny that militia units, on occasion, performed useful service, but he insists correctly that the war could not have been sustained for so many years or won without those very few long-termers who put no restraints on their participation and endured "the hardships of fatigue, starvation, cold, and nakedness" without "instantly" giving up and quitting "the service in disgust." Martin took pride in knowing how well he and his long-term comrades had served the cause of liberty. Unlike so many of their generation, they had personified the meaning of public virtue.

The American Revolution:
The Indian Story

Kenneth M. Morrison

By the time of the America Revolution, the dialectical images of Indians had already assumed mythic proportions. If these images—either as Noble Red Man or as Bloodthirsty Savage—bore any significant resemblance to the activities and diversities of native life, it was at best purely coincidental. What mattered most both emotionally and ideologically was that the white experience with the Indians could conveniently be reduced to almost a cartoon version of a very complex social reality. The Revolution, concludes Kenneth M. Morrison, professor of religious studies at Arizona State University, dramatized even more forcefully the importance of these images both to the practical conduct of the war itself—wherein most Indian nations supported the British—and to the manner in which all parties involved have come to understand its meaning. Often lost in the chorus of voices and the forest of symbols is the profound meaning that the Revolution held for native peoples. Cultural stories pitting civility against savagery, tied to the old mythic formulas of Indian captivity narratives, scarcely tell the tale. History may be, as has been argued, but "a fable agreed upon," but any final story of the American Revolution cannot even begin to be written until the Indian side is told. As the Native American writer Paul Gunn Allen has observed: "The one who tells the story rules the world."

For many Americans, the story of who they are winds back to the Revolution. It matters how we think of that event and how we see ourselves and others in the tableau. At the same time, history books tend to discount the power of that mythology and to turn the human meaning of the event into dull facts. Rather than appearing as some kind of collective creation, the Revolution is too often reduced to the product of disembodied forces, inevitable outcomes, and foreordained action. In response to that rather gray vision, impatient students have called for a new story, one that includes women and working people and that allows for human heroism. They want a story that conveys some of the passion of the age; they want history "from the bottom up!"

To write a history of the Revolution "from the bottom up" requires us to take seriously the experi-ence and perspective of American Indians. The first aspect of the Indian side of the Revolution—their contribution—is easily managed. Most Indians sided with the British and fought alongside their allies in New England, New York, Pennsylvania, the Carolinas, and the Great Lakes. This is the story of the Indians *in* the Revolution.

The Indian perspective on the Revolution is a second—and far more important—aspect of the story. This perspective tells us about Indians *and* the Revolution. To tell that tale we should begin with a single question: What can the Indians—the outsiders—teach us about the character of the Revolution? An explanation does not come easily.

An overview of the American Indian *and* the Revolution should begin with a concern for story. For years historians have struggled to include Native

Americans—people who were thought of as preliterate and therefore ahistorical—in the great American history of progress. The struggle has been marked by anguish: without written documents Native American history remained mired in sentiment and myth, and Indian people themselves stood by chiding historians that they had gotten the story wrong. This should not surprise us, for Indians were not insiders to the Revolution. They were excluded by the principal actors and they rejected involvement themselves. Except for interaction in trade and conflict over land, Native and Euro-Americans had few common experiences. The war derived from and affected people who were usually far from the tribal world.

But the revolutionary era inspired acts of storytelling that addressed the cultural divisions of Indians and whites and set the course of relations between the races far into the future. Whether spoken by Native or Euro-Americans, the stories tried to explain why brutality was the order of the day. The world was coming apart and all the old stories had to be revised.

The era of the Revolution confronted both cultures with a new age. Behind an array of shifting economic, diplomatic, and military events lay a mythic urgency. Native and Euro-Americans alike plumbed events seeking answers to new, fundamental questions: Who are we? Why are we? . . .

*   *   *

Because the Patriots failed to comprehend the Indians' need to protect themselves from individual American citizens, they constructed an Indan policy on false premises. These erroneous principles were established in the official United States' story about Indian involvement in the Revolutionary War. As expressed in treaties, laws, and executive proclamations, the story was simple, having only two themes. First, Native Americans had proven themselves incapable of friendship. They had waged an unprovoked war against the United States. And second, since they had sided with the British, the tribes were conquered when Great Britain admitted defeat. It followed, therefore, that Indians had lost ownership of their lands. In other words, the United States contended that it had waged a "just war"; the new government could call upon international law and the doctrine of conquest to further buttress its claims. It is worth comparing this story with the facts of Indian participation in the War for Independence. The official story

forgot that the war had many complex causes and that the outcome was not nearly as simple as conquest theory would have it.

In the Northeast, the Penobscot and Passamaquoddy suffered because they supported the American cause. Having survived a century of warfare with the English of Massachusetts, the two peoples aligned with their old enemies to ingratiate themselves. Both tribes, in fact, obtained written guarantees protecting their land from further encroachments in exchange for their support. During the war, the Indians' assistance was appreciated. Afterwards, Massachusetts returned to its old tactics.

Despite the fact that individuals were legally barred from settling on Indian land, Massachusetts looked the other way. Dispossession proceeded apace. Then, as the Penobscot and Passamaquoddy people found themselves in direct economic competition with English squatters, government commissioners offered them a new, protected reserve. In actual defiance of laws requiring federal participation in land transactions, Massachusetts pushed the two peoples into treaties that dispossessed them against their will. The conquest story didn't fit the Penobscot and Passamaquoddy, but it was applied anyway.

In the South we find variations on these themes. Despite British promises and the enthusiastic endorsement of the Cherokee, the boundary established in the 1760s fell before settlers and traders. John Stuart, the British Indian superintendent, used the resulting Cherokee resentment to animate them against the American cause. Still, the Cherokee followed their own interests. They concluded in 1776 that further protests to either the British or colonial governments were futile. Speaking a new language, the tribe attacked the two newest white settlements. This action flouted the British request that the Cherokee remain neutral. Nevertheless, southern governments interpreted the attack as a British plot. Instead of discussing the real issue of territorial encroachment, colonial military forces set out to teach the Cherokee a lesson. Militiamen attacked and burned Cherokee villages across the tribe's vast lands. Witnessing these harrowing events, and richly benefiting from British trade, most Creeks remained quiet on the sidelines. Indeed, except for a few Cherokee warriors who continued to resist individual settlements, most southern Indians remained neutral. After the war, the Cherokee lost half of their remaining lands, and even the Creeks accepted a new boundary.

The conquest story was directly applied against the Six Nations and their supposed allies in the Old Northwest. Here, again, the story failed to mesh with the facts. Two of the Six Nations (the Oneida and Tuscarora) not only sided with the United States, they also paid a stiff price when the other members of the confederacy attacked them as traitors. Moreover, despite promises that Oneida and Tuscarora lands would be protected, it was only a short time after the war before they too were dispossessed.

The struggle for land was so intense in the Old Northwest that it would have been self-destructive for Indians to side with the Patriots, an option Americans rarely considered. The Iroquois understood that it would be disastrous to side with Great Britain. The confederacy therefore resurrected the old play-off policy and told the new American government that the Six Nations would remain neutral. It also stipulated that its promise hinged on several conditions, all of which were soon violated. American forces engaged the British on Iroquois soil; Patriots attempted to arrest the Mohawk ally, Sir John Johnson, and forced other Loyalist friends to flee. Worse, the government did not examine long-standing Mohawk complaints that settlers were encroaching on their lands. These American refusals to meet the Iroquois halfway demonstrate that the first theme of the conquest story, Indian perfidy, was not true. The confederacy did its part in trying to keep the peace, but no government succeeded in reining in the advancing settlers.

The conquest story also directed the confederacy's actual wartime activity. Although the British provided much needed goods and war material, everyday strategy remained in Iroquois hands. Waging traditional war, the confederacy succeeded in laying waste a vast area of New York, Pennsylvania, and Virginia. Since these were agricultural regions on which revolutionary forces depended, the Iroquois thus proved themselves a formidable force. Retaliating Amerian armies inflicted comparable losses on confederacy towns but failed to dampen Iroquoian resistance. When Great Britain made peace, the Iroquois were ready to fight on. The confederacy considered itself undefeated.

The conquest story failed to account for either the causes or the course of the Indian side of the Revolutionary War. The story also made it necessary for the new United States to fight the tribes. The heritage of the Revolution produced such a clamor for land that the federal government found itself committed to the proposition that Native Americans were subjects who held their land only on sufferance. In the Old Northwest, at least, Native Americans acted to make clear their rejection of this idea. Armies under Generals Harmar and St. Clair met the assembled tribesmen and were soundly defeated in 1790 and 1791. The latter encounter cost the Americans 647 lives, more than any other Indian battle in the nation's history, including the celebrated Custer massacre of 1876. Shocked, the United States intensified its efforts and, in the process, learned an important lesson: war is more costly than diplomacy.

The conquest story had another result: Americans soon transformed their deep seated contempt for Indian people into a story of superiority and inferiority. Thomas Jefferson, for a single example, admitted that Native Americans were people. He added, however, that they were less developed and more backward than advanced Europeans. Thus, the president was equipped with a linguistic tool for dealing with head-strong Native Americans who needed restraint. Having found it too expensive to enforce its will, the federal government declared itself a father with ultimate disciplinary authority. Paternalism turned out to be the ultimate story for eroding Native American independence.

* * *

For people of the revolutionary era, brutal realities demanded effective action. As we have seen, those actions were organized around new stories that not only justified policy but also shaped it. The new stories swept away earlier beliefs in the possibility of constructive relations between Native and Euro-Americans. The old stories were now thought to be false. Native Americans apparently were doomed to dispossession and destruction. Seen in the light of historical facts (facts that fit the "stories"), the era of the American Revolution epitomizes the passive victimhood of Indians in every age.

There is another side to this story. If, as many have held, the history of Indian-white relations has been shaped by federal paternalism, we should recognize that this was not a father who knew best. Rather, we must conclude that this was a father who killed—sometimes by neglect and sometimes with righteous fury. The image is uncomfortable, but it helps us to understand better the side of the Revolution that eludes our understanding of the apparent facts. The very image of the Great White Father often hides his habit of using power with little qualm of conscience.

In actuality, both the facts of the American Revolution and the paternal symbols in which they are often expressed hide another element of the story: from their own point of view, Native Americans never accepted the role of mere victim. Before, during, and after the American Revolution, Native Americans took responsibility for defining themselves in ways that made sense to them. And, in achieving both success and failure in that struggle for identity, native peoples have a good deal to teach us about the social dynamics of the Revolution itself.

Native American failure stemmed from the inability of the tribes to effectively unite—a failing that rested partly on their economic dependence and partly on their tribal traditions. Such problems also affected the revolutionary effort: economic immaturity and states' rights troubled both the American confederation and the new republic. As it turned out, republicanism was achieved at the cost of some personal and political freedoms, a price that Native Americans largely refused to pay. Thus Native and Euro-Americans shared a similar vision of unity, but they sought to achieve it in entirely different ways.

For Indians, the era of the Revolution was sandwiched between two acts of prophecy. In the early 1760s, Neolin, a Delaware prophet, called the nations of the Old Northwest to revitalize themselves. The 1790s witnessed a number of such passionate individuals, the most prominent of which, Handsome Lake, led the way in reshaping Iroquois tradition and culture. In both the short and the long term, these religious movements were more important to tribal survival than were the militay events of the war.

Grounded in tradition as they were, prophetic stories became historic forces. They called the people themselves to renewal, reminding them that responsible action effectively countered victimhood. The Iroquois say that whenever the people find themselves up against the wall, a prophet will come forth to help them. Oral tradition trained Indian people to listen attentively to the stories such prophets related. They did not always heed the prophet, but when they did revolutionary results were possible.

The Delaware prophet was neither the first nor the last religious leader who attempted to save disintegrating tribes with a new vision. But Neolin stands out for three reasons. First, Neolin's message was a syncretism of Indian and Christian teachings mixed to speak to the crisis of the 1760s. Second, unlike the old, traditional prophet, Neolin attempted to unite religiously several independent Indian nations. Third, Neolin's teachings ideologically fueled the Indian war of 1763.

Native Americans of the Old Northwest had always believed in a supreme God who created and ruled the world. But this God was also remote from everyday affairs. When the Creator spoke to Neolin, it became clear that the Christ of the missionaries and the Indian God were one and the same. Like Christ, the Creator communicated directly with human beings; this came as a radical change in Indian religious experience. The Creator's message was radical. Unlike Christ, the Creator recognized that Indians and Euro-Americans were culturally different peoples. In this way, the Creator, working through Neolin, validated Indian culture and began to undermine Christian beliefs among the tribes.

Sometime in 1760, Neolin had a vision in which the Creator warned that the Indian peoples were in grave danger. They had rejected the Creator's teachings and would, therefore, lose everything in this world and be damned in the next. The catastrophe could be averted. Euro-Americans could be driven from Indian lands and Native peoples themselves could return to their original, reciprocal relationship with nature. In effect, the Creator called Native Americans to recognize their own responsibility for their situation. He condemned their addiction to alcohol, quarrelsomeness, and sexual licentiousness.

Most of all, the Creator declared to Neolin that Indians tolerated the settlement of their lands only because they wanted trade goods. This desire led to two kinds of moral failings. First, Indians who hunted with guns violated the reciprocity that was supposed to exist between themselves and animals. The Creator observed that he had placed animals on earth to provide the people with food. He had not intended that they be sold to Euramerican traders. Second, the Creator warned that such commercial relationships had created severe social strife even within the individual tribes. This vicious conflict was so grave a violation of kinship values that the Creator had removed the animals as a punishment. Neolin's message was clear. Either the people would repent and return to proper ways of living, or they would starve and lose their lands to the Americans.

Religious stories like Neolin's put forward a special kind of truth. In becoming the voice of truth itself, Neolin attempted to bridge the gap between absolute and relative truth. He attempted to speak from tradition to the unprecedented troubles of the 1760s. Neolin's tale shows the extreme difficulty of bridging past and present, of conserving the best of the old while changing to ensure survival.

Given the problems facing the Old Northwest tribes, Neolin's message had to have been heard with some uncertainty. It is not known whether Indians perceived themselves as dependent on trade; at least that is not the thrust of Neolin's story. Rather, the Creator demanded that Indian people act positively and take responsibility. Neolin told the people that they could return to traditional values, if they so chose.

The initially successful war of 1763 was partly based on Neolin's vision of moral and cultural liberation. The failure of that war has obscured much that is valuable in Neolin's story. Behind the failure stand the harsh facts of economic need. The tribes could not drive the British away without ammunition, but that was only one part of the situation. At the intertribal level, Neolin's story became a call to arms. But at home, where kinship mattered, the story had another meaning: Neolin urged Indians to renew themselves as family members whose first commitment had to be to each other.

Little is known about the impact of Neolin's teachings, but something of their importance can be seen in the career of the Seneca prophet, Handsome Lake. As one of the forty-nine sachems of the Iroquois Confederacy, Handsome Lake had considerable prominence. But he was also a dispirited drunk, a state of being all too common for end-of-the-century Senecas. The American Revolution had terminated an ancient way of life, bringing an end to hunting, warfare, and diplomacy and to a social life in which men and women contributed equally. The Revolution also accelerated a beginning made long before the War of Independence, when the Iroquois first selected aspects of Euramerican culture. George Washington's troops had destroyed frame houses and barns, blacksmith shops, and sawmills. The Seneca continued to draw profitably from Euramerican culture in the 1790s, but the changes sparked little optimism. And, therein lies the importance of Handsome Lake.

As a prophet, Handsome Lake focused on the Seneca's most pressing issue, the survival of the people themselves. For the Seneca, prophets exist only to call the people to moral and social renewal. It did not seem remarkable to them that Handsome Lake had been a drunk. The Seneca knew that prophetic authority derived from no merely human act and certainly not from individual choice, ability, or ambition. Rather, the prophet is called because he is representative. Handsome Lake the man had internalized both the social and psychological difficulties afflicting his people. Like other Senecas, he felt ashamed, but not even Quaker missionaries could help him, or them, to change.

Instead, Handsome Lake fell "dead." He returned transformed by power, now a vehicle and a voice of the basic reality of things. The Seneca recognized Handsome Lake's transformation in a traditional way: the prophet spoke an archaic form of their language, a style of speaking that could not have been learned in everyday speech. Handsome Lake returned with mythic truth about the sad story of Seneca life. The Seneca listened and in time they themselves were transformed.

Handsome Lake's visions spoke to the Seneca's total condition. The visions located the source of the Seneca's problems in their religious lapses. They directed the prophet to aid his people in bringing their social lives back into line with the old values. The visions thus made it possible for the Seneca to choose wisely from Euramerican culture. Because he spoke of these concerns using the concepts and language of Seneca myth, Handsome Lake's words galvanized the people in ways that Quaker missionaries had not been able to achieve. One of them reported that after hearing Handsome Lake recite his first vision the Seneca were "solid and weighty in spirit," and that he "felt the love of God flowing powerfully amongst us."

Handsome Lake's story resembled Neolin's. Its overall message—that the Seneca must accept responsibility for their sorry condition—was the same. Like Neolin, Handsome Lake pointed to antisocial behavior as the major cause of declension, and he summed up Seneca failings in four sins: whiskey, witchcraft, love-magic, and abortion medicines. In his second vision, Handsome Lake not only saw the resulting damnation of the Seneca but he also met Jesus. "Now tell your people that they will become lost when they follow the ways of the white man," was Jesus' frightening message.

Unlike Neolin, Handsome Lake devised a program of cultural change that worked within preexisting forms of cultural organization, made sense of adaptations to Euramerican culture, and led to genuine and long-range reform. Handsome Lake stressed that traditional values had to shape Seneca adjustments. In particular, the prophet's grasp of the socioreligious implications of economic change reveal the main characteristics of an effective story.

Handsome Lake squarely faced the facts. The Seneca's ancient hunting economy had been swept away. Hence, the demoralization of the men. The Seneca were also moving toward a life-style based on the nuclear, patrilineal family farm instead of the matrilineal clan. Again, the result was social strife as women repulsed male authority. Moreover, acceptance of a money economy threatened the exchange values that had always stressed putting group welfare before private profit.

The prophet identified and responded to each of these concerns. He understood that the authority of the clan mothers had to be wielded with more discretion, and he advised them to avoid interfering in their daughter's marriages. In effect, Handsome Lake validated a shift toward men and women sharing work and power. Similarly, Handsome Lake advised maternal uncles that they ought to defer to fathers in disciplining their nephews, a new rule appropriate to the new social arrangement.

More remarkably, Handsome Lake shaped the Seneca's transition to a Euramerican economy, and he did so in a way that countered the social divisiveness of capitalism. He warned the Seneca against pride in material worth, stipulated that they were not to sell agricultural produce among themselves, and required that they maintain collective ownership of tools and resources. In these ways the prophet showed the Seneca that close contact with the American people threatened communal life because it undercut the traditional value of sharing and an economy of reciprocal exchange.

Handsome Lake's story spoke to the Indians' situation with a remarkable sensitivity. The story recognized the excruciating emotional pain individuals experienced during the recent war. In doing so, it helped people to act responsibly. Specifically, the story urged Indians to take collective action: that people should work together was the main theme of Handsome Lake's tale. Moreover, the story accounted for both the psychological and the social impact of Euramerican culture. Finally, Handsome

Lake's story taught an attitude of tolerance. Unlike Neolin, whose teachings urged a violent solution, Handsome Lake recommended cooperation between Indian and Euramerican people. In all these ways, the prophet not only reinvigorated Indian identity but he also realistically confronted the fact of cultural pluralism.

*   *   *

Handsome Lake illustrates the ways in which even the most revolutionary story can actually have a conservative character. Like the Seneca revival, the American Revolution was built on old mythic foundations, particularly the precepts of Christian faith and the certainty of civilized progress. Religious and secular truths bolstered each other, thereby obscuring many of the class divisions within the Euro-Americans' social order. Revolutionaries achieved political independence, and they promulgated far-reaching republican and democratic principles. But those principles and real life were something else again. Initially, the Revolution excluded not only Native Americans but also blacks, women, and many rural and urban workers from decision making. The rights of man made for fine-sounding political rhetoric, but in the early national period those rights were limited.

Like Native American prophets, revolutionaries spoke hopeful stories—stories of freedom, stories of possibility. But Euro-Americans did not share Handsome Lake's insight that the new American order had to embrace cultural pluralism. As they were applied to Native Americans, both official and unofficial Euramerican stories camouflaged colonialism in the cover of friendly help. The Northwest Ordinance expressed the story in 1787: "The utmost good faith shall always be observed towards the Indians; their land and property shall never be taken from them without their consent. . . ." The ordinance also contained an escape clause, declaring that Indians' property and liberty would never be compromised except "in just and lawful wars authorized by Congress."

Changing the tale to suit the case, Euro-Americans sooner or later won the land, thereby alienating Indian peoples from tried and true ways of life. The result was an enduring crisis as Native Americans sought a workable synthesis of traditional values and new culture, and Euro-Americans insisted on the veracity of their revolutionary stories. Thus federal agents and missionaries hastened to reform Indians n the name of progress and Christian love even though their program ran afoul of three additional American myths.

First, even though Euro-Americans claimed to offer Indians membership in the American nation, they built a segregated society. Federal policy envisioned Native American cultural transformation but did not take into consideration either Native American culture or Euramerican reactions to having Indians as neighbors. Much of the brutality of American history can be attributed to the fact that Euro-Americans did not have Handsome Lake's appreciation of the delicate balance of Indian values, culture, and social well-being.

Moreover, the offer of civilization failed to account for the conventional reaction to Indians as the ultimate outsiders—the wilderness personified. Fear of the stranger had always fueled Indian-white distrust, and it continued to do so after the war. Since the governing American symbol was now the vigorous pioneer transforming the land, government promises of peaceful cooperation contradicted new facts. Even Christianity failed to make sense of cultural pluralism. The idea of one God contradicted the multifaceted nature of tribal solidarity. That solidarity rested on kinship, custom, and obligation, not on ideological unanimity.

The second undercutting constructive association was based on cultural ethnocentrism. Euro-Americans were convinced of the superiority of their way of life. From first contact centuries before, Native Americans had been defined in negative terms. They were not religious and had neither laws nor property. The same continued to shape federal-Indian relations. Forgetting the economic upheaval caused by massive dispossession, federal officials claimed that Indians knew nothing of agriculture and so began a program to civilize them. This story not only failed to recognize Indians' sophisticated agricultural knowledge, it also attacked tribal values directly. Unlike Handsome Lake, who strengthened the social reciprocity at the heart of Indian life, federal officials sought to detribalize Indian people. Individually held property, they argued, would transform the Indian into a citizen.

The final story line had ominous implications for Indian-white relations. Americans contended that theirs was a government of laws. They therefore failed to see that laws surrounding Indian relations often did not govern. Treaties with Indian nations were ostensibly the highest law of the land, but they were respected only in the breech. In frontier areas, lawlessness became a way of life. Individuals and states purchased Indian lands in violation of the federal government's constitutional authority. Traders used credit, shoddy goods, sweet talk, and rum to defraud Indians everywhere. Indian agents and missionaries embezzled annuity funds and skimmed the money sent out to uplift Indians morally and culturally. In these ways, the story of law became a cover for continuing oppression.

In the end, each of these stories has had a history extending from the Revolution to the present, and all three share an important characteristic. Like Neolin's tale, and unlike Handsome Lake's, the Euramerican stories that shaped Indian-white relations enshrined a fatal mistake. Neither Neolin nor the Euro-Americans were inclined to test their stories against possible contradiction. They didn't realize that their stories failed to fit the facts. Many Native Americans have understood the essential flaw: they have come to know that stories often have a hidden agenda. The Revolution, and its continuing aftermath, have refreshed for them a traditional truth: all stories have a history and, when amnesia strikes the teller, history can repeat itself. But that's another story.

The Philadelphia Story: The Founding Fathers and the Myth of Constitutional Intent

Jack N. Rakove

Since the creation of American political culture in 1787–88 by way of the writing and ratification of the Constitution, that document has traditionally functioned as a central myth of American culture, with the Founding Fathers standing foremost. The Constitution is "a machine that would run of itself"; the fifty-five Founders are collectively regarded as its great designers. Such is the oft-recited Philadelphia Story.

Even stripped of myth the constitutional era remains one of the most energized and engaging in all of American history. Animated by classic and freshly-minted political philosophy, yet practical and pragmatic in executing these ideas, the proceedings of the Constitutional Convention exhibited both high- and tough-mindedness. An assembly of delegates drawn from the ranks of the well bred, fed, read, and wed, shaped a legal and political agenda for the nation that if not fully democratic at the time held that potential within it. In arbitrating inherent tensions between the interests of nation, state, and individual; in contending with issues of property and power; in seeking to harmonize the needs of personal liberty and social stabilty; in formulating a measured balance between executive, legislative, and judicial authority, the Founders with great hope and passion creatively met fundamental and enduring public issues. As Professor Jack N. Rakove of Stanford University demonstrates, their capacity for compromise, their talent for grappling with great issues, was enormous. While imperfect, and certainly not of one mind regarding "constitutional intent" in any specific fashion, they left it to future generations to judge both the meaning and the fallibility of their work.

"There never was an assembly of men, charged with a great and arduous trust, who were more pure in their motives, or more exclusively or anxiously devoted to the object committed to them."

It probably was shortly before his death, in 1836, that Virginia's James Madison, the sole surviving Framer of the Constitution, dictated those closing words of the preface to his notes of the debates at the Constitutional Convention. This was how Madison wanted his countrymen to imagine the Convention. In many ways we have followed his wishes.

Yet, for most of this century, this popular image of the Founding has coexisted with another, less heroic portrait etched by scholars since Charles A. Beard published *An Economic Interpretation of the Constitution* (1913).

Rather than treat the Constitution as the product of a highly principled debate conducted by an extraordinary group of men who resolved *all* of the great questions before them, these historians have emphasized everything that was practical and tough-minded about the task of creating a national government: the threats and bargains that dominated the politics of the Convention, and the determination of the delegates to protect the interests of their states and, for that matter, of their own propertied class.

To strike an accurate balance between these two contrasting images is the great challenge that confronts anyone who studies the making of the Constitution.

That task is more important now than it has been at any point in our recent history. Today's controversy over constitutional jurisprudence . . . requires that Americans ask again how much weight the "original intent" of the Framers should carry in interpreting the Constitution.

One thing is clear: The 55 delegates to the Philadelphia Convention were not all cut from the same cloth. Six had signed the Declaration of Independence, 14 were land speculators, 21 were military veterans of the Revolution, at least 15 owned slaves, and 24 served in Congress. Thirty-four were lawyers.

Present were many of the most outstanding men that the new Republic could muster. Among them were Benjamin Franklin, the president of Pennsylvania's Supreme Executive Council and the leading American scientist of the century, so disabled by gout and other ailments at the age of 81 that he was carried from his lodgings to the Convention in a sedan chair borne by four convicts; Virginia's George Washington, then 55, who came to Philadelphia very reluctantly after three years of retirement from public life at Mount Vernon; New York's Alexander Hamilton, 30, Washington's wartime aide; George Mason, a 60-year-old Virginia plantation owner and (said Thomas Jefferson) "the wisest man of his generation."

Also in attendance were men of somewhat less distinction. One of the more interesting examples was Luther Martin, "the rollicking, witty, audacious Attorney General of Maryland," as Henry Adams later described him, "drunken, generous, slovenly, grand . . . the notorious reprobate genius."

Missing from the Convention were Thomas Jefferson, 44, author of the Declaration of Independence 11 years earlier, who was overseas serving as the American minister to France, and former congressman John Adams, 51, likewise engaged in England. The great firebrands of the Revolution—Samuel Adams, Thomas Paine, Patrick Henry—were also absent.

* * *

No delegates came from Rhode Island. "Rogue Island," as a Boston newspaper called it, was in the hands of politicians bent on inflating the currency to relieve farm debtors; they would have nothing to do with a strong national government and the monetary discipline it would impose. For lack of funds, New Hampshire's delegates arrived more than two months late, bringing the number of states represented to 12. Indeed, during the Convention's debates, the cost and difficulties of travel would occasionally be cited as looming obstacles to effective national government. Nearly a year, Madison predicted, would be "consumed in preparing for and travelling to and from the seat of national business."

The delegates were supposed to gather in Philadelphia on May 14, 1787, but it was the rare public assembly in 18th-century America that met on time. Only on Friday the 25th did delegates from seven states—a quorum—assemble in the spacious east room of the Pennsylvania State House, the same chamber where the Declaration of Independence had been signed. The delegates sat two or three to a desk. George Washington was immediately elected president of the Convention. Serious discussion began on the 29th. Thereafter, the delegates met six days a week until they finally adjourned on September 17, taking only one recess. It was, by contemporary standards, an arduous schedule. The delegates met for four, six, sometimes even eight hours a day.

In the afternoons, when the Convention adjourned, the delegates often repaired to local taverns—the Indian Queen, the George, the Black Horse—or turned to other amusements. These included visiting Mrs. Peale's Museum, with its fossils, stuffed animals, and portraits of the Revolution's heroes (by her husband, Charles), browsing through libraries and book and stationery shops, reading the city's eight newspapers, and watching the occasional horse race through the city streets, paved with bricks and cobblestones. Down by the busy docks and brick warehouses along the Delaware River, spectators could watch as inventor John Fitch demonstrated a novel contraption: a steam-powered boat.

Although there was a large and growing German population, the Quakers, in their broadbrim hats, still set the tone in Philadelphia, and the tone was sober but cosmopolitan. George Mason, from rural Virginia, complained after his arrival that he was growing "heartily tired of the etiquette and nonsense so fashionable in this city."

It was hot and humid that summer. "A veritable torture," moaned one French visitor. But the delegates had to keep their windows closed as they slept: Obnoxious stinging flies filled the air. The dyspeptic Elbridge Gerry of Massachusetts sent his family to the healthier clime of New York City, where the U.S. Congress was sitting. A few of his colleagues, such as Charles Pinckney, the young delegate from South Carolina, rented houses and brought their families to Philadelphia; others lived alone in rented rooms above the taverns or boarded in Mrs. Mary House's place at the corner of Fifth and Market streets near the State House. Most brought servants. George Washington was the guest of Pennsylvania delegate Robert Morris, Philadelphia's great merchant prince, who owned a large mansion a block from the State House.

A typical session of the Convention would find perhaps 35 or 40 delegates from 10 or 11 states in attendance. Some delegates came and went, others sat silently the entire time—and a few would have been better advised to say less. Washington did not so much as venture an opinion until the last day of debate. But his stern presence in the chair did much to preserve the decorum of the meeting

* * *

The debates were held in secrecy. Otherwise, candor would have been impossible, since the delegates knew that their opinions and votes, if made public, would become live ammunition in the hands of political foes back home. Moreover, the threat of deadlock would have quickly arisen had the dissidents within the Convention been allowed to stir up a hue and cry among their constituents. "Their deliberations are kept inviolably secret, so that they set without censure or remark," observed Francis Hopkinson, a Philadelphia musician and signer of the Declaration, "but no sooner will the chicken be hatch'd but every one will be for plucking a feather."

Nevertheless, we know a great deal about what was said at the Convention, thanks chiefly to the copious daily note-taking of Virginia's James Madison, then just turned 36, who is now generally regarded as the "father of the Constitution."

Were he alive today, the slight, soft-spoken Madison would probably be happily teaching history or political theory at his alma mater, Princeton University (or the College of New Jersey, as it was then known). He took a distinctively intellectual approach to politics, reinforced by a decade of experience in the Virginia legislature and the U.S. Congress. He had read deeply in the history of ancient and modern confederacies and pondered the shortcomings of the Articles of Confederation and the state constitutions. (It was Madison's frustration with the scanty archives left by earlier confederacies that prompted him to take meticulous notes at the Convention.) He arrived in Philadelphia 11 days early to begin drafting, with his fellow Virginians, the Virginia Plan. After the state's 34-year-old governor, Edmund Randolph, presented the plan on May 29, it became, in effect, the agenda of the Convention.

The starting point for all of Madison's proposals was his belief, based on the nation's unhappy experiences under the Articles and under the state constitutions, that the state legislatures could not be counted on to respect the national interest, the concerns of other states, or even the "private rights" of individuals and minorities.

Like most other Federalists, Madison thought that the legislatures were dominated by demagogues who sought office for reasons of "ambition" and "personal interest" rather than "public good." Such men—e.g., Patrick Henry, his great rival in Virginia—could always "dupe" more "honest but unenlightened representative[s]" by "veiling [their] selfish views under the professions of public good, and varnishing [their] sophistical arguments with the glowing colors of popular eloquence."

From this condemnation of state politics, Madison drew a number of conclusions that appeared in the Virginia Plan. First, unlike the existing Congress, which relied upon the good will of the states to see its resolutions carried out, the new government would have to be empowered to impose laws and levy taxes directly upon the population, and to enforce its acts though its own executive and judiciary. Second, he hoped that membership in the new Congress would result from "such a process of elections as will most certainly extract from the mass of the society the purest and noblest characters it contains."

* * *

Yet, because Madison also doubted whether popularly chosen representatives could ever be entirely trusted, he hoped to make an indirectly elected Senate (with members nominated by the legislatures ut elected by the people) the true linchpin of government. Not only would this Senate thwart the passage of ill-conceived laws by the lower house, it would manage the nation's foreign relations and appoint all major federal officials. But since even the Senate could not always be counted upon to legislate wisely, Madison sought an additional check in the form of a joint executive-judicial Council of Revision that would possess a limited veto over all acts of Congress.

Most important of all, Madison wanted to arm the national government with a "negative in all cases whatsoever" over the acts of the states. This radical veto power would be shared jointly by Congress (or the Senate) and the Council of Revision.

In Madison's mind, the whole edifice of the Virginia Plan rested on the adoption of some form of proportional representation in Congress. If the Confederation's "one state, one vote" scheme were retained, for example, each citizen of tiny Delaware (population in 1790: 59,000) would, in effect, carry the same weight in the powerful new government as 12 Virginians. Delegates from Massachusetts and Pennsylvania, the Confederation's other two largest states, reached the same conclusion.

The Pennsylvanians, in fact, wanted to deny the small states an equal vote even within the Convention. But in a private caucus held before the Convention, the Virginians persuaded Pennsylvania's leading delegates—James Wilson (the Convention's finest legal mind), Gouverneur Morris (its wiliest advocate and its most talkative delegate, with 173 speeches), and Robert Morris (the former superintendent of finance for the Confederation)—that they could prevail over the small states by force of reason. And sooner rather than later. For the large states' delegates also agreed that the problem of representation had to be solved first.

Two of the small states' leaders tried to avoid the clash: Roger Sherman, a 66-year-old Connecticut farmer and storekeeper turned politician, and John Dickinson of Delaware, who had gained fame as the "penman of the Revolution" during the late 1760s for his antitax *Letters from a Farmer in Pennsylvania*. Sherman was among the signers of the Declaration of Independence; Dickinson had refused to put his name to it, still hoping for reconciliation with Great Britain. Both men had taken leading roles in drafting the Articles of Confederation a decade before the

Convention. Now, during the early days of debate in Philadelphia, they tried to head off full discussion of the dangerous issue of representation.

Let the Convention first determine what it wanted the national government to do, they suggested. Perhaps it might vest Congress with only a few additional powers; then there would be no need to propose any changes in the system of representation.

* * *

Their opponents would not waver. "Whatever reason might have existed for the equality of suffrage when the union was a federal one among sovereign states," Madison flatly declared, "must cease when a national government should be put into the place."

Although interrupted by discussion of other issues, such as fixing the qualifications for legislative office, the struggle over representation would go on for seven grueling weeks. It lasted until July 16, when the Great Compromise, as scholars now call it, allowed the Convention to move forward.

The fight went through three phases. During the first (May 29–June 13), the large states exploited the initiative they had seized with the Virginia Plan to gain an early endorsement of the principle of proportional representation in both houses. The small-state men rallied after June 14, when William Paterson, 42, a diminutive country lawyer and New Jersey attorney general—"of great modesty," noted Georgia's William Pierce, "whose powers break in upon you and create wonder and astonishment"—presented the New Jersey Plan. This second round of debate came to a dramatic end on July 2, when the convention deadlocked (five states to five, with Georgia divided, and thus losing its vote) over a motion by Oliver Ellsworth of Connecticut to give each state an equal vote in the Senate.

Round Three began immediately, with the appointment of a committee made up of one member from each delegation and explicitly charged with finding a compromise. The Convention received its report on July 5, debated it until the 14th, and finally approved it by a narrow margin two days later.

These seven weeks were the Convention's true testing time. The tension is apparent to anyone who reads Madison's daily notes. The character of debate covered a wide spectrum, from highly principled appeals to heavy-handed threats and pokerfaced bluffs.

In the speeches of the large states' leading advocates—Madison, Wilson, and Rufus King, the 32-year-old lawyer from Massachusetts—one finds powerful and profound briefs for the theory of majority rule. Indeed, the spokesmen for the other side rarely met the arguments on their own terms. Delaware's hot-tempered Gunning Bedford, Jr., claimed, for example, that the large states would "crush the small ones whenever they stand in the way of their ambitious or interested views." But when Madison and his allies demanded to know what common interest could ever unite societies as diverse as those of Massachusetts, Pennsylvania, and Virginia, the small-state men could not come up with an answer.

What was finally at issue was a question not so much of reason as of will. John Dickinson had made sure that Madison got the point immediately after the New Jersey Plan was introduced on June 15. "You see the consequences of pushing things too far," he warned, as the delegates filed out of the chamber at the end of the day. "Some of the members from the small states wish for two branches in the general

---

THE 'NEFARIOUS INSTITUTION'

James Madison was somewhat surprised by the intensity of the debates between the large and small states at Philadelphia. After all, he told the delegates on June 30, the states were really not divided so much by size as by "the effects of their having, or not having, slaves."

Yet slavery did not become a major issue at the Constitutional Convention. In August, Gouverneur Morris passionately denounced it as "a nefarious institution." But, as John Rutledge of South Carolina quickly reminded the delegates, "the true question at present is whether the Southern states shall or shall not be parties to the union."

As they would time and again during the Convention, the delegates turned away from divisive social issues to focus on what historian James MacGregor Burns has called the "mundane carpentry" of making a constitution.

*   *   *

Abolitionist sentiment was widespread but not deep in 1787. Traffic in imported African slaves was outlawed everywhere except in Georgia and the Carolinas, yet only Massachusetts had banned slave ownership. Many delegates, Northerners and Southerners alike, disliked slavery; some also believed, as Connecticut's Oliver Ellsworth said, that the arrival of cheap labor from Europe would ultimately "render slaves useless."

Such hopes, combined with the delegates' sense of the political realities, led them to reduce the slavery issue to a series of complicated tradeoffs.

Early in June, the large states accepted the famous "three-fifths" compromise: Slaves (carefully referred to as "all other Persons") would each count as three-fifths of a free white "person" in any scheme of representation by population. In return, the Georgians and Carolinians tacitly agreed to support the large states' ideas for a strong national government.

But on August 6, a report by the Committee of Detail upset the agreement. The Committee recommended several measures that would weaken the new national government, including a ban on national taxes on exports. More important, it proposed a ban on any federal regulation of the slave trade.

The debate was heated. Rufus King of Massachusetts reminded the Southerners of the earlier bargain and added that he could not agree to let slaves be "imported without limitation and then be represented in the National Legislature." A slave influx could give undue legislative power to the South.

Another committee—the Committee of Eleven—was named to mediate the dispute. After more haggling, the ban on export taxes was retained. The government would be empowered to halt the slave trade in 1808. But the new Constitution also mandated the return to their owners of escaped slaves.

*   *   *

Congress did abolish the slave trade in 1808, but the "peculiar institution" did not die. Inevitably, the North-South division that Madison saw in 1787 widened, while the heated conflict between the large and small states faded almost as soon as the delegates left Philadelphia. The Framers' artful compromises, later denounced by abolitionists as "A Covenant with Death and an Agreement with Hell," could not contain the nation's passions over slavery.

legislature, and are friends to a good national government: but we would sooner submit to a foreign power, than submit to be deprived of an equality of suffrage in both branches of the legislature, and thereby be thrown under the domination of the large states."

*   *   *

When the large states hinted that perhaps they might confederate separately, or that the Union might dissolve if their demands were not met, Bedford retorted that the small states would "find some foreign ally of more honor and good faith, who will take them by the hand and do them justice."

In the end, it was the bluff of the large states that was called. Once the deadlock of July 2 demonstrated that the small states would not buckle, the necessity for compromise became obvious. And the committee, called the Grand Committee, that the Convention elected to that end was stacked in favor of the small states. The three members chosen for the most populous states—Elbridge Gerry of Massachusetts, Benjamin Franklin of Pennsylvania, and George Mason of Virginia—were less militant than others in their delegations.

While the Grand Committee labored, the other delegates observed the 11th anniversary of American Independence. Philadelphia marked the occasion in fine fashion. A fife-and-drum corps paraded about the city; the militia fired three cannonades. In the local taverns, revelers toasted the day.

The delegates kept their worries to themselves. "We were on the verge of dissolution," wrote Luther Martin, "scarce held together by the strength of an hair, though the public papers were announcing our extreme unanimity." Indeed, up and down the Atlantic seaboard, editors were speculating about the proceedings in Philadelphia. "With zeal and confidence, we expect from the Federal Convention a system of government adequate to the security and preservation of those rights which were promulgated by the ever memorable Declaration of Independency," proclaimed the *Pennsylvania Herald.* "The world at large expect something from us," said Gerry. "If we do nothing, it appears to me we must have war and confusion."

In Britain, France, and Spain, royal advisers awaited news from America with detached curiosity. The Spaniards were particularly interested in the proceedings at Philadelphia, for if an effective government were not formed, American settlers in the lands west of the Appalachians might fall into their orbit. Even after the adoption of the Constitution, wrote historians Samuel Eliot Morison and Henry Steele Commager, "most European observers believed that the history of the American Union would be short and stormy."

On July 5, the committee presented its report to a glum Convention. The compromise it proposed was one in name only. In return for accepting an equal state representation in the Senate, the large states would gain the privilege of having all tax and appropriations bills originate in the House of Representatives, whose members were apportioned on the basis of population, with no changes by the upper chamber allowed. (Later, the Convention decided to allow the Senate to alter tax and spending laws.) Madison and his allies dismissed the proposed trade-off as worthless, neither desirable in theory nor useful in practice; the Senate, they said, could simply reject a bill it disliked.

*   *   *

But, by this time, argument no longer mattered.

The key vote of July 16 found five states for the compromise, four against, and Massachusetts divided by Gerry and Caleb Strong, who insisted that "an accommodation must take place." The compromise won, but not by much.

Emotions were still running high. New York's two remaining delegates, Robert Yates and John Lansing, Jr., had departed on July 10, declaring that the Convention was exceeding its authority. This point was raised several times during the proceedings, and brushed aside. As James Wilson had put it, the Convention was "authorized to *conclude nothing,* but . . . at liberty to *propose anything.*"

Next on the Convention's agenda for the afternoon of July 16th was the difficult task of beginning to define the extent of the legislative authority of Congress.

But the large states' delegates were unprepared to go on. The broad powers the Virginia Plan had proposed for Congress had rested on the expectation that both houses would be selected by proportional voting. "The vote of this morning had embarrassed the business extremely," Edmund Randolph declared during the afternoon of the 16th. He suggested that the Convention adjourn to give both sides a chance to rethink their positions. Mistakenly believing that Randolph was calling for an adjournment *sine die* (indefinitely), William Paterson of New Jersey immediately jumped to his feet and enthusiastically agreed that "it was high time for the Convention to adjourn, that the rule of secrecy ought to be rescinded, and that our constituents should be consulted."

But that, Randolph apologized, was not what he had meant. All he sought was an overnight adjournment. Tempers cooled, a few members hastened to remind their colleagues that even if "we could not do what was best, in itself, we ought to do something," and the Convention broke up for the day.

*   *   *

The next morning, the large states' delegates caucused to decide whether to pull out and confederate separately. "The time was wasted in vague conversation on the subject," Madison noted, "without any specific proposition or agreement." The Convention, despite the large states unhappiness, would continue.

The critical vote of July 16, then, was not a compromise as we ordinarily use the term. One side had won its point, the other had lost. But the outcome of this struggle did cause a series of other changes and "accommodations" that profoundly affected both the structure of the future U.S. government and its powers.

In its preoccupation with representation in Congress, the Convention had barely discussed the other two branches of government. Most of the delegates agreed with Madison that the central problem was to find a way to enable the executive and the judiciary to withstand the "encroachments" of the legislature. But how was that to be accomplished?

At an early point, the Convention had rejected Madison's scheme for a joint executive-judicial Council of Revision. The judiciary could simply overturn unconstitutional laws by itself, the members felt, and it would be most effective if "free from the bias of having participated" in writing the laws.

It is remarkable how little time the Framers spent discussing the role of the judiciary. Harvard's Raoul Berger noted some years ago that "the very casualness with which the [Convention's] leadership assumed that judicial review was available . . . suggests that the leaders considered they were dealing with a widely accepted doctrine." In their focus on the powers of the other branches of government, however, the Framers never sought to prescribe either the scope of the courts' power to declare laws unconstitutional or the basis on which this power could be exercised.

Far more of the Convention's time was devoted to the subject of executive power. But here, too, it is difficult to fathom exactly what the Framers intended.

Something of the uncertainty the convention had to overcome was illustrated when the subject of the executive was first raised on June 1. After James Wilson moved that "the executive consist of a single person," the delegates sat speechless in their chairs, reluctant to begin discussing so great an issue. "A considerable pause ensuing," noted Madison, "and the chairman asking if he should put the question, Dr. Franklin observed that it was a point of great importance and wished that the gentlemen would deliver their sentiments on it before the question was put." A lively debate began, and it immediately revealed two things.

The delegates agreed that a republican executive could not be modeled on the British monarchy. Second, most members thought that considerations of efficiency and responsibility alike required an executive headed by a single person—though a few dissenting members joined Randolph in fearing that such an office would prove "the foetus of monarchy." The dissenters variously favored either a plural executive, a kind of government by committee, or some form of ministerial government, akin to the British cabinet.

The great puzzle was how the executive was to be elected.

Today, Americans regard the strange device that the Framers finally invented, the electoral college, as evidence of how far they were prepared to go to prevent a popular majority from choosing a potential tyrant. What the Framers actually feared, however, was that a scattered population could never "be sufficiently informed of characters," as Roger Sherman put it, to choose wisely among what the Framers assumed would be a large field of candidates.

Believing that popular election was impractical, then, many delegates saw no alternative to having Congress choose the executive. But this only raised other objections. An election by Congress would be "the work of intrigue, cabal, and of faction," Gouverneur Morris asserted. "Real merit" would be passed over.

Moreover, the executive could not be expected to discharge his duties conscientiously, free from improper legislative influence, unless he were made ineligible for reelection. But that, Morris noted, would "destroy the great motive to good behavior, the hope of being rewarded by a reappointment." Such an executive, he continued, would be tempted to "make hay while the sun shines."

The desire for reelection would be an incentive to good behavior. But would that not leave open the possibility that a leader's fondness for the powers and perquisites of office—or a public that had grown too used to a leader—might lead to the creation of a monarchy in everything but name?

*   *   *

Just before it recessed on July 26, the Convention agreed (six states to three, with Virginia divided) to have Congress appoint a single executive, to serve for a single seven-year term. It then turned the task of recasting all the resolutions approved thus far over to a Committee of Detail composed of Randolph, Wilson, Ellsworth, John Rutledge of South Carolina, and Nathaniel Gorham of Massachusetts.

The muggy weather continued. "At each inhaling of air," wrote one visitor to Philadelphia, "one worries about the next one. The slightest movement is painful." Many of the delegates from nearby states took the opportunity to return home. Others fled to the countryside. General Washington, in his usual terse style, recorded in his journal: "In company with Mr. Govr. Morris and in his Phaeton with my horses, went up to one Jane Moore's (in whose house we lodged) in the vicinity of Valley Forge to get Trout."

When they reconvened on August 6, the delegates were eager to move the business toward a conclusion. During the remaining six weeks, the debates became more rushed—and more focused. They centered on specific clauses and provisions; decisions that would figure prominently in later controversies over the Constitution were reached with surprisingly little discussion, revealing far less about the Framers' intentions than modern commentators would like to know.

Far and away the most momentous changes that took place were those involving the powers of the executive.

In the report of the Committee of Detail, the major duties of the president (as the committee now named the executive) were confined to seeing that the laws were "duly and faithfully executed" and to serving as commander-in-chief of the armed forces. He would also enjoy a limited veto over acts of Congress. Two of the powers that provide the foundation for much of the political authority of the modern presidency remained in the Senate: the power to make treaties and the power to appoint ambassadors and justices of the Supreme Court (and perhaps even the heads of major executive departments, though this was left unclear).

In Britain, these powers were critical elements of the royal prerogative, and the Framers were reluctant to grant them to the president. Yet, with the report of the Committee of Detail in their hands, many began to reconsider. Madison, Wilson, Gouverneur Morris, and other delegates from the large states now opposed giving sole power over foreign affairs to the Senate, a body in which the small states would enjoy disproportionate influence, and whose members would be elected by the presumably reckless state legislatures.

*   *   *

From this unhappiness with the Great Compromise over representation in Congress, a new concept of the presidency began to emerge. Though many of the Framers worried about the potential abuse of executive power, some now described the president, in Gouverneur Morris's words, as "the general guardian of the national interests." He would not only carry out the national will as it was expressed by the legislature, but also act independently to define a national interest larger than the sum of the legislators' concerns.

The best evidence for this enlarged conception of executive power is circumstantial, resting less on anything the delegates said than on the final changes that led to the adoption of the electoral college. Unfortunately, the key discussions took place within the Committee on Postponed Parts, appointed on August 31 to consider a potpourri of unresolved issues. Very little is known about what was said during its debates.

In the Committee's major report, read September 4, the president suddenly enjoyed significant responsibility for foreign affairs and the power to appoint ambassadors, judges, and other officials, with the "advice and consent" of the Senate. At the same time, his election by an electoral college promised to make the president politically independent of Congress. The report also specified a four-year term and eligibility for reelection.

The Committee had clearly sought to preserve the Great Compromise. The large states, it was assumed, would enjoy the advantage in promoting candidates for the presidency. (None of the Framers anticipated the formation of powerful political parties.) But if an election failed to produce a majority—as many delegates thought it usually would—the election would fall to the Senate. There, the small states would have greater influence.

*   *   *

James Wilson rose to object. If the Senate controlled the ultimate power of election, he warned, "the President will not be the man of the people as he ought to be, but the Minion of the Senate." Many members agreed, but nobody could find a solution that would not erode the Great Compromise.

It was only after the report had been adopted that Roger Sherman and North Carolina's Hugh Williamson had the idea of sending deadlocked elections into the House of Representatives, with the members voting by states. This had the ingenious effect of preserving both the president's independence from the Senate and the Great Compromise. The amendment was adopted almost without debate.

On September 12, George Mason broached the subject of a Bill of Rights. "It would give great quiet to the people," he argued, if trial by jury and other rights were guaranteed in the new Constitution. Roger Sherman replied that a Bill of Rights was unnecessary. The states, he said, could protect these rights: Eight of them had already incorporated such provisions into their constitutions. The discussion was brief. The Convention voted against including a Bill of Rights, 10 states to none. Only later, after several state ratifying conventions demanded it, were the guarantees that Americans now associate with the Constitution introduced in Congress and ratified by the states as the first 10 amendments.

Despite this progress, Madison was gloomy. As he informed Jefferson seven weeks later, he was discouraged because the Convention had rejected the Virginia Plan's scheme for an unlimited national veto of all state laws, instead vesting the courts with narrower powers of review. Madison was convinced that an independent judiciary, as framed by the Convention, would lack the political strength to override the improper acts of the legislatures, which could always claim to express the will of the people.

Madison had entered the Convention with higher hopes and more ambitious goals than any of the other delegates. What they saw as compromises and accommodations he regarded as defeats. He privately thought that the worst "vices of the political system" would go unchecked even if the new national government worked as planned. He did not cheer the end result.

So it fell to Benjamin Franklin to claim the privileges of age and reputation to urge the 41 delegates still present as the Convention drew to a close to make their final approval of the Constitution unanimous. That would speed its ratification by Congress and the states.

*   *   *

"When you assemble a number of men to have the advantage of their joint wisdom," Franklin reminded them, "you inevitably assemble with those men, all their prejudices, their passions, their errors of opinion, their local interests, and their selfish views. From such an assembly," he asked, "can a perfect production be expected? It therefore astonishes me, Sir, to find this system approaching so near to perfection as it does; and I think it will astonish our enemies, who are waiting with confidence to hear that our councils are confounded like those of the Builders of Babel. . . . Thus I consent, Sir, to this Constitution, because I expect no better, and because I am not sure that it is not the best."

On September 15, 1787, the delegates, voting by states, did endorse the Constitution. But Franklin's appeal failed to sway three of the delegates. Mason, Randolph, and Gerry refused, for various reasons, to sign the Constitution. Mason worried, among other things, about the extent of the president's powers and the absence of a Bill of Rights.

For what Franklin invoked was not simply the cumulative wisdom of what the Framers had wrought, but also the character of the deliberations themselves. No one could better gauge the range of intentions, honorable and otherwise, that had entered into the making of the Constitution than Franklin, who was perhaps the most worldly and calculating of all the Framers. No one could better grasp both the limits as well as the possibilities of human reason than the leading American experimental scientist of his century.

Franklin was bold enough to observe how "near to perfection" the completed Constitution came, yet he was just as prepared to concede that the objections against it might have merit. (Franklin himself favored a unicameral national legislature and a plural executive.) With his usual cleverness, he asked only that "every member of the Convention who may still have objections to it, would with me, on this occasion doubt a little of his own infallibility."

It took Madison a while to appreciate Franklin's wisdom. But when he dictated the final paragraphs of his preface to the Philadelphia debates, he took the same philosophical view. "Of the ability and intelligence of those who composed the Convention," he wrote, "the debates and proceedings may be a test." But, he went on, "the character of the work which was the offspring of their deliberations must be tested by the experience of the future, added to that of the nearly half century which has passed."

To see the Constitution as Franklin asked its very first critics to see it, or as Madison later learned to view it, does not require later generations to invest the Framers with perfect knowledge, to conclude that they had closely considered and conclusively resolved every issue and problem that they faced.

The Framers were patriotic men of varied capacities who rose above their passions and self-interest to forge a grand document. But they left Philadelphia viewing the Constitution as a hopeful experiment whose results and meanings would be made known only through time.

Nothing would have struck the Framers as more unrealistic than the notion that their original intentions must be the sole guide by which the meaning of the Constitution would ever after be determined. They did not bar future generations from trying to improve upon their work, or from using the lessons of experience to judge the "fallibility" of their reason. They asked only that we try to understand the difficulties that they had encountered and the broad array of concerns, variously noble and self-serving, that they had labored to accommodate during nearly four months of debate in the City of Brotherly Love.

The Illusion of Change: Women and the American Revolution

Joan Hoff

Revolution breaks the cake of custom. When the revolution in question is predicated on an ideology of liberty and equality, as was that of the thirteen colonies, how could it not have resulted in greater liberty and equality for women? Joan Hoff, professor of history at Indiana University, discusses why it did not. Reflecting a division of labor based on sex-role stereotyping inherited from English custom, woman's role was confined to the domestic sphere. In fact, so thoroughgoing was the belief in separate spheres for men and women that it was conceptually difficult for women even to contemplate the possibility of defining, much less realizing, liberty and equality in a political sense. Even assertive women such as Mercy Otis Warren and Abigail Adams were not "feminists"; they were not demanding—they could not yet imagine—equality in a legal sense. Even for the enlightened of the revolutionary generation, concludes Professor Hoff, the mythic idea that men and women occupied distinct spheres of worldly activity "was commonly accepted in the last half of the eighteenth century as one of the natural laws of the universe."

I will argue that certain types of female functions, leading either to the well-known exploitation of working women or to the ornamental middle-class housewife of the nineteenth century, were abetted by the American Revolution, although not caused by it.

This occurred because the functional opportunities open to women between 1700 and 1800 were too limited to allow them to make the transition in attitudes necessary to insure high status performance in the newly emerging nation. In other words, before 1776 women did not participate enough in conflicts over land, religion, taxes, local politics, or commercial transactions. They simply had not come into contact with enough worldly diversity to be prepared for a changing, pluralistic, modern society. Women of the postrevolutionary generation had little choice but to fill those low status functions prescribed by the small minority of American males who *were* prepared for modernization by enough diverse activities and experiences.

As a result, the American Revolution produced no significant benefits for American women. This same generalization can be made for other powerless groups in the colonies—native Americans, blacks, probably most propertyless white males, and indentured servants. Although these people together with women made up the vast majority of colonial population, they could not take advantage of the overthrow of British rule to better their own positions, as did the white, propertied males who controlled economics, politics, and culture. By no means did all members of these subordinate groups support the patriot cause, and those who did, even among whites, were not automatically accorded personal iberation when national liberation was won. This is a common phenomenon of revolution within subcultures which, because of sex, race, or other forms of discrimination or deprivation of the members, are not far enough along in the process toward modernization to express their dissatisfaction or frustration through effectively organized action.

Given the political and socioeconomic limitations of the American Revolution, this lack of positive societal change in the lives of women and other derived colonials is to be expected. It is also surprising that until recently most historians of the period have been content to concentrate their research efforts on the increased benefits of Lockean liberalism that accrued to a relatively small percent of all Americans and to ignore the increased sexism and racism exhibited by this privileged group both during and after the Revolution. They have also tended to ignore the various ways in which the experience of the Revolution either hastened or retarded certain long-term eighteenth-century trends already affecting women.

What has been called in England and Europe "the transformation of the female in bourgeois culture" also took place in America between 1700 and 1800. This process would have occurred with or without a declaration of independence from England. It produced a class of American bourgeoises who clearly resembled the group of middle-class women evident in England a century earlier. However, the changing societal conditions leading up to this transformation in American women were much more complex than they had been for seventeenth-century British women because of the unique roles, that is, functions, that colonial women had originally played in the settlement and development of the New World. The American Revolution was simply one event among many in this century-long process of change. It was a process that ultimately produced two distinct classes of women in the United States—those who worked to varying degrees exclusively in their homes and those who worked both inside and outside of their homes. . . .

It is true, however, for most of the period up to 1750 that conditions *out of necessity* increased the functional independence and importance of all women. By this I mean that much of the alleged freedom from sexism of colonial women was due to their initial numerical scarcity and the critical labor shortage in the New World throughout the seventeenth and eighteenth centuries. Such increased re-

productive roles (economic as well as biological) reflected the logic of necessity and *not any fundamental change* in the sexist, patriarchal attitudes that had been transplanted from Europe. Based on two types of scarcity (sex and labor), which were not to last, these enhanced functions of colonial women diminished as the commercial and agricultural economy became more specialized and the population grew.

A gradual "embourgeoisement" of colonial culture accompanied this preindustrial trend toward modern capitalism. It limited the number of high status roles for eighteenth-century American women just as it had for seventeenth-century English and European women. Alice Clark, Margaret George, Natalie Zemon Davis, and Jane Abray have all argued convincingly that as socioeconomic capitalist organization takes place, it closes many opportunities normally open to women both inside and outside of the family unit in precapitalist times. The decline in the status of women that accompanied the appearance of bourgeois modernity in England, according to Margaret George, "was not merely a relative decline. Precapitalist woman was not simply relatively eclipsed by the great leap foward of the male achiever; she suffered, rather, an absolute setback."

In the New World this process took longer but was no less debilitating. Before 1800 it was both complicated and hindered by the existence of a severe labor shortage and religious as well as secular exhortations against the sins of idleness and vanity. Thus, colonial conditions demanded that all ablebodied men, women, and children work, and so the ornamental, middle-class woman existed more in theory than in practice.

The labor shortage that plagued colonial America placed a premium on women's work inside and outside the home, particularly during the war-related periods of economic dislocation between 1750 and 1815. And there is no doubt that home industry was basic to American development both before and after 1776. It is also true that there was no sharp delineation between the economic needs of the community and the work carried on within the preindustrial family until after the middle of the eighteenth century. Woman's role as a household manager was a basic and integral part of the early political economy of the colonies. Hence she occupied a position of unprecedented importance and equality within the socioeconomic unit of the family.

As important as this function of women in the

home was, from earliest colonial times, it nonetheless represented a division of labor based on sex-role stereotyping carried over from England. Men normally engaged in agricultural production; women engaged in domestic gardening and home manufacturing—only slave women worked in the fields. Even in those areas of Massachusetts and Pennsylvania that originally granted females allotments of land, the vestiges of this practice soon disappeared, and subsequent public divisions "simply denied the independent economic existence of women." While equality never extended outside the home in the colonial era, there was little likelihood that women felt useless or alienated because of the importance and demanding nature of their domestic responsibilities.

In the seventeenth and eighteenth centuries spinning and weaving were the primary types of home production for women and children (of both sexes). This economic function was considered so important that legal and moral sanctions were developed to insure it. For example, labor laws were passed, compulsory spinning schools were established "for the education of children of the poor," and women were told that their virtue could be measured in yards of yarn. So from the beginning there was a sex, and to a lesser degree a class and educational, bias built into colonial production of cloth, since no formal apprenticeship was required for learning the trade of spinning and weaving.

It has also been recognized that prerevolutionary boycotts of English goods after 1763 and later during the war increased the importance of female production of textiles both in the home and in the early piecework factory system. By mid-1776 in Philadelphia, for example, 4,000 women and children reportedly were spinning under the "putting out system" for local textile plants. . . .

American living standards fluctuated with the unequal prosperity that was especially related to wars. Those engaging in craft production and commerce were particularly hard hit after 1750, first by the deflation and depression following the French and Indian War (1754–1763), and then by the War for Independence. In fact, not only were the decades immediately preceding and following the American Revolution ones of economic dislocation, but the entire period between 1775 and 1815 has been characterized as one of "arrested social and economic

development." These trends, combined with increased specialization, particularly with the appearance of a nascent factory system, "initiated a decline in the economic and social position of many sections of the artisan class." Thus with the exception of the innkeeping and tavern business, all of the other primary economic occupations of city women were negatively affected by the periodic fluctuations in the commercial economy between 1763 and 1812.

Women artisans and shopkeepers probably suffered most during times of economic crisis because of their greater difficulty in obtaining credit from merchants. Although research into their plight has been neglected, the documents are there—in the records of merchant houses showing women entrepreneurs paying their debts for goods and craft materials by transferring their own records of indebtedness, and in court records showing an increased number of single women, especially widows sued for their debts, or in public records of the increased number of bankrupt women who ended up on poor relief lists or in debtors' prisons or who were forced to become indentured servants or earn an independent living during hard times.

It was also a difficult time for household spinners and weavers, about whom a few more facts are known. First, this all-important economic function increasingly reflected class distinctions. In 1763 one British governor estimated that only the poor wore homespun clothes, while more affluent Americans bought English imports. Second, it was primarily poor women of the northern and middle colonies who engaged in spinning and weaving for pay (often in the form of credit rather than cash), while black slave women and white female indentured servants performed the same function in the South. Naturally women in full frontier areas had no recourse but to make their own clothing. Beginning with the first boycotts of British goods in the 1760s, women of all classes were urged to make and wear homespun. Several additional "manufactory houses" were established as early as 1764 in major cities specifically for the employment of poor women. Direct appeals to patriotism and virtue were used very successfully to get wealthier women to engage in arduous home-spinning drives, but probably only for short periods of time.

Thus all classes of women were actively recruited into domestic textile production by male patriots with such pleas as, "In this time of public distress you have each of you an opportunity not only to help to sustain your families, but likewise to call your mite into the treasury of the public good." They were further urged to "cease trifling their time away [and] prudently employ it in learning the use of the spinning wheel." Beyond any doubt the most well-known appeal was the widely reprinted 9 November 1767 statement of advice to the "Daughters of Liberty" which first appeared in the *Massachusetts Gazette*. It read in part:

> First then throw aside your high top knots of pride
> Wear none but your own country linen.
> Of economy boast. Let your pride be the most
> To show cloaths of your make and spinning.

Peak periods in prerevolutionary spinning and weaving were reached during every major boycott from 1765 to 1777. But the war and inflation proved disruptive. For example, we know that the United Company of Philadelphia for Promoting American Manufactures, which employed 500 of the city's 4,000 women and children spinning at home, expired between 1777 and 1787, when it was revived. The record of similar organizations elsewhere was equally erratic.

It is common for developing countries with a labor shortage to utilize technological means to meet production demands. After the war, the new republic proved no exception, as the inefficiency and insufficiency of household spinners became apparent. Ultimately the "putting out" system was replaced entirely by the factory that employed the same women and children who had formerly been household spinners. It took the entire first half of the nineteenth century before this process was completed, and when it was, it turned out to be at the expense of the social and economic status of female workers. . . .

Why didn't the experiences of the Revolution result in changing the political consciousness of women? Part of the answer lies in the socialized attitudes among female members of the revolutionary generation that set them apart from their male contemporaries. Their attitudes had been molded by the modernization trends encountered by most women in the course of the eighteenth century. Out of the necessity wrought by the struggle with England, women performed certain tasks that appeared revolutionary in nature, just as they had performed nonfamilial tasks out of necessity throughout the colonial period. But this seemingly revolutionary behavior is not necessarily proof of the acceptance of abstract revolutionary principles.

Despite their participation in greater economic specialization, despite their experiences with a slightly smaller conjugal household where power relations were changing, despite a limited expansion of the legal rights and somewhat improved educational opportunities for free, white women, the revolutionary generation of females were less prepared than most men for the modern implications of independence. Their distinctly different experiential level, combined with the intellectually and psychologically limiting impact of the Great Awakening and the Enlightenment on women, literally made it impossible for even the best educated females to understand the political intent or principles behind the inflated rhetoric of the revolutionary era. Words like virtue, veracity, morality, tyranny, and corruption were ultimately given public political meanings by male revolutionary leaders that were incomprehensible or, more likely, misunderstood by most women.

As the rhetoric of the revolution began to assume dynamic, emotional proportions, its obsession with "virtue" versus "corruption" struck a particularly responsive chord among literate women, as evidenced, for example, in their patriotic statements as individuals and in groups when supporting the boycott of English goods between 1765 and 1774. While these statements are impressive both in number and intensity of feeling, it can be questioned whether the idea of taking "their country back on the path of virtue" and away from "the oppression of corrupt outside forces" was understood in the same way by female and male patriots, when even men of varying Whig persuasions could not agree on them. Virtue and morality for the vast majority of Americans, but particularly women, do not appear to have had the modernizing implications of pluralistic individualism, that is, of the "acceptance of diversity, the commitment to individual action in pursuit of individual goals, the conception of politics as an arena where these goals contest and the awareness of a national government which is at once the course of political power and the framework for an orderly clash of interest." These are characteristics of "modern man."

How does one prove such a generalization about

attitudes behind the behavior of women during the Revolution? Few poor white or black women left records revealing how they felt about the war. Such women, whether Loyalists or patriots, conveyed their sentiments silently with their physical labor. Among the more articulate and educated women there is written testimony to at least an initial sense of pride and importance involved in their participation in the war effort. Thus a young Connecticut woman named Abigail Foote wrote in her diary in 1775 that carding two pounds of whole wool had made her feel "Nationly," while others recorded their contributions in similarly patriotic terms.

But the question remains: did their supportive actions prepare them to accept a vision of society anywhere near the version ultimately conveyed by James Madison's Federalist Number Ten in the fight over the Constitution of 1787? To date there is little evidence that this type of sophisticated political thought was present, either in the writings of women about the Revolution and its results or in the appeals made to them during or immediately following the war. From the popular 1767 statement of advice to the Daughters of Liberty to the 1787 one urging women to use "their influence over their husbands, brothers and sons to draw them from those dreams of liberty under a simple democratical form of government, which are so unfriendly to . . . order and decency," it is difficult to conclude that women were being prepared to understand the political ramifications of the Revolution.

The same lack of political astuteness appears to underlie even the least traditional and most overtly political activities of women, such as the fifty-one who signed the anti-tea declaration in Edenton, North Carolina, on 25 October 1774 (later immortalized in a London cartoon). The same could be said of the more than 500 Boston women who agreed on 31 January 1770 to support the radical male boycott of tea; of the Daughters of Liberty in general; and of the 1,600 Philadelphia women who raised 7,500 dollars in gold for the Continental Army. Even Mercy Otis Warren never perceived the modern political system that evolved from the Revolution. Instead she viewed the war and its aftermath as the "instrument of Providence that sparked a world movement, changing thought and habit of men to complete the divine plan for human happiness" largely through the practice of virtue.

Perhaps the most important aspect of the sup-

portive activities among women for the patriot cause was the increase in class and social distinctions they symbolized. For example, it appears unlikely that poor white or black women joined Daughters of Liberty groups, actively boycotted English goods, or participated in any significant numbers in those associations of "Ladies of the highest rank and influence," who raised money and supplies for the Continental Army. On the contrary, it may well have been primarily "young female spinsters" from prominent families and well-to-do widows and wives who could afford the time or the luxury of such highly publicized activities. The vast majority, however, of middle-class female patriots (and, for that matter, Loyalists), whether single or married, performed such necessary volunteer roles as seamstresses, nurses, hostesses, and sometime spies, whenever the fighting shifted to their locales, without any undue fanfare or praise.

The same is true of poorer women, with one important difference: they had no choice. They had all they could do to survive, and although this did lead a few of them to become military heroines, they could not afford the luxury of either "disinterested patriotism" or the detached self-interest and indulgences that some of the richer women exhibited. The very poorest, particularly those in urban areas, had no resources to fall back on when confronted with the personal or economic traumas caused by the War for Independence. As noted above, this was especially evident in the case of women wage earners who, regardless of race or class, had apparently always received lower pay than free men or hired-out male slaves, and who had suffered severely from runaway inflation during the war. Women's services were more likely to be paid for in Continental currency than with specie. Fees for male "doctors," for example, according to one Maryland family account book, were made in specie payment after the middle of 1780, while midwives had to accept the depreciated Continental currency for a longer period of time. Thus, the American Revolution hastened the appearance of greater class-based activities among "daughters of the new republic," with poor women undertaking the least desirable tasks and suffering most from the inflationary spiral that plagued the whole country. It is easy to imagine the impact that inflation had on the rural and urban poor, but it even affected those middle- and upper middle-class women who were left at home to manage businesses, states, plantations, or farms. Their activities often meant the difference between bankruptcy and solvency for male revolutionary leaders.

Probably the classic example of housewifely efficiency and economic shrewdness is found in Abigail's management of the Adams family and farm during John's long absences. But in this respect Abigail Adams stands in direct contrast to the women in the lives of other leading revolutionaries like Jefferson, Madison, and Monroe—all of whom were bankrupt by public service in part because their wives were not as capable at land management as she was. This even proved true of the most outspoken of all revolutionary wives, Mercy Otis Warren. Numerous less well-known women, however, proved equal to the increased domestic responsibilities placed upon them. Only the utterly impoverished could not resort to the traditional colonial task of household manager.

As the months of fighting lengthened into years, more and more poverty-stricken women left home to join their husbands, lovers, fathers, or other male relatives in the army encampments. Once there, distinctions between traditional male and female roles broke down. While a certain number of free white and black slave women were needed to mend, wash, and cook for officers and care for the sick and wounded, most enlisted men and their women took care of themselves and fought beside each other on many occasions. Moreover, unlike the English, German, and French commanders, American military leaders were often morally offended or embarrassed by the presence of these unfortunate and destitute women, "their hair flying, their brows beady with the heat, their belongings slung over one sholder [sic], chattering and yelling in sluttish shrills as they went and spitting in the gutters."

This puritanical, hostile attitude on the part of patriot army officers toward such a common military phenomenon insured that camp followers of the American forces were less systematically provided for than those of foreign troops. Aside from its class overtones (after all Martha Washington, Catherine Greene, and Lucy Knox were accepted as respectable camp followers), it is difficult to explain this American attitude, except that in the prevailing righteous rhetoric of the Revolution and of later historians these women were misrepresented as little better than prostitutes. In reality they were the inarticulate, invisible poor whose story remains to be told from existing pension records based on oral testimony. At any rate there is pathos and irony in the well-preserved image of Martha Washington, who visited her husband at Valley Forge during the disastrous winter of 1777–1778, copying routine military communiques and presiding over a sewing circle of other officers' wives, while the scores of combat-hardened women who died along with their enlisted men have been conveniently forgotten.

These camp followers, as well as the women who stayed at home, complained about their plight privately and publicly, and on occasion they rioted and looted for foodstuffs. Women rioting for bread or other staples never became a significant or even a particularly common revolutionary act in the New World as it did in Europe, largely because of the absence of any long-term, abject poverty on the part of even the poorest colonials. The most likely exception to this generalization came during the extreme inflation that accompanied the war. Then there is indeed some evidence of what can be called popular price control activity by groups of women who had a definite sense of what were fair or legitimate marketing practices. At the moment we have concrete evidence of only a half-dozen seemingly spontaneous instances of "a corps of female infantry" attacking merchants. Other examples will probably be discovered as more serious research into the "moral economy of the crowd" is undertaken by American historians.

What is interesting about the few known cases is that the women involved in some of them did not simply appear to be destitute camp followers passing through towns stripping the dead and looting at random for food. A few at least were women "with Silk gownes on," who were offering to buy sugar, salt, flour, or coffee for a reasonable price with Continental currency. When a certain merchant insisted on payment with specie or with an unreasonable amount of paper money, the women then, and only then, insisted on "taking" his goods at their price. These appear, therefore, to be isolated examples of collective behavior by women where there was, at the least, a very strongly held cultural notion of a moral economy.

Nevertheless, there is still no clear indication of an appreciable change in the political consciousness of such women. Perhaps it was because even the poorest who took part in popular price control actions primarily did so, like the Citoyennes Républicaines Révolutionnaires during the French Revolution, out of an immediate concern for feeding themselves and their children and not for feminist reasons growing out of their age-old economic plight as women in a patriarchal society. In addition, except for camp followers and female vagabonds, the principal concern of most members of this generation of primarily rural women remained the home and their functions there. During the home-spinning drives and during the war when their men were away, their domestic and agricultural duties became all the more demanding, but not consciousness-raising. . . .

Lastly, in explaining the failure of the equalitarian ideals of the Revolution to bear even limited fruit for women, one must analyze the narrow ideological parameters of even those few who advocated women's rights, persons such as Abigail Adams, Judith Sargent Murray, Elizabeth Southgate Bowne, Elizabeth Drinker, and Mercy Otis Warren.

These women . . . were not feminists. Like most of the better organized, but no less unsuccessful Républicaines of France, they seldom, if ever, aspired to complete equality with men except in terms of education. Moreover, none challenged the institution of marriage or defined themselves "as other than mothers and potential mothers." They simply could not conceive of a society whose standards were not set by male, patriarchal institutions, nor should they be expected to have done so. Instead of demanding equal rights, the most articulate and politically conscious American women of this generation asked at most for privileges and at least for favors—not for an absolute expansion of their legal or political functions, which they considered beyond their proper womanly sphere. Man was indeed the measure of equality to these women, and given their societal conditioning, such status was beyond their conception of themselves as individuals.

Ironically it is this same sense of their "proper sphere" that explains why the most educated female patriots did not feel obliged to organize to demand more from the Founding Fathers. It is usually overlooked that in the famous letter of 31 March 1776 where Abigail asks John Adams to "Remember the Ladies," she justified this mild request for "more generous and favourable" treatment on the grounds that married women were then subjected to the "unlimited power" of their husbands. She was not asking him for the right to vote, only for some legal protection of wives from abuses under common-law practices. "Regard us then," she pleaded with her husband, "as Beings placed by providence under your protection and in imitation of the Supreme Being make use of that power only for our happiness." Despite an earlier statement in this letter about the "Ladies" being "determined to foment a Rebellion" and refusing to be "bound by any Laws in which we have no voice, or Representation," Abigail Adams was not in any sense demanding legal, let alone political or individual, equality with men at the beginning of the American Revolution. If anything, her concept of the separateness of the two different spheres in which men and women operated was accentuated by the war and the subsequent trials of the new republic between 1776 and 1800.

This idea that men and women existed in two separate spheres or orbits was commonly accepted in the last half of the eighteenth century as one of the natural laws of the universe. While European Enlightenment theories adhered strictly to the inferiority of the natural sphere that women occupied, in colonial America they were tacitly challenged and modified by experience—as were so many other aspects of natural law doctrines. On the other hand, the degree to which educated, upper-class women in particular thought that their sphere of activity was in fact equal, and the degree to which it actually was accorded such status by the male-dominated culture, is all-important. Historians have tended to place greater emphasis on the former rather than the latter, with misleading results about the importance of the roles played by both colonial and revolutionary women.

It is true that Abigail Adams was an extremely independent-minded person who firmly criticized books by foreign authors who subordinated the female sphere to that of the male. Writing to her sister Elizabeth Shaw Peabody in 1799, she said that "I will never consent to have our sex considered in an inferior point of light. Let each planet shine in their own orbit, God and nature designed it so—if man is Lord, woman is *Lordess*—that is what I contend for." Thus, when her husband was away she deemed it was within her proper sphere to act as head of the household on all matters, including the decision to have her children inoculated against smallpox without his permission. At the same time, however, she always deferred to his ambitions and his inherent superiority, because the equality of their two separate orbits did not make them equal as individuals. In general Abigail Adams and other women of her class accepted the notion that while they were mentally equal to men their sphere of activity was entirely private in nature, except on those occasions when they substituted for their absent husbands. "Government of States and Kingdoms, tho' God knows badly enough managed," she asserted in 1796, "I am willing should be solely administered by the lords of creation. I should contend for Domestic Government, and think that best administered by the female." Such a strong belief in equal, but separate, spheres is indeed admirable for the times, but it should not be confused with feminism. . . .

Only unusual male feminists like Thomas Paine asked that women be accorded "the sweets of public esteem" and "an equal right to praise." It was Paine—not the female patriots—who also took advantage of American revolutionary conditions to attack the institution of marriage. Later, in the 1790s, only a few isolated women in the United States supported Mary Wollstonecraft's demand for the right to public as well as private fulfillment on the grounds that "private duties are never properly fulfilled unless the understanding enlarges the heart and that public virtue is only an aggregate of private. . . ." Her criticisms of marital bondage were never seriously considered by American women in this postrevolutionary decade.

The reasons for this unresponsiveness to the feminism of both Paine and Wollstonecraft are complex, for this was not only opposed by the sexist Founding Fathers, but by most women. Again we must ask—why?

The physical and mental hardships that most women had endured during the war continued to varying degrees in the economic dislocation that followed in its wake. Sheer personal survival, not rising social or material expectations, dominated the thinking and activities of lower- and even some middle- and upper-class women. Probably more important, the few well-educated American women, fortunate to have the leisure to reflect, clearly realized the discrepancy that had occurred between the theory and practice of virtue in the course of the war and its aftermath. While it was discouraging for them to view the corruption of morals of the society at large and particularly among men in public life, they could take some satisfaction in the greater consistency between the theory and practice of virtue in their own private lives. Such postrevolutionary women found

their familial duties and homosocial relationships untainted by the corruption of public life. They considered themselves most fortunate and they were, compared to their nineteenth-century descendants, who had to pay a much higher price for similar virtuous consistency and spiritual purity.

It was natural, therefore, for the educated among this generation to express disillusionment with politics, as they saw republican principles corrupted or distorted, and then to enter a stage of relative quiescence that marked the beginning of the transitional period between their war-related activities and a later generation of female reformers who emerged in the 1830s. They cannot be held responsible for not realizing the full extent of the potentially debilitating features of their withdrawal to the safety of modern domesticity—where virtue becomes its own punishment instead of reward.

A final factor that helps to explain the absence of feminism in the behavior of women during the Revolution and in their attitudes afterward is related to the demographic changes that were taking place within the family unit between 1760 and 1800. Middle- and upper-class women were increasingly subjected to foreign and domestic literature stressing standards of femininity that had not inhibited the conduct of their colonial ancestors. While the rhetoric of this new literature was that of the Enlightenment, its message was that of romantic love, glamorized dependence, idealized motherhood, and sentimentalized children within the ever-narrowing realm of family life. At poorer levels of society a new family pattern was emerging as parental control broke down, and ultimately these two trends would merge, leaving all women in lower status domestic roles than they had once occupied.

In general it appears that the American Revolution retarded those societal conditions that had given colonial women their unique function and status in society, while it promoted those that were leading toward the gradual "embourgeoisement" of late eighteenth-century women. By 1800 their economic and legal privileges were curtailed; their recent revolutionary activity minimized or simply ignored; their future interest in politics discouraged; and their domestic roles extolled, but increasingly limited.

Moreover, at the highest *and* lowest levels of society this revolutionary generation of women was left with misleading assumptions: certain educated women believing strongly in the hope that immediate improvement for themselves and their children would come with educational reform, and some lower-class women believing that improvement would come through work in the "manufactories." Both admitted, according to Mercy Otis Warren, that their "appointed subordination" to men was natural, if for no other reason than "for the sake of Order in Families." Neither could be expected to anticipate that this notion would limit their participation in, and understanding of, an emerging modern nation because the actual (as opposed to idealized) value accorded their postrevolutionary activities was not yet apparent.

A few, like Priscilla Mason, the valedictorian of the 1793 graduating class of the Young Ladies' Academy of Philadelphia, might demand an equal education with men and exhort women to break out of their traditional sphere, but most ended up agreeing with Eliza Southgate Bowne when she concluded her defense of education for women by saying: "I believe I must give up all pretension to *profundity*, for I am much more at home in my female character." And the dominate male leadership of the 1790s could not have agreed more.

For women, the American revolution was over before it ever began. Their "disinterested" patriotism (or disloyalty, as the case may be) was accorded identical treatment by male revolutionaries following the war: conscious neglect of female rights combined with subtle educational and economic exploitation. The end result was increased loss of function and authentic status for all women whether they were on or under the proverbial pedestal.

III

Myths of Nationalism and Jacksonian Democracy

As the United States launched a government under the auspices of its new Constitution, expectations at home and abroad ran high. Throughout the national period, as Americans strove to live up to the high standards set for them from both without and within, mythology was inevitable. Later historians too would see the early republic in mythic terms. As Henry Steele Commager demonstrates in the first article in this section, Americans have sought to find in the nation's earlier decades a "usable past."

In this search, the Jacksonian period served for a long time to represent an unfolding of the democratic implications of the Revolution. Democracy, it seemed, arrived with the election of Andrew Jackson in 1828. After Abraham Lincoln, Jackson ranks as perhaps the greatest of the nation's political folk heroes. A substantial mythology, along with a certain symbolism and mystique, surrounds our historical understanding of both these men. In the case of Andrew Jackson, historical judgment suffers most from the notion that he was the country's first "popular" President. Jackson's popularity stemmed not so much from the degree to which his countrymen came to admire him (for certainly George Washington before him was thus admired), but rather from the degree to which he is said to have represented the "common man." For example, Jackson was the first President seemingly close enough to the people to be known by a nickname—"Old Hickory." So close an association between Old Hickory and the masses has been traditionally supposed that, in fact, the era of his presidency was long affectionately labeled the "Age of the Common Man."

It is precisely that affinity between Andrew Jackson and the "common man" that recent historical scholarship has sought to reexamine. Legitimate questions have been raised as to the extent of democratization during Jackson's presidency, whether Jackson was a cause or consequence of his age, and whether he himself was in fact a Jacksonian. Was Jacksonian society noticeably and distinctly egalitarian, or is that view a result of popular and historical mythology?

The Legendary Washington: His Apotheosis. *(Courtesy, Library of Congress)*

The Verdict of the People: Age of the Common Man? *(Courtesy, Library of Congress)*

The Invention of America: The Search for a Usable Past

Henry Steele Commager

Henry Steele Commager, distinguished historian at Amherst College, explores the conditions that served to evoke a national consciousness in Americans during the period from the Revolution to the Civil War. Arguing that American self-consciousness was deliberately created and fostered, Commager sees that American nationalism, myths included, "was, to an extraordinary degree, a literary creation. . . ." It was poets and storytellers who created the fund of culture, tradition, and experience so necessary to bind national sentiments.

The United States was the first of the "new" nations. As the American colonies were the first to rebel against a European "mother country," so the American states were the first to create—we can use Lincoln's term, to bring forth—a new nation. Modern nationalism was inaugurated by the American, not the French, Revolution. But the new United States faced problems unknown to the new nations of nineteenth-century Europe—and twentieth. For in the Old World the nation came before the state; in America the state came before the nation. In the Old World nations grew out of well-prepared soil, built upon a foundation of history and traditions; in America the foundations were still to be laid, the seeds still to be planted, the traditions still to be formed.

The problem which confronted the new United States then was radically different from that which confronted, let us say, Belgium, Italy, Greece, or Germany in the nineteenth century, or Norway, Finland, Iceland, and Israel in the twentieth. These "new" states were already amply equipped with history, tradition, and memory—as well as with many of the other essential ingredients of nationalism except political independence. Of them it can be said that the nation was a product of history. But with the United States, history was rather a creation of the nation, and

it is suggestive that in the New World the self-made nation was as familiar as the self-made man.

It is unnecessary to emphasize anything as familiar as the importance of history, tradition, and memory to successful nationalism. On this matter statesmen, historians, and philosophers of nationalism are all agreed. It was the very core of Edmund Burke's philosophy: the nation—society itself—is a partnership of past, present, and future; we (the English) "derive all we possess as an inheritance from our forefathers." It is indeed not merely the course of history but of nature itself. Thus Friedrich von Schlegel, trying to quicken a sense of nationalism in the Germans, urged that "nothing is so important as that the Germans . . . return to the course of their own language and poetry, and liberate from the old documents of their ancestral past that power of old, that noble spirit which . . . is sleeping in them." And Mazzini, in his struggle for the unification of Italy, was ever conscious that "the most important inspiration for nationalism is the awareness of past glories and past sufferings."

So, too, with the philosophers of nationalism, and the historians as well. Listen to Ernest Renan. In that famous lecture "What Is a Nation?" he emphasized "the common memories, sacrifices, glories, fflictions, and regrets," and submitted that the worthiest of all cults was "the cult of ancestors." So, too, with the hard-headed John Stuart Mill, across the Channel. "The strongest cause [for the feeling of nationality] is identity of political antecedents, the possession of a national history, and consequent community of recollections, collective pride and humiliation, pleasure and regret."

But if a historical past and a historical memory are indeed essential ingredients for a viable nationalism, what was the new United States to do in 1776, or in 1789, or for that matter at almost any time before the Civil War? How does a country without a past of her own acquire one, or how does she provide a substitute for it? Where could such a nation find the stuff for patriotism, for sentiment, for pride, for memory, for collective character? It was a question that came up very early, for Americans have always been somewhat uncomfortable about their lack of history and of antiquity, somewhat embarrassed about being historical *nouveaux riches*.

It was Henry James who put the question in most memorable form. I refer to the famous passage about the historical and intellectual environment in which the young Nathaniel Hawthorne found himself in 1840. It takes a great deal of history to make a little literature, said James, and how could Hawthorne make literature with a history so meager and so thin: "No state, in the European sense of the word, and indeed barely a specific national name. No sovereign, no court, no personal loyalty, no aristocracy, no church, no clergy, no army, no diplomatic service, no country gentlemen, no palaces, no castles, nor manors, nor old country houses, nor parsonages, nor thatched cottages, nor ivied ruins; no cathedrals, nor abbeys, nor little Norman churches; no great Universities, nor public schools, no Oxford nor Eton nor Harrow; no literature, no novels, no museums, no pictures, no political society, no sporting class—no Epsom nor Ascot!"

There is almost too much here; the indictment, as James himself remarked, is a lurid one, and he noted, too, with some satisfaction, that Hawthorne had not been wholly frustrated by the thinness of his materials—how he managed was, said James wryly, our private joke. It is suggestive that James' famous outburst was inspired by Hawthorne himself; he had, so he wrote, delighted in a place—his own dear native land—which had "no shadow, no antiquity, no mystery, no picturesque and gloomy wrong, nor

anything but a commonplace prosperity, in broad and simple daylight, as is happily the case with my dear native land." It is worth dwelling on this for a moment, for this is from the author of *The Scarlet Letter*, and of *The House of the Seven Gables*, and of a score of stories which did precisely dwell on shadows, antiquities, gloomy wrongs—witchcraft, for example. If a Hawthorne, who all his life felt it necessary to immerse himself in New England antiquities and inherited wrongs, could yet contrast his own dear native land with the Old World in these terms, think how unshadowed were the lives of most Americans—or how empty, if you want to adopt the James point of view.

A host of Americans had anticipated all this, but with different emphasis. Thus the poet Philip Freneau, introducing the abbé Robin's *New Travels in America*: "They who would saunter over half the Globe to copy the inscription on an antique column, to measure the altitude of a pyramid, or describe the ornaments on the Grand Seigneur's State Turban, will scarcely find anything in American Travels to gratify their taste. The works of art are there comparatively trivial and inconsiderable, the splendor of pageantry rather obscure, and consequently few or none but the admirers of simple Nature can either travel with pleasure themselves or read the travels of others with satisfaction, through this country." And half a century later James Fenimore Cooper, caught in that dilemma of New World innocence and Old World corruption so pervasive in the first century of our history, admitted that in America "there are no annals for the historian; no follies beyond the most vulgar and commonplace for the satirist; no manners for the dramatist; no obscure fictions for the writer of romance; no gross and hardy offenses against decorum for the moralist; nor any of the rich artificial auxiliaries of poetry."

But if there were "no annals for the historian," and if a historical past was necessary to nation-making, what were Americans to do?

Americans had, in fact, several courses open to them, and with characteristic self-confidence, took them all.

Over a century before the Revolution it had been observed of the Virginians that they had no need of ancestors, for they themselves were ancestors. The variations on this theme were infinite, but the theme was simple and familiar: that Americans had no need of a past because they were so sure of a future. Goethe had congratulated them on their good fortune in a famous but almost untranslatable poem: *Amerika, du hast es besser:* "no ruined castles, no venerable stones, no useless memories, no vain feuds [he said]. . . . May a kind providence preserve you from tales of knights and robber barons and ghosts."

Americans took up the refrain with enthusiasm. The romantic artist Thomas Cole observed that though American scenery was "destitute of the vestiges of antiquity" it had other features that were reassuring, for "American associations are not so much with the past as of the present and the future, and in looking over the uncultivated scene, the mind may travel far into futurity."

This theme runs like a red thread through early American literature and oratory, and finally connects itself triumphantly with Manifest Destiny. It began, appropriately enough, with Crèvecoeur: "I am sure I cannot be called a partial American when I say that the spectacle afforded by these pleasing scenes must be more entertaining and more philosophical than that which arises from beholding the musty ruins of Rome. Here everything would inspire the reflecting traveller with the most philanthropic ideas; his imagination, instead of submitting to the painful and useless retrospect of revolutions, desolations, and plagues, would, on the contrary, wisely spring forward to the anticipated fields of future cultivation and improvement, to the future extent of those generations which are to replenish and embellish this boundless continent." Washington Irving's friend and collaborator, James Paulding, entertained the same sentiment: "It is for the other nations to boast of what they have been, and, like garrulous age, muse over the history of their youthful exploits that only renders decrepitude more conspicuous. Ours is the more animating sentiment of hope, looking forward with prophetic eye."

Best of all is Cooper's John Cadwallader in *Notions of the Americans*, rebuking his travelling companion, the bachelor Count, for his unmanly longing for antiquity: "You complain of the absence of association to give its secret, and perhaps greatest charm which such a sight is capable of inspiring. You complain unjustly. The moral feeling with which a man of sentiment and knowledge looks upon the plains of your [Eastern] Hemisphere is connected with his recollections; here it should be mingled with his hopes. The same effort of the mind is as equal to the one as to the other."

The habit of looking forward instead of back blended readily enough with Manifest Destiny. Thus John Louis O'Sullivan, who all but invented Manifest Destiny, dismissed the past in favor of the future: "We have no interest in scenes of antiquity, only as lessons of avoidance of nearly all their examples. The expansive future is our arena. We are entering on its untrodden space with the truth of God in our minds, beneficent objects in our hearts, and with a clear conscience unsullied by the past. We are the nation of human progress, and who will, what can, set limits on our onward march? . . . The far-reaching, the boundless future will be the era of American greatness. . . ."

There was nothing surprising in Emerson's conclusion that America had no past. "All," he said, "has an outward and prospective look." For transcendentalism—the first genuine expression of the American temperament in philosophy, or New England's at least—was impatient with origins, put its confidence in inspiration, looked upon each day as a new epoch and each man as an Adam. It is difficult to exaggerate the impatience of the transcendentalists with the past. It was not so much that they were opposed to it as they found it irrelevant. And note that New England's major historians—Bancroft, Prescott, Ticknor, Motley, and Parkman—were all outside the mainstream of transcendentalism.

This was all very well, this confidence in the future. But it was, after all, pretty thin fare for nationalism to feed on at a time when other self-conscious nations were rejoicing in an ancient and romantic past. To be sure, the past became ancient and the future became present more rapidly in America than anywhere else: thus Thomas Jefferson could write from Paris in 1787 that much was to be said for keeping the "good, old, venerable, fabrick" of the six-year-old Articles of Confederation. And thus, too, John Randolph, in the Virginia ratifying convention, could "take farewell of the Confederation, with reverential respect, as an old benefactor."

Happily, there was a second formula to which Americans had recourse, and one no less convenient than the first: that America had, in fact, the most impressive of all pasts; *all* Europe was the American past. After all, we speak the tongue that Shakespeare spake—and for good measure, the tongues of Luther and Racine and Dante and Cervantes as well. Just because Americans had crossed the Atlantic Ocean did not mean that they had forfeited or repudiated their heritage. Americans enjoyed, in fact, the richest and most varied of all heritages. Other benighted peoples had only their past—the Danes a Danish, the Germans a German—but Americans had them all. Were we not in very truth a teeming nation of nations? Edward Everett asserted this as early as 1820: "We suppose that in proportion to our population Lord Byron and Walter Scott are more read in America than in England, nor do we see why we are not entitled to our full share of all that credit which does not rest . . . in the person of the author. . . ." Whitman made this the burden of "Thou Mother With Thy Equal Brood":

Sail, sail thy best, ship of Democracy,
Of value is thy freight, 'tis not the Present only,
The Past is also stored in thee,
Thou holdest not the venture of thyself alone,
　　not of the Western Continent alone,
Earth's résumé entire floats on thy keel O ship,
　　is steadied by thy spars. . .
Steer then with good strong hand, and wary eye
　　O helmsman, thou carriest great companions,
Venerable priestly Asia sails this day with thee,
And royal feudal Europe sails with thee.

All very well, but a risky business, this assimilation of the Old World past. For could the Old World be trusted? Could the past be trusted? We come here to one of the major themes of American intellectual history, and one of the most troublesome of all the problems in the creation of a usable past.

The theme of New World innocence and Old World corruption emerged early, and persisted all through the nineteenth century: it is a constant of American literature as of American politics, and if it no longer haunts our literature, it still bedevils our politics and diplomacy.

How deeply they were shocked, these innocent Americans, by the goings on in Europe! Benjamin Franklin, after a long residence in England, could deprecate the notion of a reconciliation between the Americans and the mother country on moral grounds: "I have not heard what Objections were made to the Plan in the Congress, nor would I make more than this one, that, when I consider the extreme Corruption prevalent among all Orders of Men in this old rotten State, and the glorious publick Virtue so predominant in our rising Country, I cannot but apprehend more Mischief than Benefit from a closer Union." Dr. Benjamin Rush, who had studied in Edinburgh and in London, never ceased to preach the danger of contamination from abroad. With Jefferson—surely the most cosmopolitan American of his generation—New World innocence and Old World corruption was almost an *idée fixe.* How illuminating, that famous letter to John Banister about the education of his son. "Why send an American youth to Europe for education? . . . Let us view the disadvantages. . . . To enumerate them all, would require a volume. I will select a few. If he goes to England, he learns drinking, horse racing, and boxing. These are the peculiarities of English education. The following circumstances are common to education in that, and the other countries of Europe. He acquires a fondness of European luxury and dissipation, and a contempt for the simplicity of his own country; he is fascinated with the privileges of the European aristocrats and sees, with abhorrence, the lovely equality which the poor enjoy with the rich, in his own country; he contracts a partiality for aristocracy or monarchy; he forms foreign friendships which will never be useful to him . . . he is led, by the strongest of all the human passions, into a spirit for female intrigue, destructive of his own and others' happiness, or a passion for whores, destructive of his health, and, in both cases, learns to consider fidelity to the marriage bed as an ungentlemanly practice. . . . It appears to me, then, that an American coming to Europe for education, loses in his knowledge, in his morals, in his health, in his habits, and in his happiness. . . ."

The theme, and the arguments, persisted. Hezekiah Niles wrote on the eve of the War of 1812 that "the War, dreadful as it is, will not be without its benefits in . . . separating us from the *strumpet governments of Europe.*" It is the most persistent theme in American literature from Crèvecoeur to Tocqueville, from Hawthorne's *Marble Faun* to James' *Daisy Miller* and *Portrait of a Lady,* from *Innocents Abroad* to *The Sun Also Rises.* Something of its complexity and difficulty can be seen in the position of the expatriate. Here Americans long maintained a double standard; it was taken for granted not only that European immigrants to the United States give up their nationality and identify themselves with their adopted country, but that they do so exuberantly. But for Americans to give up their nationality and identify themselves with a foreign country was another matter.

Needless to say, there are philosophical and psychological implications here which we ignore at our peril. For this concept of New World innocence and Old World corruption encouraged that sense of being a people apart which nature herself had already sufficiently dramatized. How characteristic that Jefferson should have combined nature and morality in his first inaugural: "Kindly separated by nature from one quarter of the globe; too high-minded to endure the degradations of the others. . . ." To this day Americans are inclined to think that they are outside the stream of history, exempt from its burden.

But quite aside from the theme of Old World corruption, the availability of the European past was not a simple matter of chronological assimilation or absorption. It was available, to be sure, but only on limited terms. It was there more for purposes of contrast than for enrichment; it pointed the moral of American superiority, and adorned the tale of American escape from contamination. It was there, too, as a museum, a curio shop, and a moral playground. But for practical purposes it contributed little to the juices of American Life.

Americans had a third choice: They could use what they had. "We have not, like England and France, centuries of achievements and calamities to look back on," wrote the indefatigable diarist George Templeton Strong, "but being without the eras that belong to older nationalities—Anglo-Saxon, Carolingian, Hohenstaufen, Ghibelline, and so forth—we dwell on the details of our little all of historic life and venerate every trivial fact about our first settlers and colonial governors and revolutionary heroes." Not all Americans struck so modest a pose. All their past lacked, after all, was antiquity, and antiquity was relative; in any event, this meant that the American past was better authenticated than the European.

Nothing in the history of American nationalism is more impressive than the speed and lavishness with which Americans provided themselves with a usable past: history, legends, symbols, paintings, sculpture, monuments, shrines, holy days, ballads, patriotic songs, heroes, and—with some difficulty— villains. Henry James speaks of Emerson dwelling for fifty years "within the undecorated walls of his youth." To Emerson they did not seem undecorated, for he embellished them with a profusion of historical association and of memory: the author of "Concord Hymn" was not unaware of the past.

Not every American, to be sure, was as deeply rooted as Emerson, but even to newcomers America soon ceased to be undecorated. Uncle Sam was quite as good as John Bull, and certainly more democratic. The bald eagle (Franklin sensibly preferred the turkey, but was overruled) did not compare badly with the British lion and was at least somewhat more at home in America than the lion in Britain. The Stars and Stripes, if it did not fall straight out of heaven like Denmark's *Dannebrog,* soon had its own mythology, and it had, besides, one inestimable advantage over all other flags, in that it provided an adjustable key to geography and a visible evidence of growth. Soon it provided the stuff for one of the greatest of all national songs—the tune difficult but the sentiments elevated—and one becoming to a free people. The Declaration of Independence was easier to understand than Magna Carta, and parts of it could be memorized and recited—as Magna Carta could not. In addition it had a Liberty Bell to toll its fame, which was something the British never thought of. There were no less than two national mottoes—*E pluribus unum,* selected, so appropriately, by Franklin, Jefferson, and John Adams, and *Novus ordo seclorum,* with their classical origins. There were no antiquities, but there were shrines: Plymouth Rock, of course, and Independence Hall and Bunker Hill and Mount Vernon and Monticello; eventually there was to be the Log Cabin in which Lincoln was born, as indestructible as the hull of the *Mayflower.*

These were some of the insignia, as it were, the ostentatious manifestations of the possession of a historical past. The stuff of that past was crowded and rich; it is still astonishing that Americans managed to fill their historical canvas so elaborately in so short a time. The colonial era provided a remote past: Pocahontas saving John Smith; the Pilgrims landing on the sandy coast of Plymouth, and celebrating the first Thanksgiving; Roger Williams fleeing through the wintry storms to Narragansett Bay; William Penn treating with the Indians; Deerfield going up in flames, its captives trekking though the snow to Canada; Franklin walking the streets of Philadelphia, munching those "three great puffy rolls" that came to be permanent props.

The Revolution proved a veritable cornucopia of heroic episodes and memories: Washington crossing the Delaware; Washington dwelling at Valley Forge; the signing of the Declaration; Captain Parker at Lexington Common: "If they mean to have a war, let it begin here!"; Prescott at Bunker Hill: "Don't fire until you see the whites of their eyes!"; John Paul ones closing with the *Serapis:* "I have not yet begun to fight!"; Nathan Hale on the gallows: "I only regret that I have but one life to lose for my country"; Tom Paine writing the first *Crisis* on the flat of a drum, by the flickering light of campfires; George Rogers Clark wading through the flooded Wabash bottom lands to capture Vincennes; Washington at Yorktown: "The World Turned Upside Down"; Washington, again, fumbling for his glasses at Newburgh: "I have grown gray in your service, and now find myself growing blind"; Washington even in Heaven, not a pagan Valhalla but a Christian Heaven, doubly authenticated by a parson and a historian—one person to be sure—the incomparable Parson Weems.

The War of 1812, for all its humiliations, made its own contributions to national pride. Americans conveniently forgot the humiliations and recalled the glories: Captain Lawrence off Boston Harbor: "Don't give up the ship"; the *Constitution* riddling the *Guerière;* Francis Scott Key peering through the night and the smoke to see if the flag was still there; Perry at Put-in-Bay: "We have met the enemy and they are ours"; the hunters of Kentucky repulsing Pakenham—

There stood John Bull in Martial pomp
But here was old Kentucky.

No wonder Old Hickory went straight to the White House.

The West, too—not one West but many—provided a continuous flow of memories and experiences and came to be, especially for immigrants, a great common denominator. There was the West of the Indian; of Washington at Fort Necessity; the West of Daniel Boone; of Lewis and Clark; of the Santa Fe Trail and the Oregon Trail and the California Gold Rush; the West of the miner and the cowboy; the West of the Union Pacific trail and the other transcontinentals. "If it be romance, if it be contrast, if it be heroism that we require," asked Robert Louis Stevenson, "what was Troytown to this?" What indeed?

And richest of all in its contribution to the storehouse of American memory was the Civil War, with its hero, Lincoln: it produced the best literature and the best songs of any modern war; it was packed with drama and with heroism. To one part of America it gave the common bond of defeat and tragedy, but a defeat that fed sentiment so powerful that it was metamorphosed into victory. It gave to the whole of America a dramatic sense of unity; to Negroes it

associated national unity with freedom; and to all it gave the most appealing of national heroes, probably the only modern hero to rank with Alfred and Barbarossa and Joan of Arc. Certainly, of all modern heroes it is Lincoln who lends himself most readily to mythology; his birth humble and even mysterious; his youth gentle and simple; his speech pithy and wise; his wit homely and earthy; his counsels benign. He emerged briefly to save his nation and free the slaves, and died tragically as the lilacs bloomed; no wonder the poets and the mythmakers have exhausted themselves on this theme.

No less remarkable was the speed and comprehensiveness with which the new nation provided itself with an artistic record. From the beginning, to be sure, Americans had been fortunate in this realm; no other nation, it is safe to say, has had its entire history so abundantly recorded as the American, from the first contributions by Le Moyne and De Bry and John White to the realism of the Ash Can school of the early twentieth century. Never before in recorded history had anything excited the imagination like the discovery of the New World—O brave new world, O strange new world, new world that was Utopia and Paradise. Everything about it excited the explorers and conquerors: the Patagonian giants and the Amazons of Brazil and the pygmies of the Far North; the mountains that soared fifty miles into the clouds and lakes as vast as continents and the caves of solid gold; the natives who were descended from the Chinese or the Jews or the Norwegians or the Welsh; the flora and fauna so strange they all but defied description. How to make clear the wonder and the terror of it all?

All the explorers were historians, to be sure; almost all of them were artists as well, and soon all Europe could share the wonder of those who had seen what men had never seen before. It was as if cartographers had given us maps of the voyages of the Phoenicians or of the Vikings; it was as if artists had pictured Hector and Agamemnon before the walls of Troy or Romulus founding the city that would bear his name, or Hengist and Horsa on the shores of Ebbsfleet!

Political independence brought with it artistic freedom, and an ardent preoccupation with the birth of the nation created the stirring political drama; the scenes of battle, lurid and triumphant; the Founding Fathers, grave, as became men occupying a sure place in history. In a generation when Franklin doubted the possibility and John Adams the propriety of art, a host of artists emerged, as if in defiance of counsels too sober; if they were not Rembrandts or Turners, they were better than anyone had any right to expect. It is not, however, their artistic merits that interest us, but their historical function. John Singleton Copley gave us a rich and crowded portrait gallery of colonial society in the process of becoming American—the merchants, the statesmen, the captains, and their ladies as well. John Trumbull regarded himself as the official painter of the Revolution and covered that chapter of history systematically though not comprehensively. Scarcely less impressive was the contribution of the versatile Charles Willson Peale, who left us a whole gallery of Founding Fathers as well as an academy of artistic sons, while the achievement of Gilbert Stuart in impressing on future generations his image of the Father of His Country is almost without parallel in the history of art. This school of artistic historians came to an end when its work was done, when it had provided posterity with artistic archives and monuments of its birth and its youth. Then the new nation, secure in the possession of an artistic record, could afford to indulge the romanticism of an Allston or a Cole, of the Hudson River school, or of genre painters like the puckish John Quidor—worthy companion to Washington Irving—or William Sidney Mount.

The celebration of independence and the founding of the republic was but one chapter in the history of the creation of an artistic image of the American past. Another school seized, almost instinctively, on the inexhaustible theme of the Indian and the winning of the West. Thus, while scores of American artists sailed for the Italian Arcadia, others, untrained, or trained in the irrelevant school of Dusseldorf, moved quite as confidently across the Alleghenies and on to the prairies and the plains and the mountains of the West. What a romantic group they were: the Swiss Carl Bodmer, who went with Prince Maximilian of Wied up the Missouri River in the early 1830's, and who gave us a crowded gallery of Sioux, Crees, Assiniboins, and Mandans; the indefatigable George Catlin with his hundreds of Indian portraits—surely the fullest artistic re-creation of the West before photography; Alfred Jacob Miller, who was the artist for Captain Stewart's explorations in the Far West and who sketched not only Indians but the landscape—Chimney Rock and Independence Rock and the Tetons and the Wind River Mountains;

the luckless John Mix Stanley, who was ubiquitous, from the lead mines of Galena to the Cherokee country, with Kearny on the Santa Fe Trail, one thousand miles by canoe up the Columbia, even to distant Hawaii—the work of a lifetime lost in the great Smithsonian fire of 1865.

Not all of these artists of the early West recreated the past for their own generation. Miller, for example, was not really known in his own day, nor was Stanley. Far more important in the creation of the popular image of America were two artist-ornithologists, Alexander Wilson and John James Audubon, who captured for all time the flora and fauna of America in its pastoral age. Wilson's nine-volume *American Ornithology* was perhaps the most ambitious work of science in the early republic. Soon came Audubon's *Birds of America*, less scientific than Wilson's Ornithology but more splendid, "the most magnificent monument" said Cuvier, "which art has ever raised to ornithology." And Audubon, of course, contributed more: his own extraordinary life and legend.

The sumptuous paintings of Wilson and Audubon reached the public only gradually, and in cheap reproductions. More effective was the impact of the almost forgotten school of panoramists. The hapless John Vanderlyn, who had dared display his nude *Ariadne* to an outraged public, introduced the panorama, in a specially built rotunda in New York's City Hall Park. But it was Versailles and Athens and Mexico which he chose to display; perhaps that is why he failed. His successors preferred to reveal America, and particularly the Father of Waters, which had the advantage of being almost the only object of nature longer than their paintings. One John Rowson Smith did a panorama of the Mississippi as early as 1844; when he displayed it at Saratoga Springs, New York, he took in twenty thousand dollars in six weeks. Soon there were a dozen rivals in the field: John Banvard, for example, who claimed that his Mississippi panorama was three miles long (actually it was only a quarter of a mile—a bad calculation, that). Poor John Stanley, who had so little luck with his Indian paintings, scored a tremendous success with a panorama of the *Western Wilds*, forty-two episodes, no less, requiring a minimum of two hours to view! Greatest of all the panoramists was Henry Lewis, who managed to cover almost three quarters of a mile of canvas with his paintings; his earnings from his great panorama enabled him to settle in Dusseldorf and learn to paint. Whatever their artistic merits, or demerits, the panoramas helped give a whole generation of Americans some feeling for the spaciousness and the beauty of the early West.

Writing in 1841, Emerson had lamented that "banks and tariffs, the newspaper and caucus, Methodism and Unitarianism, are flat and dull to dull people but rest on the same foundations of wonder as the town of Troy and the temple of Delphi. . . . Our logrolling, our stumps and their politics, our fisheries, our Negroes and Indians, our boasts and our repudiations . . . the northern trade, the southern planting, the western clearing, Oregon and Texas, are yet unsung. Yet America is a poem in our eyes; its ample geography dazzles the imagination." Poets and artists had responded, but none had quite encompassed American nature. Even Whitman and Winslow Homer could not quite do that. For nature played a special role in American history and in the process of creating a sense of history and a national consciousness. Since the seventeenth century, Europeans have not had to concern themselves energetically with the conquest of nature, for nature, like history, was given. For Americans, on the other hand, the relationship to nature was more personal, and more complex. They had an empty continent to settle and successive frontiers to conquer, and for them nature had always played a twofold role: her ruggedness was a challenge, and her richness a manifestation of divine favor. How suggestive it is that for over two hundred years Europeans could not make up their minds whether the New World was Paradise or an accursed place, whether its natives were Noble Savages or degenerate men without souls. But however nature was to be interpreted—and by the nineteenth century the paradisiacal interpretation had triumphed—it was, in a peculiar way, the great common denominator and the great common experience. Virginians, Pilgrims, and Quakers alike could rejoice in the abundance of nature, and generations of pioneers, even those who were not *Mayflower* descendants or FFV'S, could cherish the common memory of hardship endured and overcome.

Because they had conquered nature, Americans came in time to think that they had created it and to display toward it a proprietary interest. The stupendous flow of Niagara, the luxuriance of the Bluegrass, the power and majesty of the Father of Waters, the limitless expanse of prairie and plain, the glory of the Rockies—all of these came to be regarded as national attributes, and failure to appreciate them, like failure to appreciate political attributes, an affront. How interesting that from "Swanee River" to "Ol' Man River" songs celebrating nature have usurped the place of formal patriotic music— "Dixie," for example, or "My Old Kentucky Home," or "On the Banks of the Wabash," or "Home on the Range," or best of all, "America, the Beautiful."

And how interesting, too, that where in other countries topography is local, in America it is national. In the Old World, plains, valleys, and mountains belong to the people who happen to inhabit them, but in America the whole country, "from sea to shining sea," belongs to the whole people. The Italians and Germans traditionally celebrate their own cities, their particular churches or bridges; the English write two-volume works on Fly-casting in the Dart, or Cricket in Lower Slaughter, but until recently there has been little of this local possessiveness about Americans. "We have so much country that we have no country at all," Hawthorne lamented back in 1837, but Hawthorne was far from typical, and newcomers who could find little satisfaction in the slums of New York or the coal mines of Pennsylvania or the steel mills of Gary might yet rejoice in the Great Lakes and Yosemite. Movement, especially westward movement, is an essential ingredient in the American memory. When John F. Kennedy hit on the slogan, "Get America moving," he touched a responsive chord.

The task of providing themselves with a historical past was peculiarly difficult for Americans because it was not something that could be taken for granted, as with most peoples, or arranged once and for all. It was something that had to be done over and over again, for each new wave of newcomers, and that had to be kept up to date, as it were, continually reinvigorated and modernized. Above all, it had to be a past which contained an ample supply of easily grasped common denominators for a heterogeneous people, English and German, Irish and Norse, white and black, gentile and Jew, Protestant, Mormon, and Catholic, old stock and newcomer. Almost inevitably the common denominators tended to be pictorial and symbolic: the Pilgrims and Valley Forge, Washington and Lincoln, cowboy and Indian, and along with them ideas and institutions like Democracy, Liberty, Equality, the American Dream, and the American Way of Life.

One consequence of this emphasis on the simple, the symbolic, and the ideological is that American patriotism tended to be more artificial, labored, and ostentatious than that of most Old World peoples. It was almost inevitably calculated and artificial: after all, the process of drawing the juices of tradition for a German boy newly arrived in America was very different from that for a French or an English lad at home, where everything could be taken for granted, or left to nature. Tradition in America had to be labored, for it was not born into the young; it did not fill the horizon, as the glory of Joan of Arc or the fame of Nelson filled the horizons of French and English boys and girls. The American past could not be absorbed from childhood on in the art and architecture of every town and village, in song and story and nursery rhyme, in novel and history, in the names of streets and squares and towns. Growing up in Pittsburgh or Chicago was a very different experience, historically, from growing up in London or Edinburgh, Paris or Rome. And patriotism probably had to be ostentatious; in any event, it is. Ostentation characterizes new wealth, and new loyalties as well. This is doubtless one reason there is so much emphasis on the overt observance of patriotism in America. Americans dedicate a large number of days to ceremonial patriotism: the Fourth of July, Memorial Day, Confederate Memorial Day, Veterans Day, Washington's Birthday, Lincoln's Birthday, Columbus Day, Loyalty Day, and many others, and for good measure many states have their own special holidays—Patriots' Day in Massachusetts or Texas Independence Day. Americans require children to "pledge allegiance to the flag," impose loyalty oaths for every conceivable occasion, and march in "I Am an American Day" parades, and there is no W. S. Gilbert to satirize what so many take with passionate seriousness. Perhaps nowhere else in the Western world is loyalty such a touchstone as in the United States, perhaps nowhere else are there so many organizations dedicated to fostering patriotism: the Daughters of the American Revolution, the Sons of the American Revolution, the Colonial Dames, the United Daughters of the Confederacy, the Americanism committees of the great veterans' organizations, and, more recently, the Minute Women.

The process of acquiring a usable past was immensely facilitated by two extraordinary circumstances. The first was the eagerness of almost all newcomers from every part of the globe to slough off their pasts and take on an American habit, an eagerness so avid and so pervasive that it made nonsense of the compunctions and fears of native Americans from Fisher Ames to Thomas Bailey Aldrich a century later. Perhaps no other society in the process of transforming itself into a nation had more cooperative material to work with. The American newcomer, as he told us over and over again, was under both moral and practical compulsions to achieve acceptance for himself and for his children by becoming completely American as rapidly and as thoroughly as possible. Crèvecoeur, who saw so much, saw this, and so too the magisterial Tocqueville, but it is a lesson that has had to be relearned in every generation.

That it was *possible* for newcomers to become American overnight was the second circumstance. The explanation here lies in large part in the high degree of literacy that obtained in America, even in the eighteenth century, and the tradition of literacy and of education that flourished in that and the next century. Schools proved, in the long run, the most effective agencies for the creation and the transmission of an American memory. If they did not deliberately inculcate Americanism, that was because they did not need to: Noah Webster's Spellers, McGuffey's many Readers, Jedidiah Morse's Geographies and Peter Parley's Histories—these and scores of books like them conjured up an American past and provided, for generations of children, the common denominators, the stories and songs and poems, the memories and symbols. And it was the children, in turn, who educated the parents, for America is the only country where, as a matter of course, it is assumed that each new generation is wiser and more sophisticated than the old, and where parents adopt the standards of their children rather than children adopting those of their parents. For newcomers too old for school, and too inflexible to learn from their children, the work of providing an American past was carried on by voluntary organizations which have always performed the most miscellaneous of social tasks: churches, political parties, labor unions, lyceums, fraternal and filiopietistic organizations, and so forth.

What this meant was that the sentiment of American nationalism was, to an extraordinary degree, a literary creation, and that the national memory was a literary and, in a sense, a contrived memory. The contrast here with the Old World is harp. There the image of the past was conjured up and sustained by a thousand testimonials: folklore and folk song, the vernacular and the patois, church music and architecture, monuments, paintings and murals, the pageantry of the court and of popular feasts and holidays. To be sure, literature—poetry and drama and formal histories—came to play a role, but only when it was quarried from cultural foundations that went deep. In America the image of the past was largely the creation of the poets and the story-tellers, and chiefly of the New England–New York group who flourished between the War of 1812 and the War for the Union, that group familiar to an earlier generation through the amiable game of Authors: Irving, Cooper, and Bryant; Longfellow, Hawthorne, and Whittier; Emerson, Lowell, and Holmes. These were the Founding Fathers of American literary nationalism, and their achievement was scarcely less remarkable than that of the Founding Fathers of political nationalism.

In a single generation these men of letters gave Americans the dramas, the characters, the settings, which were to instruct and delight succeeding generations: Uncas and Deerslayer and Long Tom Coffin; Rip Van Winkle and the Headless Horseman; Miles Standish, Paul Revere, Evangeline, and Hiawatha; Goodman Brown, the Grey Champion, and Hester Prynne, as well as the Salem Customs House, the House of the Seven Gables, the Old Manse, and the Great Stone Face; Skipper Ireson and Concord Bridge and Old Ironsides and the One-Hoss Shay and Hosea Biglow with all his Yankee company.

Note that this image of the past which the literary Founding Fathers created and imposed upon Americans was very largely a New England image, and much that was most distinctive about American nationalism was to be conditioned by this circumstance.

It meant that Americans on Iowa prairies or the plains of Texas would sing *"I love thy rocks and rills, thy woods and templed hills"* with no sense of incongruity; that Plymouth would supplant Jamestown as the birthplace of America; that Thanksgiving Day would be a New England holiday; that Paul Revere would be the winged horseman of American history and Concord Bridge the American equivalent of the Rubicon; that Boston's Statehouse would vindicate its claim—or Holmes'—to be the "hub of the solar system." If all this was hard on the South, southerners had only themselves to blame for their indifference to their own men of letters. The most familiar of southern symbols came from the North: Harriet Beecher Stowe of New England gave us Uncle Tom and Little Eva and Topsy and Eliza, while it was Stephen Foster of Pittsburgh who sentimentalized the Old South, and even "Dixie" had northern origins.

The literary task of creating a usable past was largely performed by 1865; after that date perhaps only Mark Twain, Bret Harte, and Louisa May Alcott added anything substantial to the treasure house of historical memories. This was, in perspective, the most significant achievement of American literature and one almost without parallel in the literature of any other country in a comparable period. How interesting that a people supposed to be indifferent to literature—supposed by some to have no literature—should depend so largely upon literature for the nourishment of its historical self-consciousness. Certainly the speed and effectiveness with which Americans rallied their resources to supply themselves with a historical past cannot but excite astonishment. And what a past it was—splendid, varied, romantic, and all but blameless, in which there were heroes but no villains, victories but no defeats—a past that was all prologue to the Rising Glory of America.

Parson Weems, the Cherry Tree, and the Patriotic Tradition

Nicholas Cords

While George Washington had some part in the creation of the myths concerning him (subjects usually do), one man, more than any other, was responsible for a vast part of his mythic monument. Mason Locke Weems was such a successful mythmaker that he too has passed into folklore. This article by Nicholas Cords, one of this book's editors, briefly discusses Parson Weems, his times, the genesis and development of his *Life of Washington*, some of his techniques, and the emphasis on patriotism that was common throughout this national period. No attempt is made to destroy either the Parson or his myths. Much is to be learned—even about George Washington—from the literary father of the Father of Our Country.

American historical writing after the Revolution came to be dominated by the Federalist-Whig tradition. Its proponents were of the upper-middle-class leisured group, and were highly selective in the materials they included in their histories. They accepted the view of the Revolution as put forth in the Whig publication, the *Annual Register,* and were anti-Jeffersonian. Local loyalties continued but were overshadowed by nationalistic fervor.

The new national spirit demanded of the historian that he express the ideals of the Republic and affirm its virtues and destiny. As the Revolution was the foundation of this new national spirit, its men and events provided the subject matter for most patriotic writing. Many authors played heavily on the Whig-influenced patriotic theme. Even literary figures such as Joel Barlow and Washington Irving sang the refrain. The man who is the subject of this article, however, did more to enhance the patriotic tradition than any of the others. If he did not exactly fit into the Federalist-Whig mold, it was probably because he was the type of person who did not fit well into any fixed category. What he lacked in social conservatism

and selectivity, he made up for in patriotism. Who was this figure? "I can't tell a lie"; it was Parson Weems.

Mason Locke Weems was born on October 11, 1759, at Marshes Seat, Herring Bay, Anne Arundel County, Maryland. His father was of a Scottish noble family (Wemyss) and had emigrated sometime before 1722. Little is known of Weems' early life, although legends abound. He is said to have made some voyages on his brothers' ships, and he studied medicine at Edinburgh or London. By 1783 Weems was back in London where he studied for the Episcopal ministry. He was ordained in 1784 by the Archbishop of Canterbury, only after the oath of allegiance law had been abrogated (he had refused to take the oath). While in London he had correspondence with John Adams and Benjamin Franklin. On his return to Maryland he was rector of the All Hallows Parish (1785–89) and St. Margaret's (1791–94).

In 1794 Weems left the permanent ministry and pursued what was to become part of his life's work—bookselling. Striking up a relationship with Mathew Carey, a young Philadelphia publisher, Weems acted as his selling agent for practically the remainder of his life. His bookselling career was accompanied by one of editing and writing. He edited a series of improving books and wrote political pamphlets, biographies and tracts. He traveled between New York and Savannah, and became a well-known figure throughout the entire area.

Mason Weems did not exactly belong to the Federalist-Whig historical tradition; mainly because of his attraction to, and constant dealings with, the common people. Although he got along well with people of all classes, he was more at home and more successful with those of the lower groups. The upper class tended to resent his crusading zeal, breadth of view in matters of dogma, outbursts of liberalism and lack of dignity. Also, his affinity for the Negro did not suit upper-class taste in the South. He conducted services for them every other Friday and once said concerning preaching to them, "Oh, it is sweet preaching, when people are desirous of hearing. Sweet feeding the flock of Christ, when they have so good an appetite." Bishop Meade referred to Weems as a "curious oddity," and to his family as "interesting and pious." What really irked Meade was the fact that Weems sold books in taverns on election and Court-House days, and extolled Tom Paine from the pulpit. Weems had once said concerning Paine, "Divinity, for this climate sh'd be very rational and liberal. . . ."

If Weems did not represent the socially conservative side of the Federalist-Whig tradition, he certainly had the patriotic line well in hand. His writings exude patriotism, embroidered with religion and morality. Concerning the Revolution, the Whig theory was easy for him to accept. The war had been cruelly made on the American people and its cause was simple to ascertain—"the king wanted money for his hungry relations and the ministers stakes for their gaming tables or diamond necklaces for their mistresses." Thus armed with these views, Weems, a merrily disposed white-haired individual, preached, prayed and sold his way back and forth across the southern half of the country. His saddlebags always contained a manuscript on which he was working, and he was constantly ready to dance or play the violin (Weems' family disclaimed that he ever played his violin on the road).

Weems' patriotic historical writing—as well as his talent for mythbuilding—is best typified by his biography of George Washington. The first known meeting between the two men occurred in 1787 and

is recorded in Washington's diary for March 3rd of that year. Correspondence between them continued until Washington's death and Weems, always a businessman, used the acquaintanceship to his own advantage. Washington wrote a testimonial to an improving book edited by Weems, *The Immortal Mentor* (1796); the Parson immediately had it printed on the back of the title page. In 1799 Weems published *The Philanthropist; or A Good Twenty-five cents worth of Political Love Powder, for Honest Adamsites and Jeffersonians.* In this book Weems, brandishing his nationalism, pleaded for toleration in politics and recognition of what true equality meant. He defended John Adams and even Jefferson, of whom he was not particularly enamored. Washington's written praise of the effort appeared on the title page under the heading: "With the Following Recommendation by George Washington."

Upon Washington's death in 1799, the floodgates were released on the already swelling tide of legend concerning him. Here was an opportunity for Mason L. Weems and a torrent of other authors to expound the traditions, values and goals of the new nation in terms of the life and character of its most important citizen.

Parson Weems preached a eulogy at Pohick Church in Truro Parish, seven miles from Mount Vernon. This eulogy was expanded to eighty pages and published as a pamphlet under the title: A *History of the Life and Death, Virtues and Exploits of General George Washington.* The good Parson spent much of the remainder of his life expanding this work and bringing out new editions (twenty-nine before his death). The second edition added to the title: "faithfully taken from authentic documents." The fifth edition (1806) contained the cherry tree story and claimed that Weems was the "former rector of Mount Vernon Parish." Later the author went all out and called himself "former rector of General Washington's parish"—based on the fact that on a few occasions he had preached at the church Washington attended before the Revolution.

Weems is quite clear as to his purposes in the *Life of Washington.* The title of a later edition is helpful: *The Life of George Washington, with curious anecdotes equally honorable to himself and exemplary to his young countrymen. . . .* In a letter to a publisher (1800) Weems said he wanted to bring out "his [Washington's] Great Virtues. 1 His Veneration for the Diety [*sic*], or Religious Principles. 2 His Patriotism. 3d His

Magninimity [*sic*]. 4 his Industry. 5 his Temperance and Sobriety. 6 his Justice, &^{c} &^{c}." Another goal of Weems, interesting in light of criticism leveled at him for creating much of the Washington myth, was to get at the real Washington. He stated: "In most of the elegant orations pronounced to his praise, you see nothing of Washington below *the clouds* . . . 'tis only Washington the HERO, and the Demigod . . . Washington the *sun beam* in council, or the *storm* in war." The actual result of his effort, of course, was that Weems created a Washington which all research scholars have been unable to erase and with whom they must come to grips—"a figure of truly terrifying piosities and incredible perfections." According to Senator Albert Beveridge, at times this Washington was an "impossible and intolerable prig."

Washington's characteristics and accomplishments, as put forth by the Parson, are exhausting just to contemplate. He had the old-fashioned virtues, loved his parents, loved and feared God, was a leader, a good student, and was born to be a soldier. He proved that duty leads to advantage, he did not drink or gamble, he was talented and a case of smallpox marked him agreeably. He had a great sense of patriotism and duty combined with religiosity, he had intuitive perception, was a good writer, was benevolent, industrious and a gentleman. After all this—and more—Weems' readers were probably not surprised to find Washington, upon his death, ascending to heaven amidst choirs of angels to meet, among others, Benjamin Franklin and General Wolfe.

Reading two hundred and twenty-five pages of such material would not be too rewarding if it were not for Parson Weems' racy style, vivid descriptions and ever-present sense of humor. Throughout it all his delightful ability to adorn a tale keeps the narrative alive and interesting. One is tempted to agree with Sidney Fisher, who said: "Reckless in statement, indifferent to facts and research, his books are full of popular heroism, religion and morality, which you at first call trash and cant and then, finding it extremely entertaining, you declare with a laugh, as you lay down the book, what a clever rogue."

Weems used the anecdotal method extensively. Considering the general literacy level of the day and the fact that his reading public consisted mainly of lower-class southern people, this seems a wise choice. Besides, the anecdotal method gave Weems a better chance to moralize and inspire; it also sold more books. The *Life of Washington* was laden with

these anecdotes, the most famous of which is the one concerning the cherry tree incident. George was blessed with a kindly old homily-laden father who, although not intellectually endowed, was a wonderful man and a great teacher. He early had told little George that he would rather see him dead than to see him become a liar:

> Hard, indeed, would it be to me to give up my son, whose little feet are always so ready to run about with me, and whose fondly looking eyes, and sweet prattle make so large a part of my happiness. But still I would give him up, rather than see him a common liar.

When George was six years old, he was given a hatchet with which he blithely tripped around chopping everything that came in his way—including his mother's pea-sticks. One day, in Weems' words, "he unluckily tried the edge of his hatchet on the body of a beautiful young English cherry tree, which he barked so terribly, that I don't believe the tree ever got the better of it." When asked by his father if he knew who had done it, George gave the reply every schoolchild knows:

> "I can't tell a lie, Pa; you know I can't tell a lie. I did cut it with my hatchet."—"Run to my arms, you dearest boy," cried his father in transports, "run to my arms; glad am I, George, that you killed my tree; for you have paid me for it a thousand fold. Such an act of heroism in my son is more worth than a thousand trees, though blossomed with silver, and their fruits of purest gold."

The documentation for this and other of the anecdotes was "an aged lady, who was a distant relative, and, when a girl, spent much of her time in the family." Although the consensus of opinion seems to be that the incident originated with Weems in 1806, Emily Ford Skeel, in her work on the Parson, shows an illustration of a pottery mug with the incident depicted on it; the mug is dated 1776 and is believed to have been made in Germany. Irrespective of this, certainly it was Weems who popularized the tale.

As to Washington's patriotism, Weems left no doubt. He quotes the general on his deathbed:

> Your government claims your utmost confidence and support. Respect for its authority, compliance with its laws, acquiescence in its measures, are duties enjoined by the fundamental maxims of true liberty. The basis of our political system is the right of the people to make and alter their constitution of government. But the constitution, which at any time exists, until

changed by an explicit and authentic act of the whole people, is sacredly obligatory upon all.

Again Washington is quoted upon hearing that his plantation manager had given supplies to a British frigate commander in order to avert the destruction of Mount Vernon:

> Sir—It gives me extreme concern to hear that you furnished the enemy with refreshments. It would have been a less painful circumstance to me, to have heard that, in consequence of your non-compliance with their request, they had laid my plantation in ruins.

Weems was also concerned with the relationship of patriotism and religion, and thus Washington was. The book informed the reader that in the "Farewell to the People of the United States," Washington dwelled chiefly on the union and brotherly love. For Washington, in Weems' words, this combination appeared as "the one thing needful, the spring of political life, and bond of perfection."

The author outdid himself when it came to discussing the death of Washington. No normal death for the father of the country; after the rest of the book this would have been an anticlimax. After seeking the face of God (like Moses) and hesitating to quit the earth, Washington humbled himself (like Christ) and submitted to his fate. After death the following came to pass:

> Swift on angels' wings the brightening saint ascended; while voices more than human were warbling through the happy regions, and hymning the great procession towards the gates of heaven. His glorious coming was seen afar off; and myriads of mighty angels hastened forth, with golden harps, to welcome the honoured stranger.

Weems also wrote tracts. These were against a variety of things—bachelorhood, adultery, gambling, infidelity. They fit into the patriotic theme because of Weems' connection of good government with religion and morality. An uplifted and improved people would be more patriotic. Lack of time and space do not permit a discussion of the tracts here; however, the full title of one tells a great deal about this aspect of the Parson's literary efforts.

> The Drunkard's Looking Glass—Reflecting a faithful likeness of the drunkard, in sundry very interesting attitudes, with lively representations of the many strange capers which he cuts at different stages of his disease:
>
> At first, when he has only "a drop in his eye;" second, when he is "half shaved;" third, when he is getting "a little on the staggers or so;" and fourth and fifth, and so on, till he is "quite capsized;" or "snug under the table with the dogs," and can "stick to the floor without holding on."
>
> By Mason L. Weems

Mason Locke Weems has escaped relatively unscathed from over a century and a half of criticism. His acceptance by writers during the past fifty years has usually run the range from apathy to captivation. Marcus Cunliffe refers to Weems as a Victorian before the Victorian era. Washington had all the nineteenth-century virtues from courage to punctuality, from modesty to thrift. Lawrence C. Wroth claims that Weems was successful because Americans wanted an exciting vagabond writer—an American Marlowe or Villon. Wroth goes on to say that the Parson's influence on American youth has been favorable, citing the influence on Lincoln as an example. Harold Kellock sees Weems as the first American salesman, with the instinct for giving the public what it wants. Weems did once say: "God knows there is nothing I so dread as Dead stock, dull sales, back loads, and blank looks. But the joy of my soul is quick & clear sales—Heavy pockets, and light hearts." Sidney Fisher claimed that Weems was a mixture of Scriptures, Homer, Virgil and backwoods. His history was all wrong but then so were all the other histories of the Revolutionary period. The Parson at least helped religion and youth. Walter B. Norris has come under the influence of Weems' sense of humor. He wrote of a hypothetical S.P.P.C.T. (Society for the Protection and Preservation of *Cherished* Traditions) with Weems as chief *preserver*. He went on to say that the cherry tree incident could have taken place, offering as proof the known colonial regard for fruit trees and the fact that Virginia passed laws to protect them. He also suggested that, if the incident were false, the people living in Washington's home area would have disclaimed it.

There are other ways to judge the importance of a historian than to study his critics. Assuming success in sales and number of readers are valid criteria, perhaps we must agree with Sidney Fisher who viewed Weems as "a writer of the highest order of popularity, and in that sense and influence the ablest historian we have ever produced. Prescott, Motley and Parkman are mere children when compared with him."

Weems' contribution to American historical mythology is considerable; on the subject of George Washington he is without peer. Attempts to destroy his credibility generally have proved to be exercises in futility—perhaps they are even superfluous; ignoring him is impossible. This article has discussed the Parson, his times, some of his works, his "creative" techniques and his strong concern for patriotism, religion, and morality.

Father Serra, Sexuality, and the California Mission Myth

Albert L. Hurtado

As heir to the ventures of Christopher Columbus, Spain, far earlier than either England or France, established a cultural presence in the New World. The history of America from the beginning had a strong and identifiable Hispanic character. By the late 1500s, first in Latin and Central America and Mexico, and later in what is now a goodly portion of the United States, Spanish military and administrative authority was being exercised. In Florida (Spanish for the "flowery land"), and in what the Spanish had come to call New Mexico, both political and religious officials worked to establish New Spain. By 1609, colonial authorities had founded La Villa Real de la Santa Fé de San Francisco—"the royal town of the holy faith of St. Francis"—soon known simply as Santa Fé. As can be judged by the name chosen for the official seat of government for the colony, Spanish motives were simultaneously political and religious, making native Indians subject to the King of Spain and converting them to Christianity. In fact, Christian missionaries had been in the colonial vanguard, having entered the area by the 1580s. Such was the pattern—God and Glory, Conversion and Conquest—of an expanding Spanish empire.

The imperial design was replicated later, beginning in 1769, in California, with the arrival of Father Junipero Serra, founder of the California missions. Over subsequent decades, until the end of the Franciscan mission era in the 1830s, the number of California settlements grew to include twenty-one missions and a half dozen presidios (military garrisons), and pueblos—such as that of San Francisco, established in 1776. As Albert L. Hurtado of Arizona State University evaluates it, this entire process especially in California is generally viewed in epic terms, aptly accented by the benign qualities of the good Padres. Not only does this mythic version of Hispanic history effectively force Indian peoples off center stage, but it fails to account for the ill results of the Spanish "mission." The impact of Spanish imperialism was the spread of disease in the native population that the Spanish had concentrated. Emblematic of Spanish policy was the imposition of alien attitudes toward matters of sexuality. In alignment with orthodox Catholic standards of "monogamy, permanence and fidelity," the missionaries were appalled by the native peoples' vastly different cultural habits—and especially the institution of the *berdache*—male homosexual transvestism. However unintended, the only changes to result in Indian culture from the imposition of the missionary's morality was the rampant spread of sexually transmitted disease and increased prostitution. The history of California's missions bred cultural consequences that serve as a microcosm of the enduring impact of myth, morals, and misunderstanding that often existed between conquerors and conquered in the New World.

For a long time now, the Franciscan missions have figured prominently in the popular history of California and in the palmy brochures of the tourist industry. In the twentieth century, there has grown a powerful myth that is known to every schoolchild and traveler in the Golden State: In 1769, good Father Junipero Serra led to California a band of pious missionaries who Christianized the awed Indians, peacefully recruited them to the missions, and made the grateful neophytes into useful citizens of the Spanish empire. The kindly friars worked selflessly to make life—and afterlife—better for the Indians. When Mexico broke from Spain and took over California, jealous private citizens broke up the missions, took the land, and abused the mission Indians, thus undoing the religious work of half a century. The mission ruins remained, the story concludes, as crumbling and quaint reminders of California's humane and idealistic beginnings.

Like all good myths, there is some truth in this tale. Its main shortcoming, however, is that it pays so little attention to the Indians who were the objects of the missionaries' attention. Few historians have looked carefully at the impact of the missions on the native people. Fewer still have examined the motives and responses of Indians who chose to enter or remain outside the mission. These scholars have, however, unearthed the alarming population history of the missions that challenges the California mission myth. In 1769, there were about three hundred thousand Indians in California, with perhaps sixty thousand living between San Francisco Bay and San Diego, where the missions were located. By the end of the mission era in the 1830s, there were perhaps one hundred fifty thousand Indians left in the entire state. Disease was the principal cause of this appalling destruction, for Indians had little resistance to the maladies that Spaniards brought to California. Evidently the missions facilitated the spread of illnesses because they concentrated native populations that had formerly been dispersed. This tragic outcome, of course, was not what the fathers had intended. Nevertheless, missions became agencies of native destruction, even as they held out the promise of eternal salvation.

This essay will examine an aspect of the mission experience that has not received much attention— Indian sexuality and Franciscans' attempts to control it. Sexuality is only one aspect of Spanish-Indian relations, but it is important for several reasons. First,

sexual relations are a universal feature of human existence that not only replicate life, but society as well. Second, anything that affects fertility is of particular importance in the study of a population like the California Indians, who were in rapid, prolonged decline. Third, because sexual relations are intensely human experiences, knowledge of sexuality provides insight into the historical life of the individual. Finally, an analysis of this one aspect of Spanish-Indian interaction provides a way to better understand population dynamics that advance beyond ungovernable environmental factors—such as disease—and delves into the realm of human choice.

Before Father Junipero Serra founded California's Franciscan missions, he led a religious revival in Mexico's Oaxaca region. Francisco Palóu, Serra's companion and biographer, approvingly reported that Serra's religious work produced concrete results. He reformed an adultress who at the tender age of fourteen had begun to cohabit with a married man whose wife lived in Spain. This sinful arrangement had lasted for fourteen years, but upon Serra's order the woman left the house of her lover. The man was desolate. He threatened and begged her to return, but to no avail. Then "one night in desperation," Palóu related, "he got a halter, took it with him to the house where she was staying, and hung himself on an iron gate, giving over his soul to the demons." At the same moment a great earthquake shook the town whose inhabitants trembled with fear. Thereafter, the woman donned haircloth and penitential garb and walked the streets begging forgiveness for her shamful past. "All were edified and touched at seeing such an unusual conversion and subsequent penance," the friar wrote. "Nor were they less fearful of divine Justice," he added, "recalling the chastisement of that unfortunate man." Thus, Palóu believed, the tragedy brought "innumerable conversions . . . and great spiritual fruit" to Serra's Oaxaca mission.

This story was a kind of parable that prefaced Palóu's glowing account of Serra's missionary work in California. It demonstrated not only the presence of sexual sin in Spain's American colonies—which is not especially surprising—but that priestly intervention could break perverse habits, and that public exposure and sincere repentance could save souls. This incident is especially important to us because, on the eve of his expedition to California, Palóu linked Serra's Mexican missionary triumph with the rectification of sexual behavior. Thus, a discussion of exuality in the California missions is not merely a rurient exercise, but goes to the heart of the missionries' intentions. While errant sexuality was not the nly concern of priests, the reformation of Indian exual behavior was an important part of their endeavor to Christianize and Hispanicize native Californians. Their task was fraught with difficulty, peril, nd tragedy for Indians and Spaniards alike.

Changing Indian behavior was difficult because ative people already behaved according to sexual orms that, from their point of view, worked perctly well. From north of San Francisco Bay to the resent Mexican border, tribespeople regulated sexal life so as to promote productive family relationhips that varied by tribe and locality. Everywhere, he conjugal couple and their children formed the asic household unit, which was sometimes augnented by aged relatives and unmarried siblings. ndian families, however, were not merely a series of uclear units, but were knit into a complex set of ssociations that comprised native society. Kinship lefined the individual's place within the cultural ommunity, and family associations suffused every spect of life. . . .

Re-creating the sexual behavior of any historic >eople is difficult, but it is especially difficult in ocieties that lacked a written record. Still, modern nthropology and historical testimony make a plauible—if partial—reconstruction of intimate native ife. California Indians regulated sexual behavior >oth in and out of marriage. Premarital sex does not eem to have been regarded with disapproval, so virginity was not a precondition for selecting a repectable mate. After marriage, spouses expected idelity from their husbands and wives, possibly beause of the importance of status inheritance. Consequently, adultery was a legitimate cause for divorce, nd husbands could sometimes exact other punishnents for sexual misbehavior by their wives. Chunash husbands sometimes whipped errant wives. An Esselin man could repudiate his wandering wife, or turn her over to her new lover who had to pay the cuckold an indemnity, usually the cost of acquiring a new bride. A wronged Gabrielino husband could retaliate by claiming the wife of his wife's lover, and could even go so far as to kill an adulterous spouse, >ut such executions were probably rare.

Women were not altogether at the mercy of jealous and sadistic husbands, for they could divorce husbands who mistreated them, a circumstance that probably meant they could leave if their husbands committed sexual indiscretions. Chumash oral narratives reveal that women often initiated sex and ridiculed inadequate partners. When it suited them, some women killed their husbands. It is impossible to know how frequently adulterous liaisons and subsequent divorces took place, but anthropologists characterize the common Gabrielino marital pattern as serial monogamy with occasional polygyny, indicating that separations were common. It is not unreasonable to suppose that, because so many marriages were arranged in youth, some California Indians subsequently took lovers after meeting someone who struck deeper emotional chords than their initial partners had. Nor is it implausible to speculate that some grievances were overlooked completely in the interest of maintaining family harmony and to keep intact the economic and diplomatic advantages that marriage ties were meant to bind. Prostitution was extremely rare in California, and before the arrival of the Spaniards, was noted only among the Salinan Indians. This lack of a flesh trade may indicate that such outlets were simply not needed because marital, premarital, and extramarital associations provided sufficient sexual opportunities.

Another sexual practice recorded among a few California Indian groups was male homosexual transvestism, or the so-called *berdache* tradition, which was evident in some other North American tribes. The berdache dressed like women and generally assumed many female gender roles, but they were not thought of as homosexuals. Instead, it appears that some Indian groups believed that they belonged to a third gender that combined both male and female aspects. In sex, they took the female role, and they often married men who were regarded as heterosexual males. Sometimes a chief took a berdache for a "second wife" because it was believed that such a person worked harder.

Horrified by existing social and marital patterns among the Indians they encountered, Serra and the secular colonizers of Spain's northern frontier narrowly based their familial concepts on a Spanish model that was in some respects internally contradictory. The state regarded marriage as a contract that—among other things—transferred property and guaranteed rights to sexual service. On the other hand, the Church regarded marriage as a sacrament before God and sought to regulate alliances according to religious principles.

In theory, if not always in practice, Spanish society forbade premarital sex and required marital fidelity. Marriages were monogamous and lasted for life; the Church granted divorces only in the most extraordinary cases, although remarriage of widows and widowers was permitted. The Church regarded all sexual transgressions with a jaundiced eye, but held some acts in special horror. By medieval times Christian theologians had worked out a scheme of acceptable sexual behavior that also reflected their abhorrence of certain practices. Of course, fornication, adultery, incest, seduction, rape, and polygamy were sins, but far worse than any of these were the execrable "sins against nature," which included masturbation, bestiality, and homosexual copulation. The Church allowed married intercourse only in the missionary position; other postures were unnatural because they made the woman superior to her husband, thus thwarting God's universal plan. Procreation, not pleasure, was God's purpose in creating the human sexual apparatus in the first place. Therefore, to misuse the instruments of man's procreative destiny was to thwart the will of God. Medieval constraints on intimate behavior began to erode in the early modern period, but Catholic proscriptions against "unnatural" sexual behavior remained a part of canon law when Spain occupied California.

Such was the *formal* sexual ideology that Franciscans, soldiers, and *pobladores* brought to California. All unapproved sexual practices were considered sinful lust. Maintaining sexual orthodoxy in the remotest reaches of the empire, however, proved to be a greater task than Franciscan missionaries and secular officials could accomplish. Part of the problem was that Spaniards also brought to California an informal sexual ideology rooted in Mediterranean folkways that often ran counter to the teachings of the Church. In this informal scheme, honor was an important element in determining family and individual social ranking, and male status was linked to sexual prowess. To seduce a woman was to shame her and to dishonor her family, while it conferred honor on her consort and asserted his dominant place in the social hierarchy. This double standard arose, in part, because men viewed women as sexually powerful creatures who could lead them astray, and more importantly, dishonor their families. Spanish society controlled female sexual power by segregating women, sometimes going so far as to sequester them behind locked doors, to assure that they would

not sully the family escutcheon with lewd conduct. Thus, Catholic priests labored to restrict sexual activity in a world of philanderers, concubines, prostitutes, lovers, and lawful spouses.

California's Spanish colonizers brought with them these formal and informal ideas about sexuality that were riven with contradictions. The conquest of the New World and its existing alien sexual conventions made matters even more complicated but did not keep Spaniards from intimate encounters with native women. From the time of Cortés, the Crown and the Church encouraged intermarriage with native people, and informal sexual amalgamation occurred with great regularity. Throughout the Spanish empire, interracial sex resulted in a large mixed-race (mestizo) population. Ordinarily, the progeny of these meetings attached themselves firmly to the religion and society of their Spanish fathers. Thus, sexual amalgamation was an integral part of the Spanish colonial experience that served to disable native society and strengthen the Hispanic population, as it drew Indians and their mixed-race children into the colonial orbit. This was the world that Serra had tried to reform in Oaxaca; yet it was a world that he and fellow Spaniards would unwittingly replicate in California.

In 1775 Father Serra wrote thoughtfully to the Viceroy of New Spain about interracial marriages. Three Catalan soldiers had already married neophyte women, and three more were "making up their minds to marry soon." Serra approved of new Spanish regulations that subsidized such marriages with a seaman's salary for two years and provided rations for the mixed-race couple for five years. Such families, it was agreed, should be attached permanently to the wife's mission and receive some livestock and a piece of land from the royal patrimony, provided the husband had "nothing else to fall back upon." To Father Serra these marriages symbolized the foundation of Spanish society. The new families formed "the beginnings of a town," because all the families lived in houses so placed as to form two streets. The little town of Monterey, Serra observed, also included the mission buildings, and "all together make up a square of their own, in front of our little residence and church." They noted happily that children were already beginning to appear in the little town, thus assuring that the community would have a future. Serra's idealistic vision of colonization incorporated Spanish town building and Catholic marriages that tamed the sinful natures of Spaniards and Indians and harnessed them to Spanish imperial goals. If Serra had had his way, however, the only sexual activity in California would have occurred in the few sanctified marriage beds that were under the watchful eye of the friars.

But that was not to be. Serra recognized that Spanish and Indian sexual transgressions occurred, and they troubled him. Common Indian sexual behavior, viewed in light of Catholic mores, amounted to serious sins that merited the friars' solemn condemnation. Perhaps the worse cases were the berdache, who seemed to be ubiquitous in some parts of California. Their so-called "sins against nature" challenged religious and military leaders alike. While Serra extolled the virtues of marriage, Captain Pedro Fages in 1775 reported that Chumash Indians were "addicted to the unspeakable vice of sinning against nature," and that each *rancheria* had a transvestite "for common use." Fages, reflecting common Spanish and Catholic values, apologized for even mentioning homosexuality, because it was "an excess so criminal that it seems even forbidden to speak its name." Similarly, the missionary Pedro Font observed "sodomites addicted to nefarious practices" among the Yuma and concluded that "there will be much to do when the Holy Faith and the Christian religion are established among them."

Civil and Church officials agreed on the need to eradicate homosexuality as an affront to God and Spanish men alike. At Mission Santa Clara, the fathers noticed an unconverted Indian who, though dressed like a woman and working among women, seemed to have undeveloped breasts, an observation easily made because Indian women traditionally wore only necklaces above the waist. The curious friars conspired with the corporal of the guard to take this questionable person into custody, where he was completely disrobed, confirming that he was indeed a man. The poor fellow was "more embarrassed than if he had been a woman," said one friar. For three days the soldiers kept him nude—stripped of his gender identity—and made him sweep the plaza near the guard house. He remained "sad and ashamed" until he was released under orders to abjure feminine clothes and stay out of women's company. Instead, he fled from the mission and reestablished a berdache identity among gentiles.

The Spanish soldiers thoroughly misconstrued what they were seeing and what they had done. The soldiers no doubt thought they had exposed an impostor who was embarrassed because his ruse had been discovered. They did not realize that their captive himself—and his people—regarded him as a woman, and he reacted accordingly when stripped and tormented by men. Humiliated beyond endurance and required to renounce a sexual preference that had never raised an eyebrow in Indian society, the Santa Clara transvestite was forced to flee, but perhaps he was more fortunate than he knew. Father Francisco Palóu reported a similar incident at the Mission San Antonio, where a berdache and another man were discovered "in an unspeakably sinful act." A priest, a corporal, and a soldier "punished them," Palóu revealed, "although not as much as they deserved." When the horrified priest tried to explain how terrible this sin was, the puzzled Indians told him that it was all right because they were married. Palóu's reaction to this news is not recorded, but it is doubtful that he accepted it with equanimity. After receiving a severe scolding, the homosexual couple left the mission vicinity. Palóu hoped that "these accursed persons will decrease, and such an abominable vice will be eradicated," as the Catholic faith increased "for the greater Glory of God and the good of those pitiful, ignorant people."

The revulsion and violence that ordinary Indian sexual relations inspired in the newcomers must have puzzled and frightened the native people. Formerly accepted by some Indian groups as an unremarkable part of social life, berdache faced persecution at the hands of friars and soldiers. To the Spaniards, homosexual behavior was loathsome, one of the many traits that marked California Indians as a backward race. In a word, they were "incomprehensible" to Father Geronimo Boscana. The "affirmative with them is negative," he thought, "and the negative, the affirmative," a perversity that was clearly reflected in the open Indian practice of homosexuality. In frustration, Boscana compared the California Indians "to a species of monkey."

For Spaniards and California Indians alike, the early days of colonization created a confused sexual landscape, but Spanish intolerance of homosexuality was not the only cause of this. In order to convert the Indians, the Franciscans had to uproot other aspects of the normative social system that regulated Indian sexuality and marriage. At the very least, the missionaries meant to restructure Indian marriage to conform to orthodox Catholic standards of monogamy, permanence, and fidelity, changes in intimate conduct that engendered conflict in the California frontier.

At the outset, friars had to decide what to do about married Indians who became mission neophytes. Even the acerbic Father Boscana believed that monogamous Indian marriages were lawful and should be permanently binding on neophytes, except for couples who were united against their will. But what about marriages where one partner became a Christian while the other remained a heathen? And what should be done about polygynous unions? Missionaries worked out the answers according to canon law and its application to Indian converts in Mexico. Neophyte couples remarried in the Catholic Church, and when indigenous marriages were divided by religious beliefs, the Christian partner was permitted to take a new Christian spouse. . . .

Christian ceremonies did not automatically eliminate older cultural meanings of Indian marriage, nor did they necessarily engender Catholic values in the Indian participants. Dissident neophyte runaways sometimes abandoned their old wives and took new ones according to tribal custom. When fathers forbade specific neophyte marriages, unhappy Indians found ways to insist on having the relationship that they preferred. In 1816, for example, an Indian man, probably Chumash, left Mission San Buenaventura to be with the woman he wanted at Santa Barbara. "This happens," Father Jose Senan revealed, "every time his shackles are removed." It is not clear if the missionaries had shackled the man for previously running off to his lover or for some other offense, but Senan allowed that it would be best to permit the couple to wed quietly. If, however, the Indian made mischief, "send him back to us." . . .

Neophytes who failed to live up to Catholic standards ran afoul of the missionaries, who imposed corporal punishment. When, for example. Chumash neophytes at Mission Santa Barbara reverted to polygyny—which the friars evidently regarded as concubinage after Christian conversion—Father Esteban Tapis first admonished the offenders. On the second offense, Tapis laid on the whip, and when this did not convince the Indians of the error of their ways, he put them in shackles.

Franciscans believed they had a right to use corporal punishment to correct unruly Indians. Indeed, the lash was used as an instrument of discipline throughout Spanish society. Eighteenth-century Spanish parents whipped children; teachers whipped pupils; magistrates whipped civil offenders; pious Catholics whipped themselves as penance. Although many Indians appeared to have deeply resented corporal punishment, some neophytes accepted the lash as a fact of mission life when their sexual transgressions caught the watchful eyes of the friars, but the Spanish and Catholic understanding of the whip as an instrument of correction, teaching mortification, and purification no doubt eluded them. In Indian society corporal punishment as a means of social control was rare. Some tribes permitted husbands to physically punish adulterous wives, who were judged not only to have violated moral codes but to have threatened the economic and diplomatic role of the family.

Indian sexuality was not the only carnal problem that the fathers had to contend with in California. Civilians and soldiers brought to California sexual attitudes and behavior that were at odds with both Catholic and Indian values. Rape was a special concern of friars, who persistently condemned Spanish deviant sexual behavior in California. As early as 1772, Father Luis Jayme complained about some of the soldiers, who deserved to be hanged for "continuous outrages" on the Kumeyaay women near Mission San Diego. "Many times," he asserted, the Indians were on the verge of attacking the mission because "some soldiers went there and raped their women." The situation was so bad that the Indians fled from the priests, even risking hunger "so the soldiers will not rape their women as they have already done so many times in the past."

Father Jayme thought Spaniards' assaults were all the worse because the Kumeyaay Indians had become Christians and had presumably given up polygyny. According to Jayme, married neophytes did not commit adultery, and bachelors were celibate. "If a man plays with a woman who is not his wife," Jayme explained, "he is scolded and punished by his captains." Kumeyaay sexual behavior was not only the result of the missionaries' teachings, but a reflection of their traditional belief that adultery was bad. An unconverted Indian told Jayme that "although we did not know that God would punish us in Hell, [we] considered [adultery] to be very bad, and we did not do it, and even less now that we know that God will punish us if we do so." When the missionary heard this, he "burst into tears to see how these gentiles were setting an example for us Chrisans." Jayme's version of the Kumeyaay statement seems to confuse rape and adultery, a problem that may have stemmed from linguistic and cultural misunderstanding. In any case, Jayme described two rapes and their consequences. In one instance three soldiers raped an unmarried woman who became pregnant. She was ashamed of her condition and ultimately killed the newborn infant, an act that horrified and saddened Father Jayme. The second incident occurred when four soldiers and a sailor went to a *rancheria* and dragged off two women. The sailor refused to take part and left the four to complete the assault. Afterwards, the soldiers tried to convert the act from rape to prostitution by paying the women with some ribbon and a few tortillas. They also paid a neophyte man who had witnessed the assault and warned him not to divulge the incident. Insulted and angry, the Indians were not overawed by the rapists' threats. They told Jayme. In retaliation the soldiers locked the neophyte man in the stocks, an injustice that outraged Jayme, who personally released him.

The situation at San Diego was not unique. "There is not a single mission where all the gentiles have not been scandalized," Jayme wrote, "and even on the road, so I have been told." The Spaniards' sexual behavior also did not escape the eye of Father Serra, who asserted that "a plague of immorality had broken out." He had heard the bitter complaints of the friars who wrote to him of disorders at all the missions. Serra worried especially about the muleteers who traversed the vast distances between missions with their pack trains. Serra feared the consequences of allowing unbridled characters among the Indians. There were so many Indian women on the road that Serra expected sexual transgressions, for "it would be a great miracle, yes, a whole series of miracles, if it did not provoke men of such low character to disorders which we have to lament in all our missions; they occur every day." Serra came perilously close to blaming the women for the sexual assaults they suffered. Nevertheless, he believed rapes could imperil the entire mission enterprise by alienating the Indians, who would "turn on us like tigers." Serra was right. In 1775 some eight hundred neophyte and non-Christian Kumeyaays, fed up with sexual assaults and chafing under missionary supervision, attacked Mission San Diego. They burned the mission and killed three Spaniards, including Father Jayme, beating his face beyond recognition. As Jayme and Serra predicted, sexual abuse

against Indians made California a perilous place. Still, the revolt did not dissuade some Spaniards from sexual involvement with Indian women. In 1779, Serra was still criticizing the government for "unconcern in the matter of shameful conduct between the soldiers and Indian women," a complaint that may have been directed at mutual as well as rapacious liaisons.

Serra's argument implied that without supervision, some Spaniards acted without sexual restraint. As we have seen, Spaniards believed in a code of honor that rewarded sexual conquest. Soldiers may have asserted their ideas about honor and status by seducing California Indian women, but there was no honor in rape. Honorable sexual conquest required a willing partner who was overcome by the man's sensuality, masculinity, and magnetism, not merely his brute ability to overpower her. Recall the San Diego rapists who tried to mitigate their actions by making a payment to their victim; Serra argued that these were men of bad character who could not control their urges.

Rape, however, is a violent, complex act that requires more than opportunity and a supposed super-heightened state of sexual tension. Recent research shows that rape is an act of domination carried out by men who despise their victims, in this case because of their race, as well as their gender. Stress, anger, and fear also motivate some rapists.

It should not be forgotten that Spaniards were fearful of California Indians. The soldiers were outnumbered and surrounded by Indians who seemed capable of overwhelming them at any moment. Frequent minor skirmishes, livestock thefts, and occasional murders reinforced the Spanish conception of the Indian enemy. As late as 1822 one missionary thought it was impossible to know how many troops were necessary to defend the Mission San Buenaventura because there were so many unchristianized Indians in the interior. "May God keep our neophytes peaceful and submissive," he wrote "for they would not want for allies if they should rise against our Saint and our charity!" It is not difficult to imagine that some men, sent to a dangerous frontier outpost, violently used Indian women as objects to ward off fear and to express their domination over the numerous native people that the Spanish Crown and Catholic Church sought to subdue, colonize, and convert.

Sexuality, unsanctioned and perversely construed as a way to control native people, actually threatened Spain's weak hold on California by angering the Indians and insulting their ideas about sexuality, rectitude, and justice. It is impossible to know how many rapes occurred in Spanish California, but sexual assaults affected Indian society beyond their absolute numbers. Moreover, Indian rape victims likely displayed some of the somatic and emotional symptoms of rape trauma syndrome, including physical wounds, tension, sleeplessness, gastrointestinal irritations, and genitourinary disturbances. In our own time, rape victims are often stricken with fear, guilt, anger, and humiliation, and some women who have suffered rape develop a fear of normal sexual activity. There is no reason to believe that Indian women did not react to rape in similar ways. Fear of assault may also have affected many women who were not themselves victims, but who tried to help friends and relatives cope with the consequences of rape. Sexual assaults echoed in the Indian social world, even as they frightened friars who feared the consequences of an outraged Indian population.

It is impossible to know how many free-will assignations occurred in California during the mission period, but it is safe to assume that such cross-cultural trysts were fraught with misunderstanding. Indian women, accustomed to looking outside their communities for husbands, likely viewed Spaniards as potential mates who could bring them and their families increased power, wealth, and status. Some women may have hoped that sex would lead to marriage, but it seldom did.

Indians responded to Spanish sexual importunities in several ways. Physical resistance to missionization, as happened at San Diego and on the Colorado River, was one way to deal with rapists and other unwanted intruders. Marriage to a Spaniard was another strategy that could protect women, but evidently only some Indians, a small minority, were able to use this tactic. Other Indians withdrew from Spanish-controlled areas to avoid any infringement on their social life and values. On the other hand, some women might have entered the missions for the protection from sexual abuse that the mission setting provided.

There is also reason to believe that Indians altered their sexual practices as a result of meeting the Spanish. Prostitution, which had been rare among the Indians, became common. In 1780, Father Serra complained about Nicolas, a neophyte who procured

women for the soldiers at San Gabriel. A few years later, a Spanish naturalist observed that the Chumash men had "become pimps, even for their own wives, for any miserable profit."

Nicolas and other Indians had several reasons to resort to prostitution. Spanish men seduced and raped their female kinfolk, but did not marry them. Perhaps Indians were recovering lost bride prices through prostitution. Perhaps, since some Hispanic men were willing to pay for sex, prostitution seemed a logical way to enhance the economic value of wives and daughters, who were expected to be productive. Perhaps, prostitution was simply a means of economic survival, taken out of desperation. How women felt about being so used is not known, but the missions would have been one avenue of escape for those who were unhappy with these new conditions. In the early years of colonization, Indian women outnumbered male neophytes, indicating that females found the mission especially attractive in a rapidly changing world.

Another California Indian reaction to a new sexual world was physiological: they contracted syphilis and other venereal diseases, maladies they had not previously been exposed to. So rapidly did syphilis spread among Indians that in 1792 a Spanish naturalist traveling in California believed the disease was endemic among the Chumash. Twenty years later, the friars recorded it as the most prevalent and destructive disease in the missions. Syphilis was particularly deadly among the Indians because its weakened victims became easy prey for other epidemic diseases that periodically swept the missions. In addition, stillbirths increased, and syphilitic women died more frequently in childbirth. If the women bore live children, the infants were likely to have congenital syphilis. . . .

The combination of virulent endemic syphilis and sexual promiscuity created a fatal environment that killed thousands of mission Indians and inhibited the ability of survivors to recover population losses through reproduction. Franciscans and some of their critics believed that the carnal disintegration of the California missions occurred because the Indians simply continued to observe the sexual customs of their native society. According to the missionaries, the Indians were unrestrained libertines who had learned nothing of Catholic moral behavior in the missions, and were incapable of realizing that syphilis was killing them. This view is incomplete because t assumes that sexual behavior was unregulated in native society and that Indian sexual behavior was unchanged during sixty-five years of mission experience.

Perhaps mission Indian sexuality was a response to new conditions. Who would have understood disparate demographic conditions at the missions better than the neophytes themselves? Locked into a system that seemed to assure their ultimate destruction, dying rapidly from unheard-of diseases, perhaps neophytes chose procreation as a means of group survival. Sadly, they failed, but it was not for want of trying. . . .

Whatever the causes of mission sexuality, neophytes relied on old ways and new ones to solve difficult problems in a new setting. In the end, efficacious solutions eluded them, but it is not accurate to say that Indians were immoral, amoral, or incapable of assimilating the message that the missionaries brought them. The mission experience demonstrates that Indians were simultaneously resolute and unsure, conservative and radical, forward looking and bound to tradition. They exemplified, in other words, the human condition.

Ultimately, the history of California's missions is a sad story of human misunderstandings and failures and terrible unintended consequences. That Spaniards and Indians were often incapable of comprehending each other should hardly be surprising, because they came from radically different cultures. As was so often the case in the history of the Western Hemisphere, Indians and newcomers talked past each other, not with each other. This was true even of their most personal contacts in California. Sacred and profane, intimate, carnal, spiritual, ecstatic, bringing life and death—Indian and Spanish sexuality embodied the identity and paradox of their all-too-human encounter.

Hope and Heritage:
Myth and Thomas Jefferson

Gordon S. Wood

Some time ago a popular magazine ran a brief piece entitled "Which Jefferson do you quote?" In 1960, on a loftier level, there appeared Merrill Peterson's book *The Jefferson Image in the American Mind*. Both dealt with the wide range of the author of the Declaration of Independence and the third President of the United States.

Over the course of history Jefferson's image, or influence, has appeared mainly favorable. The father of American liberalism was idolized by succeeding Presidents, including Madison, Monroe, Adams, Jackson, Lincoln, and on through the twentieth-century pantheon—Roosevelt, Wilson, Roosevelt, Kennedy, Truman, and beyond. There are some obvious reasons for this. The tension that still exists between national and state political power, for example, Jefferson handled in an equitable manner over a long career, as he almost seamlessly moved back and forth between the two. His massive intelligence, philosophical mind, and extensive correspondence, all make for a highly interesting and complex figure. His catholicity of practical and artistic interests adds to the mix. The lionizing of Jefferson reached its scholarly height with the writings of Vernon Louis Parrington in the 1920s. Perhaps Jefferson's continuing popularity was epitomized in the statement of President John F. Kennedy to a group of assembled intellectual and artistic glitterati at the White House to the effect that more collective intelligence is gathered in this room this evening than has ever assembled here, except, of course, when Jefferson dined alone.

Accepting all this, Professor Gordon S. Wood of Brown University here concerns himself with a persistent, and currently flowering unfavorable view of the Jeffersonian image, Jefferson's "darker side." This involved, among other things, racism, political opportunism, and petulance. For scandalmongers there was the alleged Sally Hemings affair, offering the remote possibility that Jefferson had fathered seven children by one of his slaves. Professor Wood implores us to look at Jefferson first as a human being, replete with warts, foibles, and even hypocrisy—a man of his or any time. Ultimately, Jefferson's most real and lasting legacy is his faith in people and democracy, and their role in the future.

Americans seem to have forgotten nothing about Thomas Jefferson, except that he was once a living, breathing human being. Throughout our history, Jefferson has served as a symbol of what we as a people are, someone invented, manipulated, turned into something we like or dislike within ourselves—whether it is populism or elitism, agrarianism or racism, atheism or liberalism. We continually ask ourselves whether Jefferson still survives, or what still lives in his thought, and we quote him on nearly every side of every major question in our history. No figure in our past has embodied so much of our heritage and so many of our hopes.

In his superb *The Jefferson Image in the American Mind* (1960), Merrill Peterson showed that American culture has always used Jefferson as "a sensitive reflector . . . of America's troubled search for the image of itself." The symbolizing, the image-mongering, and the identifying of Jefferson with America has not changed a bit since Peterson's book was published, even though the level of professional historical scholarship has never been higher. If anything the association of Jefferson with America has become more complete. During the past three turbulent decades many people, including some historians, have concluded that something is seriously wrong with America and, therefore, that something has to be wrong with Jefferson.

The opening blast in this criticism of Jefferson was probably Leonard Levy's *Jefferson and Civil Liberties: The Darker Side* (1963). No subtle satire, no gentle mocking of the ironies of Jefferson's inconsistencies and hypocrisies, Levy's book was a prosecutor's indictment. Levy ripped off Jefferson's mantle of libertarianism to expose his "darker side": his passion for partisan persecution, his lack of concern for basic civil liberties, and a self-righteousness that became at times out-and-out ruthlessness. Far from being the skeptical enlightened intellectual, allowing all ideas their free play, Jefferson was portrayed by Levy and others as something of an ideologue, eager to fill the young with his political orthodoxy while censoring all those books he did not like.

Not only did Jefferson lack an original or skeptical mind; he could in fact be downright doctrinaire, an early version of a "knee-jerk liberal." In this respect he was very different from his more skeptical and inquisitive friend James Madison. Jefferson, for example, could understand the opening struggles of the French Revolution only in terms of a traditional liberal antagonism to an arrogant and overgrown monarchy. He supported the addition of a bill of rights to the federal Constitution not because he had thought through the issue the way Madison had but largely because he believed that a bill of rights was what good governments were supposed to have. All of his liberal aristocratic French friends said so; indeed, as he told his fellow Americans, "the enlightened part of Europe have given us the greatest credit for inventing this instrument of security for the rights of the people, and have been not a little surprised to see us so soon give it up." One almost has the feeling that Jefferson advocated a bill of rights in 1787–88 out of concern for what his liberal French associates would think. One sometimes has the same feeling about his antislavery statements, many of which seem to have been shaped to the expectations of enlightened foreigners.

It is in fact his views on black Americans and slavery that have made Jefferson most vulnerable to modern censure. If America has turned out to be wrong in its race relations, then Jefferson had to be wrong too. Samuel Johnson with his quip, "How is it that we hear the loudest yelps for liberty from the drivers of Negroes?" had nothing on modern critics. Who could not find the contrast between Jefferson's great declarations of liberty and equality and his life-long ownership of slaves glaringly inconsistent? Jefferson undoubtedly hated slavery and believed that the self-evident truths that he had set forth in 1776 ought eventually to doom the institution in the United States. Early in his career he tried unsuccessfully to facilitate the manumission of slaves in Virginia, and in the 1780s he worked hard to have slavery abolished in the new western territories. But unlike George Washington, he was never able to free all of his slaves. More than that, as recent historians have emphasized, he bought, bred, and flogged his slaves, and he hunted down fugitives in much the same way his fellow Virginia planters did—all the while declaring that American slavery was not as bad as that of the ancient Romans.

* * *

Some recent historians even claim that Jefferson's attitudes and actions toward blacks were so repugnant that identifying the Sage of Monticello with antislavery discredits the reform movement. Jefferson could never truly imagine freed blacks living in a white man's America, and throughout his life he insisted that the emancipation of the slaves be accompanied by their expulsion from the country. He wanted all blacks sent to the West Indies, or Africa, or anywhere out of the United States. In the end, it has been said, Jefferson loaded such conditions on the abolition of slavery that the antislavery movement could scarcely get off the ground. In response to the pleas of younger men that he speak out against slavery, he offered only excuses for delay.

His remedy of expulsion was based on racial fear

and antipathy. While he had no apprehensions about mingling white blood with that of the Indian, he never ceased expressing his "great aversion" to miscegenation between blacks and whites. When the Roman slave was freed, Jefferson wrote, he "might mix with, without staining the blood of his master." When the black slave was freed, however, he had "to be removed beyond the reach of mixture." Although Jefferson believed that the Indians were uncivilized, he always admired them and made all sorts of environmental explanations for their differences from whites. Yet he was never able to do the same for the African American. Instead, he lastingly clung to the view that blacks were inherently inferior to whites in both body and mind.

It has even been suggested that Jefferson's obsession (shared by so many other Americans) with black sensuality was largely a projection of his own repressed—and, perhaps in the case of his attractive mulatto slave Sally Hemings, not-so-repressed—libidinal desires. The charge that Jefferson maintained Hemings as his mistress for decades and fathered several children by her was first made by an unscrupulous newspaperman, James Callender, in 1802. Since then, historians and others have periodically resurrected the accusation. In fact, in the most recent study of Jefferson's political thought, political scientist Garrett Ward Sheldon treats Jefferson's "keeping of a black mistress" as an established fact, a "common transgression of his class."

In her 1974 psychobiography of Jefferson the late Fawn Brodie made the most ingenious and notorious use of Callender's accusation, building up her case for the passionate liaison between Jefferson and his mullato slave largely through contrived readings of evidence and even the absence of evidence. In accord with our modern soap-opera sensibilities, Brodie naturally turned the relationship into a secret love affair. Brodie's suggestion of a love match aroused a great deal of controversy, perhaps because so many people believed it or at least were titillated by it. A novel based on Brodie's concoctions was written, and there was even talk of a TV movie.

These may seem like small and silly matters, but they are not—not where Jefferson is involved—for the nature of American society itself is at stake. The relationship with Sally Hemings may be implausible to those who know Jefferson's character intimately. He was, after all, a man who never indulged his passions but always suppressed them. But whether he had a relationship with Hemings, there is no denying that Jefferson presided over a household in which miscegenation took place, a miscegenation that he believed was morally repugnant. Thus any attempt to make Jefferson's Monticello a model patriarchal plantation is compromised at the outset.

Everyone, it seems, sees America in Jefferson. When Garry Wills in his *Inventing America* (1978) argued that Jefferson's Declaration of Independence owed less to the individualism of John Locke and more to the communitarian sentiments of the Scottish moralist Francis Hutcheson, one critic accused Wills of aiming "to supply the history of the Republic with as pink a dawn as possible." So too the shame and guilt that Jefferson must have suffered from his involvement in slavery and racial mixing best represents the shame and guilt that white Americans feel in their tortured relations with blacks. Where Jefferson for Vernon Louis Parrington and his generation of the 1920s, '30s, and '40s had been the solution, Jefferson for this present generation has become the problem. The Jefferson that emerges out of much recent scholarship therefore resembles the America that many critics have visualized in the past three decades—self-righteous, guilt-ridden, racist, doctrinaire, and filled with liberal pieties that under stress are easily sacrificed.

Quite clearly, no historical figure can bear this kind of symbolic burden and still remain a real person. Beneath all the images, beneath all the allegorical Jeffersons, there once was a human being with very human frailties and foibles. Certainly Jefferson's words and ideas transcended his time, but he himself did not.

*   *   *

The human Jefferson was essentially a man of the 18th century, a very intelligent and bookish slaveholding southern planter, enlightened and progressive no doubt, but like all human beings possessing as many weaknesses as strengths, inclined as much to folly as to wisdom. Like most people caught up in fast-moving events and complicated changing circumstances, the human Jefferson was as much a victim as he was a protagonist of those events and circumstances. Despite all his achievements in the Revolution and in the subsequent decades, he was never in control of the popular forces he ostensibly led; indeed, he never even fully comprehended these forces. It is the ultimate irony of Jefferson's life, in a life filled with ironies, that he should not have understood the democratic revolution that he himself supremely spoke for.

It is true that much of Jefferson's thinking was conventional, although, as historian William Freehling points out, he did have "an extraordinary gift of lending grace to conventionalities." He had to be conventional or he could never have had the impact he had on his contemporaries. His writing of the Declaration of Independence, he later correctly recalled, was "not to find out new principles, or new arguments, never before thought of . . . ; but to place before mankind the common sense of the subject, in terms so plain and firm as to command their assent, and to justify ourselves in the independent stand we are compelled to take."

*　　*　　*

Jefferson's extraordinary impressionability, learning, and virtuosity were the source of his conventionality. He was very well-read and extremely sensitive to the avant-garde intellectual currents of his day. And he was eager to discover just what was the best, most politically correct, and most enlightened in the world of the 18th century. It was his insatiable hunger for knowledge and his remarkable receptivity to all that was new and progressive that put him at the head of the American Enlightenment.

The 18-century Enlightenment represented the pushing back of the boundaries of darkness and what was called Gothic barbarism and the spreading of light and knowledge. This struggle occurred on many fronts. Some saw the central battle taking place in natural science and in the increasing understanding of nature. Some saw it occurring mostly in religion, with the tempering of enthusiasm and the elimination of superstition. Others saw it happening mainly in politics—in driving back the forces of tyranny and in the creating of new free governments. Still others saw it in the spread of civility and refinement and in the increase in the small, seemingly insignificant ways that life was being made easier, politer, more comfortable, more enjoyable for more and more people. In one way or another, the Enlightenment activities involved the imposition of order and reason on the world. To contemplate aesthetically an ordered universe and to know the best that was thought and said in the world—that was enlightenment.

Jefferson participated fully in all aspects of the 18th-century Enlightenment. He was probably the American Revolutionary leader most taken with the age's liberal prescriptions for enlightenment, gentility, and refinement. He was born in 1743 the son of a wealthy but uneducated and ungenteel planter from western Virginia. He attended the College of William and Mary, the first of his father's family to attend college. Like many of the Revolutionary leaders who were also the first of their family to acquire a liberal arts education in college, he wanted a society led by an aristocracy of talent and taste. For too long men had been judged by who their fathers were or whom they had married. In a new enlightened republican society they would be judged by merit and virtue and taste alone.

Jefferson was not one to let his feelings show, but even today we can sense beneath the placid surface of his autobiography, written in 1821 at the age of 77, some of his anger at all those Virginians who prided themselves on their genealogy and judged men by their family background.

In its opening pages Jefferson tells us that the lineage of his Welsh father was lost in obscurity: He was able to find in Wales only two references to his father's family. His mother, on the other hand, was a Randolph, one of the distinguished families of Virginia. The Randolphs, he said with about as much derision as he ever allowed himself, "trace their pedigree far back in England & Scotland, to which let everyone ascribe the faith & merit he chooses." He went on to describe his efforts in 1776 in Virginia to bring down that "distinct set of families" who had used several legal devices to confine the inheritance of property both to the eldest son (primogeniture) and to special lines of heirs (entail) so as to form themselves "into a Patrician order, distinguished by the splendor and luxury of their establishments." Historians have often thought Jefferson exaggerated the power of primogeniture and entail and this "Patrician order." Not only was the setting aside of entails very common in Virginia; the "Patrician order" seemed not all that different from its challengers. But Jefferson clearly saw a difference, and it rankled him. The privileges of this "aristocracy of wealth," he wrote, needed to be destroyed "to make an opening for the aristocracy of virtue and talent"— of which he considered himself a prime example.

*　　*　　*

To become a natural aristocrat, one had to acquire the attributes of a natural aristocrat—enlightenment, gentility, and taste. We will never understand the young Jefferson until we appreciate the intensity and earnestness of his desire to become the most cosmopolitan, the most liberal, the most genteel, and the most enlightened gentleman in all of America. From the outset he was the sensitive provincial quick to condemn the backwardness of his fellow colonials. At college and later in studying law at Williamsburg he played the violin, learned French, and acquired the tastes and refinements of the larger world. At frequent dinners with Governor Francis Fauquier and his teachers, William Small and George Wythe, Jefferson said he "heard more good sense, more rational and philosophical conversations than in all my life besides." Looking back, he called Williamsburg "the finest school of manners and morals that ever existed in America." Although as a young man he had seen very few works of art, he knew from reading and conversation what was considered good; and in 1771 he wrote a list, ranging from the Apollo Belvedere to a Raphael cartoon, of those celebrated paintings, drawings, and sculptures that he hoped to acquire in copies. By 1782, "without having left his own country," this earnest autodidact with a voracious appetite for learning had become, as the French visitor Chevalier de Chastellux noted, "an American who . . . is at once a musician, a draftsman, an astronomer, a geometer, a physicist, a jurist and a statesman."

* * *

In time Jefferson became quite proud of his gentility, his taste, and his liberal brand of manners. In fact, he came to see himself as a kind of impresario for America rescuing his countrymen from their "deplorable barbarism" by introducing them to the finest and most enlightened aspects of European culture. When Americans in the 1780s realized that a statue of Washington was needed, "there could be no question raised," he wrote from Paris, "as to the Sculptor who should be employed, the reputation of Monsr. Houdon of this city being unrivalled in Europe." No American could stand up to his knowledge. When Washington timidly expressed misgivings about Houdon's doing the statue in Roman style, he quickly backed down in the face of Jefferson's frown, unwilling, as he said, "to oppose my judgment to the taste of Connoisseurs."

Jefferson's excitement over the 16th-century Ital-

ian, Andrea Palladio, whose *Four Books of Architectu[re]* was virtually unknown in America, was the excite[ment] of the provincial discovering the cosmopolita[n] taste of the larger world. He became ashamed of th[e] "gothic" Georgian architecture of his native Virgini[a] and he sought in Monticello to build a house tha[t] would do justice to those models that harked back t[o] Roman antiquity. In the 1780s he badgered his Vi[r]ginia colleagues into erecting as the new state cap[i]tol in Richmond a magnificent copy of the Maiso[n] Carrée, a Roman temple from the first century A.[D] at Nîmes, because he wanted an American publi[c] building that would be a model for the people'[s] "study and imitation" and "an object and proof [of] national good taste." Almost singlehandedly he be[-]came responsible for making America's public build[-]ings resemble Roman temples.

No American knew more about wine than Jeffer[-]son. During his trips around Europe in 1787–88 h[e] spent a great deal of time investigating French, Ital[-]ian, and German vineyards and wineries and makin[g] arrangements for the delivery of wine to the Unite[d] States. Everyone in America acknowledged his ex[-]pertise in wine, and three presidents sought his ad[-]vice about what wine to serve at presidential dinners[.] In everything—from gardening and food to music[,] painting, and poetry—Jefferson wanted the lates[t] and most enlightened in European fashion.

It is easy to make fun of Jefferson and his par[-]venu behavior. But it would be a mistake to dismis[s] Jefferson's obsession with art and good taste merel[y] as a trivial affectation, or as the simple posturing an[d] putting on of airs of an American provincial wh[o] would be the perfect gentleman. Jefferson migh[t] have been more enthusiastic about such matters tha[n] the other Revolutionary leaders, but he was by n[o] means unique in his concern for refining his ow[n] sensibilities as well as those of other American citi[-]zens. This was a moral and political imperative of al[l] of the Founding Fathers. To refine popular taste wa[s] in fact a moral and political imperative of all th[e] enlightened of the 18th century.

The fine arts, good taste, and even good manners had political implications. As the English philoso[-]pher Lord Shaftesbury had preached, morality and good taste were allied: "The science of virtuosi and that of virtue itself become, in a manner, one and the same." Connoisseurship, politeness, and genteel re[-]finement were connected with public morality and political leadership. Those who had good taste were enlightened, and those who were enlightened were virtuous.

But note: *virtuous in a modern, not an ancient, manner*. Politeness and refinement tamed and domesticated the severe classical conception of virtue. Promoting social affection was in fact the object of the civilizing process. This new social virtue was less Spartan and more Addisonian, less the harsh self-sacrifice of antiquity and more the willingness to get along with others for the sake of peace and prosperity. Virtue in the modern manner became identified with politeness, good taste, and one's instinctive sense of morality. As the 18th-century Scottish philosopher Lord Kames said, "a taste in the fine arts goes hand in hand with the moral sense, to which indeed it is nearly allied."

*   *   *

Indeed, there was hardly an educated person in all of 18th-century America who did not at one time or another try to describe people's moral sense and the natural forces of love and benevolence holding society together. Jefferson's emphasis on the moral sense was scarcely peculiar to him.

This modern virtue that Jefferson and others extolled was very different from that of the ancient republican tradition. Classical virtue had flowed from the citizen's participation in politics; government had been the source of his civic consciousness and public spiritedness. But modern virtue flowed from the citizen's participation in society, not in government, which the liberal-minded increasingly saw as the source of the evils of the world. "Society," said Thomas Paine in a brilliant summary of this common enlightened separation, "is produced by our wants and government by our wickedness; the former promotes our happiness positively by uniting our affections, the latter negatively by restraining our vices. The one encourages intercourse, the other creates distinctions." It was society—the affairs of private social life—that bred sympathy and the new domesticated virtue. Mingling in drawing rooms, clubs, and coffeehouses—partaking of the innumerable interchanges of the daily comings and goings of modern life—created affection and fellow-feeling, which were all the adhesives really necessary to hold an enlightened people together. Some of Jefferson's contemporaries even argued that commerce, that tradi-

tional enemy of classical virtue, was in fact a source of modern virtue. Because it encouraged intercourse and confidence among people and nations, commerce, it was said, actually contributed to benevolence and fellow-feeling.

Jefferson could not have agreed more with this celebration of society over government. Indeed, Paine's conventional liberal division between society and government was the premise of Jefferson's political thinking—his faith in the natural ordering of society, his belief in the common moral sense of ordinary people, his idea of minimal government. "Man," said Jefferson, "was destined for society. His morality, therefore, was to be formed to this object. He was endowed with a sense of right and wrong, merely relative to this. . . . The moral sense, or conscience, is as much a part of a man as his leg or arm. . . ." All human beings had "implanted in our breasts" this "love of others," this "moral instinct"; these "social dispositions" were what made democracy possible.

The importance of this domesticated modern virtue to the thinking of Jefferson and of other Americans can scarcely be exaggerated. It laid the basis for all reform movements of the 19th century and for all subsequent liberal thinking. We still yearn for a world in which everyone will love one another.

*   *   *

Probably no American leader took this belief in the natural sociability of people more seriously than Jefferson. His scissors-and-paste redoing of the New Testament in the early years of the 19th century stemmed from his desire to reconcile Christianity with the Enlightenment and at the same time to answer all of those critics who said that he was an enemy of all religion. Jefferson discovered that Jesus, with his prescription for each of us to love our neighbors as ourselves, actually spoke directly to the modern enlightened age. Jefferson's version of the New Testament offered a much-needed morality of social harmony for a new republican society.

Jefferson's faith in the natural sociability of people also lay behind his belief in minimal government. In fact, Jefferson would have fully understood the Western world's present interest in devolution and localist democracy. He believed in nationhood but not the modern idea of the state. He hated all bureaucracy and all the coercive instruments of government, and he sometimes gave the impression that government was only a device by which the few attempted to rob, cheat, and oppress the many. He certainly never accepted the modern idea of the state as an entity possessing a life of its own, distinct from both rulers and ruled. For Jefferson there could be no power independent of the people, in whom he had an absolute faith.

Although he was not a modern democrat, assuming as he did that a natural aristocracy would lead the country, he had a confidence in the capacity and the virtue of the people to elect that aristocracy that was unmatched by any other of the Founding Fathers. Jefferson like the other Founding Fathers had doubts about all officials in government, even the popularly elected representatives in the lower houses of the legislatures ("173 despots would surely be as oppressive as one"); but he always thought that the people, if undisturbed by demagogues or Federalist monarchists, would eventually set matters right. It was never the people but only their elected agents that were at fault.

Not only did Jefferson refuse to recognize the structure and institutions of a modern state; he scarcely accepted the basic premise of a state, namely, its presumed monopoly of legitimate control over a prescribed territory. For him during his first presidential administration (1801–1804) the United States was really just a loosely bound confederation, not all that different from the government of the former Articles of Confederation. Hence his vision of an expanding empire of liberty over a huge continent posed no problems for his relaxed idea of a state. As long as Americans continued to believe certain things, they remained Americans. Jefferson could be remarkably indifferent to the possibility that a western confederacy might break away from the eastern United States. What did it matter? he asked in 1804. "Those of the western confederacy will be as much our children & descendants as those of the eastern."

It was Jefferson's extraordinary faith in the natural sociability of people as a substitute for the traditional force of government that made the Federalists and especially Alexander Hamilton dismiss him as a hopeless pie-in-the-sky dreamer. The idea that, "as human nature shall refine and ameliorate by the operation of a more enlightened plan," government eventually "will become useless, and Society will subsist and flourish free from its shackles" was, said

Hamilton in 1794, a "wild and fatal . . . scheme," even if its "votaries" like Jefferson did not always push such a scheme to the fullest.

*   *   *

Jefferson and other Revolutionary leaders believed that commerce among nations in international affairs was the equivalent to affection among people in domestic affairs. Both were natural expressions of relationships that needed to be freed of monarchical obstructions and interventions. Hence in 1776 and in the years following, Jefferson and other Revolutionary idealists hoped to do for the world what they were doing for the society of the United States— change the way people related to one another. They looked forward to a rational world in which corrupt monarchical diplomacy and secret alliances, balances of power, and dynastic rivalries would be replaced by the natural ties of commerce. If the people of the various nations were left alone to exchange goods freely among themselves, then international politics would become republicanized and pacified, and war itself would be eliminated. Jefferson's and the Republican party's "candid and liberal" experiments in "peaceful coercion"—the various efforts of the United States to use nonimportation and ultimately Jefferson's disastrous Embargo of 1807–09 to change international behavior—were the inevitable consequences of this sort of idealistic republican confidence in the power of commerce.

Conventional as Jefferson's thinking might often have been, it was usually an enlightened conventional radicalism that he espoused. So eager was he to possess the latest and most liberal of 18th-century ideas that he could easily get carried away. He, like "others of great genius," had "a habit," as Madison gently put it in 1823, "of expressing in strong and round terms impressions of the moment." So he alone of the Founding Fathers was unperturbed by Shays's rebellion in 1786–1787. "I like a little rebellion now and then," he said. "It is like a storm in the Atmosphere." It was too bad that some people were killed, but "the tree of liberty must be refreshed from time to time with the blood of patriots and tyrants. It is its natural manure." Similar rhetorical exaggeration accompanied his response to the bloody excesses of the French Revolution. Because "the liberty of the whole earth" depended on the success of the French Revolution, he wrote in 1793, lives would have to be lost. "Rather than it should have failed, I would have seen half the earth desolated. Were there but an Adam & an Eve left in every country, & left free, it would be better than as it now is." Unlike Coleridge and Wordsworth and other disillusioned European liberals, Jefferson remained a champion of the French Revolution to the end.

He saw it, after all, as a movement on behalf of the rights of man that had originated in the American Revolution. And to the American Revolution and the rights of man he remained dedicated until his death. In the last letter he wrote he described the American Revolution as "the signal of arousing men to burst the chains under which monkish ignorance and superstition had persuaded them to bind themselves, and to assume the blessings and security of self-government."

* * *

Yet during Jefferson's final years in retirement these expressions of confidence in the future progress of the Enlightenment came fewer and farther between. The period between Jefferson's retirement from the presidency in 1809 and his death in 1826 was a tumultuous one in American history—marked by war with the British and Indians, a severe commercial panic, the rapid growth of democracy and evangelical religion, and the Missouri crisis over the spread of slavery. It was also not a happy time for Jefferson. To be sure, there was the Sage of Monticello relaxing among his family and friends and holding court on top of his mountain for scores of visiting admirers. There was his reconciliation with John Adams and the wonderful correspondence between the two old revolutionaries that followed. And there was his hard-fought establishment of the University of Virginia. But there was not much else to comfort him.

The world around him, the world he helped to create, was rapidly changing, and changing in ways that Jefferson found bewildering and sometimes even terrifying. The American Revolution was unfolding with radical and unexpected developments. American society was becoming more democratic and more capitalistic, and Jefferson was not prepared for either development. By the end of his life Jefferson had moments of apprehension that the American Revolution, to which he had devoted his life, was actually in danger of failing. In response his speech

and action often did not accord with what we now like to think of as Jeffersonian principles. He turned inward and began spouting dogmas in a manner that many subsequent historians and biographers have found embarrassing and puzzling.

After Jefferson retired from public life in 1809, he became more narrow-minded and localist than he had ever been in his life. He had always prided himself on his cosmopolitanism, yet upon his retirement from the presidency he returned to Virginia and never left it. In fact, he virtually never again lost sight of his beloved Blue Ridge. He cut himself off from many of the current sources of knowledge of the outside world, and became, as one of his visitors George Ticknor noted, "singularly ignorant & insensible on the subjects of passing politics." He took only one newspaper, the Richmond *Enquirer*, and seemed to have no strong interest in receiving his mail. In all this he differed remarkably from his friend and neighbor James Madison. Madison, said Ticknor, "receives multitudes of newspapers, keeps a servant always in waiting for the arrival of the Post—and takes anxious note of all passing events."

Jefferson's turn inward was matched by a relative decline in the place of Virginia in the union. Decay was everywhere in early 19th-century Virginia, and Jefferson felt it at Monticello. Despite his life-long aversion to public debts, his private debts kept mounting, and he kept borrowing, taking out new loans to meet old ones. He tried to sell his land, and when he could not he sold slaves instead. He feared that he might lose Monticello and complained constantly of his debts, but he refused to cut back on his lavish hospitality and expensive wine purchases.

Unable to comprehend the economic forces that were transforming the country and destroying the upper South, Jefferson blamed the banks and the speculative spirit of the day for both his and Virginia's miseries. It is true that he accepted the existence of commerce and, after the War of 1812, even some limited manufacturing for the United States. But the commerce he accepted was tame and traditional stuff compared to the aggressive commerce that was taking over northern America in the early 19th century. Jefferson's idea of commerce involved little more than the sale abroad of agricultural staples—wheat, tobacco, and cotton. His commerce was not the incessant trucking and trading, the endless buying and selling with each other, that was coming to characterize the emerging northern Yankee world. That kind of dynamic domestic commerce and all the capitalistic accouterments that went with it—banks, stock markets, liquid capital, paper money—Jefferson feared and despised.

*   *   *

He did indeed want comforts and prosperity for his American farmers, but like some modern liberals he had little or no appreciation of the economic forces that made such prosperity and comforts possible. He had no comprehension of banks and thought that the paper money issued by banks was designed "to enrich swindlers at the expense of the honest and industrious part of the nation." He could not understand how "legerdemain tricks upon paper can produce as solid wealth or hard labor in the earth." As far as he was concerned, the buying and selling of stocks and the raising of capital were simply licentious speculation and wild gambling—all symptoms of "commercial avarice and corruption."

The ultimate culprit in the degeneration of America, he thought, was the corrupt and tyrannical course of the national government. The Missouri Crisis of 1819–1820, provoked by northern efforts to limit the spread of slavery in the West, was to Jefferson "a fire bell in the night," a threat to the union and to the Revolutionary experiment in republicanism. He believed that the federal government's proposed restriction on the right of the people of Missouri to own slaves violated the Constitution and threatened self-government. Only each state, he said, had the "exclusive right" to regulate slavery. If the federal government arrogated to itself that right, then it would next declare all slaves in the country free, "in which case all the whites within the United States south of the Potomac and Ohio must evacuate their States, and most fortunate those who can do it first."

Jefferson became a bitter critic of the usurpations of the Supreme Court and a more strident defender of states' rights than he had been even in 1798 when he penned the Kentucky Resolution justifying the right of a state to nullify federal laws. While his friend Madison remained a nationalist and upheld the right of the Supreme Court to interpret the Constitution, Jefferson lent his support to the most dogmatic, impassioned, and sectional-minded elements in Virginia, including the arch states'-rightists Spencer Roane and John Randolph. He became parochial and alarmist, and his zeal for states' rights, as even

his sympathetic biographer Dumas Malone admits, "bordered on fanaticism."

For someone as optimistic and sanguine in temperament as Jefferson usually was, he had many gloomy and terrifying moments in these years between 1809 and 1826. What happened? What accounts for these moments of gloom and these expressions of fanaticism? How can we explain Jefferson's uncharacteristic but increasingly frequent doubts about the future?

Certainly his personal troubles, his rising debts, the threat of bankruptcy, the fear of losing Monticello, were part of it, but they are not the whole explanation. Something more is involved in accounting for the awkwardness of his years of retirement than these outside forces, and that something seems to lie within Jefferson himself—in his principles and outlook, in his deep and long-held faith in popular democracy and the future.

No one of the Revolutionary leaders believed more strongly in progress and in the capacity of the American people for self-government than did Jefferson. And no one was more convinced that the Enlightenment was on the march against the forces of medieval barbarism and darkness, of religious superstition and enthusiasm. So sure was he of the future progress of American society that he was intellectually and emotionally unprepared for what happened in the years following his retirement from public office. He was unprepared for the democratic revolution that he himself had inspired. In the end Jefferson was victimized by his overweening confidence in the people and by his naive hopefulness in the future. The Enlightenment and the democratic revolution he had contributed so much to bring about and his own liberal and rosy temperament finally did him in.

Jefferson's sublime faith in the people and the future is the source of that symbolic power he has had for succeeding generations of Americans. He was never more American than when he told John Adams in 1816 that he liked "the dreams of the future better than the history of the past." He was always optimistic; indeed, he was a virtual Pollyanna about everything. His expectations always outran reality, whether they concerned French aristocrats who turned out to be less liberal than his friend Lafayette, or garden vegetables that never came up, or misbehaving students at the University of Virginia who violated their honor code, or an American Revolution that actually allowed people to pursue their pecuniary happiness. He was the pure American innocent. He had little understanding of man's capacity for evil and had no tragic sense whatsoever.

Through his long public career, while others were wringing their hands, Jefferson remained calm and hopeful. He knew slavery was a great evil, but he believed his generation could do little about it. Instead he counseled patience and a reliance on the young who would follow. When one of those younger men, Edward Coles, actually called on Jefferson in 1814 to lend his voice in the struggle against slavery, he could only offer his confidence in the future. "The hour of emancipation is advancing, in the march of time. It will come. . . ."

It was the same with every difficulty. In one way or other he expected things to work out. In 1814 he saw his financial troubles coming at him and his household like "an approaching wave in a storm; still I think we shall live as long, eat as much, and drink as much, as if the wave had already glided under the ship. Somehow or other these things find their way out as they come in, and so I suppose they will now." Was not progress on the march, and were not science and enlightenment everywhere pushing back the forces of ignorance, superstition, and darkness? The future, he felt, was on his side and on the side of the people. A liberal democratic society would be capable of solving every problem, if not in his lifetime, then surely in the coming years.

But Jefferson lived too long, and the future and the coming generation were not what he had expected. Although he continued in his public letters, especially to foreigners, to affirm that progress and civilization were still on the march, in private he became more and more apprehensive of the future. He sensed that American society, including Virginia, might not be getting better after all, but actually going backward. The American people were not becoming more refined, more polite, and more sociable; if anything, he believed, they were more barbaric and factional. Jefferson was frightened by the divisions in the country and by the popularity of Andrew Jackson, whom he regarded as a man of violent passions and unfit for the presidency. He felt overwhelmed by the new paper-money business culture that was sweeping through the country and never appreciated how much his democratic and egalitarian principles had contributed to its rise.

Ordinary people, in whom he placed so much

confidence, more certainly than his friend Madison had, were not becoming more enlightened. In fact, superstition and bigotry, which Jefferson identified with organized religion, were actually reviving, released by the democratic revolution he had led. He was temperamentally incapable of understanding the deep popular strength of the evangelical forces that were seizing control of American culture in these early decades of the 19th century. He became what we might call a confused secular humanist in the midst of real moral majorities. While Jefferson in 1822 was still predicting that there was not a young man now alive who would not die a Unitarian, Methodists and Baptists and other evangelicals were gaining adherents by the tens of thousands in the Second Great Awakening. In response all Jefferson could do was blame the defunct New England Federalists and an equally bewildered New England clergy for spreading both capitalism and evangelical Christianity throughout the country.

*   *   *

Jefferson's solution to this perceived threat from New England and its "pious young monks from Harvard and Yale" was to hunker down in Virginia and build a university that would perpetuate true republican principles. "It is in our seminary," he told Madison, "that that vestal flame is to be kept alive." Yet even building the university brought sorrow and shock. The Virginia legislature was not as eager to spend money for higher education as he had expected. His support of the university became more of a political liability in the legislature than an asset.

The people in fact seemed more sectarian and less rational than they had been at the time of the Revolution. They did not seem to know who he was, what he had done. Was this the new generation on which he rested all his hopes? During the last year of his life, at a moment, says his biographer Malone, of "uneasiness that he had never known before," Jefferson was pathetically reduced to listing his contributions during 61 years of public service in order to justify a legislative favor. No wonder he sometimes felt cast off. "All, all dead!" he wrote to an old friend in 1825, "and ourselves left alone midst a new generation whom we know not, and who knows not us."

These were only small cracks in his optimism, only tinges of doubt in his democratic faith, but for an innocent like him these were enough. Jefferson went further in states' rights principles and in his fears of federal consolidation than his friend Madison did because he had such higher expectations of the Revolution and the people. He had always invested so much more of himself intellectually and emotionally in the future and in popular democracy than Madison had. Jefferson was inspired by a vision of how things could and should be. Madison tended to accept things as they were. Madison never lost his dark foreboding about the America yet to come, and he never shed his skepticism about the people and popular majorities. But Jefferson had nothing but the people and the future to fall back on; they were really all he ever believed in. That is why we remember Jefferson, and not Madison.

The Louisiana Purchase: A Dangerous Precedent

Walter LaFeber

The nation had made an auspicious anti-imperialist beginning. As early as the Confederation Period of the 1780s, Congress, following Jefferson's leadership, set an anti-imperialist course for the Northwest Territory. States within the territory would ultimately emerge and enjoy equal status with the original thirteen, the inhabitants receiving equal citizenship. During Washington's presidency a policy of noninvolvement in "entangling alliances" and other muscular foreign activities was enunciated and to a large extent followed. So far so good.

In 1803, however, with Jefferson president, an opportunity presented itself that was impossible to refuse. Napoleon's offer to sell all Louisiana to the United States for approximately fifteen million dollars proved irresistible to the President. Jefferson was not brimming over with expansionist fever, but was faced with the possibility of ample space for his yeoman farmers' advance. There were problems. Jefferson had been a champion of state over national rights; to buy Louisiana would contradict his previous stance. Also came the question of constitutionality: Where did that document contain the authority to double the existing size of the country? Influenced by advisers and news that Napoleon might change his mind, Jefferson without resort to constitutional amendment presented his decision to the Senate for advice and consent. After that body consented, House of Representatives' reservations were steamrollered, and the deed was done. One of the House reservations dealt with Jefferson's decision, in contrast to that in the Northwest Ordinance, to allow black slavery. Arthur Schlesinger, Jr., in his book *The Imperial Presidency* posits that whenever Presidents act decisively in foreign affairs—and particularly during wartime—the powers of the executive branch grow very rapidly. In accordance with Schlesinger's thesis, Walter LaFeber of Cornell University, raises serious doubt as to the advisibility of such precedent-setting activity in the purchase of Louisiana. LaFeber sees a mythic path laid out for subsequent unilateral actions: President Polk in the Mexican War, President McKinley in 1898, and President Truman in Korea. Panama, Grenada, and the Persian Gulf are clear additions.

Thomas Jefferson was one of the greatest expansionists in an American history full of ardent expansionists. But then, he believed the success of America's great experiment in democracy demanded an expanding territory. In the Virginian's mind, the republic must be controlled by ambitious, independent, property-holding farmers, who would form the incorruptible bedrock of democracy. As he wrote in 1785 in his *Notes on the State of Virginia*, "Those who labour in the earth are the chosen people.... Corruption of [their] morals ... is a phenomenon of which no age nor nation has furnished an example." Americans who worked the land would never become dependent on factory wages. "De-

123

pendence begets subservience and venality," Jefferson warned in *Notes*, "and prepares fit tools for the designs of ambition."

But Jefferson's virtuous farmers needed land, and their population was growing at an astonishing rate. Jefferson and his close friend and Virginia neighbor, James Madison, had studied the birthrate carefully. The two men rightly perceived that Americans were nearly doubling their population every 25 to 27 years. Moreover, the number of immigrants seemed to be increasing so quickly that as early as 1785 Jefferson had actually suggested restricting their numbers. Virginia provided a striking example of how fast land was being peopled. The region on the state's western frontier had filled with settlers so quickly that in 1792 it became the state of Kentucky. Unless something was done, Jefferson declared, Virginia would within the next century be burdened with "nearly the state of population in the British islands." Given Jefferson's convictions about the corruption to be found in Britain's cities, the analogy was damning.

During his first term as President (1801–1805), Jefferson had the chance to obtain that "extension of territory which the rapid increase of our numbers will call for" by purchasing Louisiana, an area larger than Western Europe. In a single step he could double the size of the United States and open the possibility of an "empire for liberty," as he later described it, of mind-boggling proportions.

The President was playing for large stakes. Louisiana stretched from the Mississippi westward to the Rocky Mountains, and from Canada's Lake of the Woods southward to the Gulf of Mexico. If annexed, these 825,000 square miles would give the new nation access to one of the world's potentially richest trading areas. The Missouri, Kansas, Arkansas and Red rivers and their tributaries could act as giant funnels carrying goods into the Mississippi and then down to New Orleans. Even in the 1790s, with access to the Mississippi only from the east, the hundreds of thousands of Americans settled along the river depended on it and on the port of New Orleans for access to both world markets and imported staples for everyday living. "The Mississippi is to them everything," Secretary of State James Madison observed privately in November 1802. "It is the Hudson, the Delaware, the Potomac, and all the navigable rivers of the Atlantic formed into one stream."

Louisiana had long been a focus for imperial ambitions. The French had largely controlled the region until 1763 when, after losing the so-called Seven Years War, they were forced to cede it to Spain. But in 1799 Napoleon Bonaparte became head of the French government, and the next year he seized the opportunity to retake the territory. In exchange for his promise to make the Spanish royal family rulers of Tuscany, Spain handed over Louisiana. Though Bonaparte never bothered to carry out his end of the bargain, he set in motion plans for a New World colonial empire that would make Louisiana the food source for the rich French sugar island of Saint Domingue (Haiti) in the Caribbean.

Jefferson and Madison reacted with alarm. A decaying Spanish empire along the western American border was little threat. But Napoleon was something else. He would dam up American expansionism and perhaps attract settlements east of the Mississippi away from the United States. In 1801, after hearing rumors of Napoleon's bargain with Spain, Jefferson ordered Robert R. Livingston to Paris as the new U.S. minister. He instructed Livingston to talk Napoleon out of occupying Louisiana or, if that was impossible, to buy New Orleans. By 1802 both Jefferson and Livingston began to mention the possibility of acquiring not just the port, but also its vast interior.

Jefferson told Livingston that if France insisted on occupying New Orleans, he would consider an Anglo-American alliance against France. That threat was probably empty. But others were not. In February the Senate authorized Jefferson to create an 80,000-man army to defend the Mississippi. Although the House adjourned before acting on the measure, the President had already been strengthening forts along the river. He sent three artillery and four infantry companies into position north of New Orleans. The commander of these forces, William C.C. Claiborne, assured him that these troops could seize New Orleans if they attacked before French forces arrived to strengthen the Spanish garrison.

But just as war with Napoleon loomed in the early months of 1803, Jefferson faced a crisis of quite another kind. He knew that the Constitution had no provision giving him the power to take New Orleans—let alone an area such as Louisiana that would double the nation's size—and he believed he could take no action not explicitly authorized by the Constitution.

This conviction was no mere infatuation with

theory. As George Washington's secretary of state from 1790 until 1793, Jefferson had fought Secretary of the Treasury Alexander Hamilton's attempt to interpret the Constitution's phrases in broad terms. Beaten by Hamilton over such critical issues as whether the Constitution permitted the United States to create a national bank, or the federal government to assume state debts, Jefferson resigned from the cabinet. He retired to Monticello and—even as Vice-President under the Federalist President John Adams—organized the Republican Party to take power and, as he saw it, restore the Constitution's true meaning. "The powers not delegated to the United States," he wrote in a debate with Hamilton in 1790 and 1791, "are reserved to the States respectively, or to the people." He warned, in words that were later to cause him anguish, that "to take a single step beyond the boundaries thus specially drawn around the powers of Congress is to take possession of a boundless field of power, no longer susceptible of any definition."

In 1798 Jefferson's fears seemed to come true. Enmeshed in undeclared war with France on the high seas, the Federalists tried to force Americans to cooperate with Adam's war plans by passing the Alien and Sedition Acts. These measures gave President John Adams the power to arrest and imprison his critics. Jeffersonians believed the acts were aimed at them—and with good reason: the 14 indictments and 10 convictions that occurred under the act were against members of the Republican Party. In secret, Jefferson and Madison helped the Virginia and Kentucky legislatures draft resolutions that condemned the Federalists for enlarging central government—especially presidential—powers beyond the limits set by the Constitution. The resolutions argued that a state should have the power to decide whether federal governmental acts were constitutional or not. Demanding that Congress support a strict construction of the 1787 document, Jefferson won what he called "the revolution of 1800," which threw Adams and the Hamiltonians out of office. The "sum of good government," he observed in his 1801 inaugural address, was small and limited government.

Thus Jefferson's dilemma in January and February 1803. As he and his closest advisers agreed, nothing in the Constitution explicitly permitted the government to annex and govern new territory—let alone a territory so immense that it would transform the nation's political balance. Reading that power into the Constitution's general wording, Jefferson warned, could so twist and distort the document that American liberty would be threatened. "Our peculiar security is in possession of a written Constitution," he wrote privately to a close friend. "Let us not make it a blank paper by construction." By no means, however, was he willing to turn away Louisiana.

In January 1803, Jefferson discussed these difficulties with Attorney General Levi Lincoln and the brilliant young secretary of the treasury, Albert Gallatin. Lincoln suggested that Jefferson have the French, if they sold any part of the territory, designate it as an extension of the Mississippi Territory or the state of Georgia. Gallatin retorted that if the central government lacked the constitutional power to annex new territory, then so did the states. By mid-January he had given Jefferson his rather Hamiltonian view of the matter: "1st. That the United States as a nation have an inherent right to acquire territory. 2nd. That whenever that acquisition is by treaty, the same constituted authorities in whom the treaty-making power is vested [that is, in the President and the Senate] have a constitutional right to sanction the acquisition. 3rd. That whenever the territory has been acquired, Congress have the power either of admitting into the Union as a new State, or of annexing to a State with the consent of that State, or of making regulations for the government of such territory."

In acquiring a territorial empire over the next century, Americans were to follow precisely these principles. But Gallatin's views did little to quell Jefferson's uneasiness, which reached a climax on July 3 when he learned that the two U.S. diplomats in Paris, Robert R. Livingston and James Monroe, had signed a treaty in which Napoleon sold Louisiana to the United States for $11,250,000. A separate agreement stipulated that the United States would assume $3,750,000 more for claims of U.S. citizens against France. The two diplomats also agreed that for 12 years French and Spanish ships would receive special tariff rates over other foreign ships and merchandise in New Orleans. The inhabitants of the vast territory, moreover, were to receive full constitutional rights as soon as possible.

These last provisions were to bedevil Jefferson. Giving French and Spanish traders preferences in New Orleans violated the Constitution's provisions that duties be levied uniformly throughout the nation. Granting full constitutional rights to the many non-Americans, especially nonwhites, in this vast area went against Jefferson's better judgment—not to mention the devout wishes of conservative and increasingly agitated New Englanders.

On July 16, Jefferson placed the agreements before his cabinet (or "executive council" as it was then known) and suggested that Congress "be obliged to ask from the people an amendment to the Constitution authorizing their receiving the province into the Union, and providing for its government." Gallatin, Madison, Lincoln, Secretary of War Henry Dearborn and Secretary of the Navy Robert Smith vigorously disagreed. They did not share the President's constitutional sensitivities.

The council pointed out a more immediate danger: the treaty provided for an exchange of ratifications within six months of the signing on April 30, 1803. No constitutional amendment could be passed by the necessary two-thirds vote in both houses of Congress and the three fourths of the states in the time remaining. But if there were any delay, Napoleon could renounce the agreement and recommence his empire building along the Mississippi. The advisers urged that Jefferson call a special session of Congress in October and rush the treaty and conventions through without mentioning the amendment.

Jefferson's friends warned him that if he so much as hinted at the need for an amendment, the treaty's enemies—most notably, New England Federalists whose fear of a vast western empire beyond their control was matched only by their hatred of Jefferson—would delay and probably kill the agreements. The President realized this. Nevertheless, that summer he tried to write at least two drafts of an amendment. He admitted to his close friend, Senator John Breckinridge of Kentucky, that in agreeing to the purchase he had gone far beyond what the Constitution permitted. Breckinridge, who had written the Kentucky Resolutions with Jefferson just four years earlier, disagreed. He had long nurtured the ambition to control New Orleans and the trans-Mississippi—an ambition that in the 1790s had led him to plot secretly (and in some Easterners' eyes, treasonously) with a French agent to gain control of the river without the knowledge or approval of the Washington administration. In any case, the President's desire for empire was becoming overwhelming. "I infer," he wrote Madison later in August, "that the less we say about constitutional difficulties respecting Louisiana the better, and that what is necessary for surmounting them must be done sub silentio."

Jefferson found these "constitutional difficulties" distinctly less important after he received two letters. In the first, which arrived from Paris on August 17, Livingston warned that Napoleon now regretted having signed the treaty. The French leader was searching for any excuse ("the slightest alteration" made by the United States, in the envoy's words) to avoid carrying it out. If Congress did not act within the six-month limit, the First Consul would renounce the deal. The second letter carried a long-expected message from the Spanish minister in Washington, Marquis de Casa Yrujo. It reached Jefferson on September 12. The king of Spain, Yrujo wrote, was shocked that Napoleon had sold Louisiana. The French leader had no right to do so. The President now had to fear that either his majesty or Napoleon might use this message as an excuse to reclaim New Orleans and the interior.

Livingston's note decided Jefferson, and Yrujo's protest reinforced his determination. The President concluded that although it would be advisable to push for an amendment, it could be done only after Congress had acted on the agreements and the territory was safely in hand. In the meantime, he told Gallatin, Congress should approve the documents "without talking."

Jefferson needed two thirds of the Senate to ratify his treaty and a simple majority of the House to carry the agreements into effect. In the Senate, where his forces were led by the loyal Breckinridge, his party held 25 seats to the Federalists' nine; in the House the numbers were also overwhelming—103 to 39. Jefferson, however, left nothing to chance. Regularly working 10 to 13 hours a day to ensure that his wishes were carried out, he became the most powerful party leader in the republic's short history. Such a regimen left, according to this remarkably organized man, "an interval of 4 hours for riding, dining, and a little unbending." Even then he used the dinner hour several times a week to invite congressional members, stoke them with excellent food and wine and, as Jefferson delicately put it, exchange information for the sake of the "public interest."

Many, New England Federalists feared the idea of annexing a vast territory whose people would over time develop immense political power—and, no doubt, be forever grateful to Jeffersonians. A Boston Federalist newspaper sniffed that Louisiana was nothing more than "a great waste, a wilderness un-peopled with any beings except wolves and wandering Indians. . . . We are to give money of which we have too little for land of which we already have too much." Senator William Plumer, a Federalist from New Hampshire, warned that New England would not "tamely shrink into a state of insignificance."

On October 17, 1803, Jefferson told the Congress he had summoned into session that he was sending it the treaty and the accompanying agreements. Nothing was said about a constitutional amendment. The measures were being whipped through after only three days of debate when a crisis developed. Senate Federalists demanded that Jefferson send the documents proving that Napoleon had rightfully obtained Louisiana from Spain and so had the power to sell the territory. This demand presented a problem: the documents did not exist. Republicans nevertheless closed ranks and "with unblushing front" (as Plumer sarcastically commented) voted down the resolution on the grounds that such information was not needed. The agreements were then rammed through, 24 to 7. "The Senate," Plumer complained, "have taken less time to deliberate on this most important treaty than they allowed themselves on the most trivial Indian contract."

Next the papers went to the House for legislation that would authorize monetary payments to carry out the agreements. Again the Federalists demanded documents, particularly a deed of cession from Spain to France. The request touched a nerve. Seven years earlier, Madison, then the Jeffersonian leader in a Federalist-dominated House of Representatives, had tried to kill the Jay treaty with Great Britain by demanding all appropriate documents. President Washington had refused on the grounds that the House was obliged to carry out treaties that, under the Constitution, only the Senate had to ratify. Madison protested, but he was beaten in a showdown vote that had large implications for the constitutional role the House was to play in future U.S. foreign policy. Now, in 1803, the roles were reversed. As the Federalists demanded the deed, Samuel Mitchill of New York rose to reply on behalf of the Jeffersonians that if the President had thought the House needed to see any more papers, he certainly would have sent them. After that disingenuous response, the House voted down the Federalist demand by two votes.

In his pioneering analysis of how rapidly presidential power grew during the Jeffersonian years, Abraham Sofaer argues that the Virginian set a precedent in refusing to acknowledge the Federalists' call for the documents. President Washington had taken the position that, yes, papers that Congress had requested did exist, but, no, he did not have to send certain confidential papers to Congress. The Jeffersonians had responded vigorously that such official information could be demanded and used by the people's representatives in the legislature. In 1803, however, (and again during the treason trial of former Vice-President Aaron Burr in 1807) Jefferson took the position that it was unnecessary to tell the Congress (or the court) that such papers even existed. Instead, he labeled the documents "private" or "confidential" and kept them out of sight. The people's representatives in Congress apparently had a limited right to know, and the limits were determined by the President.

This embarrassment eased in December 1803 when Jefferson learned that Napoleon had finally pressured Spain into giving him official possession of Louisiana. In January 1804, the forces Jefferson had dispatched under Claiborne's command a year earlier controlled the region. The Stars and Stripes replaced the French Tricolor over New Orleans.

One major obstacle remained, however. Jefferson had to create, and Congress approve, a government for this vast territory. The region held fewer than 100,000 inhabitants, and Jefferson believed, rightly as it turned out, that only half of those were white and that the remainder were largely Indian and African-American. The President indicated from the start of the debate that he thought only whites could govern the territory. But even some of them were suspect. New Orleans had attracted renegades and runaways, like former New York district attorney, Edward Livingston, who had moved to New Orleans after he was suspected of having illegally siphoned money from his office. Roman Catholic groups, long protected by Spain, were fearful and suspicious of Jefferson's intentions. As for the large population of Creoles (those with French ancestry born in Louisiana), the President believed they were "as yet as incapable of self-government as children." When a Creole delegation traveled to Washington to demonstrate its ability to lobby, it was turned away.

Congress divided the region into two districts: Orleans (the future state of Louisiana) and Louisiana. Late in 1803 the President sent Congress a bill for governing the area during the next year. This measure gave the inhabitants guarantees for their "liberty, property, and religion," which the treaty had obligated him to grant. There was, however, no self-government, no indication that, to repeat one of Jefferson's earlier principles, governments derived "their just powers from the consent of the governed." Military officers, chosen by the President, were to rule in the iron-handed manner of the former Spanish governor. They were responsible to no local authorities, but only to the President in the faraway city of Washington. Senator John Quincy Adams, who had just won election from Massachusetts, supported the annexation, but he was appalled that the Constitution was being interpreted as giving the President authority to rule the territory as a colony. When Adams moved that a constitutional amendment be considered to make such rule legitimate, no senator seconded his proposal. Jefferson's governing bill passed the Senate 26 to 6.

The House's view of Jefferson's constitutional powers was revealed when angry Federalists attacked the treaty provision that gave French and Spanish merchants trade preferences in New Orleans. Joseph H. Nicholson of Maryland replied for the Jeffersonians that the whole of Louisiana "is in the nature of a colony whose commerce may be regulated without any reference to the Constitution" and its provision that duties be uniformly imposed throughout the Union. Madison, with his sensitivity to such issues, excused the Jeffersonians' tough approach by granting that while "Republican theory" would not immediately govern the newly annexed people, "it may fairly be expected that every blessing of liberty will be extended to them as fast as they shall be prepared and disposed to receive it." The secretary of state was known for choosing his words carefully.

From January through March 1804, Congress discussed Jefferson's plans for a more permanent government, which would last until both sections of Louisiana had enough white settlers to be entrusted with regular territorial government. Few problems arose in the debates until Senator James Hillhouse of Connecticut proposed that slavery be prohibited from both parts of the purchase. A struggle erupted in the Senate that previewed some of the arguments that later threatened to splinter the Union. When one slave-state senator tried to stop the uproar by saying, "I am unwilling to think let alone speak on this subject," another grimly warned that "if we leave it, it will follow us." Jefferson notably refused to support Hillhouse, and Senator James Jackson of Georgia led the opposition to the Connecticut senator by declaring that Louisiana could "not be cultivated" without slavery. He urged that the people on the scene (many of whom owned slaves) be allowed to decide. "You cannot prevent slavery. . . . Men will be governed by their interest not the law." In the end, though, Congress again broadly construed its power by recognizing slavery where it existed in the purchase, while allowing a previous act to stand that stringently limited the slave trade. Provisions were added to prevent Orleans, a center of the foreign slave trade, from becoming a state until after the 1810 census. This delay not only appeased New England Federalists but also prevented Orleans' entry as a state until after 1808 when, as the Constitution provided, the foreign trade in slaves was to end.

The final bill gave the President the power to appoint governors over Orleans and Louisiana who, with a small legislative body they were to choose, would rule autocratically. The rights of the inhabitants were not "self-evident," as Jefferson had once described them, but were granted by the will of the central government. The law became effective October 1, 1804.

In less than one year Jefferson had enlarged the central government's constitutional powers more broadly than had Washington and Adams in 12 years. He had set a dangerous precedent, moreover, by arguing that when time was of the essence, the President and Congress could ignore, perhaps violate, the Constitution if they considered it to be in the national interest. Critics called Jefferson's government in Louisiana "about as despotic as that of Turkey in Asia." The President and his supporters responded that such a government was, unfortunately, necessary to ensure that the vast territory would remain orderly until enough white Americans could populate the region. The new states would then prosper as a part of the Union with rights equal to those of the older parts.

Critics were not reassured. "We rush like a comet into infinite space," Fisher Ames of Massachusetts warned. "In our wild career we may jostle some other world out of its orbit, but we shall, in every event, quench the light of our own." John Randolph of Virginia had a less apocalyptic response to Jefferson's actions. He had helped the President push the Louisiana legislation through the House. But by 1806 he had turned against his fellow Virginian for having overthrown Republican constitutional doctrine. There were only "two parties in all States," Randolph concluded, "the *ins* and the *outs*." The ins construed governmental power broadly for the gain of their own "patronage and wealth," while the outs tried to limit such power. "But let the *outs* get in . . . and you will find their Constitutional scruples and arguments vanish like dew before the morning sun."

As the ins, Jefferson and his supporters realized larger objectives than "patronage and wealth." They succeeded in transforming the Constitution into an instrument for imperial expansion, which made it possible for Jefferson to resolve the crisis in his great democratic experiment.

But the transformation of the Constitution for the sake of "enlarging the empire of liberty" had a price.

The President, as Jefferson had demonstrated, could find in the Constitution virtually any power he needed to carry out the most expansive foreign policy, especially if his party commanded a majority in Congress. Loose construction was given the seal of bipartisanship as the Republicans, now the ins, out-Hamiltoned Hamilton in construing the 1787 document broadly. Such loose construction would be used by others, among them President James K. Polk from 1845 to '46 as he maneuvered Mexico into a war in order to annex California, President William McKinley between 1898 and 1901 when he expanded U.S. power into the Philippines and landed troops in China, and President Harry S Truman when he claimed the authority to wage war in Korea. Jefferson's experiment in democracy cast long shadows.

The Jacksonian Revolution: Myth and Reality

Robert V. Remini

Historical legend holds that a coalition of circumstances following the War of 1812—the rise of the West as a political force, the growing democracy of the frontier, and a new rough-hewn style of American politics—brought Andrew Jackson to the nation's center stage; from Tennessee to Washington, D.C, from the backwoods to national political leadership. Without doubt Jackson was a remarkable charismatic figure, but much of his image owes to a complex blend of sentimentality, folklore, and misinformation. Finding a clear path through the wilderness of Jacksonian scholarship is the task of Robert V. Remini, professor of history at the University of Illinois, Chicago Circle.

"What?" cried the outraged North Carolina lady when she heard the dreadful news. "Jackson up for president? *Jackson? Andrew* Jackson? The Jackson that used to live in Salisbury? Why, when he was here, he was such a rake that my husband would not bring him into the house! It is true, he *might* have taken him out to the stable to weigh horses for a race, and might drink a glass of whiskey with him *there*. Well, if Andrew Jackson can be president, anybody can!"

Indeed. After forty years of constitutional government headed by presidents George Washington, John Adams, Thomas Jefferson, James Madison, James Monroe, and John Quincy Adams, the thought of Gen. Andrew Jackson of Tennessee—"Old Hickory" to his devoted soldiers—succeeding such distinguished statesmen came as a shock to some Americans in 1828. And little did they know at the time that Old Hickory would be followed in succession by the Little Magician, Tippecanoe and Tyler too, Young Hickory, and then Old Rough and Ready.

What had happened to the American political process? How could it come about that the Washingtons, Jeffersons, and Madisons of the world could be replaced by the Van Burens, Harrisons, Tylers,

and Taylors? What a mockery of the political system bequeathed by the Founding Fathers!

The years from roughly 1828 to 1848 are known today as the Age of Jackson or the Jacksonian era. To many contemporaries, they initiated a "revolution," a shocking overthrow of the noble republican standards of the founders by the "common people," who in 1828 preferred as president a crude frontiersman like Andrew Jackson to a statesman of proven ability with a record of outstanding public service like John Quincy Adams.

Over the forty years following the establishment of the American nation under the Constitution, the United States had experienced many profound changes in virtually all phases of life. Following the War of 1812, the industrial revolution took hold and within thirty years all the essential elements for the creation of an industrial society in America were solidly in place. At the same time, a transportation revolution got underway with the building of canals, bridges, and turnpikes, reaching a climax of sorts in the 1820s with the coming of the railroads. The standard of living was also improved by numerous new inventions. Finally, many of the older eastern states began to imitate newer western states by democratizing their institutions, for example, amending their constitutions to eliminate property qualifications for voting and holding office, thereby establishing universal white manhood suffrage.

The arrival of many thousands of new voters at the polls in the early nineteenth century radically changed American politics. In the past, only the wealthy and better educated were actively involved in government. Moreover, political parties were frowned upon by many of the Founding Fathers. Parties stood for factions or cliques by which greedy and ambitious men, who had no interest in serving the public good, could advance their private and selfish purposes. John Adams spoke for many when he declared that the "division of the republic into two great parties . . . is to be dreaded as the greatest political evil under our Constitution."

But times had changed. An entirely new generation of politicians appeared at the outbreak of the War of 1812, men like Henry Clay, John C. Calhoun, Martin Van Buren, and Daniel Webster, who regarded political parties more favorably. Indeed, the party structure that had emerged before the end of President Washington's administration had been their corridor to power, since none of them could offer to their constituents a public record to match what the founders had achieved. None had fought in the Revolution. None had signed the Declaration or participated in the debates leading to the writing and adoption of the Constitution. Some of them—Martin Van Buren is probably the best example—actually considered parties to be beneficial to the body politic, indeed essential to the proper working of a democratic society. Through the party system, Van Buren argued, the American people could more effectively express their will and take measures to ensure that that will was implemented by their representatives. "We must always have party distinctions," he wrote," "and the old ones are the best. . . . Political combinations between the inhabitants of the different states are unavoidable and the most natural and beneficial to the country is that between the planters of the South and the plain Republicans of the North."

In supporting Andrew Jackson for the presidency in 1828 and trying to win support from both planters and plain Republicans, Van Buren affirmed his belief in the American need for a two-party system. Jackson's election, he told Thomas Ritchie, editor of the Richmond *Enquirer*, "as the result of his

military services without reference to party, and, as far as he alone is concerned, scarcely to principle, would be one thing. His election as the result of combined and concerted effort of a political party, holding in the main, to certain tenets and opposed to certain prevailing principles, might be another and far different thing."

Van Buren eventually formed an alliance with John C. Calhoun and a number of other southern politicians, and led the way in structuring a political organization around the presidential candidacy of Andrew Jackson. That organization ultimately came to be called the Democratic Party. Its leaders, including Jackson, Van Buren, Calhoun, and Thomas Hart Benton, claimed to follow the republican doctrines of Thomas Jefferson. Thus they opposed both a strong central government and a broad interpretation of the Constitution, and they regarded the states, whose rights must be defended by all who cared about preserving individual liberty, as a wholesome counterweight to the national government. Many of them opposed the idea of the federal government sponsoring public works, arguing that internal improvements dangerously inflated the power of the central government and jeopardized liberty. As president, Andrew Jackson vetoed the Maysville road bill and contended that the national government should avoid internal improvements as a general practice, except for those essential to the national defense.

The political philosophy these Democrats espoused was fundamentally conservative. It advocated economy in operating the government because a tight budget limited government activity, and Jackson swore that if ever elected president he would liquidate the national debt. True to his word, he labored throughout his administration to cut expenditures by vetoing several appropriations bills he tagged as exorbitant, and he finally succeeded in obliterating the national debt altogether in January 1835—a short-lived accomplishment.

The organization of the Democratic Party in its initial stages included a central committee, state committees, and a national newspaper located in Washington, D.C., the *United States Telegraph,* which could speak authoritatively to the party faithful. In time it was said that the Democratic organization included "a chain of newspaper posts, from the New England States to Louisiana, and branching off through Lexington to the Western States." The supporters of Jackson's election were accused by their opponents of attempting to regulate "the popular election by means of organized clubs in the States, and organized presses everywhere."

Democrats took particular delight in celebrating the candidacy of Andrew Jackson. They found that Old Hickory's personality and military accomplishments made him an attractive and viable candidate for the ordinary voter. Indeed his career and personality stirred the imagination of Democratic leaders around the country and they devised new methods, or improved old ones, to get across the message that Andrew Jackson was a "man of the people." "The Constitution and liberty of the country were in imminent peril, and he has preserved them both!" his supporters boasted. "We can sustain our republican principles . . . by calling to the presidential chair . . . ANDREW JACKSON."

Jackson became a symbol of the best in American life—a self-made man, among other things—and party leaders adopted the hickory leaf as their symbol. Hickory brooms, hickory canes, hickory sticks shot up everywhere—on steeples, poles, steamboats, and stage coaches, and in the hands of all who could wave them to salute the Old Hero of New Orleans. "In every village, as well as upon the corners of many city streets," hickory poles were erected. "Many of these poles were standing as late as 1845," recorded one contemporary, "rotten momentoes [sic] of the delirium of 1828." The opponents of the Democratic Party were outraged by this crude lowering of the political process. "Planting hickory trees!" snorted the Washington *National Journal* on May 24, 1828. "Odds nuts and drumsticks! What have hickory trees to do with republicanism and the great contest?"

The Democrats devised other gimmicks to generate excitement for their ticket. "Jackson meetings" were held in every county where a Democratic organization existed. Such meetings were not new, of course. What was new was their audience. "If we go into one of these meetings," declared one newspaper, "of whom do we find them composed? Do we see there the solid, substantial, moral and reflecting yeomanry of the country? No. . . . They comprise a large portion of the dissolute, the noisy, the discontented, and designing of society." The Democratic press retorted with the claim that these so-called dissolute were actually the "bone and muscle of American society. They are the People. The real People who understand that Gen. Jackson is one of them and will defend their interests and rights."

The Jacksonians were also very fond of parade and barbecues. In Baltimore a grand barbecue wa scheduled to commemorate the successful defense o the city when the British attacked during the War o 1812. But the Democrats expropriated the occasior and converted it into a Jackson rally. One parad started with dozens of Democrats marching to th beat of a fife and drum corps and wearing no othe insignia save "a twig of the sacred [hickory] tree ir their hats." Trailing these faithful Jacksonians cam "gigantic hickory poles," still live and crowned witl green foliage, being carted in "on eight wheels for th purpose of being planted by the democracy on th eve of the election." These poles were drawn by eigh horses, all decorated with "ribbons and mottoes." Perched in the branches of each tree were a dozer Democrats, waving flags and shouting, "Hurrah fo Jackson!"

"Van Buren has learned you know that the *Hurre Boys* were for Jackson," commented one critic, "anc to my regret they constitute a powerful host." Indeec they did. The number of voters in the election of 182 rose to 1,155,340, a jump of more than 800,000 ovei the previous presidential election of 1824.

*   *   *

The Hurra Boys brought out the voters in 1828 but at considerable cost. The election set a low mark for vulgarity, gimmickry, and nonsensical hijinks Jackson's mother was accused of being a prostitute brought to America to service British soldiers, anc his wife was denounced as an "adulteress" and biga mist. "Ought a convicted adulteress and her para mour husband to be placed in the highest offices oi this free and Christian land?" asked one editor. Bui the Democrats were no better, accusing John Quincy Adams of pimping for the czar of Russia.

The tone and style of this election outraged many voters who feared for the future of American politics With so many fresh faces crowding to the polls, the old republican system was yielding to a new demo cratic style and that evolution seemed fraught with all the dangers warned against by the Founding Fathers. Jackson's subsequent victory at the polls gave some Americans nightmares of worse things to come.

At his inauguration people came from five hun dred miles away to see General Jackson, wrote Danie Webster, "and they really seem to think that the country is rescued from some dreadful danger!"

They nearly wrecked the White House in their exuberance. Their behavior shocked Joseph Story, an associate Justice of the Supreme Court, and sent him scurrying home. "The reign of KING MOB seemed triumphant," he wailed. But a western newspaper disagreed. "It was a proud day for the people," reported the *Argus of Western America*. "General Jackson is *their own* President."

Jackson himself was fiercely committed to democracy. And by democracy he meant majoritarian rule. "The people are the government," he wrote, "administering it by their agents; they are the Government, the sovereign power." In his first message to Congress as president, written in December 1829, Jackson announced: "The majority is to govern." To the people belonged the right of "electing their Chief Executive." He therefore asked Congress to adopt an amendment that would abolish the College of Electors. He wanted all "intermediary" agencies standing between the people and their government swept away, whether erected by the Founding Fathers or not. "The people are sovereign," he reiterated. "Their will is absolute."

So committed was Jackson to the principle of popular self-rule that he told historian-politician George Bancroft that "every officer should in his turn pass before the people, for their approval or rejection." And he included federal judges in this sweeping generalization, even justices of the Supreme Court. Accordingly, he introduced the principle of rotation, which limited government appointments to four years. Officeholders should be regularly rotated back home and replaced by new men, he said. "The duties of all public officers are . . . so plain and simple that men of intelligence may readily qualify themselves for their performance." Otherwise abuse may occur. Anyone who has held office "a few years, believes he has a life estate in it, a vested right, & if it has been held 20 years or upwards, not only a vested right, but that it ought to descend to his children, & if no children then the next of kin—This is not the principles of our government. It is rotation in office that will perpetuate our liberty." Unfortunately, hack politicians equated rotation with patronage and Jackson's enemies quickly dubbed his principle "the spoils system."

But it was never meant to be a spoils system. Jackson wanted every office of government, from the highest to the lowest, within the reach of the electorate, arguing that "where the people are every-

thing . . . there and there only is liberty." Perhaps his position was best articulated by Alexis de Tocqueville, the French visitor in the 1830s whose *Democracy in America* remains one of the most profound observations about American life in print. "The people reign in the American political world," declared Tocqueville, "as the Deity does in the universe. They are the cause and aim of all things; everything comes from them, and everything is absorbed in them." The "constant celebration" of the people, therefore, is what Jackson and the Democratic Party provided the nation during his eight years in office. It is what Jacksonian Democracy was all about.

As president, Jackson inaugurated a number of important changes in the operation of government. For example, he vetoed congressional legislation more times than all his predecessors combined, and for reasons other than a bill's presumed lack of constitutionality. More importantly, by the creative use of his veto power he successfully claimed for the chief executive the right to participate in the legislative process. He put Congress on notice that they must consider his views on all issues before enacting them into law or run the risk of a veto. In effect he assumed the right to initiate legislation, and this essentially altered the relationship between the executive and the Congress. Instead of a separate and equal branch of the government, the president, according to Jackson, was the head of state, the first among equals.

Jackson also took a dim view of the claim that the Supreme Court exercised the final and absolute right to determine the meaning of the Constitution. When the court decided in *McCulloch v. Maryland* that the law establishing a national bank was constitutional, Jackson disagreed. In his veto of a bill to recharter the Second National Bank in 1832, he claimed among other things that the bill lacked authority under the Constitution, despite what the high court had decided. Both the House and the Senate, as well as the president, he continued, must decide for themselves what is and what is not constitutional before taking action on any bill. The representatives of Congress ought not to vote for a bill, and the president ought not to sign it, if they, in their own good judgment, believe it unconstitutional. "It is as much the duty of the House of Representatives, of the Senate, and of the President to decide upon the constitutionality of any bill or resolution which may be presented to them for passage or approval as it is of the supreme judges when it may be brought before them for judicial decision." Jackson did not deny the right of the Supreme Court to judge the constitutionality of a bill. What he denied was the presumption that the Court was the final or exclusive interpreter of the Constitution. All three branches should rule on the question of constitutionality, Jackson argued. In this way the equality and independence of each branch of government is maintained. "The authority of the Supreme Court," he declared, "must not, therefore, be permitted to control the Congress, or the Executive when acting in their legislative capacities, but to have only such influence as the force of their reasoning may deserve." What bothered Jackson was the presumption that four men could dictate what 15 million people may or may not do under their constitutional form. To Jackson's mind that was not democratic but oligarchic. But that was precisely the intention of the Founding Fathers: to provide a balanced mix of democratic, oligarchic, and monarchical forms in the Constitution.

Of course Jackson was merely expressing his own opinion about the right of all three branches to pass on the constitutionality of all legislation, an opinion the American people ultimately rejected. The great fear in a democratic system—one the Founding Fathers knew perfectly well—was the danger of the majority tyrannizing the minority. Jackson would take his chances. He believed the American people were virtuous and would always act appropriately. "I for one do not despair of the republic," he wrote. "I have great confidence in the virtue of a great majority of the people, and I cannot fear the result. The republic is safe, the main pillars [of] virtue, religion and morality will be fostered by a majority of the people." But not everyone shared Jackson's optimism about the goodness of the electorate. And in time—particularly with the passage of the Fourteenth Amendment—it fell to the courts to guard and maintain the rights of the minority.

Jackson summed up his assertion of presidential rights by declaring that he alone—not Congress, as was usually assumed—was the sole representative of the American people and responsible to them. After defeating Henry Clay in the 1832 election, he decided to kill the Second National Bank by removing federal deposits because, as he said, he had received a "mandate" from the people to do so. The Senate objected and formally censured him, but Jackson, in response, merely issued another statement on presidential

rights and the democratic system that had evolved over the last few years.

By law, only the secretary of the treasury was authorized to remove the deposits, so Jackson informed his secretary, William Duane, to carry out his order. Duane refused pointblank. And he also refused to resign as he had promised if he and the president could not agree upon a common course of action with respect to the deposits. Thereupon, Jackson sacked him. This was the first time a cabinet officer had been fired, and there was some question whether the president had this authority. After all, the cabinet positions were created by Congress and appointment required the consent of the Senate. Did that not imply that removal also required senatorial consent—particularly the treasury secretary, since he handled public funds that were controlled by Congress? The law creating the Treasury Department never called it an "executive" department, and it required its secretary to report to the Congress, not the president. None of this made a particle of difference to Andrew Jackson. All department heads were *his* appointees and they would obey *him* or pack their bags. The summary dismissal of Duane was seen by Jackson's opponents as a presidential grab for the purse strings of the nation. And in fact presidential control over all executive functions gave the chief executive increased authority over the collection and distribution of public funds.

* * *

By the close of 1833 many feared that Andrew Jackson was leading the country to disaster. Henry Clay regularly pilloried the president on the Senate floor. On one occasion he accused Jackson of "open, palpable and daring usurpation" of all the powers of government. "We are in the midst of a revolution," Clay thundered, "hitherto bloodless, but rapidly tending towards a total change of the pure republican character of the Government."

A "revolution"—that was how the opposition Whig Party characterized Jackson's presidency. The nation was moving steadily away from its "pure republican character" into something approaching despotism. What the nation was witnessing, cried Clay, was "the concentration of all power in the hands of one man." Thereafter Whig newspapers reprinted a cartoon showing Jackson as "King Andrew the First." Clad in robes befitting an emperor, he was shown wearing a crown and holding a scepter in one hand and a scroll in the other on which was written the word "veto."

Democrats, naturally, read the "revolution" differently. They saw it as the steady progress of the country from the gentry republic originally established by the Founding Fathers to a more democratic system that mandated broader representation in government and a greater responsiveness to popular will.

Andrew Jackson did not take kindly to Clay's verbal mauling. "Oh, if I live to get these robes of office off me," he snorted at one point, "I will bring the rascal to a dear account." He later likened the senator to "a drunken man in a brothel," reckless, destructive, and "full of fury."

Other senators expressed their opposition to this "imperial" president and seconded Clay's complaints. John C. Calhoun, who by this time had deserted to the enemy camp, adopted the Kentuckian's "leading ideas of revolution" and charged that "a great effort is now making to choke and stifle the voice of American liberty." And he condemned Jackson's insistence on taking refuge in democratic claims. The president "tells us again and again with the greatest emphasis," he continued, "that he is the immediate representative of the American people! What effrontery! What boldness of assertion! Why, he never received a vote from the American people. He was elected by electors . . . who are elected by Legislatures chosen by the people."

Sen. Daniel Webster and other Whigs chimed in. "Again and again we hear it said," rumbled Webster, "that the President is responsible to the American people! . . . And this is thought enough for a limited, restrained, republican government! . . . I hold this, Sir, to be a mere assumption, and dangerous assumption." And connected with this "airy and unreal responsibility to the people," he continued, "is another sentiment . . . and that is, that the President is the direct representative of the American people." The sweep of his language electrified the Senate. And "if he may be allowed to consider himself as the sole representative of all the American people," Webster concluded, "then I say, Sir, that the government . . . has already a master. I deny the sentiment, and therefore protest against the language; neither the sentiment nor the language is to be found in the Constitution of this Country."

Jackson's novel concept that the president served as the people's tribune found immediate acceptance by the electorate, despite the warnings of the Whigs. In effect, he altered the essential character of the presidency. He had become the head of government, the one person who would formulate national policy and direct public affairs. Sighed Senator Benjamin W. Leigh of Virginia: "Until the President developed the faculties of the Executive power, all men thought it inferior to the legislature—he manifestly thinks it superior: and in his hands [it] . . . has proved far stronger than the representatives of the States."

*   *   *

From Jackson's own time to the present, disagreement and controversy over the significance of his presidency have prevailed. In the twentieth century the disagreements intensified among historians. Confusion over the meaning of Jacksonian Democracy, varying regional support for democratic change, and the social and economic status of the Democrats and Whigs have clouded the efforts of scholars to reach reliable conclusions about the Old Hero and the era that bears his name.

Andrew Jackson himself will always remain a controversial figure among historians. That he can still generate such intense partisan feeling is evidence of his remarkable personality. He was an aggressive, dynamic, charismatic, and intimidating individual. And although modern scholars and students of history either admire or dislike him intensely, his rating as president in polls conducted among historians over the past thirty years varies from great to near great. He carries an enormous burden in winning any popularity contest because of his insistence on removing the eastern Indians west of the Mississippi River and on waging a long and vicious war against the Second National Bank of the United States.

His first biographer, James Parton, wrote a three-volume *Life of Andrew Jackson* (1859, 1860), and came away with mixed feelings about the man and his democracy. At times Parton railed against the mindless mob "who could be wheedled, and flattered, and drilled," but at other times he extolled democracy as the mark of an enlightened society. What troubled Parton particularly was the spoils system. Rotation, he wrote, is "an evil so great and so difficult to remedy, that if all his other public acts had been perfectly wise and right, this single feature of his administration would suffice to render it deplorable rather than amiable."

William Graham Sumner's *Andrew Jackson* (1882)

was relentlessly critical of his subject, deploring in particular Jackson's flawed moral charter and emotional excesses. Sumner and other early historians, such as Herman von Holst and James Schouler, constituted what one student of the Jacksonian age called a "liberal patrician" or "Whig" school of history. These individuals came from European middle- or upper middle-class families with excellent backgrounds of education and public service. Because their class had been ousted from political power, these historians were biased against Jacksonian Democracy, and their books reflect their prejudice.

The interpretation of Old Hickory and his adherents took a sharp about-face with the appearance in 1893 of the vastly influential article by Frederick Jackson Turner, "The Significance of the Frontier in American History." Turner argued that American democracy emerged from the wilderness, noting that universal white manhood suffrage guaranteed by the new western states became something of a model for the older, eastern states. Naturally Jackson and his followers were seen as the personification of this frontier democracy. The thesis was advanced and sometimes amplified by Charles A. Beard, Vernon L. Parrington, and other western and southern historians of the early twentieth century who were caught up in the reform movement of the Progressive era. They dubbed the Jacksonian revolution an age of egalitarianism that produced the rise of the common man. Jackson himself was applauded as a man of the people. Thus the liberal patrician school of historiography gave way to the Progressive school.

This interpretation dovetailed rather well with the views of Tocqueville. During his visit, Tocqueville encountered a widespread belief in egalitarianism but worried that majoritarian rule could endanger minority rights. There are so many sharp and accurate insights into American society and institutions in *Democracy in America* that it ought to be the first book anyone reads in attempting to understand the antebellum period of American history. Among other things, he catches the American just as he is emerging from his European and colonial past and acquiring many of the characteristics [that] are generally regarded as typically American today.

Tocqueville's democratic liberalism, augmented by the works of the Progressive historians—especially Turner, Beard and Parrington—dominated historical thought about the American past for the next fifty years or more. Almost all the Progressive histo-

rians stressed the role of geographic sections in the nation, and Turner at one point even denied any class influence in the formation of frontier democracy. The only important negative voice concerning Jackson during this period came from Thomas P. Abernethy, whose *From Frontier to Plantation in Tennessee: A Study in Frontier Democracy* (1932) insisted that Jackson himself was a frontier aristocrat, an opportunist, and a land speculator who strongly opposed the democratic forces in his own state of Tennessee.

The virtual shattering of the Progressive school's interpretation of Jacksonian Democracy came with the publication of one of the most important historical monographs ever written concerning American history: *The Age of Jackson* (1945), by Arthur M. Schlesinger, Jr. This classic work virtually rivals in importance the frontier thesis of Frederick Jackson Turner. It is a landmark study and represents the beginning of modern scholarship on Jackson and his era.

Schlesinger argued that class distinctions rather than sectional differences best explain the phenomenon of Jacksonian Democracy. He interpreted Jackson's actions and those of his followers as an effort of the less fortunate in American society to combat the power and influence of the business community. The working classes in urban centers as well as the yeoman farmers, he argued, were the true wellsprings of the Jacksonian movement. Jacksonian Democracy evolved from the conflict between classes and best expressed its goals and purposes in the problems and needs facing urban laborers. Schlesinger singled out the bank war as the most telling example of the conflict and as the fundamental key to a fuller understanding of the meaning of Jacksonian Democracy. What attracted many historians to this path-breaking study, besides its graceful and majestic style, was Schlesinger's perceptive definition of Jacksonian Democracy and a precise explanation of its origins.

The reaction to Schlesinger's work was immediate and dramatic. It swept the historical profession like a tornado, eliciting both prodigious praise and within a relatively short time, fierce denunciations. Bray Hammond, in a series of articles as well as his *Banks and Politics in America from the Revolution to the Civil War* (1957), and Richard Hofstadter, in his *The American Political Tradition and the Men Who Made It* (1948), contended that the Jacksonians were not the champions of urban workers or small farmers but rather ambitious and ruthless entrepreneurs principally concerned with advancing their own economic and political advantage. They were "men on the make" and frequently captains of great wealth. According to Hofstadter, the Jacksonians were not so much hostile to business as they were hostile to being excluded from entering the confined arena of capitalists. Where Schlesinger had emphasized conflict in explaining the Jacksonian era, Hofstadter insisted that consensus best characterized the period. The entrepreneurial thesis, as it was called, found strong support among many young scholars who constituted the Columbia University school of historians. In a series of articles and books produced by these critics, Jackson himself was described as an inconsistent opportunist, a strikebreaker, a shady land speculator, and a political fraud. Marvin Meyers, in his *The Jacksonian Persuasion* (1957), provides a slight variation on the entrepreneurial thesis by arguing that Jacksonians did indeed keep their eyes on the main chance but yearned for the virtues of a past agrarian republic. They hungered after the rewards of capitalism but looked back reverentially on the blessings of a simpler agrarian society.

A major redirection of Jacksonian scholarship came with the publication of Lee Benson's *The Concept of Jacksonian Democracy: New York as a Test Case* (1961). This work suggested a whole new approach to the investigation of the Jacksonian age by employing the techniques of quantification to uncover solid, factual data upon which to base an analysis. Moreover, Benson emphasized social questions and found that such things as ethnicity and religion were far more important than economics in determining how a person voted or which party won his allegiance. He dismissed Jacksonian rhetoric about democracy and the rights of the people as "claptrap" and contended that local issues in elections meant more to the voters than national issues. Andrew Jackson himself was dismissed as unimportant in understanding the structure and meaning of politics in this period. In time, some college textbooks virtually eliminated Jackson from any discussion of this period except to mention that he opposed social reforms and that his removal of the Indians was one of the most heinous acts in American history.

An ethnocultural school of historical writing soon emerged that rejected class difference as an important factor in political determinism. German and Irish Catholics, for example, were more likely to vote Democratic because of their ethnicity and religion than anything else. Besides, some argued, Whigs were not materially richer than Democrats. Edward Pessen, in a series of books and articles took the argument one step further and insisted that Jacksonian America was not particularly egalitarian in terms of wealth, as Tocqueville had stated. He rejected the argument that the common man politically came into his own during the Jacksonian age. In a nice turn of phrase concluding his *Jacksonian America: Society, Personality, and Politics* (1969), Pessen declared that there was only "*seeming* deference to the common man by the uncommon men [the rich and powerful] who actually ran things."

By the end of the 1970s the ethnocultural approach had quieted down and was replaced by newer kinds of social analyses, most particularly by cultural Marxists who reemphasized class conflict in understanding voter preference. Other historians took a different approach and sought to describe what might be called a "political culture" for the period. However, many of the insights of Benson and the other students of the ethnocultural school have been incorporated into the whole to form a more sophisticated analysis. Joel Silbey, Sean Wilentz, Harry L. Watson, and others have shown that the electorate normally develops a wide set of values based on class, religion, nationality, family, residence, and several other factors and then invariably votes to safeguard those values as they perceive them. Watson particularly has demonstrated by his study of North Carolina politics that national issues did in fact matter in general elections. Even Jackson has been somewhat restored to his former importance, if not his former heroic stature. My own three-volume life of Old Hickory, *Andrew Jackson and the Course of American Empire, 1767–1821; Andrew Jackson and the Course of American Freedom, 1822–1832; Andrew Jackson and the Course of American Democracy, 1833–1845* (1977, 1981, 1984) highlights Schlesinger's findings and Jackson's faith and commitment to liberty and democracy. I contend that Jackson was in fact a man of the people, just as the Progressive historians had argued, and that he actively attempted to advance democracy by insisting that all branches of government, including the courts, reflect the popular will. I also tried to show that, for a number of reasons, the president's policy of Indian removal was initiated to spare the Indian from certain extinction. And Francis Paul Prucha has argued persuasively that Indian removal was probably the only policy possible under the circumstances.

The study of the Jacksonian era is essential for any serious examination of the evolution of the American presidency. This has been widely recognized since the avalanche of articles and books triggered by the appearance of Schlesinger's monumental work. Jackson himself has never lost his ability to excite the most intense passions and interest among students of American history. No doubt scholars and popular writers will continue to debate his role as a national hero and as an architect of American political institutions.

The Egalitarian Myth and American Social Reality

Edward Pessen

The historical reputation of the Jacksonian era, and a centerpiece of belief about it, have been that it was an especially propitious time for upward social and economic mobility. The resultant notion persists that doors of opportunity swung open ever more widely for common, ordinary folk (exclusive of women, blacks, and Indians). According to the social historian Edward Pessen, late Distinguished Professor of History at Baruch College and the City University of New York Graduate Center, quantitative data evinces slim evidence that equality reigned. Elitism persisted in the Age of the Common Man. It was an age neither "of egalitarianism nor of the Common Man."

The bedrock of the egalitarian theory is the belief that in Jacksonian America a rough equality prevailed. The very first words in Tocqueville's classic set forth this view: "Among the novel objects that attracted my attention during my stay in the United States, nothing struck me more forcibly than the general equality of condition among the people." This equality was not simply one among a number of equally important features of American life. Rather it was "the fundamental fact from which all others seem to be derived and the central point at which all . . . [his] observations constantly terminated." Tocqueville was both too sophisticated and, for all his predilection for theorizing, too observant to believe that wants were satisfied equally here. He spoke, after all, of a general, not an absolute, equality. He allows for differences.

Any attempt, however, to dilute Tocqueville's observation, to water it down to a belief in mere equality of opportunity, flies in the face of his numerous assertions to the contrary. For the United States to him was not simply a manifestation of Benjamin Constant's liberal bourgeois ideal, a society whose "careers were open to talents." What made it a unique society, among other things, was its demo-cratic distribution of life's good things. While riches and poverty existed here as elsewhere, America was marked by the relative absence of extremes. If the social ladder could be easily ascended here, it was due not only to the absence of both aristocratic restraints and a restrictive political order, but ultimately, to an abundance that made all other benefits possible. Many of Tocqueville's contemporaries and later commentators alike, as I mentioned at the outset, shared his belief that an essential equality of condition was the norm.

A strong case can be made, however, that not equality but disparity of condition was the rule in Jacksonian America. It was manifested above all in the nation's cities which were becoming increasingly important in an era marked by a great urban expansion. Old cities grew at an unprecedented rate while new ones were built seemingly overnight. Rochester was not the only city in which tree stumps could be found in the cellars of the buildings that had been put up around them. In the West, too, cities became increasingly important, attracting large amounts of speculative capital, providing their classic economic functions for their hinterlands, and acting as a magnet to settlers, many of whom "came across the

139

mountains in search of promising towns as well as good land." Turner's frontier, as Richard C. Wade has shown, also included Cincinnati, Lexington, Pittsburgh, St. Louis, and Louisville.

The housing of the urban rich, as a case in point, set them apart from the great majority of town dwellers. In western cities choice locations were pre-empted by the well-to-do; "other people moved to less desirable areas." In the East, observers commented on the "genteel dwelling houses [of the rich]," made of fine stone or brick, with white marble increasingly used for doorsteps, window sills, lintels, and entire first stories. Pure silver ornaments and "costly European importations [that] decorated the homes of the rich," led one almost abject admirer of this country to concede that there was something in such refinements "very unlike republican simplicity."

Working people lived very differently. According to Mathew Carey, the wealthy philanthropist, working-class families in Philadelphia were squeezed together, 55 families to a tenement, lacking "the accommodation of a privy for their use." Their houses, according to a recent study, "were strung along, side to side as boxcars . . . obscured from the street view. . . ." Their tenants typically had one room per family, living "huddled to the rear . . . victims of a parsimonious building policy which meant crowding, noise, inadequate sanitation, lack of facilities for rubbish removal." The fresh water newly pumped from the Schuylkill—and which was so admired by many European travelers—went into the homes of the wealthy but not to the working classes. According to the labor press, the major cities of the nation abounded with dismal alleys, "the abodes of the miserable objects of grinding poverty." Andrew Jackson and Nicholas Biddle, on the other hand, could repair to the "Hermitage," outside of Nashville, or "Andalusia," near Philadelphia, similar in their opulence for all the political differences of their owners.

Glaring disparities were not confined to housing alone. If beggars were not readily apparent on the streets, they could be discerned in less public places. Bell had seen "scores of destitute homeless wretches lying on bulks or under the sheds about the markets of New York and Philadelphia." Fellow travelers claimed they saw as much poverty here as elsewhere. Statistical studies confirmed the rising rates of pauperism and of those too poor to pay a minimal tax.

Nor does the evidence indicate that membership these forlorn groups was swelled by the drama failure of eminent men. Rather some poor men came poorer. Imprisonment for debt was also on rise, in some cities evidently accounting for the n jority of men in jail. This abuse was shortly to outlawed, in large part because its negative effe were felt by businessmen as well as by the poor. the Jacksonian era, however, its main victims w men who owed debts of $20 or less. Abject pove was not the characteristic lot of Americans who w not wealthy, but neither was it a negligible proble One labor newspaper edited by the respected Geoi Henry Evans—who was to become "the heart a soul" of the land reform movement of the 1840's estimated that in Boston in 1834 more than 5,0 persons were "aided annually as paupers." The re able Edward Abely reported that not only was pa perism increasing in the nation's major cities, but th "there . . . [was] little reason to hope it . . . [could] checked by the judicious application of charity."

The great bulk of Americans living in towns a cities were neither paupers nor debtors facing ii prisonment. They were for the most part artisans mechanics, to a lesser extent small business peo and less than wealthy professionals. If they did r live in penury, the nation's journeymen lived a worked under conditions of extreme difficulty, removed indeed from the "general equality of con tion" mentioned by visitors who merely glanc their way. For the better part of the period, artisa put in a working day that rivalled the farmers' sunt to sundown. The spectre of unemployment haunt them, particularly in the cold weather months short working days. And when they did work, ar sans were paid in a paper currency that invariat was not worth its face value. They had little to f back on when their shops closed down. In the deca of inflation that preceded the Panic of 1837, worke discovered that their wages did not keep up wi runaway prices. The depression that came on t heels of the Panic kept perhaps one third of t working classes unemployed for long periods in t early 1840's. Quite apart from the depression yea labor fared poorly during the Jacksonian era. Mc modern studies indicate that real wages stood st during an otherwise exuberant economic surge in t 1830's, at best approximating what they had been the turn of the century.

Most Americans during the era were farmers, an estimated two thirds or more of the American working population making its living in agriculture. The income of farmers is notoriously hard to come by. In the case of people who largely consume their own product, income is by no means the most relevant clue to standard of living. Nor is the relatively unrevealing census data for the years before 1840 particularly helpful. And of course there were farmers and farmers, with successful but atypical operators of huge farms and plantations at one extreme and a much larger number of slaves at the other. Wages of farm hands and farm labor were even lower than those earned by urban workers. Impressionistic evidence, in the form of diaries and journals left by moderately successful independent farm families in different sections of the country, suggests the monotony, the hard work and the generally poor quality of life enjoyed by the nation's yeomanry during the era. Thomas Coffin's family in New Hampshire worked hard, lived frugally and had little leisure. Ridding the farm of vermin constituted an amusement or form of recreation for the young. A large farm that was regarded as "fairly well improved," located on one of the "better developed farm communities" in Iredell County, North Carolina, characteristically eked out a living, its "produce yielding only a small return for the work involved, while prices of necessities bought were high." Living conditions were indeed discouraging to men who found that their incomes from sales frequently only balanced their purchases. American farmers in the antebellum period were also convinced that their status was low. The "agrarian myth" that romanticized rural life was either unknown to most farmers or disbelieved by them.

The leaders of the labor organizations that formed several years before the great depression spoke of the daily worsening of the American working man's condition. Most people, they said, would suffer hunger and ruin "if sickness or want of employment should intervene for any length of time." Such sources did not provide an objective study of American conditions, focusing as they did on the grimmer aspects of American life. Yet contemporary reports by government and private sources, accounts by visitors, and modern studies confirm not only the difficult situation faced by most skilled and semiskilled artisans, but the truly dismal lot of most factory operatives.

It was not only radical labor leaders who charged that real equality did not exist in the United States. The point was also made by conservative Americans of the highest standing. John Quincy Adams had told Tocqueville that while in the north there was "a great equality before the law, . . . it ceases absolutely in the habits of life. There are upper classes and working classes." In Philadelphia Tocqueville had been advised by an eminent attorney, "There is more social equality with you at home [in France] than with us. Here . . . wealth gives a decided preeminence." Peter Duponceau confirmed Adams' point "that equality exists only on the street. Money creates extreme inequalities in society." But such comments seem to have made little impression on a mind that was busy creating theories based on very different assumptions. Some years later James Fenimore Cooper would assert that in the United States "inequality . . . [existed] and in some respects, with stronger features than it is usual to meet with in the rest of christendom." Thomas Hamilton would not go so far: the United States was no worse than Britain in this regard. But it was nonsense to call this country the land of equality merely because it lacked a "privileged order." Chevalier, too, impressed as he was by the absence here of aristocratic titles or an idle rich, concluded that great inequalities in income were becoming more and more the rule, dividing society as forcefully as name and land did in Europe. Even Mrs. Trollops, who had been willing to concede an equality of condition for which she had no admiration, came to the conclusion that the American poor were "kept in a state of irritation by feeling that their boasted equality is a falsehood." For all the absence of aristocratic distinctions in this country, it enjoyed only a "fictitious equality."

The case for egalitarianism is a subtle one, depending on a number of propositions that have nothing to do with wealth as such. But its underlying axiom, alleging the slightness of disparities in material condition, does not come off too well. The American rich lived a most distinctive life of relative comfort and splendor that differed dramatically, not only from the lives of the poor, but from the experience of the great majority of ordinary citizens. True, the rich were few in number. Moses Beach's list of New York City's rich men, the Boston list of the most heavily taxed, Philadelphia's roster of wealthy citizens, contained closer to 2 percent than 5 of their cities' populations. But that is precisely the case in most societies marked by inequality. Were the rich more typical, yea-sayers could quite rightly make much of the great amount of room at the top available in the egalitarian society they admire.

The egalitarian theory is also based on certain assumptions concerning social class and its role. It does not deny the existence of classes but rather stresses the ease of movement between them. The term "class" has been variously defined, of course. Sociologists have come to no agreement: one school emphasizing wealth and income; another, occupation; another, family; another, such intangibles as prestige and standing; another, style of life; another, religion and nationality; Miss Nancy Mitford recently redirected attention to the importance of speech; while eclectics have combined some or all of these plus other attributes to fashion their concept of class. In this discussion, the term will assume a group that is distinguished from others mainly by its members' means of making a living, the costliness and quality of the life they command, and the comparative influence and prestige they enjoy.

E. Digby Baltzell has sensibly written that "leadership and some form of stratification are inherent in all human social organization." When we leave the drawing board or the realm of the purely theoretical, there are no classless societies, certainly not in the civilized world. The important questions concerning a society have to do not with whether classes exist, but with the extent of class differences, the relative ease of access to the most favored class, and the degree of power and influence wielded by the latter. Where differences are slight, upward mobility is great, and power is with the middling orders, the society can properly be adjudged socially democratic. Jacksonian society, of course, enjoys just such a reputation.

The case for social fluidity, as might have been expected, was put most forcefully by Tocqueville. "In America," he wrote, "most of the rich men were formerly poor." It is a striking idea, of profound importance, not least because for later periods in American history it does not seem to be true. Stephan Thernstrom's recent study of working people in the Massachusetts town of Newburyport, for the period 1850 to 1880, shows that while parents were pleased at the rise to more prestigious working-class occupations that was made by some of their sons, no dramatic movement to the top took place. Earlier studies

of the social backgrounds of rich men of the late 19th and 20th centuries disclosed that, for the most part, they were sons of men of unusual wealth, prestige, education, favored religious denomination and other attributes of high rank. If Tocqueville was right, then the Jacksonian era stands alone for the 19th century. He may yet turn out to be right, but unfortunately his assertions are based not on substantial evidence, but rather on his own deductions, largely from what one informant told him concerning the disappearance of the law of entail in this country.

Of course the egalitarian thesis does not depend on so exaggerated a statement as Tocqueville's. If a substantial minority of the rich were born poor, America would have been unusual enough. To date, however, claims to an amazing social fluidity have not been substantiated. As always, Tocqueville's logic was excellent, for certainly it followed that in a dynamic social democracy, "the conditions of life are very fluctuating, men have almost always recently acquired the advantages which they possess. . . . [A]t any moment the same advantages may be lost." The fact was, however, that the United States and his ideal democracy were two most unlike things. Buckingham may have been closer to the mark when he wrote that "the greater number [of America's social elite] . . . inherit land, or houses, or stock, from their parents."

Alexandra McCoy's recent study of Wayne County, Michigan, for the latter part of the Jacksonian era, defines mobility as "the achievement of wealth by men of lower class origins," and finds very little evidence of the phenomenon. The economic elite of that important area were not self-made men. Like the successful men of a half century later, shown by William Miller and his students to be fortunate sons of wealthy fathers, Wayne County's rich seem to have "enjoyed an advantaged early environment to enable them to start a business in the west." Plebeians could not afford the five or six thousand dollars required. If the wealthy were born of the rich, they also tended to remain in that closed circle. "Those [in Wayne County] who were at the top in 1844 tended to stay there. Only one took a fall." The eminent modern historian, Oscar Handlin, long ago disclosed that Boston in the 1830's and 1840's "offered few opportunities to those who lacked the twin advantages of birth and capital." Boston was not unique.

A wide gulf existed between the classes. At the top of the urban social structure was an upper crust, some of whose members came of old family and long-established wealth, others of whom were considered parvenu and shunned by their social betters. Both groups lived and moved in a world apart from the one inhabited by those below. One informant told Tocqueville that rich Americans might be democratic enough to receive a man of talent but they would make him aware that he was not rich and refuse to receive his wife and children. Large merchants scorned small, while in a number of cities merchants of any sort would receive neither mechanics nor their children.

Richard Wade has shown that even in the youthful cities of the West, at the beginning of the era, merchants made up a distinctively wealthy and socially prominent group. "Their wives belonged to the same clubs, their children went to the same schools, and they participated in the same amusements and recreations." They lived in their own districts, physically separated from others; "by 1830, social lines could be plotted on a map of the city." They went to great pains to match the lavish living of the older upper classes of the eastern cities, succeeding to a large degree. Many of them lived in "villas." Expensive furniture, overloaded tables, fancy dress for dinner, extravagant entertainment, elegant carriages, ornate cotillions led by dancing masters imported from the East, characterized merchant life in the "frontier towns." Wade notes dryly that in the first decades of the 19th century, "local boosters talked a great deal about egalitarianism in the West, but urban practice belied the theory. Social lines developed very quickly and although never drawn as tightly as in Eastern cities, they denoted meaningful distinctions." Vigne found "an aristocracy in every city of the Union; and perhaps as many as four or five different sects or circles, notwithstanding their boasted equality of condition." Logan would have reduced the number of elite strata to three.

The behavior of the eastern social elite was vividly, in some cases ludicrously, influenced by class bias. Grund found that it was not simply that the fashionable would not mingle with the vulgar. In Boston, good society would not permit itself to be seen publicly. Women of society, more expert than men in the finer points of snobbishness, curtsied according to their wealth or circumstances. Not only was seating in theatres arranged according to class, applause was given by class. Class distinction was worse here than in England, it was said, manifesting

itself in exquisite attention to nuances. Thus the "second society" of Boston—itself unacceptable to the first—with a vulgarity peculiar to itself, in turn displayed contempt for its inferiors. The fine gradations within society were of a complexity that only a mathematician could analyze. Grund found such behavior repellent but he did not think it was confined to Boston. Other visitors, while conceding the pretentiousness of Boston and even of New York, gave the nod to Philadelphia as the most exclusive of American cities. Bell was told that there were "nine or ten distinct ranks in the city, beginning at the lower class of traders and ending in the dozen or so who keep . . . a large establishment; each of these circles, repelling and repelled, carefully keeps itself apart, and draws a line that no one of doubtful status may pass." Murray believed that these lines were drawn tighter than ever. Even Tocqueville made the uncharacteristic admission, at the close of his second chapter, that "the picture of American society has . . . a surface covering of democracy, beneath which the old aristocratic colors sometimes peep out."

Americans, too, were aware that class distinctions were important here. In *Home As Found*, Cooper wrote a biting satire directed in part against the varieties of class snobbishness practiced in American cities and villages. In western cities, "people felt them [distinctions] and contemporaries thought them important." Contemporaries, of course, thought a variety of things, their viewpoints about class running the gamut from denial of its existence to enthusiastic recognition of class division. A few would maintain, even try to widen, the existing cleavage. The era's workingmen's parties and trade unions were led by men who believed that America was torn by class conflict. According to the labor spokesmen, the capitalist's attempt to beguile workers into the false belief that social harmony prevailed here was only a stratagem in the unremitting, if subtle, class warfare waged by the rich. In view of upper class control of the major parties, the press, and all other influential institutions, workers had no alternative to recognizing the harsh fact of American life: that class conflict existed here. Labor's way out was not to deny the fact but to accept it and rely on its own efforts in order to change it. Since most of the labor radicals had earned leadership in their movement precisely because their views were well known, it would appear they spoke not for themselves alone but at least in part for their memberships.

That some persons evidently believed American society was under the tight control of a small upper class is more a sign of the proneness of zealots to exaggerate than of anything else. The charge was poorly documented, flies in the face of good sense, and cannot be taken seriously—except as a clue to the state of mind of those who believed it. In the latter sense, however, it was significant testimony that many of the nation's workingmen believed America to be a class society dominated by a powerful few. While extant evidence proves nothing so extreme, it does appear to show that wealthy men commanded an inordinate political influence over American society.

The egalitarian theory is in part based on the belief that the common man dominated Jacksonian politics. Popular suffrage meant to Tocqueville the "sovereignty of the people. . . . The people reign in the American political world," he wrote, "as the Deity does in the universe." Chevalier called America a "popular despotism." By this theory of politics, near oligarchies which regularly send 95 percent or better of their citizenry to the polls, are actually ruled by their voters. It is not necessary to subscribe to an ultrarealist view of politics to detect the naïveté in such an analysis.

In Jacksonian America, the common man's possession of the suffrage subjected him to much flattery by political leaders, for it is quite true that his votes decided whether this or that one would take office. (Tocqueville, who was no great admirer of the common man, hoped that direct elections would be increasingly replaced by indirect ones, thus minimizing the dangers of the manhood suffrage.) In his brilliant book of two decades ago, Arthur M. Schlesinger, Jr., synthesized, updated, and gave new life to a traditional interpretation which held that since the party battles of the era were fought over great social and economic principles, the common man's choice of Jackson over his enemies was fraught with crucial political significance and was as well a demonstration of popular power. That is not the view, however, of many of the excellent studies of the past 20 years. They tell a tale of major parties during the Jacksonian era, which, for all the difference in their political rhetoric, were more like than unlike, not least in the extent to which their basic structures and policymaking apparatus were controlled by unusually wealthy men.

How much power could the common man exer-

cise when there was little real choice left open to him by the parties that counted? In the states, small groups of insiders had a tight control over nominations and policymaking, with popular influence more nominal than real. Whether in New York or Mississippi, Pennsylvania or South Carolina, Michigan or New Jersey, Massachusetts or Florida, Tennessee or Ohio, Democratic leaders, more often than not, were speculators, editors, lawyers, the "land office crowd," coming from the "wealthier elements in the society," typically of the same economic background as their Whig opponents. For that matter, Andrew Jackson himself, not to mention the men who launched him in presidential politics, were uncommonly wealthy. As Robert V. Remini has noted, "it cost a great deal of money to enter politics." Jackson may have spoken in ringing terms of the common man's right to high office, as well as his ability to perform its tasks, but in point of fact Jackson, like his "aristocratic" predecessors, filled Cabinet and high civil service posts with men who possessed unusual wealth and social eminence. This is not to say that the era's leaders dealt with political issues primarily in terms of class interest. Rich men no more than poor live by bread alone. It is not farfetched, however, to interpret the lack of real issues on the national level in the decade of the 1820's, or the ambiguity of issues in the subsequent decades of the Jacksonian era, as due in part to the backgrounds of the era's leaders.

Wealth exerted political power most directly on the local level. At a time when local boards of government typically received small salaries or none at all, wealthy merchants sat in the seats of municipal power, determining policies and expenditures. The way of life of the town dweller was significantly affected by upper class decisions to build wharves or expensive market houses rather than improve the night watch or drain pools. Robert Dahl's recent study of New Haven politics underscores these points. In that small eastern city, prior to 1842, "public office was almost the exclusive prerogative of the patrician families. . . . Wealth, social position and education" were the main determinants of patrician status. During this period, according to Dahl, control over such a factor as wealth enabled the individual who enjoyed it, to "be better off in almost every other resource"—such as "social standing and control over office." The prime beneficiaries of this "cumulative inequality" were the old merchant elite. A revolution of sorts was to take place in 1842 with the election of a wealthy manufacturer to the office of mayor, ushering "in a period during which wealthy entrepreneurs dominated public life almost without interruption for more than half a century." I am not sure whether the Jacksonian era was still in force when new wealth replaced older in the City Hall of New Haven, but in the one case as in the other, working people and so-called "ethnic groups" made up nothing better than a passive electorate. Until well after the middle of the 19th century, the city's aldermen continued to be composed almost entirely of wealthy professionals and businessmen in the entrepreneurial as during the patrician phase of their city's political evolution. Nor was New Haven atypical. Elite upper classes controlled mayors' offices and municipal councils or boards of aldermen in New York City and Boston as well as in Detroit and the cities of the South and West for most of the era.

The Jacksonian era witnessed no breakdown of a class society in America. If anything, class lines hardened, distinctions widened, tensions increased. Wade noted that while, with the passage of time, "new families entered the circle [of the merchant elite] and older ones fell out," there was also a "heightened . . . sense of separateness, . . . the circle itself becoming tighter and more distinct." Communities already stratified, "found lines sharpened, class division deepened," as they grew in size and as their economies became more specialized. The wealthiest merchants, according to the testimony of their own diaries and of travelers' accounts, became even more class conscious. Their children had absorbed so well the lesson of social exclusiveness that, if anything, they "moved in an even more insulated circle than their parents." In eastern cities it has also been noted that social stratification intensified during the Jacksonian era.

Has the time not come, then, to discard the label, the Era of the Common Man? Like its companion designation, the Age of Egalitarianism, it has rested on questionable assumptions. Struck by surface examples of popular influence or by the absence of aristocratic titles in America, we have jumped to unwarranted conclusions. The absence of a caste system has been interpreted as though it denoted the absence of a class system. It is true that, theoretically, individuals could move freely up the social ladder, actually doing so if they had the talent and good fortune. But these restless men on the make should

not be confused with the bulk of the nation's workingmen or small farmers. An expanding capitalistic society everywhere dips into the less privileged strata to provide some of the manpower it requires for entrepreneurial leadership. There is no evidence, however, that during the Jacksonian era the poor made dramatic movement up the social ladder in greater numbers than they made the move westward to Turner's frontier and its alleged safety valve.

The belief that the era was dominated by the common man has rested on political assumptions that have been pretty well demolished. That white men without property had won the right to vote, even before Andrew Jackson stood for the presidency, is something that every politician knew. Shrewd men in politics, therefore, paid lip service to the common man, managing to explain their own origins, their careers, and their political beliefs in terms that were highly flattering to Tom, Dick, and Harry. Though Jackson spoke of turning high office over to ordinary men, he did not do so. The men surrounding the Old General, like those who ran his party on the state level, were decidedly uncommon or wealthy. Common men there were in abundance. That pragmatists in high places addressed them artfully, however, is less proof that the common man held power than that skillful politicians knew how to delude him into believing that he did.

An age is not ordinarily named after its most typical members, regardless of their real power. For if it were, almost every age would have to be known as the era of the ordinary man. Whatever it might have been, the era named after Andrew Jackson was neither an age of egalitarianism nor of the common man. . . .

The era that bears his name was not really the age of Jackson. The label has been attached too long for it to be torn off, however, and it continues to be most satisfactory to a people who like to think their history was made by mythic figures of heroic stature who imposed their will on their times. Were the name of an era determined by a scholarly process that assigned a proper weight to all the relevant factors that shaped it, it would be apparent that no individual, not even Andrew Jackson, dominated the period 1825 to 1845. Certainly he was not the typical man of the time. For all his towering personality, his own and his party's influence even on the politics of the period have been exaggerated. That in hundreds of places the name Jackson was invoked by men eager to win office bespeaks not real influence so much as the power of propaganda and popular hero worship. The notion that the era was his has also rested on a belief that an indissoluble bond connected the Hero and the common man, to whom Jacksonian Democracy ostensibly gave power. But in fact Jacksonian Democracy gave power not to Tom, Dick, and Harry but to the shrewd, ambitious, wealthy, and able politicians who knew best how to flatter them.

Nor was it the age of the common man. If talk alone determined the character of an era then there would be much reason to think that it was. Politicians who sought the common man's vote bombarded him with praise. Romantic artists, whether using pen or brush, extolled his simplicity and his innate wisdom. The American style of life, for all its unloveliness, seemed to be shaped by his mannerisms, his interests, his limitations. Scandalmongering journalism, coarse public manners, the frenzied pursuit of things, the indifference to learning and unconcern with quality, were only some of the characteristics of American civilization that bore the stamp of the ordinary man. Since it was primarily the surface aspect of things that he influenced most—precisely those phenomena that caught the eye of outsiders passing through—visitors understandably concluded that here the common man was sovereign. But he was not.

Political authority belonged not to him but to the uncommon men who typically controlled the major parties at every level. It goes without saying that unusual men will emerge as leaders, even in the most democratic society conceivable. The era's political leaders were distinctive, however, not only in their ability but also in the possession of status and wealth that were unrepresentative of the mass of men. The seats of power in society and the economy were also filled by men whose origins and outlook were not plebeian. Self-made men *were* in greater abundance here than in the Old World. The relative absence of a feudal tradition meant that in the 1830's as before, individual Americans of whatever origins might move to positions of eminence that in Europe were unattainable to men of like background. But their numbers were not legion. The weight of the evidence is that family ties and a form of nepotism played an important part in singling out fortune's favorites. Andrew Jackson's own political appointments were heavily influenced by such considerations.

The era's egalitarianism seems also to have been more apparent than real. American farmers and working men *were* better off than their European counterparts. Their material condition was superior as were their opportunities, their status, and their influence. Yet this remained a class society. The small circles that dominated the life in the great cities of the East as well as the new towns of the West, lived lives of relative opulence, while socially during the Jacksonian era they became, if anything, more insulated against intrusion by the lower orders. Social lines were drawn even tighter in the slave states. For all the era's egalitarian reputation, evidence is lacking that movement up the social ladder was any more commonplace than it was in subsequent periods of American life; eras whose reputations for social fluidity have been largely deflated by modern empirical studies that characteristically reveal that the race was to the well born. Tocqueville's influential insight that the American rich man was typically born poor was not a conclusion drawn from evidence but an undocumented inference, characteristic of the brilliant French visitor's flair for generalizing from unproven assumptions. James Fenimore Cooper and Michel Chevalier were among the contemporaries who observed that money increasingly tended to be concentrated in relatively few hands, widening the gulf between classes for all the brave talk to the contrary.

It is impossible to know whether people believed that their chances for success were as great as some contemporaries claimed they were. Certainly most Americans seemed to throw themselves into the race for gain, undeterred by religious enthusiasms which cheerfully approved worldly success. Materialism and a love of money were perhaps their most noticeable traits. An ambivalence may be detected in the fact that while the nation participated in a speculative orgy whose goals were selfish and material, reform movements designed to enhance the quality of American life and end social injustice, also flourished. But the two "movements" had different memberships. The movements to uplift slaves, the poor, and the conditions of the weak have caught the eye of scholars—themselves relatively perfectionist when their values are compared to those of more unreflective men. The reform cause was not insignificant. But it was led and kept alive by unusual men whose values were outside the mainstream of American life. The mass of Americans seemed far more interested in personal enrichment than in moral uplift.

The depression that followed the great panic at

the end of the 1830's temporarily halted the economic growth that had moved the young nation into a prominent place in the world economy. It also dampened if it did not completely suppress the exuberant mood that characterized the earlier period. Optimism had by no means been totally misplaced. The great enhancement of profit-making opportunities only reflected solid advances in the nation's technology, its agricultural and industrial capacity, and above all in the scope and quality of its internal transportation system. Currency was a problem to a country whose opportunities far outstripped its gold supply and whose urge to profit was so overwhelming. Americans, said by discerning observers to value quantity over quality, were content to use vast amounts of paper currency as though it were solid coin. In the absence of sufficient precious metals, the system was not without redeeming social value. Yet it was a precarious one. In a sense, the great Bank War represented the brushing aside of an agency that would restrain the flood of paper desired by the community of profit seekers, although Jackson had not intended such a result.

The nation's modern political system was born during the era, reflecting beautifully the traits of the people it served. Dominated by pragmatic parties which placed electoral success above principle while managing to remain distinctive from one another—in part because of differences in policy as well as in style—it was marked by extravagant campaign techniques, sordid manipulation, brilliant organization, marvelous rhetorical flourishes and a degree of popular participation that were unknown on the Continent. It was not as democratic a system as it seemed, however. Not only were large numbers denied the suffrage by virtue of sex or color, but astute party managers devised ways of confining real control to small cliques of insiders, just as corporate managers would later use widespread stock ownership as a means of tightening their control over business organizations. While the rhetorical excesses of demagogues had little relationship to their parties' actual achievements, real issues were not altogether avoided, in part because of the clamor of dissenters. Characteristically the great parties dealt with the great issues not by meeting them squarely but by indirection.

Tocqueville thought that the American people were essentially conservative. For all their restless temper, their hunger to change both their lot and their locales, they had no interest in drastic alteration of their society. They loved change (in their personal status) but dreaded revolution. The American exceptions to this rule were fascinating but in view of their small numbers and unrepresentativeness, their influence was slight. The dominant values, like the dominant political, economic, and social tendencies of the Jacksonian era, were essentially conservative. Moralistic dissenters, unhappy with the era's prevalent opportunism, like social radicals displeased with its inequality, got equally short shrift.

It is undoubtedly too late to try to change the name of the Jacksonian era. If it could be done, my idea of a new label would not be a catchy one. For one thing the era was too heterogeneous to be captured by any simple rubric. If the attempt were made nevertheless to capture its spirit in a phrase, there is something to be said for calling it an age of materialism and opportunism, reckless speculation and erratic growth, unabashed vulgarity, and a politic *seeming* deference to the common man by the uncommon men who actually ran things.

IV

Myths of Sectionalism, Slavery, and Expansionism

"The South" is more than a geographical expression. It denotes a recognition that the region is different from the rest of the nation—"Uncle Sam's other province," as the poet Allen Tate once put it; "not a nation within a nation, but the next thing to it," to quote Wilbur Cash. A theory holds that a sense of regional difference between North and South may have begun around the time of the Revolution. A more conventional idea has it that southern regional identity, and the cultural configuration of Cavalier and Yankee, are largely the product of the political and social conflict from about 1820 to 1861, the age of the sectional controversies of the pre–Civil War decades. Whenever the moment the South as an entity appeared, it gradually became a section convinced that it was cultivating both a way of life and a mind of its own. It remains a region struck by a sense of its uniqueness—proud of its distinctive past, its tragic yet heroic traditions, and its special taste for ceremonial style and public ritual. Burdened with a history of frustration, poverty, defeat, and guilt, born of the inheritance of slavery and racial prejudice, in a nation optimistically addicted to wealth, victory, and assumed innocence, the southern sectional imagination has made even defeat itself, the Lost Cause, the occasion of myth.

The antebellum view of a hospitable and mannered society populated by contented blacks, aristocratic cavaliers, and virtuous belles came to supplant the South's true historical experience. As the historian Vernon Louis Parrington has said:

> A golden light still lingers upon the old plantation. Memories are still too dear to the Virginian to suffer any lessening of the reputed splendor of antebellum days. The tragedy of a lost cause has woven itself into the older romance and endowed the tradition with an added sanction. It has long since spread beyond the confines of Virginia and become a national possession. North as well as South is so firmly convinced of its authenticity that realism has never had the temerity to meddle with it.

Another mythic South meanwhile was forming, notably in the rich imagination of William Faulkner: a South soaked in guilt and blood, secret in half-knowledge of crimes against slaves, and of families of mixed race. These southerners have lived with guilt in a fierce, defiant pride. It was their unique lot, in the case of some of them, to overcome it—not with the bright confidence of liberal rationalism but with so massive an acceptance of the region's wrong, brave, loyal past as to hope to receive, someday, a specific redemption, their fate, fixed in the inseparability of the two tortured and mutually torturing people. The Faulknerian myth is myth in the best sense, not a slick and selective exaltation of history but the imaginative drawing from history of genuinely dark and redemptively moral and courageous components, which the mythmaker arranges in poetic or dramatic economy.

Uncle Tom's Cabin: Mythic Tableau of the Antebellum South. *(Courtesy, Library of Congress)*

The Cherokee Trail of Tears. *(Courtesy, Library of Congress)*

William Sidney Mount, *The Banjo Player.*
(Courtesy, Museum at Stony Brook)

Isabella Van Wagner as "Sojourner Truth."
(Courtesy, Library of Congress)

Southern Indians and the Myth of True Womanhood

Theda Perdue

At least one useful means of dealing with American Indians in a more historically sensitive fashion is to transcend myth and stereotype by acknowledging significant cultural differences among distinct Indian groups. The study of southern Indians offers a case in point: Their cultural experience differs markedly from that of native Americans of, say, the Plains or the Southwest. Using the specific case of the Cherokee as the focus of her study, Professor Theda Perdue of the University of Kentucky examines the self-directed cultural transformation of the tribe from a matriarchy to a form that embraced the developing central white myth of "the cult of true womanhood." Cherokee culture was co-opted by this mythic cult purveyed by Protestant missionaries and government officials precisely because it appeared to be to the Cherokees' practical advantage—cultural harmony with the majority white culture—to adopt it. The ideology of women's "separate sphere" was so powerful a cultural myth in the nineteenth century as to encourage these Indians to refashion their culture in the image of another.

Southern Indians stand apart culturally and historically from other native Americans. Building of temple mounds, an elaborate ceremonial life, a complex belief system, riverine agriculture, and matrilineal descent characterized their aboriginal culture. Southern Indians embraced European culture with such enthusiasm and success that they came to be known as the "five civilized tribes." They acquired this sobriquet in the half-century after the ratification of the United States Constitution, a time when many southern Indians came to believe that their physical survival depended on adopting an Anglo-American lifestyle and value system. These Indians gradually abandoned hunting and subsistence agriculture, the practice of blood vengeance, their traditional religious beliefs and practices, and other aspects of their aboriginal way of life. Some individual Indians succeeded so well that they became culturally indistinguishable from their white neighbors. They owned large plantations, operated successful businesses, attended Christian churches, promoted formal legal and judicial systems, and wrote and conversed in the English language.

An integral part of this cultural transformation was redefinition of gender roles. Just as men could no longer follow their aboriginal pursuits of hunting and warfare, women could no longer behave in what was perceived to be a "savage" or "degraded" way. Instead, they had to attempt to conform to an Anglo-American ideal characterized by purity, piety, domesticity, and submissiveness. By the second quarter of the nineteenth century, the glorification of this ideal had become so pervasive in American society that the historian Barbara Welter has called it the "cult of true womanhood." A true woman was essentially spiritual rather than physical. She occupied a separate sphere apart from the ambition, selfishness, and materialism that permeated the man's world of business and politics. Her proper place was the home, and because of her spiritual nature, she imbued her home with piety, morality, and love. The home was a haven from the outside world, and in its operation a true woman should excel. Openly submissive to men, a true woman influenced them subtly through her purity and piety.

Traditionally southern Indians had a very different view of womanhood. Indian women occupied a separate sphere from that of men, but they had considerable economic, political, and social importance. While men hunted and went to war, women collected firewood, made pottery and baskets, sewed clothes, cared for children, and cooked the family's food. These tasks certainly fell within the nineteenth-century definition of domesticity, but the sphere of Indian women extended beyond home and hearth to encompass economic activities that seemed far less appropriate to their sex. In particular, women farmed in a society that depended primarily on agriculture for subsistence, and women performed most of the manual labor with men assisting only in clearing fields and planting corn. This inequitable division of labor elicited comments from most Euro-American observers. In 1775, Bernard Romans described the women he encountered on a journey through east and west Florida: "Their strength is great, and they labor hard, carrying very heavy burdens great distance." On his 1797 tour of the Cherokee country, Louis-Philippe, who later would become king of France, observed: "The Indians have all the work done by women. They are assigned not only household tasks; even the corn, peas, beans, and potatoes are planted, tended, and preserved by the women." in the economy of southern Indians, therefore, women did what Euro-Americans considered to be work—they farmed—while men did what was considered sport—they hunted.

This arrangement was amazing in that women did not seem to object to doing most of the work. In the early nineteenth century, a missionary commented on the willingness with which the women toiled: "Though custom attached the heaviest part of the labor of the women, yet they were cheerful and voluntary in performing it. What others have discovered among the Indians I cannot tell, but though I have been about nineteen years among the Cherokees, I have perceived nothing of that slavish, servile fear, on the part of women, so often spoke of." One reason women may have worked so gladly was that they received formal recognition for their economic contribution and they controlled the fruit of

their labor. In the Green Corn Ceremony, the southern Indians' most important religious event, women ritually presented the new crop, which was sacrificed to the fire, and when Europeans occasionally purchased corn from Indians in the eighteenth century, they bought it from women. Women may also have labored without complaint because farming was one of the determinants of gender. Southern Indians distinguished between the sexes on other than merely biological grounds. Women were women not only because they could bear children but because they farmed, and men who farmed came to be regarded sexualiy as women. Men hunted, therefore, because hunting was intrinsically linked to male sexuality; women farmed because farming was one of the characteristics that made them women.

The matrilocal residence pattern of southern Indians probably contributed to the association of women and agriculture. A man lived in the household of his wife's lineage, and buildings, garden plots, and sections of the village's common field belonged to her lineage. A man had no proprietary interest in the homestead where he lived with his wife or in the land his wife farmed. Nor was a husband necessarily a permanent resident in the household of his wife's lineage. Polygamy was common, and he might divide his time between the lineages of his wives. Furthermore, southeastern Indians frequently terminated their marriages, and in the event of divorce, a man simply left his wife's household and returned to his mother's house and his own lineage. Because southeastern indians were also matrilineal, that is, they traced kinship only through the female line, children belonged to the mother's lineage and clan rather than to the father's, and when divorce occurred, they invariably remained with their mothers. Men, therefore, had no claim on the houses they lived in or the children they fathered.

John Lawson tried to explain matrilineal lineage, which he considered an odd way of reckoning kin, by attributing it to "fear of Imposters; the Savages knowing well, how much Frailty possesses *Indian* women, betwixt the Garters and the Girdle." Women in southern Indian tribes did enjoy considerable sexual freedom. Except for restraints regarding incest and menstrual taboos, Indian women were relatively free in choosing sexual partners, engaging in intercourse, and dissolving relationships. All southern Indians condoned premarital sex and divorce, which were equally female or male prerogatives, but atti-

tudes toward adultery varied from one tribe to another.

Indian women usually displayed a sense of humor and a lack of modesty regarding sexual matters.
One member of Lawson's expedition took an Indian
"wife" for a night. The couple consummated their
marriage in a room occupied by other members of
the company and guests at the wedding feast. In the
morning the groom discovered that both his bride
and his shoes were gone. So brazen and skilled were
most Cherokee women that Louis-Philippe concluded that "no Frenchwomen could teach them a
thing." When his guide made sexual advances to
several Cherokee women in a house they visited, he
recorded in his journal that "they were so little embarrassed that one of them who was lying on a bed
put her hand on his trousers before my eyes and said
scornfully, *Ah, sick.*"

Compared to the other southern Indians, Louis-
Philippe decided, the Cherokees were "exceeding
casual" about sex. Although all southern Indians had
certain common characteristics—they were matrilineal and matrilocal, women farmed, and both sexes
enjoyed some sexual freedom—Cherokee women
had the highest degree of power and personal autonomy. The trader James Adair maintained that the
Cherokees "have been a considerable while under a
petticoat-government." In Cherokee society, women
spoke in council and determined the fate of war
captives. Some even went on the warpath and earned
a special title, "War Woman." In fact, Cherokee
women were probably as far from the "true women"
of the early nineteenth-century ideal as any women
Anglo-Americans encountered on the continent.
When the United States government and Protestant
missionaries undertook the "civilization" of native
Americans in the late eighteenth century, however,
the Cherokees proved to be the most adept at transforming their society. Because the Cherokees provide
the greatest contrast between the aboriginal role of
women and the role that emerged in the early nineteenth century as a consequence of civilization, I will
examine the impact of the cult of true womanhood
on the status of Cherokee women.

Until the late eighteenth century, Europeans had
few relations with Cherokee women other than sexual ones. Europeans were primarily interested in
Indian men as warriors and hunters and considered
women to be of little economic or political significance. After the American Revolution, native alli-

ances and the deerskin trade diminished in importance. All the Indians still had that Europeans valued
was land. George Washington and his advisers devised a plan which they believed would help the
Indians recover economically from the depletion of
their hunting grounds and the destruction experienced during the Revolution while making large
tracts of Indian land available for white settlement.
They hoped to convert the Indians into farmers living
on isolated homesteads much like white frontiersmen. With hunting no longer part of Indian economy, the excess land could be ceded to the United
States and opened to whites.

The Cherokees traditionally had lived in large
towns located along rivers. These towns were composed of many matrilineal households containing
several generations. A woman was rarely alone: her
mother, sisters, and daughters, with their husbands,
lived under the same roof, and other households
were nearby. Beyond the houses lay large fields
which the women worked communally. Originally,
these towns had served a defensive purpose, but in
the warfare of the eighteenth century, they became
targets of attack. In the French and Indian War
and the American Revolution, soldiers invaded the
Cherokee country and destroyed towns and fields.
As a result, Cherokees began abandoning their towns
even before the United States government inaugurated the civilization program. When a government
agent toured the Cherokee Nation in 1796, he passed
a number of deserted towns; at one site he found a
"hut, some peach trees and the posts of a town
house," and at another there was only a "small field
of corn, some peach, plumb and locust trees."

Agents appointed to implement the civilization
program encouraged this trend. They advised the
Cherokee to "scatter from their towns and make
individual improvements also of cultivating more
land for grain, cotton &c. than they could while
crowded up in towns." The Cherokees complied:
"They dispersed from their large towns,—built convenient houses,—cleared and fenced farms, and soon
possessed numerous flocks and herds." By 1818 missionaries complained that "there is no place near us
where a large audience can be collected as the people
do not live in villages, but scattered over the country
from 2 to 10 miles apart." The breaking up of Cherokee towns resulted in a very isolated existence for
women because new households often consisted of
only one nuclear family. This isolation occurred just

at the time when the work load of women was increasing.

In a letter of 1796, George Washington advised the Cherokees to raise cattle, hogs, and sheep. He pointed out that they could increase the amount of corn they produced by using plows and that they could also cultivate wheat and other grains. Apparently addressing the letter to the men, Washington continued: "To these you will easily add flax and cotton which you may dispose of to the White people, or have it made up by your own women into clothing for yourselves. Your wives and daughters can soon learn to spin and weave." Washington apparently knew nothing about traditional gender roles, and the agents he sent usually had little sympathy for the Indian division of labor. They provided plows to the men and instructed them in clearing fields, tilling soil, and building fences. Women received cotton cards, spinning wheels, and looms.

The women, politically ignored in the eighteenth century and bypassed in the earlier hunting economy, welcomed the opportunity to profit from contact with whites. In 1796, agent Benjamin Hawkins met with a group of Cherokee women and explained the government's plan. He reported to Washington that "they rejoiced much at what they had heard and hoped it would prove true, that they had made some cotton, and would make more and follow the instruction of the agent and the advice of the President." According to a Cherokee account, the women proved far more receptive to the civilization program than the men: "When Mr. Dinsmore, the Agent of the United States, spoke to us on the subject of raising livestock and cotton, about fifteen years ago, many of us thought it was only some refined scheme calculated to gain an influence over us, rather than to ameliorate our situation, and slighted his advice and proposals; he then addressed our women, and presented them with cotton seeds for planting; and afterwards with cards, wheels and looms to work it. They acquired the use of them with great facility, and now most of the clothes we wear are of their manufacture." Two censuses conducted in the early nineteenth century reveal the extent to which women accepted their new tasks. In 1810 there were 1,600 spinning wheels and 467 looms in the Cherokee Nation; by 1826 there were 2,488 wheels and 762 looms.

In 1810, one Cherokee man observed that the women had made more progress toward civilization than the men: "The females have however made much greater advances in industry than the males; they now manufacture a great quantity of cloth; but the latter have not made proportionate progress in agriculture; however, they raise great herds of cattle, which can be done with little exertion." At the same time, women continued to do most of the farming, and many even raised livestock for market. This extension of woman's work concerned government agents because many men were not acquiring the work habits considered essential to "civilized" existence. They had not been able to accomplish a shift in gender roles merely by introducing the tools and techniques of Western culture. Gender roles as well as many other aspects of Cherokee culture proved extremely difficult to change.

Cultural change came more easily, however, among Cherokees who already had adopted the acquisitive, materialistic value system of white Americans. Turning from an economy based on hunting, they took advantage of the government's program and invested in privately owned agricultural improvements and commercial enterprises. They quickly became an economic elite separated from the majority of Cherokees by their wealth and by their desire to emulate whites. In the early nineteenth century, members of this economic elite rose to positions of leadership in the Cherokee Nation because of the ease and effectiveness with which they dealt with United States officials. Gradually they transformed Cherokee political institutions into replicas of those of the United States. This elite expected Cherokee women to conform to the ideals of the cult of true womanhood, that is, to be sexually pure, submissive to fathers and husbands, concerned primarily with spiritual and domestic matters, and excluded from politics and economic activities outside the home. In 1818, Charles Hicks, who later would become principal chief, described the most prominent men in the nation as "those who have kept their women & children at home & in comfortable circumstances." Submissive, domestic wives were a mark of prominence.

Cherokees learned to be true women primarily through the work of Protestant missionaries whom tribal leaders welcomed to the nation. In 1800 the Moravians arrived to open a school, and in the second decade of the nineteenth century Congregationalists supported by the interdenominational American Board of Commissioners for Foreign Missions, Baptists, and Methodists joined them. Except for the Methodists, missionaries preferred to teach children in boarding schools, where they had "the influence of example as well as precept." In 1819 President James Monroe visited the American Board's Brainerd mission and approved "of the plan of instruction; particularly as the children were taken into the family, taught to work, &c." This was, the president believed, "the best, & perhaps the only way to civilize and Christianize the Indians." For female students, civilization meant becoming true women.

Mission schools provided an elementary education for girls as well as boys. Either single women or the wives of male missionaries usually taught the girls, but all students studied the same academic subjects, which included reading, writing, spelling, arithmetic, geography, and history. Examinations took place annually and were attended by parents. The teachers questioned students in their academic subjects as well as Bible history, catechism, and hymns, and "the girls showed specimens of knitting, spinning, mending, and fine needlework."

Mastery of the domestic arts was an essential part of the girls' education because, according to one missionary, "all the females need is a proper education to be qualified to fill any of the relations or stations of domestic life." The children at the mission schools performed a variety of tasks, and the division of labor approximated that in a typical Anglo-American farming family. The boys chopped wood and plowed fields, and the girls milked, set tables, cooked meals, washed dishes, sewed clothing, knitted, quilted, did laundry, and cleaned the houses. Because their fathers were wealthy, many students were not accustomed to such menial labor. Missionaries endeavored to convince them that "the charge of the kitchen and the mission table" was not degrading but was instead a "most important station," which taught them "industry and economy."

The great advantage of teaching Cherokee girls "industry and economy" was the influence they might exert in their own homes. One girl wrote: "We have the opportunity of learning to work and to make garments which will be useful to us in life." Another girl expressed gratitude that missionaries had taught the students "how to take care of families that when we go home we can take care of our mother's house." A missionary assessed the impact of their work: "We cannot expect that the influence

of these girls will have any great immediate effect or their acquaintance—but I believe in each case it is calculated to elevate the families in some degree with which they are connected." Although missionaries and students expected the domestic arts learned in the mission schools to improve the parental home they believed that the primary benefit would be to the homes the girls themselves established. Missionary Sophia Sawyer specifically hoped to "raise the female character in the Nation" so that "Cherokee gentlemen" could find young women "sufficiently educated for companions." In 1832 missionaries could report with satisfaction that the girls who had married "make good housewives and useful members of society."

The marriages missionaries had in mind were not the Cherokees' traditional polygamous or serial marriages. Louis-Philippe had believed that such a marriage "renders women contemptible in men's eyes and deprives them of all influence." A monogamous marriage was supposedly liberating to women because these "serve exclusively to heighten the affections of a man." Although the Cherokee elite accepted most tenets of Western civilization, some balked at abandoning the practice of polygamy. The chief justice was one who had more than one wife, but these marriages differed from traditional ones in which a man lived with his wives in their houses. Polygamous members of the elite headed more than one patriarchal household. They recognized the desirability of monogamous unions, however, encouraged others to enter into them, and sent their children to mission schools where they were taught that polygamy was immoral.

In practice, religious denominations confronted the problem of polygamy in different ways. Moravians apparently allowed converts to keep more than one wife. The American Board required a man "to separate himself from all but the first." Perhaps because some of their chief supporters were polygamists, the governing body in Boston advised missionaries in the field to be "prudent and kind" when dealing with this "tender subject" and to instruct polygamous converts "in the nature and design of marriage, the original institution, and the law of Christ, that they may act with an enlightened conviction of duty." American Board ministers sometimes remarried in a Christian service couples who had lived for years in "a family capacity." Missionaries also rejoiced when they united in matrimony young couples of "industrious habits & reputable behavior" who were "very decent and respectable in their moral deportment."

Achieving "moral deportment" at the mission schools was no simple matter, but missionaries considered the teaching of New England sexual mores to be one of their chief responsibilities. According to some reports, they enjoyed success. In 1822, American Board missionaries reported: "Mr. Hall thinks the moral influence of the school has been considerable. . . . The intercourse between the young of both sexes was shamefully loose. Boys & girls in their teens would strip & go into bathe, or play ball together naked. They would also use the most disgustingly indecent language, without the least sense of shame. But, when better instructed, they became reserved and modest." To maintain decorum, the missionaries tried to make certain that girls and boys were never alone together: "When the girls walk out any distance from the house they will be accompanied by instructors." Male and female students normally attended separate classes. When Sophia Sawyer became ill in 1827 she reluctantly sent the small girls to the boys' school but taught the larger girls in her sickroom. Miss Sawyer so feared for the virtue of the older girls that she asked the governing board "could not the boys at Brainerd be at some other school." The Moravians did resort to separate schools. The American Board, however, simply put locks on the bedroom doors.

Even with these precautions, difficulties arose. In 1813 the Moravians recorded in their journal: "After prayer we directed our talk toward Nancy, indirectly admonishing her to abstain from the lust which had gripped her. She seemed not to have taken it to heart, for instead of mending her ways she continues to heap sin upon sin." Nancy Watie later moved to an American Board mission along with her cousin Sally Ridge. Their fathers were prominent in the Cherokee Nation, and they had left strict instructions that their daughters be supervised constantly and their purity preserved. A problem occurred when teenage boys in the neighborhood began calling on the girls at the mission. At first, the young people decorously sat in front of the fire under the watchful eyes of the missionaries, but soon the conversation shifted from English to Cherokee, which none of the chaperons understood. Suspecting the worst, the missionaries ordered the suitors to "spend their evenings in some other place." A year later, however, the missionaries

reported that despite their care, the girls "had given themselves up to the common vices."

The missionaries did not, of course, intend to cloister the young women to the extent that they did not meet suitable young men. Sophia Sawyer observed: "Like all females they desire the admiration of men. They can easily be shown that the attention, or good opinion of men without education, taste, or judgment is not worth seeking, & to gain the affection or good opinion of the opposite character, their minds must be improved, their manner polished, their persons attended to, in a word they must be qualified for usefulness." Attracting the right young men was permissible and even desirable.

The girls' appearance was another concern of the missionaries. Ann Paine related an attempt to correct the daughter of a particularly prominent Cherokee: "Altho' her parents supplied her with good clothes, she was careless and indifferent about her appearance.—I often urged her attention to these things and offered as a motive her obligation to set a good example to her nation as the daughter of their chief. Told her how the young ladies of the North were taught to govern their manners and tempers and of their attention to personal appearance. She never appeared more mortified than in hearing of her superiority of birth, and of the attention she ought to pay to her personal appearance." Paine soon had "the satisfaction of witnessing her rapid improvement." Four years later, Sophia Sawyer complained about the female students in general: "I have had to punish several times to break bad habits respecting cleanliness in their clothes, books, & person—I found them in a deplorable situation in this respect. The largest girls I had in school were not capable of dressing themselves properly or of folding their clothes when taken off." Sometimes concern for the students' appearance went beyond clothing. One girl wrote a correspondent: "Mr. Ellsworth told me I had better alter my voice. He said I spoke like a man."

In addition to a neat, feminine appearance, respectable men presumably also admired piety in young women and probably expected them to be more pious than they themselves were. The missionaries clearly believed that the female students in mission schools were more serious about religion than the male students, and they encouraged this emotion. Nancy Reece wrote her northern correspondent that "after work at night the girls joined for singing a special hymn Mr. Walker wrote for them and then go to worship services." Many of the girls wrote about their spiritual lives. A ten-year-old confided in a letter that "some of the girls have been serious about their wicked hearts and have retired to their Chambers to pray to God. . . . I feel as though I am a great sinner and very wicked sinner."

The piety of the girls at the mission station was manifest in other ways. They organized a society to raise money to send missionaries into heathen lands. The American Board agreed to pay them for clothing they made, and they in turn donated the money to mission work. They also sold their handwork to local Cherokee women. The piety of the girls extended beyond the school and into the community. Once a month, neighboring women would gather at the mission for a prayer meeting "that missionary labors may be blessed." One missionary reported with satisfaction that "the females have a praying society which is well attended, and they begin to do something by way of benevolence."

Of the several hundred Cherokee girls who attended mission schools, the best example of "true womanhood" was Catharine Brown. She was sixteen or seventeen years old when she arrived at the Brainerd mission. She had some European ancestry, and although she had grown up in a fairly traditional Cherokee household, she spoke and read a little English. The missionaries reported that, despite the absence of a Christian influence in her childhood, "her moral character was ever good." Her biographer added: "This is remarkable, considering the looseness of manners then prevalent among the females of her nation, and the temptations to which she was exposed, when during the war with the Creek Indians, the army of the United States was stationed near her father's residence. . . . Once she even fled from her home into the wild forest to preserve her character unsullied." When she applied for admission to Brainerd, the missionaries hesitated because they feared that she would object to the domestic duties required of female students. They later recalled that she was "vain, and excessively fond of dress, wearing a profusion of ornaments in her ears." Catharine "had no objection" to work, however, and shortly after her admission, her jewelry disappeared "till only a single drop remains in each ear." After she became a part of the mission family, Catharine became extremely pious: "She spent much time in reading the Scriptures, singing, and prayer." She attended weekly prayer meetings and helped instruct the

younger girls in the Lord's Prayer, hymns, and catechism. In 1819, Catharine received baptism. Her intellectual achievements were also remarkable, and soon the missionaries sent her to open a female school at the Creek Path Mission station. There she fulfilled not only her spiritual and educational responsibilities but also her domestic ones. Visitors reported: "We arrived after the family had dined, and she received us, and spread a table for our refreshment with the unaffected kindness of a sister." When her father proposed to take the family to Indian territory, Catharine was appropriately submissive. Although she did not want to go, she acquiesced to his wishes and prepared to leave for the West. Catharine's health, however, was fragile. She became ill, and "as she approached nearer to eternity her faith evidently grew stronger." In July 1823, "this lovely convert from heathenism died."

Few women in the Cherokee Nation could equal Catharine Brown, and perhaps the majority of Cherokee women had little desire to be "true women." The historical record contains little information about the Cherokee masses, but from the evidence that does exist, we can infer that many Cherokees maintained a relatively traditional way of life. Continuing to exist at the subsistence level, they rejected Christianity and mission schools and relied on local councils rather than the central government dominated by the elite. Borrowing selectively from the dominant white society, a large number of women also maintained a semblance of their aboriginal role. As late as 1817, a council of women petitioned the Cherokee National Council to refrain from further land cessions, and in 1835 at least one-third of the heads of households listed on the removal roll were women. Some probably were like Oo-dah-less who, according to her obituary, accumulated a sizable estate through agriculture and commerce. She was "the support of a large family" and bequeathed her property "to an only daughter and three grand children." Other women no doubt lived far more traditionally, farming, supervising an extended household, caring for children and kinsmen, and perhaps even exercising some power in local councils.

Although the feminine ideal of purity, piety, submissiveness, and domesticity did not immediately filter down to the mass of Cherokees, the nation's leaders came to expect these qualities in women. Therefore, the influence of the cult of true womanhood probably far exceeded the modest number of women trained in mission schools. The Cherokee leaders helped create a new sphere for women by passing legislation that undermined matrilineal kinship and excluded women from the political process. In the first recorded Cherokee law of 1808, the national council, which apparently included no women, established a police force "to give their protection to children as heirs to their father's property, and to the widow's share." Subsequent legislation gave further recognition to patrilineal descent and to the patriarchal family structure common among men of wealth. In 1825 the council extended citizenship to the children of white women who had married Cherokee men, another act that formally reordered descent. Legislation further isolated women by prohibiting polygamy and denied women the right to limit the size of their families by outlawing the traditional practice of infanticide. In 1826 the council decided to call a constitutional convention to draw up a governing document for the tribe. According to legislation that provided for the election of delegates to the convention, "No person but a free male citizen who is full grown shall be entitled to vote." Not surprisingly, when the convention met and drafted a constitution patterned after that of the United States, women could neither vote nor hold office. The only provisions in the Cherokee legal code reminiscent of the power and prestige enjoyed by aboriginal women were laws that protected the property rights of married women and prohibited their husbands from disposing of their property without consent.

The elite who governed the Cherokee Nation under the Constitution of 1827 regarded traditionalists with considerable disdain. Having profited from the government's civilization program, most truly believed in the superiority of Anglo-American culture. Some leaders and, to an even greater extent, United States officials tended to question the ability of traditionalists to make well-informed, rational decisions. This lack of faith provided a justification for those highly acculturated Cherokees who in 1835, without tribal authorization, ceded Cherokee land in the Southeast contrary to the wishes of the vast majority of Indians. The failure of many Indian women to conform to the ideals of womanhood may well have contributed to the treaty party's self-vindication. Perhaps they believed that the land could have little meaning for the Cherokees if women controlled it, that the Indians must still depend primarily on

hunting if women farmed, and that the Indians had no notion of ownership if men had no proprietary interest in their wives.

Of all the southern tribes, the Cherokees provide the sharpest contrast between the traditional role of women and the role they were expected to assume in the early nineteenth century. In this period, the Cherokees excluded women, who originally had participated in tribal governance, from the political arena. Women in other tribes had been less active politically; consequently, their status did not change as dramatically. All southern nations, however, did move toward legally replacing matrilineal with patrilineal descent and restricting the autonomy of women. In 1824, for example, the Creeks passed one law prohibiting infanticide and another specifying that upon a man's death, his children "shall have the property and his other relations shall not take the property to the injury of His children."

Men of wealth and power among the Creeks, Choctaws, and Chickasaws as well as the Cherokees readily accepted the technical assistance offered through the government's civilization program and gradually adopted the ideology it encompassed. Although these changes occurred at different rates among southern Indians, women began to fade from economic and political life in the early nineteenth century. Just as the traditional female occupation, farming, became commercially viable, men took over and women became only secondarily involved in subsistence. Women, of course, still had their homes and families, but their families soon became their husbands' families, and domesticity brought influence, not power. Similarly, purity and piety seemed almost anachronistic in a culture and age that tended to value the material above the spiritual. Perhaps all that remained for women was what historian Nancy Cott has called "bonds of womanhood," but Indian women did not even develop closer ties to other women. Living a far more isolated existence than ever before, they no longer shared labor and leisure with mothers, daughters, and sisters. Instead they spent most of their time on remote homesteads with only their husbands and children.

This separate sphere in which Indian women increasingly lived in the nineteenth century could hardly give rise to a women's rights movement, as some historians have suggested it did among white women, because true womanhood came to be associated with civilization and progress. Any challenge to the precepts of the cult of true womanhood could be interpreted as a reversion to savagery. Ironically, by the end of the century, some white Americans had come to view the traditional status of Indian women in a far more favorable light. In 1892 the author of an article in the *Albany Law Review* applauded the revision of property laws in the United States to protect the rights of married women and noted that such a progressive practice had long existed among the Choctaw and other southern Indians. This practice, however, was only a remnant of a female role that had been economically productive, politically powerful, and socially significant but had been sacrificed to the cult of true womanhood.

The Myth of the "Cavalier" South

Wilbur J. Cash

Of those myths peculiar to the pre–Civil War South, none has proved more enduring than the belief in a historically continuous southern aristocracy. According to the romantic myth of the Old South, country gentlemen of courtliness and stately hospitality presided over southern society during the antebellum period. The late Wilbur Cash, freelance writer and former associate editor of the Charlotte (North Carolina) *News*, notes that two critical facts were perpetually at odds with the idea of an all-pervasive Cavalier society—the element of time and the ever present frontier environment. To the degree that subtle notions of class did begin to manifest themselves in the Old South, such social distinctions were linked not to lineage but rather to property ownership. The southern "aristocracy" of the Old Regime was a creation of the mind of the South.

Though . . . nobody any longer holds to the Cavalier thesis in its overt form it remains true that the popular mind still clings to it in essence. Explicit or implicit in most considerations of the land, and despite a gathering tendency on the part of the more advanced among the professional historians, and lately even on the part of popular writers, to cast doubt on it, the assumption persists that the great South of the first half of the nineteenth century—the South which fought the Civil War—was the home of a genuine and fully realized aristocracy, coextensive and identical with the ruling class, the planters; and sharply set apart from the common people, still pretty often lumped indiscriminately together as the poor whites, not only by economic condition but also by the far vaster gulf of a different blood and a different (and long and solidly established) heritage.

To suppose this, however, is to ignore the frontier and that *sine qua non* of aristocracy everywhere—the dimension of time. And to ignore the frontier and time in setting up a conception of the social state of the Old South is to abandon reality. For the history of this South throughout a very great part of the period from the opening of the nineteenth century to the Civil War (in the South beyond the Mississippi until long after that war) is mainly the history of the roll of frontier upon frontier—and on to the frontier beyond.

Prior to the close of the Revolutionary period the great South, as such, has little history. Two hundred years had run since John Smith had saved Jamestown, but the land which was to become the cotton kingdom was still more wilderness than not. In Virginia—in the Northern Neck, all along the tidewater, spreading inland along the banks of the James, the York, the Rappahannock, flinging thinly across the redlands to the valley of the Shenandoah, echoing remotely about the dangerous water of Albemarle—in South Carolina and Georgia—along a sliver of swamp country running from Charleston to Georgetown and Savannah—and in and around Hispano-Gallic New Orleans, there was something which could be called effective settlement and societal organization.

Here, indeed, there was a genuine, if small, aristocracy. Here was all that in aftertime was to give color to the legend of the Old South. Here were silver and carriages and courtliness and manner. Here were great houses—not as great as we are sometimes told, but still great houses: the Shirleys, the Westovers, the Stratfords. Here were the names that were some time to flash with swords and grow tall in thunder—the Lees, the Stuarts, and the Beauregards. Charleston, called the most brilliant of American cities by Crève-coeur, played a miniature London, with overtones of La Rochelle, to a small squirarchy of the rice planta-tions. In Virginia great earls played at Lord Bountiful, dispensing stately hospitality to every passer-by—to the barge captain on his way down the river, to the slaver who had this morning put into the inlet with a cargo of likely Fulah boys, to the wandering Yankee peddling his platitudinous wooden nutmeg, and to other great earls, who came, with their ladies, in canopied boats or in coach and six with liveried outriders. New Orleans was a pageant of dandies and coxcombs, and all the swamplands could show a social life of a considerable pretension.

It is well, however, to remember a thing or two about even these Virginians. (For brevity's sake, I shall treat only of the typical case of the Virginians, and shall hereafter generally apply the term as em-bracing all these little clumps of colonial aristocracy in the lowlands.) It is well to remember not only that they were not generally Cavaliers in their origin but also that they did not spring up to be aristocrats in a day. The two hundred years since Jamestown must not be forgotten. It is necessary to conceive Virginia as beginning very much as New England began— as emerging by slow stages from a primitive back-woods community, made up primarily of farmers and laborers. Undoubtedly there was a sprinkling of gentlemen of a sort—minor squires, younger sons of minor squires, or adventurers who had got them-selves a crest, a fine coat, and title to huge slices of the country. And probably some considerable part of the aristocrats at the end of the Revolution are to be explained as stemming from these bright-plumed birds. It is certain that the great body of them cannot be so explained.

The odds were heavy against such gentle-men—against any gentlemen at all, for that matter. The land had to be wrested from the forest and the intractable red man. It was a harsh and bloody task, wholly unsuited to the talents which won applause in the neighborhood of Rotten Row and Covent Gar-den, or even in Hants or the West Riding. Leadership,

for the great part, passed inevitably to rough and ready hands. While milord tarried at dice or lan-guidly directed his even more languid workmen, his horny-palmed neighbors increasingly wrung profits from the earth, got themselves into position to extend their holdings, to send to England for redemptioners and convict servants in order to extend them still further, rose steadily toward equality with him, at-tained it, passed him, were presently buying up his bankrupt remains.

The very redemptioners and convict servants were apt to fare better than the gentleman. These are the people, of course, who are commonly said to explain the poor whites of the Old South, and so of our own time. It is generally held of them that they were uniformly shiftless or criminal, and that these characters, being inherent in the germ plasm, were handed on to their progeny, with the result that the whole body of them continually sank lower and lower in the social scale. The notion has the support of practically all the standard histories of the United States, as for example those of John Bach McMaster and lames Ford Rhodes. But, as Professor G. W. Dyer, of Vanderbilt University, has pointed out in his monograph, *Democracy in the South Before the Civil War*, it has little support in the known facts.

In the first place, there is no convincing evidence that, as a body, they came of congenitally inferior stock. If some of the convicts were thieves or cut-throats or prostitutes, then some of them were also mere political prisoners, and so, ironically, may very well have represented as good blood as there was in Virginia. Perhaps the majority were simply debtors. As for the redemptioners, the greater number of them seem to have been mere children or adoles-cents, lured from home by professional crimps or outright kidnapped. It is likely enough, to be sure, that most of them were still to be classed as laborers or the children of laborers; but it is an open question whether this involves any actual inferiority, and cer-tainly it involved no practical inferiority in this fron-tier society.

On the contrary. Most of them were freed while still in their twenties. Every freeman was entitled to a headright of fifty acres. Unclaimed lands remained plentiful in even the earliest-settled areas until long after the importation of bound servants had died out before slavery. And to cap it all, tobacco prices rose steadily. Thus, given precisely those qualities of physical energy and dogged application which, in the absence of degeneracy, are preeminently the heritage of the laborer, the former redemptioner (or convict, for that matter) was very likely to do what so many other men of his same general stamp were doing all about him: steadily to build up his capital and become a man of substance and respect. There is abundant evidence that the thing did so happen. Adam Thoroughgood, who got to be the greatest planter in Norfolk, entered the colony as an indentured servant. Dozens of others who began in the same status are known to have become justices of the peace, vestrymen, and officers of the militia—positions reserved, of course, for gentlemen. And more than one established instance bears out *Moll Flanders*.

In sum, it is clear that distinctions were immensely supple, and that the test of a gentleman in seventeenth-century Virginia was what the test of a gentleman is likely to be in any rough young society—the possession of a sufficient property.

Aristocracy in any real sense did not develop until after the passage of a hundred years—until after 1700. From the foundations carefully built up by his father and grandfather, a Carter, a Page, a Shirley began to tower decisively above the ruck of farmers, pyramided his holdings in land and slaves, squeezed out his smaller neighbors and relegated them to the remote Shenandoah, abandoned his story-and-a-half house for his new "hall," sent his sons to William and Mary and afterward to the English universities or the law schools in London. These sons brought back the manners of the Georges and more developed and subtle notions of class. And the sons of these in turn began to think of themselves as true aristocrats and to be accepted as such by those about them—to set themselves consciously to the elaboration and propagation of a tradition.

But even here the matter must not be conceived too rigidly, or as having taken place very extensively. The number of those who had moved the whole way into aristocracy even by the time of the Revolution was small. Most of the Virginians who counted themselves gentlemen were still, in reality, hardly more than superior farmers. Many great property-holders were still almost, if not quite, illiterate. Life in the greater part of the country was still more crude than not. The frontier still lent its tang to the manners of even the most advanced, all the young men who were presently to rule the Republic having been more or less shaped by it. And, as the emergence of Jeffer-

sonian democracy from exactly this milieu testifies, rank had not generally hardened into caste.

But this Virginia was not the great South. By paradox, it was not even all of Virginia. It was a narrow world, confined to the areas where tobacco, rice, and indigo could profitably be grown on a large scale—to a relatively negligible fraction, that is, of the Southern country. All the rest, at the close of the Revolution, was still in the frontier or semi-frontier stage. Here were no baronies, no plantations, and no manors. And here was no aristocracy nor any fully established distinction save that eternal one between man and man.

In the vast backcountry of the seaboard states, there lived unchanged the pioneer breed—the unsuccessful and the restless from the older regions; the homespun Scotch-Irish, dogged out of Pennsylvania and Maryland by poverty and the love of freedom; pious Moravian brothers, as poor as they were pious; stolid Lutheran peasants from northern Germany; ragged, throat-slitting Highlanders, lusting for elbow-room and still singing hotly of Bonnie Prince Charlie; all that generally unpretentious and often hard-bitten crew which, from about 1740, had been slowly filling up the region. Houses, almost without exception, were cabins of logs. Farms were clearings, on which was grown enough corn to meet the grower's needs, and perhaps a little tobacco which once a year was "rolled" down to a landing on a navigable stream. Roads and trade hardly yet existed. Life had but ceased to be a business of Indian fighting. It was still largely a matter of coon-hunting, of "painter" tales and hard drinking.

Westward, Boone had barely yesterday blazed his trail. Kentucky and Tennessee were just opening up. And southward of the Nashville basin, the great Mississippi Valley, all that country which was to be Alabama, Mississippi, western Georgia, and northern Louisiana, was still mainly a wasteland, given over to the noble savage and peripatetic traders with an itch for adventure and a taste for squaw seraglios.

Then the Yankee, Eli Whitney, interested himself in the problem of extracting the seed from a recalcitrant fiber, and cotton was on its way to be king. The despised backcountry was coming into its own—but slowly at first. Cotton would release the plantation from the narrow confines of the coastlands and the tobacco belt, and stamp it as the reigning pattern on all the country. Cotton would end stagnation, beat back the wilderness, mow the forest, pour black men and plows and mules along the Yazoo and the Arkansas, spin out the railroad, freight the yellow waters of the Mississippi with panting stern-wheelers—in brief, create the great South. But not in a day. It was necessary to wait until the gin could be proved a success, until experience had shown that the uplands of Carolina and Georgia were pregnant with wealth, until the rumor was abroad in the world that the blacklands of the valley constituted a new El Dorado.

It was 1800 before the advance of the plantation was really under way, and even then the pace was not too swift. The physical difficulties to be overcome were enormous. And beyond the mountains the first American was still a dismaying problem. It was necessary to wait until Andrew Jackson and the men of Tennessee could finally crush him. [Then] 1810 came and went, the battle of New Orleans was fought and won, and it was actually 1820 before the plantation was fully on the march, striding over the hills of Carolina to Mississippi—1820 before the tide of immigration was in full sweep about the base of the Appalachians.

From 1820 to 1860 is but forty years—a little more than the span of a single generation. The whole period from the invention of the cotton gin to the outbreak of the Civil War is less than seventy years—the lifetime of a single man. Yet it was wholly within the longer of these periods, and mainly within the shorter, that the development and growth of the great South took place. Men who, as children, had heard the war-whoop of the Cherokee in the Carolina backwoods lived to hear the guns at Vicksburg. And thousands of other men who had looked upon Alabama when it was still a wilderness and upon Mississippi when it was still a stubborn jungle, lived to fight—and to fight well, too—in the ranks of the Confederate armies.

The inference is plain. It is impossible to conceive the great South as being, on the whole, more than a few steps removed from the frontier stage at the beginning of the Civil War. It is imperative, indeed, to conceive it as having remained more or less fully in the frontier stage for a great part—maybe the greater part—of its antebellum history. However rapidly the plantation might advance, however much the slave might smooth the way, it is obvious that the mere physical process of subduing the vast territory which was involved, the essential frontier process of wresting a stable foothold from a hostile environment, must have consumed most of the year down to 1840. . . .

*   *   *

How account for the ruling class, then? Manifestly, for the great part, by the strong, the pushing, the ambitious, among the old coon-hunting population of the backcountry. The frontier was their predestined inheritance. They possessed precisely the qualities necessary to the taming of the land and the building of the cotton kingdom. The process of their rise to power was simplicity itself. Take a concrete case.

A stout young Irishman brought his bride into the Carolina up-country about 1800. He cleared a bit of land, built a log cabin of two rooms, and sat down to the pioneer life. One winter, with several of his neighbors, he loaded a boat with whisky and the coarse woolen cloth woven by the women and drifted down to Charleston to trade. There, remembering the fondness of his woman for a bit of beauty, he bought a handful of cotton seed, which she planted about the cabin with the wild rose and the honeysuckle—as a flower. Afterward she learned, under the tutelage of a new neighbor, to pick the seed from the fiber with her fingers and to spin it into yarn. Another winter the man drifted down the river, this time to find the halfway station of Columbia in a strange ferment. There was a new wonder in the world—the cotton gin—and the forest which had lined the banks of the stream for a thousand centuries was beginning to go down. Fires flared red and portentous in the night—to set off an answering fire in the breast of the Irishman.

Land in his neighborhood was to be had for fifty cents an acre. With twenty dollars, the savings of his lifetime, he bought forty acres and set himself to clear it. Rising long before day, he toiled deep into the night, with his wife holding a pine torch for him to see by. Aided by his neighbors, he piled the trunks of the trees into great heaps and burned them, grubbed up the stumps, hacked away the tangle of underbrush and vine, stamped out the poison ivy and the snakes. A wandering trader sold him a horse, bony and half-starved, for a knife, a dollar, and a gallon of whisky. Every day now—Sundays not excepted—when the heavens allowed, and every night that the moon came, he drove the plow into the earth, with uptorn roots bruising his shanks at every step. Behind him came his wife with a hoe. In a few years the land was beginning to yield cotton—richly, for the soil was fecund with the accumulated mold of centuries. Another trip down the river, and he brought home a mangy black slave—an old and lazy fellow reckoned of no account in the ricelands, but with plenty of life in him still if you knew how to get it out. Next year the Irishman bought fifty acres more, and the year after another black. Five years more and he had two hundred acres and ten Negroes. Cotton prices swung up and down sharply, but always, whatever the return, it was almost pure velvet. For the fertility of the soil seemed inexhaustible.

When he was forty-five, he quit work, abandoned the log house, which had grown to six rooms, and built himself a wide-spreading frame cottage. When he was fifty, he became a magistrate, acquired a carriage, and built a cotton gin and a third house—a "big house" this time. It was not, to be truthful, a very grand house really. Built of lumber sawn on the place, it was a little crude and had not cost above a thousand dollars, even when the marble mantel was counted in. Essentially, it was just a box, with four rooms, bisected by a hallway, set on four more rooms bisected by another hallway, and a detached kitchen at the back. Wind-swept in winter, it was difficult to keep clean of vermin in summer. But it was huge, it had great columns in front, and it was eventually painted white, and so, in this land of wide fields and pinewoods it seemed very imposing.

Meantime the country around had been growing up. Other "big houses" had been built. There was a county seat now, a cluster of frame houses, stores, and "doggeries" about a red brick courthouse. A Presbyterian parson had drifted in and started an academy, as Presbyterian parsons had a habit of doing everywhere in the South—and Pompeys and Caesars and Ciceros and Platos were multiplying both among the pickaninnies in the slave quarters and among the white children of the "big houses." The Irishman had a piano in his house, on which his daughters, taught by a vagabond German, played as well as young ladies could be expected to. One of the

Irishman's sons went to the College of South Carolina, came back to grow into the chief lawyer in the county, got to be a judge, and would have been Governor if he had not died at the head of his regiment at Chancellorsville.

As a crown on his career, the old man went to the Legislature, where he was accepted by the Charleston gentlemen tolerantly and with genuine liking. He grew extremely mellow in age and liked to pass his time in company, arguing about predestination and infant damnation, proving conclusively that cotton was king and that the damyankee didn't dare do anything about it, and developing a notable taste in the local liquors. Tall and well made, he grew whiskers after the Galway fashion—the well-kept whiteness of which contrasted very agreeably with the brick red of his complexion—donned the longtailed coat, stove-pipe hat, and string tie of the statesmen of his period, waxed innocently pompous, and, in short, became a really striking figure of a man.

Once, going down to Columbia for the inauguration of a new Governor, he took his youngest daughter along. There she met a Charleston gentleman who was pestering her father for a loan. Her manner, formed by the Presbyterian parson, was plain but not bad, and she was very pretty. Moreover, the Charleston gentleman was decidedly in hard lines. So he married her.

When the old man finally died in 1854, he left two thousand acres, a hundred and fourteen slaves, and four cotton gins. The little newspaper which had recently set up in the county seat spoke of him as "a gentleman of the old school" and "a noble specimen of the chivalry at its best"; the Charleston papers each gave him a column; and a lordly Legaré introduced resolutions of respect into the Legislature. His wife outlived him by ten years—by her portrait a beautifully fragile old woman, and, as I have heard it said, with lovely hands, knotted and twisted just enough to give them character, and a finely transparent skin through which the blue veins showed most aristocratically.

Myths of American Slavery

Thomas C. Holt

A great measure of the South's mythology not only results from the undeniable strength of the region's collective beliefs, social codes, and cultural rituals but also emanates from its mythology based on race. The peculiar nature of the institutution of slavery adds to the ambiguities that plague clear understanding of both region and nation. Drawing special attention to the perpetual interplay of historical facts and theoretical interpretations by historians, Thomas C. Holt, professor of history at the University of Chicago, argues that the usual image of slavery as rather exclusively a southern phenomenon must be adjusted in favor of a national perspective. Holt emphasizes the many points of debate still to be judged. Assumptions about the nature and meaning of slavery almost always reflect the preoccupations of the lives in which the institution is being interpreted. Resting solidly at the center, for those seeking to explain the black experience, are recurring questions about the profitability of slavery; its relationship to paternalism and capitalism; and its effects upon black as well as white culture, identity, community, and social institutions. No subject in American history is more myth-laden than that of slavery.

It was a sociological work published during World War II that probably introduced black history to most white Americans. In 1944 Gunnar Myrdal's *American Dilemma* detailed not only the current conditions and future prospects but much of the history of blacks in America. It was at once a work of scholarship and a protest, a brutally objective examination of the black condition and a passionate call for national action. It won general acceptance as the major work of the century on American race relations and black life in America.

Myrdal's report also attracted critics, however. Among them was Ralph Ellison, soon to be a prizewinning novelist. In a review published several years later, Ellison applauded many of Myrdal's findings but took exception to the overall theme and tone of the report. Its effort to move the nation to action by highlighting the cruel oppression of blacks had the unintended effect of rendering a portrait of black life that Ellison could not recognize. After the oppressions and "meannesses" of white racism had been detailed, all that remained was "a sociological Negro," or what Ellison referred to in another context as "an image drained of humanity." Surely, he protested, black life was more than the sum of white oppression. "Can a people," he asked, "live and develop for over three hundred years simply by *reacting*? Are American Negroes simply the creation of white men, or have they at least helped to create themselves out of what they found around them?"

Anyone reviewing the historiography of Afro-American history in the post–World War II period might be surprised by the pervasive influence of Ellison's protest on historical scholarship. The novelist's query struck home, especially with the generation of white and black scholars emerging from the tumultuous 1960s. Consequently, in sharp contrast with the century of scholarship that preceded it, that of the 1970s and 1980s gave its attention almost exclusively to the problem of understanding black history as black people experienced it. No longer would black history be simply the history of relations between the races or of black contributions to the nation's life and progress. It would be the history of black communities, churches, schools, businesses, families, and folk culture. In that history blacks would no longer be relegated to nonspeaking roles, the passive victims of white hostility or beneficiaries of white benevolence. They would be actors with top billing, creating institutions, sustaining communal values, and passing on a legacy of struggle and creativity to their posterity.

The result has been a veritable explosion of histories on almost every conceivable facet of black life, by no means all of which can be examined here. But there are three major watersheds in the history of blacks in America: enslavement and forced migration from Africa, followed by almost a century and a half of bondage; emancipation, followed by more than a half-century of sharecropping and tenancy; and finally, the great twentieth-century northern migrations that produced the contemporary black urban communities and a second emancipation. Although the subject matter of Afro-American history has grown voluminous and tremendously complex, these three periods provide the essential contexts for the black experience; at the same time, they are key to any comprehensive study of the American experience generally. The black experience has ceased to be a peripheral topic in American history; it is now among the central phenomena of the national experience.

*   *   *

Arguably, slavery was the central and determining phenomenon shaping the first century of American history. Of course, one might also make claims for the Constitution, the ideology of freedom and equality, the expanding frontier, and immigration, but each of these was profoundly shaped by the fact that the nation was half slave and half free. Consequently, much of American historical literature is devoted to the study of the institution of slavery, its origins, and the causes of its destruction in the nation's bloodiest war.

Because slavery is obviously central to the black experience in America, students of Afro-American history are concerned with many of the same issues regarding slavery's rise and fall as are students of general American history: the work regime on slave plantations; the profitability of slavery as an investment of capital; the nature of the master's relation with the slave; the conditions of material and social life in the slave quarters; and the nature and incidence of slave resistance. But the focus of Afro-American history is often different. In a general American history survey the objective might be to discern the personality and motives of the slavemaster in order to explain, for example, the causes of the Civil War. Afro-American history is more likely concerned to explain how slavery affected the slave or, more broadly, to examine slavery as the formative experience of Afro-American life and culture. The two lines of inquiry are necessarily interrelated and mutually dependent; there can be no adequate history of the master that neglects the slave, and vice versa. Nevertheless, it is important to bear these different tendencies in mind as one surveys the historiography of slavery, because the emphasis has shifted perceptibly over the past quarter-century.

Modern scholarship on slavery in the United States begins with U. B. Phillips's *American Negro Slavery* (1918). Drawing on meticulous research into a vast repository of plantation records, Phillips's treatment was long considered the definitive interpretation. That interpretation, however, reflected Phillips's own southern racist convictions as much as it did his research. He portrayed slavery as a benign institution. The masters were kindly, interested less in making a profit than in a way of life. The slaves did not work hard, did not suffer material deprivations, did not miss the pleasures—in their fashion—of leisure. Resistance was insignificant and rebellions infrequent; when they did occur, the former reflected merely the laziness and malingering characteristic of a childlike race, the latter its criminal tendencies when not properly disciplined. Writing at the height of European colonial expansion into Africa, Phillips justified slavery as a rescue of blacks from African barbarism. It was a kind of "school" in which they would be readied for civilized life.

Although a number of black historians took exception to such an interpretation, it was not until Kenneth Stampp published *The Peculiar Institution* in 1955 that Phillips's views came under systematic, full-scale attack. With scholarship even more meticulous and thorough, Stampp demolished each of his predecessor's arguments. Slavery was a labor system above all else, he declared; it was "a systematic method of controlling and exploiting labor." Slaveowners were calculating capitalists out to make a killing, and they frequently did. The food, clothing, housing, and medical care given to slaves was inadequate by any standard of decency. They were driven to work under the lash from sunup to sundown, and there was little time left for leisure activities after the long, grueling day. Their family, religious, and community life was practically destroyed by the all-pervasive and systematic power of masters who sought only "to make them stand in fear." The slave plantation was not a schoolhouse; it was a factory run with prison labor. Yet despite—indeed because of—the harshness and hopelessness of the system, slaves did resist, frequently and with effect. They broke tools, malingered, struck work, ran away, and not infrequently raised their hands in violence against their owners.

Seldom has the historical profession witnessed such a thorough and completely successful revision of a major work of scholarship. Stampp's success must be credited not solely to his scholarship, however, but to the fact that the prevailing ideology of the time was ripe for this message. Europe was fast losing its grip on its African colonial empire; racist theories of human behavior were in retreat; and American segregation was under assault in federal courts and on southern streets. The racist assumptions that shaped Phillips's inquiry were replaced by a "race blind" creed in Stampp's. At the outset, Stampp declared his intellectual and personal faith: "I have assumed that the slaves were merely ordinary human beings, that innately Negroes *are,* after all, only white men with black skins, nothing more, nothing less."

Stampp's assumption expressed an admirable sentiment that resonated with contemporary black struggles to be recognized as "just like whites," deserving basic civil rights and decent treatment. His announced purpose was to understand "what slavery meant to the Negro and how he reacted to it [in order to] comprehend his recent tribulations." Thus Stampp shifted the focus of slavery studies away from questions of sectional conflict toward a concern for its meaning for Afro-American history and its legacy to black Americans. Given his starting point—the assumption that blacks shared the motivations

and aspirations of white men and women—the legacy he found was heroic resistance to a brutal system.

Four years later Stanley Elkins made entirely different assumptions and posed different questions in *Slavery: A Study of American Institutional and Intellectual Life* (1959). Blacks could not be just like whites because the experience of enslavement had to have changed them. Contemporary observers—planters and northern travelers—had left descriptions of slavish personality type, a "Sambo" character who lied, stole, shirked work, played the fool, and generally acted like a child before his master. There must be some truth to such a ubiquitous portrait, Elkins thought, so he set out to demonstrate how such personality could have been formed.

In striking and deliberate contrast with Phillips and Stampp, Elkins did no new research into plantation archives. Rather, he drew on existing comparative studies of slavery in the United States and Latin America, which generally concluded that U.S. slavery was the harshest, most oppressive system in the Western Hemisphere This he coupled with findings about the effects of the Nazi concentration camps on Jewish inmates. The concentration camp, he argued, provided an appropriate analogy to the slave plantation, and the psychological damage inflicted on the camps' inmates was a good guide to the impact of slavery on the slave. The camps created infantilized docile Jews; the plantations produced infantilized docile blacks. Like SS guard and Jewish inmate, master and slave were bound in a closed circle with the former exercising total power. Slaves were stripped of their African culture, their family life, or any other institution that might have checked the master's power or held a different mirror in which the slave could catch more than a distorted image of himself. The only person of significance in the slave's world was his master. Impressed with the neatness of his paradigm, Elkins insisted that only exceptional slaves were able to escape the psychological distortion that resulted from the calculated brutality of the system. To their descendants slaves bequeathed not a legacy of resistance but broken families, damaged minds, and a perverted culture.

Much of the recent literature on slavery has been stimulated, directly or indirectly, by the controversies provoked by Elkins's book. Detailed and thorough studies of slavery in Latin America and the Caribbean as well as in the United States have demolished key parts of his thesis. The contrasts between

North and South America were not as great and the relations between masters and slaves were much more complex than Elkins had portrayed them. Nevertheless, his contribution had been to frame slave *mentalité* as a problematic research question. Rising to his challenge, historians have sought out new sources and new methods of investigation. There have been quantitative studies not only of plantation economies but of runaways and family life. Sources have been uncovered that give a better approximation of what slaves thought, felt, and valued: their songs and stories, their autobiographies and oral histories.

Emerging from these studies is a consensus that despite the harshness of the system, slaves were able to create communities beyond their masters' total control. They fashioned institutions and a cultural ethos that were functional to their needs, that enabled them to survive the rigors of slavery and bequeath a legacy of resistance to their posterity. The reexamination of two key institutions—the family and the church—provided much of the evidentiary basis for this consensus. In *Slave Community* (1972), John Blassingame reported Freedmen's Bureau statistics from the 1860s showing that most slaves lived in two-parent households. In *The Black Family in Slavery and Freedom* (1975), Herbert Gutman went much further, showing not only that most slaves grew up with two parents but that their parents were often joined in enduring, though unlegalized, unions. Obviously, marriage and family were valued realities of slave life, despite the system. But more important, Gutman saw evidence suggesting complex relationships and networks of kinship within plantation quarters. Contrary to Elkins's assumptions, slaves identified with one another, not the master. The names they chose for their children, the affection they expressed for their families, the bonds they forged among kin and non-kin alike could not be reconciled with a thesis that the white master was the only "significant other" in the slave's world.

Studies of slave religious life have reinforced this view. Albert Raboteau and Eugene Genovese describe a rich and complex belief system from which slaves gained dignity and purpose in the world. Theirs was not a masters' Christianity, justifying racial subordination, but a slaves' Christianity, affirming that they were the children of God. Some historians argue further that their religion provided the basis for collective resistance and revolt. Others,

especially Genovese, assert on the contrary that religion turned the slave's resistance into channels that were basically nonpolitical and nonviolent. It reaffirmed their sense of worth and blunted the master's racist message, but it did not provide the millennial or even political consciousness that might have authorized revolution. Religion made slaves men, but it did not make them fight.

Beyond the consensus that slaves succeeded in creating a semi-autonomous community with alternative values and sanctions, there are conflicting interpretations about the nature and functioning of the slave system. Historians have arrived at the consensus view by different routes. Blassingame argued that the masters recognized their pecuniary interests in encouraging slave families, and the slaves seized the resultant opportunity to forge a network of family and community. In that community, like any other, lived diverse personality types in addition to "Sambo," including "Nat" the rebel and "Jack" the pragmatist, who accommodated to the system when he had to and fought it when he could. In *Time on the Cross* (1972), Robert Fogel and Stanley Engerman went much further. The productivity of slave labor showed that the system functioned efficiently, they argued. Therefore, planters must have been rational managers who relied on incentives and good treatment to get the best work out of their charges. In return for protection of their families, above-average subsistence, and various rewards and incentives, slaves worked hard and well. This portrait has much in common with that of U. B. Phillips, except that the result is black Horatio Algers instead of Sambos.

To date, the most coherent and comprehensive thesis is that offered by Eugene Genovese in *Roll, Jordan, Roll* (1974). In contrast with slaveowners in many other parts of the hemisphere (except colonial Brazil), American planters lived on their estates and developed personal relations with their bondsmen. That relationship was basically paternalistic, with both master and slave recognizing a reciprocity of duties and rights. Paternalism in this usage does not imply kindness or benevolence, however; Genovese finds a great deal of cruelty and sadism on plantations. But cruelty was not the norm. The norm was defined by an implicit bargain in which masters accepted responsibility for the slave's welfare (food, housing, medical care) in return for their labor. For the planters this bargain justified their predominant place in society, their life-style, and slavery itself;

theirs was a view similar to that presented by U. B. Phillips. But slaves interpreted the bargain by their own lights. For them the linkage of their subsistence with their labor was not apparent. Often, what planters saw as payments for work or gifts for faithful service, slaves came to regard as rights and entitlements.

The virtue of Genovese's work is that it attempts to comprehend both master and slave within the same system. Indeed, it was the struggle between master and slave that defined the system. It was, of course, an uneven struggle. But for Genovese, not only was the masters' power predominant in the slaves' world, but the masters determined the terms in which the world was seen. Thus, the slaves' world view emerges as merely a mirror reflection of the masters'. Slaves did not simply accommodate to the paternalistic ethos; they internalized it. But despite Genovese's impressive dialectical reasoning, this part of his argument remains an inference rather than an established fact. The letters and diaries he consults give us a better view of the master's thought than the slave's. For the latter he consults the recollections of former slaves collected by the WPA in the 1930s. Among the problems of these sources is that they do not convey the slave's thought and experience with the same immediacy as does a master's diary; they present a world not as it was lived but as it was remembered.

In *Black Culture, Black Consciousness* (1977), Lawrence Levine evades this difficulty, finding more direct entrée into the slaves' construction and interpretation of their experiences through their stories, songs, riddles, and jokes. These sources evince "a far greater degree of self-pride and group cohesion than the system they lived under ever intended for them

to [have]," writes Levine. "Upon the hard rock of racial, social, and economic exploitation and injustice black Americans forged and maintained a culture they formed and maintained kinship networks made love, raised and socialized children, built a religion, and created a rich expressive culture in which they articulated their feelings and hopes and dreams." Indeed, the best of the most recent studies of slavery have focused on the plantation household and the roles of black women as the key architects of the culture Levine invokes. Though differing in perspective and approach, the works of Deborah Gray White (*Ar'n't I a Woman*), Jacqueline Jones (*Labor of Love, Labor of Sorrow*), and Elizabeth Fox-Genovese (*Within the Plantation Household*) together provide a detailed and highly nuanced portrait of life in the slave huts and the Big House, and the interaction between the two. Perhaps the black world they and Levine describe is one that Ralph Ellison would recognize.

The consensus that slaves played a crucial role in making their own world is the beginning point for most recent scholarship in Afro-American history. For example, Charles Joyner's study of slavery in the Carolina low-country, *Down by the Riverside*, details the economic and social environment that permitted slaves to fashion a distinctive culture. Barbara J. Fields's *Slavery and Freedom on the Middle Ground* shows how black initiatives during the Civil War set in motion the inexorable process of slavery's destruction. Moreover, by following the black experience from slavery through emancipation, Fields suggests the continuity into the post–Civil War era of a tradition of resistance fashioned under slavery conditions. Thus the consensus on slavery resonates throughout later periods of Afro-American history.

The Antislavery Myth

C. Vann Woodward

Layers of fantasy and romance have come to cloud the historical reality of the northern position on slavery before the Civil War. Marshaling his facts with sophistication and skill, C. Vann Woodward, Sterling Professor of History Emeritus at Yale, reviews the antislavery question. Noting that the antislavery myth gained its greatest measure of vitality only after the Civil War, Woodward takes direct aim at the mythological trappings that still adhere to the Underground Railroad and, more importantly, at the notion that racial discrimination was a condition only to be found in the prewar South. Woodward's thesis suggests that the antislavery myth was a northern exercise in atonement for guilt. In the antebellum nation the Mason-Dixon Line did not successfully divide slavery from freedom.

Slavery and the Civil War were prolific breeders of myth, and their fertility would seem to wax rather than wane with the passage of time. Neither the proslavery myths of the South nor the antislavery myths of the North ceased to grow after the abolition of the Peculiar Institution. In fact they took on new life, struck new roots and flourished more luxuriantly than ever. Both myths continually found new sources of nourishment in the changing psychological needs and regional policies of North and South. The South used the proslavery myth to salve its wounds, lighten its burden of guilt and, most of all, to rationalize and defend the system of caste and segregation that was developed in place of the old order. The North, as we shall see, had deeply felt needs of its own to be served by an antislavery myth, needs that were sufficient at all times to keep the legend vital and growing to meet altered demands.

In late years the proslavery myth and the plantation legend have been subjected to heavy critical erosion from historians, sociologists and psychologists. So damaging has this attack been that little more is heard of the famous school for civilizing savages, peopled with happy slaves and benevolent masters. Shreds and pieces of the myth are still invoked as props to the crumbling defenses of segregation, but conviction has drained out of it, and it has

been all but relegated to the limbo of dead or obsolescent myths.

Nothing like this can be said of the antislavery myth. Its potency is attested by a steady flow of historical works by journalists and reputable scholars. It is obvious that the myth can still dim the eye and quicken the pulse as well as warp the critical judgment. Apart from the fact that it is a creation of the victor rather than the vanquished, there are other reasons for the undiminished vitality of the antislavery myth. One is that it has not been subjected to as much critical study as has the proslavery myth.

Before turning to certain recent evidence of the exuberant vitality of the antislavery myth, however, it is interesting to note two penetrating critical studies of some of its components. Larry Gara, in *The Liberty Line: The Legend of the Underground Railroad*, addresses himself to a limited but substantial element of the myth. No aspect of the myth has so deeply engaged the American imagination and entrenched itself in the national heritage as the Underground Railroad, and no aspect so well reflects what we fondly believe to be the more generous impulses of national character. It is a relief to report that Mr. Gara is a temperate scholar and has avoided handling his subject with unnecessary rudeness. By the time he finishes patiently peeling away the layers of fantasy and romance, however, the factual substance is painfully reduced and the legend is revealed as melodrama. Following the assumptions that the better critics of the proslavery legend make about the slave, he assumes that "abolitionists, after all, were human," and that the "actual men and women of the abolition movement, like the slaves themselves, are far too complex to fit into a melodrama."

One very human thing the authors of the melodrama did was to seize the spotlight. They elected themselves the heroes. It was not that the abolitionists attempted to stage *Othello* without the princely Moor, but they did relegate the Moor to a subordinate role. The role assigned him was largely passive—that of the trembling, helpless fugitive completely dependent on his noble benefactors. The abolitionist was clearly the hero, and as Gerrit Smith, one of them, put it, the thing was brought off by the "Abolitionists and the Abolitionists only." As Mr. Gara points out, however, it took a brave, resourceful and rebellious slave to make good an escape, not one temperamentally adapted to subordinate roles—no Uncle Tom, as abolitionists often discovered. Moreover, by the time he reached the helping hands of the Underground Railroad conductors—if he ever did in fact—he had already completed the most perilous part of his journey, the southern part.

Another important actor in the drama of rescue who was crowded offstage by the abolitionists was the free Negro. According to the antislavery leader James G. Birney, the assistance of the fugitives was "almost uniformly managed by the colored people. I know nothing of them generally till they are past." The fugitive slaves had good reason to mistrust any white man, and in the opinion of Mr. Gara the majority of those who completed their flight to freedom did so without a ride on the legendary U.G.R.R.

Still another human failing of the legend-makers was exaggeration, and in this the abolitionists were ably assisted by their adversaries, the slaveholders, who no more understood their pecuniary losses than the abolitionists underestimated their heroic exploits. Under analysis the "flood" of fugitives diminishes to a trickle. As few as were the manumissions, they were double the number of fugitives in 1860 according to the author, and by far the greater number of fugitives never got out of the slave states. Another and even more fascinating distortion is the legend of conspiracy and secrecy associated with the U.G.R.R. The obvious fact was that the rescue of

fugitive slaves was the best possible propaganda for the antislavery cause. We are mildly admonished that the U.G.R.R was "not the well-organized and mysterious institution of the legend." "Far from being secret," we are told, "it was copiously and persistently publicized, and there is little valid evidence for the existence of a widespread underground conspiracy."

But there remains the haunting appeal and enchantment of the secret stations, the disguised "conductors," and the whole "underground" and conspiratorial aspect of the legend that is so hard to give up. "Stories are still repeated," patiently explains Mr. Gara, "about underground tunnels, mysterious signal lights in colored windows, peculiarly placed rows of colored bricks in houses or chimneys to identify the station, and secret rooms for hiding fugitives." These stories he finds to be without basis in fact. While we must continue to bear with our Midwestern friends and their family traditions, we are advised that "hearsay, rumor, and persistent stories handed down orally from generation to generation are not proof of anything."

The most valuable contribution this study makes is the revelation of how the legend grew. It was largely a postwar creation, and it sprang from a laudable impulse to be identified with noble deeds. Family pride, local pride and regional pride were fed by abolitionist reminiscences and floods of memoirs and stories. "Every barn that ever housed a fugitive, and some that hadn't," remarks Mr. Gara, "were listed as underground railroad depots." There were thousands of contributors to the legend, but the greatest was Professor Wilbur H. Siebert, whose first book, *The Underground Railroad from Slavery to Freedom*, appeared in 1898. In the nineties he painstakingly questioned hundreds of surviving antislavery workers, whose letters and responses to questionnaires Mr. Gara has reexamined. Mr. Siebert accepted their statements at face value "on the ground that the memories of the aged were more accurate than those of young people." The picture that emerged in his big book was that of "a vast network of secret routes," connecting hundreds of underground stations, operated by 3,200 "conductors"—the very minimum figure, he insisted. This work fathered many subsequent ones, which borrowed generously from it. There has been no lag in legend-building since. "The greater the distance," observes Mr. Gara, "the more enchantment seems to adhere to all aspects of the underground railroad, the legend that grew up around it, and its role in America's heritage."

A second and more elaborate aspect of the antislavery myth is the legend that the Mason and Dixon Line not only divided slavery from freedom in antebellum America, but that it also set apart racial inhumanity in the South from benevolence, liberality and tolerance in the North. Like the Underground Railroad Legend, the North Star Legend (for lack of another name) was a postwar creation. Looking back through a haze of passing years that obscured historical realities, the myth-makers credited the North with the realization in its own society of all the war aims for which it fought (or eventually proclaimed): not only Union and Freedom, but Equality as well. True, the North did not win the third war aim (or if it did, quickly forfeited it), but it nevertheless practiced what it preached, even if it failed to get the South to practice it, and had been practicing it in exemplary fashion for some time.

For a searching examination of the North Star Legend we are indebted to Leon F. Litwack, *North of Slavery: The Negro in the Free States, 1790–1860*, He starts with the assumption that, "The inherent cruelty and violence of southern slavery requires no further demonstration, but this does not prove northern humanity." On racial attitudes of the two regions he quotes with approval the observation of Tocqueville in 1831: "The prejudice of race appears to be stronger in the states that have abolished slavery than in those where it still exists." White supremacy was a national, not a regional credo, and politicians of the Democratic, the Whig and the Republican parties openly and repeatedly expressed their allegiance to the doctrine. To do otherwise was to risk political suicide. "We, the Republican party, are the white man's party," declared Senator Lyman Trumbull of Illinois. And, as Mr. Litwack observes, "Abraham Lincoln, in his vigorous support of both white supremacy and denial of equal rights for Negroes, simply gave expression to almost universal American convictions." These convictions were to be found among Free Soil adherents and were not unknown among antislavery and abolitionist people themselves.

One reason for the unrestrained expression of racial prejudice from politicians was that the Negro was almost entirely disfranchised in the North and was therefore politically helpless. Far from sharing the expansion of political democracy, the Negro often suffered disfranchisement as a consequence of white manhood suffrage. By 1840 about 93 percent of the free Negroes in the North were living in states that excluded them from the polls. By 1860 only 6 percent of the Northern Negro population lived in the five states that provided legally for their suffrage. In only three states were they allowed complete parity with whites in voting. Even in those New England states doubts lingered concerning the practical exercise of equal political rights. As late as 1869, the year before the ratification of the 15th Amendment, New York State voted against equal suffrage rights for Negroes. Four Western states legally excluded free Negroes from entry.

In Northern courtrooms as at Northern polls racial discrimination prevailed. Five states prohibited Negro testimony when a white man was a party to a case, and Oregon prohibited Negroes from holding real estate, making contracts or maintaining lawsuits. Only in Massachusetts were Negroes admitted as jurors, and that not until the eve of the Civil War. The absence of Negro judges, jurors, witnesses and lawyers helps to explain the heavily disproportionate number of Negroes in Northern prisons.

Custom, extralegal codes and sometimes mob law served to relegate the Negro to a position of social inferiority and impose a harsh rule of segregation in Northern states. According to Mr. Litwack:

> In virtually every phase of existence, Negroes found themselves systematically separated from whites. They were either excluded from railway cars, omnibuses, stagecoaches, and steamboats or assigned to special "Jim Crow" sections; they sat, when permitted, in secluded and remote corners of theaters and lecture halls; they could not enter most hotels, restaurants, and resorts, except as servants; they prayed in "Negro pews" in white churches, and if partaking of the sacrament of the Lord's Supper, they waited until the whites had been served the bread and wine. Moreover, they were often educated in segregated schools, punished in segregated prisons, nursed in segregated hospitals, and buried in segregated cemeteries.

Housing and job opportunities were severely limited. A Boston Negro wrote in 1860 that "it is five times as hard to get a house in a good location in Boston as it is in Philadelphia; and it is ten times as difficult for a colored mechanic to get work here as it is in Charleston." The earlier verdict of Tocqueville continued to ring true. "Thus the Negro is free," he wrote, "but he can share neither the rights, nor the pleasures, nor the labor, nor the afflictions, nor the tomb of him whose equal he has been declared to be; and he cannot meet him upon fair terms in life or in death."

In Northern cities with large Negro populations, violent mob action occurred with appalling frequency. Between 1832 and 1849 mobs touched off five major anti-Negro riots in Philadelphia. Mobs destroyed homes, churches and meeting halls, and forced hundreds to flee the city. An English Quaker visiting Philadelphia in 1849 remarked that there was probably no city "where dislike, amounting to hatred of the coloured population, prevails more than in the city of brotherly love!"

The Southern historian will be struck with the remarkable degree to which the South recapitulated a generation later the tragic history of race relations in the North. Once slavery was destroyed as a means of social control and subordination of the Negro, and Reconstruction was overthrown, the South resorted to many of the devices originally developed in the North to keep the Negro in his "place." There was more delay in the resort to segregation than generally supposed, but once it came toward the end of the century it was harsh and thorough. One important difference was that in the antebellum North the Negro was sometimes free to organize, protest and join white sympathizers to advance his cause and improve his position. His success in these efforts was unimpressive, however, for by 1860, as Mr. Litwack says, "despite some notable advances, the Northern Negro remained largely disfranchised, segregated, and economically oppressed." The haven to which the North Star of the legend guided the fugitive from slavery was a Jim Crow haven.

While these two studies of the antislavery myth are valuable and significant, they are slight in scope and modest in aim when compared with the far more ambitious—and traditional—book of Dwight Lowell Dumond, *Antislavery: The Crusade for Freedom in America.* Elaborately documented, profusely illustrated and ornately bound, this massive volume is easily twice the bulk of an average-sized book. It covers the entire scope of the organized antislavery movement in this country, as well as preorganizational beginnings, and is the most extensive work on the subject in print. Represented as the result of "more than thirty years" of research by the Michigan historian, it is the outcome of a lifetime absorption in

antislavery literature. It is doubtful that any other scholar has lavished such devoted study upon this vast corpus of writings.

The author's total absorption with his source materials is, indeed, the key to the theory of historiography upon which this remarkable work would appear to be based. That theory is that the purest history is to be derived from strict and undivided attention to source materials—in this case chiefly the writings, tracts and propaganda, running to millions upon millions of words, of the antislavery people themselves. If the author is aware of any of the scholarly studies of slavery and antislavery that have appeared in the last generation or more, he does not betray awareness by reference to the questions they have raised, by use of methods they have developed, or by incorporation of findings they have published. Neither the problems of slavery and antislavery that have been pressed upon the historian by new learning in psychology, anthropology, sociology and economics, nor the questions that have been raised by fresh encounters with Africa and Afro-Americans and by new experience with reformers and revolutionists and their motivation, receive any attention from the author. It is difficult to comment intelligently upon a work that so persistently and successfully avoids engagement with the contemporary mind, its assumptions, its preoccupations, its urgent questions, its whole frame of reference.

Mr. Dumond's treatment of slavery and the abolitionists admits of no complexities or ambiguities beyond the fixed categories of right and wrong. All of his abolitionists are engaged in a single-minded crusade wholly motivated by a humanitarian impulse to destroy an evil institution and succor its victims. They are moral giants among the pygmies who cross their will or fail to share their views. The single exception is William Lloyd Garrison, for whom he shares the strong distaste of his onetime collaborator Gilbert H. Barnes, the Midwestern historian. "In fact," writes Dumond (the italics are his), *"he was a man of distinctly narrow limitations among the giants of the antislavery movement."* Why Garrison falls so far short of the stature of the giants is not quite clear, but we are assured that he was "insufferably arrogant," given to "cheap cynicism" and withal "a timid soul except when safely behind the editorial desk."

Apart from Garrison, the antislavery leaders command Mr. Dumond's unqualified admiration, and his praise of them is unbounded. "What a combination of intellect, courage, and Christian faith!" he exclaims in describing the founders of the American Antislavery Society. The abolitionists are indeed due a redress of grievances at the hands of the historians, for they have had something less than justice from the craft. They are remembered more as pictured by caricatures such as Henry James drew in *The Bostonians* than for their good works and genuine merits. The wild eccentricities, the fierce come-outerism, the doctrinaire extravagances and the armchair bloodlusts of some of the abolitionists have been stressed and repeated to the neglect of the dedicated and fearless work they did in the face of ridicule, mob violence and all the pressures that wealth and established order can bring to bear upon dissenters. Their cause was just, and among their numbers were men and women of courage, intelligence and moral force. They deserve their due and need a sympathetic defender.

The trouble with Mr. Dumond as historian of the antislavery movement is his total involvement. This involvement extends beyond hatred of slavery and approval of abolition. It commits him as well to the style and tone and temper, the immediacy of indignation, the very idiom and rhetoric of a movement of thought that took its shape from intellectual influences and social conditions existing nearly a century and a half ago. The effect is startling. The rhythm and color of his prose is in perfect keeping with the style and tone of the scores of lithographs and prints from old abolitionist tracts that serve appropriately to illustrate the book. The author paints just what he sees, but he sees everything through the eyes of the 1830's. The result is more than an anachronism. It gives the effect of a modern primitive, a Henri Rousseau of historiography.

Any treatment of the antislavery movement necessarily involves some treatment of the institution it opposed. Mr. Dumond's conception of slavery would seem to have taken shape in considerable degree from the antislavery literature he has so thoroughly mastered. At any rate, he quotes liberally from this literature in characterizing slavery. Among other things, he quotes a poem by Timothy Dwight, published in 1794, the year before he became president of Yale. The last stanza of it reads as follows:

Why shrinks yon slave, with horror, from his meat?/ Heavens! 'tis his flesh, the wretch is whipped to eat./

Why streams the life-blood from that female's throat?/ She sprinkled gravy on a guest's new coat!

"Poetic license?" asks the historian. "Exaggeration? Fantasy? *Only half the truth, if a thousand witnesses are to be believed."* And they, he assures us, are to be believed.

Mr. Dumond selects Theodore Dwight Weld's *American Slavery As It Is*, published in 1839, as "the greatest of the antislavery pamphlets," and still the best historical authority on slavery. "It is an encyclopedia of knowledge. It is a book of horrors," he writes. Weld himself correctly described it as "a work of incalculable value" to the abolitionist cause. "Facts and testimonies are troops, weapons and victory, all in one," he wrote. The principles governing its composition are suggested by a letter to Weld from two editorial advisors, Sereno and Mary Streeter: "Under the head of personal cruelty [you] will be obliged to reject much testimony; and this is not because the facts are not well authenticated but because those which are merely horrid must give place to those which are absolutely diabolical." Absolutely diabolical or not, in the opinion of Professor Dumond, "It is as close as history can come to the facts." According to his theory of historical evidence, "Diaries and plantation records are largely worthless because slaveholders never kept a record of their own evil ways."

The strong sexual theme that pervades antislavery literature often took a prurient turn, but in Mr. Dumond's hands the pruriency is transmuted by bold treatment. The presence of miscegenation is attested by the Census of 1860 and the proportion of the colored population of the South that was of mixed blood. But to Mr. Dumond, sexual exploitation becomes very nearly the basis of the institution of slavery. "Its prevalence leads to the inescapable conclusion," he writes, "that it was the basis—unspoken to be sure—of much of the defense of the institution." Ulrich B. Phillips, the Southern historian of slavery, doubtless betrayed a certain blindness when he reported that in all the records he studied he could find only one instance of deliberate "breeding" of slaves, and that an unsuccessful one in colonial Massachusetts. To Mr. Dumond, however, it is plain as day that the "breeding" was practiced by all slaveholders: "That is exactly what slave owners did with the slaves, and there were no exceptions." To the Georgia historian there were no instances, to the

Michigan historian no exceptions! What is one to tell the children?

Mr. Dumond's main subject, of course, is not slavery but antislavery. In his treatment of this great theme the myth is slightly muted, but it nevertheless pulses powerfully through the whole narrative. The Underground Railroad is described as "a highly romantic enterprise" that became "well organized." In these pages it operates with all the enchanting conspiracy and secrecy of the legend, with fugitive slaves, "secreted in livery stables, in attics, in storerooms, under featherbeds, in secret passages, in all sorts of out of the way places." There was one hayloft in Detroit that "was always full of Negroes."

In Professor Dumond's history the North Star Legend is given very nearly full credence. In striking contrast with the account rendered in detail by Mr. Litwack, we are informed that Negroes "continued to vote without interruption in New Hampshire, Vermont, Rhode Island, and in the two slave states of New York and New Jersey," and that there were never "any distinctions whatever in criminal law, judicial procedure, and punishments" in any New England states. "Negroes were citizens in all of these [free?] states," he writes (leaving it unclear how many). "They were citizens by enjoyment of full political equality, by lack of any statements to the contrary in any constitution or law, by complete absence of legal distinctions based on color, and by specific legal and constitutional declaration, and any statements to the contrary by courts, federal or state, were contrary to historical fact and are worthless as historical evidence." There is no hint of the thoroughgoing system of Northern segregation described by Mr. Litwack. It is admitted that one might "find a less liberal attitude toward free Negroes" in the Midwestern states, but that is easily accounted for: "There was a preponderance of Southern immigrants in the populations." In spite of this, we learn that in Jackson's time, "the Northern people, freeing themselves of the last vestiges of slavery, moved forward in a vast liberal reform movement."

The theory Mr. Dumond applies to the antislavery movement colors and coerces his reading of the whole of American history from the Revolution through the Civil War. This reading amounts to a revival of the long discredited theory of the Slave Power Conspiracy, a dominant hypothesis two or three generations ago. Slavery, we are told, "gave clay feet to Patrick Henry . . . and I suspect to Wash-

ington and Jefferson as well." Of the Revolutionary leaders he writes: "Those men were perfectly willing to spread carnage over the face of the earth to establish their own claim to freedom, but lacked the courage to live by their assertion of the natural rights of men." Of the Presidential contest of 1800 we are told: "This election enabled Jefferson to lay solidly the foundations of the party of agrarianism, slavery, and decentralization." Any mention of Jefferson is accompanied by a reminder that he owned slaves. The achievement of a group is discredited with the phrase, "slaveholders all." The Virginia Dynasty, its heirs and successors of the next three decades, and most of their acts and works including the Constitution, fare pretty harshly under this restricted historical criterion.

The whole sectional conflict that eventually erupted in the Civil War is construed, of course, in terms of right versus wrong, North against South. Civil War historians will be interested to learn that "there was complete coordination by the Congress, the President, and the field commanders of the Army" in their mutual determination to abolish slavery at the earliest possible moment. This revelation will require a good deal of revision in accepted views, which take into account a great lack of coordination among those distracted branches of the wartime government.

It is possible that Professor Dumond's interpretations of American history might be traced directly to an unfortunate theory of historical method. Neither this nor the extended criticism of his work already undertaken would be worth the effort, however, were it not for what the book reveals about the present vitality and amazing persistence of the antislavery myth. His book is the latest and fullest embodiment of the myth. Yet it comes with endorsements of unqualified praise from leading authorities in the field. The wide flaps of the dust jacket bear such recommendations from the three foremost present-day historians of the American Civil War, followed by the equally enthusiastic praise of prominent historians from four of our most respected universities. These are not men who share Mr. Dumond's restrictive concepts of historiography, nor are they given to bestowing praise lightly. They undoubtedly mean what they say. What two of them say is that this book is "definitive," and all agree that from their point of view it is wholly satisfying.

One would like to know more about their rea

soning. Several of them refer directly or obliquely to present-day social problems that are a heritage of slavery, meaning segregation and the movement for Negro rights. But surely one can establish his position upon such clear-cut contemporary moral problems as these without compromising the standards of historical criticism. And by this time, one hopes, it is possible to register a stand on the slavery issue without feigning the apocalyptic rages of a John Brown. No, these are not adequate or convincing explanations, at least for the reactions of these particular historians.

In all probability the real reason why this ponderous, fierce and humorless book is handled with such piety and solemnity is the very fact that it does embody one of the great American myths. We have never faced up to the relationship between myth and history. Without tackling the semantic difficulties involved, we know that *myth* has more than pejorative usages and that it can be used to denote more than what one deems false about the other man's beliefs. In the non-pejorative sense myths are images, or collections of them, charged with values, aspirations, ideals and meanings. In the words of Mark Schorer, they are "the instruments by which we continually struggle to make our experience intelligible to ourselves." Myths can be, in short, "a good thing." No man in his right mind, and surely not a responsible historian, will knowingly and wantonly destroy a precious thing. And no doubt some would hesitate to lay hands on a book that, improperly though it may be, got itself identified as a repository of cherished values.

Serious history is the critique of myths, however, not the embodiment of them. Neither is it the destruction of myths. One of the great national myths is the equality of man, embodied in the Declaration of Independence. Tocqueville's study of equality in America is a valid critique of the myth, with neither the intention nor the effect of destroying it or doing it injury. Henry Nash Smith's *Virgin Land* provides a valid critique of the West's Myth of the Garden and symbols of the frontier without succumbing to impulses of iconoclasm. There is no comparable critique of the more elaborate myth—one might say mythology—of the South. What has been done in this respect has been mainly the work of imaginative writers rather than historians of the South. Historians have made a beginning, however, and a recent contribution by William R. Taylor, *Cavalier and Yankee*, which illuminates the legend of aristocratic grandeur, is an excellent illustration of what is needed.

As a result of such studies, intelligent, contemporary Americans can speak of the myth of equality without self-consciousness or cynicism, and embrace it without striking the pose of a defiant Jacksonian of the 1830's. Contemporary westerners are able to cherish and preserve frontier values without assuming the role of a Davy Crockett. And southerners can even salvage some of the aristocratic heritage without wallowing in the Plantation Legend.

As yet, however, the Yankee remains to be fully emancipated from his own legends of emancipation. Confront him with a given set of symbols and he will set his sense of humor aside, snap to attention and come to a full salute. In the ensuing rigidities of that situation, conversation tends to lag. The pertinent interjections by Mr. Gara on the U.G.R.R. and by Mr. Litwack on the North Star Legend, already noticed, may help to break the ice, but the thawing will probably be slow. The provocative suggestions of Stanley M. Elkins, in *Slavery: A Problem in American Institutional and Intellectual Life,* have been gravely rebuked for impropriety, if not impiety. The orthodox text is obviously still the gospel according to Mr. Dumond.

The big assignment on the Antislavery Myth still awaits a taker. The eventual taker, like any historian who would make myth the proper subject of his study, should be involved without running the risks of total involvement. It would help a great deal if he could contrive to bring detachment as well as sympathy to his task. It is also to be hoped that he might make legitimate use of irony as well as compassion. And, finally, no aspirant with inappropriate regional identifications need apply.

America's Forgotten War: The War with Mexico

Robert W. Johannsen

Fables of the frontier, it is said, have functioned as the central cultural myths of the American experience, offering a storied, always shifting locale, inhabited by heroic individuals, wherein civilization and savagery contend. Such narratives dramatize the grand test of individual and national resources against the great unknown or the great challenge. The mythic impulse that successively drew to various wilderness utopias pathfinders, adventurers, hunters, trappers, mountain men, pioneers, yeoman farmers, land developers, soldiers, and empire builders exerted its greatest influence in the decades of the 1830s and 40s—the age of Texas independence, manifest destiny, and the Mexican War. During this era the prospect of extending the area of freedom to the Pacific captured the cultural imagination. An empire of the mind, what one political leader at the time called "the Green Tree of Empire," rooted in the cultural logic of manifest destiny, created a set of political, diplomatic, and military conditions ultimately responsible for war with Mexico.

As Robert W. Johannsen, J. G. Randall Distinguished Professor of History at the University of Illinois, assesses it a century and a half after it began, the Mexican War has become a footnote to American history. When not forgotten, it has been rather cavalierly dismissed as the nation's first imperial venture or its first unpopular war. The truth about the conflict, and its effect upon the nation, is far more complex— and interesting. The war was not an imperial aberration, but rather the fulfillment of longstanding ambitions and impulses. Lapsing into a self-righteous rhetoric of peace, thereby working to sustain the myth of the U.S. as a nonviolent nation, a great many political and military leaders with the notable exception of Ulysses S. Grant allowed this country's cultural conceit to express itself in territorial piracy against the Republic of Mexico in the Treaty of Guadalupe Hidalgo. The march to Matamoros, Buena Vista, Vera Cruz, and Mexico City, and the resultant victory over our southern neighbor orchestrated by President James K. Polk in 1846, and conducted by generals Zachary Taylor and Winfield Scott in 1846–47, did much to fulfill the mythical dreams of manifest destiny even as it left a significant legacy of hate among Mexicans and Chicanos toward their Anglo conquerors.

"Long after we are dead," wrote the popular mid-19th-century novelist George Lippard, "History will tell the children of ages yet to come, how the hosts gathered for the Crusade, in the year 1846."

One hundred and fifty years ago, the United States took up arms against Mexico, engaging in a war fought wholly on foreign soil for the first time in its history. It was a conflict fraught with significance for both nations. Yet for all its importance (and despite Lippard's confident prediction), the war with Mexico has become America's forgotten war. Few today can recite its causes. Few Americans even recall the battlefield triumphs. If remembered at all, it is thought of, wrongly, as an unpopular war, in large part because certain luminaries of the day, including Ralph Waldo Emerson and Henry David Thoreau, inveighed so eloquently against it.

To be sure, wars often create more problems than they settle, and the Mexican War was no exception. A bitter and divisive sectional struggle over the issue of slavery's expansion into the territories gained from Mexico was an unintended consequence of the conflict. Many Amreicans were later convinced, as was Ulysses S. Grant (himself a participant in the war), that "the Southern rebellion was largely an outgrowth of the Mexican War." Writing 40 years after the fact, failing in health, the old general influenced much subsequent thinking about the war when he charged that it was "one of the most unjust ever waged by a stronger against a weaker nation." The Civil War, he declared, was "our punishment." The war with Mexico, when it was viewed at all, was considered within the context of the struggle over slavery and as a precursor to what Grant called "the most sanguinary and expensive war of modern times."

*   *   *

But the Mexican War had importance far beyond its contributions to the outbreak of the Civil War—and in its day was viewed far more favorably than subsequent opinion would have us think. The first major national crisis faced during a period of unprecedented economic and social change, it came at a crucial moment in the young life of the United States. Rapid commercial and industrial expansion, with new opportunities for material advancement, was changing people's lives. Social reformers, utopian visionaries, political theorists, and religious enthusiasts were offering a host of projects and schemes in their quest for individual improvement. Questions were being raised about the true nature and purpose of republican government, as older values of patriotism and civic virtue—the heart of classical republicanism—seemed to be giving way before the new "spirit of gain."

The United States at midcentury was a nation in search of itself, and the war with Mexico became an important step toward self-definition. For a time and for some people, the war offered reassurance, giving new meaning to patriotism, providing a new arena for heroism, and reinforcing popular convictions regarding the superiority of republican government. The war was seen as a test of democratic institutions, as legitimizing America's mission as the world's "model republic."

*   *   *

The outbreak of the Mexican War had a long and complex background in years of uneasy relations between the two countries. To many Americans, the frequency of revolutions in Mexico rendered that country's republican government more a sham than a reality. The United States had lodged claims against Mexico for losses incurred by American citizens during the revolutions, but even though the claims were arbitrated in 1842 at Mexico's request, they remained unpaid.

Yet for all the moments of irritation and tension, the cause of the Mexican War might be simply stated in a single word—Texas. The United States wanted Texas, and Mexico did not mean for the Americans to have it. From the moment Texas gained its independence from Mexico in 1836, Mexico blamed the United States for its loss and nurtured hopes for its recapture. The boundary with the United States, as far as Mexico was concerned, continued to be the Sabine River, which separated Louisiana and Texas. For the United States, it was the Rio Grande, the "traditional" line claimed in the 1803 treaty with France, which suggested that Texas was a part of the Louisiana Purchase, and confirmed by John Quincy Adams in his 1819 negotiations with Spain. The land between the two rivers—the Sabine and the Rio Grande—was the disputed territory.

Sentiment in support of the annexation of Texas to the United States gained strength as it was linked with questions of western settlement and territorial expansion. John L. O'Sullivan, outspoken New York journalist and editor of the *Democratic Review*, reflecting the romantic idealism of the time, placed the issue in broader perspective (and unwittingly coined a phrase that soon became a popular American idiom) when he asserted that America's claim to Texas was "by right of our manifest destiny to overspread and possess the whole of the continent which Providence has given us for the development of the great experiment of liberty and federated self government."

Any action by the United States aimed at acquiring Texas, Mexican authorities repeatedly warned, would be regarded as a declaration of war against Mexico. When Congress passed a joint resolution annexing Texas, on March 1, 1845, Mexico broke diplomatic relations with the United States. As he left Washington, the Mexican minister angrily denounced annexation as an act of aggression against Mexico, "the most unjust which can be found recorded in the annals of modern history."

The ensuing year was marked by the rapid breakdown of relations, by threats and ultimatums, by military movements and countermovements, by bellicose invective and futile peace feelers. Mexico's repeated threats of invasion, the mobilization of its armed forces, the massing of Mexican troops on the south bank of the Rio Grande, and the appeals from Austin for protection following the official acceptance of annexation prompted President James K. Polk to order General Zachary Taylor's army into Texas. Taylor's force crossed the Sabine River and by late August 1845 was camped near the village of Corpus Christi.

* * *

The outbreak of hostilities now appeared certain. In a last-ditch effort to avert war, Polk dispatched John Slidell to Mexico City with authority to negotiate the differences between the two countries, a futile gesture that only inflamed anti-American feeling. Slidell was rebuffed, and a short time later Mexico's government was toppled by a revolution led by military hardliners who pledged to defend Mexican territory as far east as the Sabine River.

The admission of Texas to statehood in December 1845 raised the stakes. When news of Slidell's failure reached Washington shortly afterward, an impatient President Polk ordered General Taylor to move his army to the Rio Grande. By the end of March 1846, the troops were in position on the river opposite the Mexican town of Matamoros. Taylor had been instructed not to treat Mexico as an enemy unless its forces committed an "open act of hostility."

Within weeks of Taylor's movement, the new Mexican president, General Mariano Paredes, declared a "defensive war" against the United States, and the Mexican commander on the Rio Grande informed Taylor that hostilities had commenced. A Mexican force crossed the Rio Grande and ambushed a detachment of American dragoons on a reconnais-

sance mission, killing and wounding a number of them in the process. When Polk received the news on May 9, he summoned his cabinet into an emergency meeting. On May 11, he submitted his war message to Congress. Within two days, both houses had concurred, authorizing the president to raise 50,000 volunteers and appropriating $10 million to meet the expenses.

* * *

What neither Polk nor Congress could know was that the Mexican army had already crossed the Rio Grande in force and had engaged Taylor's army in the first major battles of the war, Palo Alto and Resaca de la Palma, in and near the present city of Brownsville. In both engagements, Taylor's outnumbered soldiers sent the invaders reeling in disorganized retreat back across the river.

The call for volunteers coincided with the news reports of the victories on the Rio Grande. The response was electric. Quotas, initially assigned to those states nearest the scene of operations, were quickly oversubscribed. Thousands of young men had to be turned back; Illinois provided enough men for 14 regiments when only four were called. The rush of volunteers, according to one writer, confirmed the superior nature of republican government: "We had to show the Mexicans that a people without being military, may be *warlike*."

The volunteers came from all walks of life. Individuals from the upper ranks of society—sons of Henry Clay and Daniel Webster, a descendant of John Marshall, and Edward Everett's nephew, as well as scions of families with proud Revolutionary War connections—mixed with farmers, merchants, lawyers, journalists, members of fire companies, students, recent immigrants, and even a sprinkling of American Indians. As one Illinois volunteer looked about him at a rendezvous where recruits had gathered, he noted "lead-miners from Galena; wharf rats and dock loafers from Chicago; farmers on unpurchased lands from the interior; small pattern politicians, emulous of popularity; village statesmen, pregnant with undeveloped greatness, and anxious to enlarge the sphere of their influence by a military *accouchement*; briefless lawyers and patientless physicians; and a liberal allowance of honest, hard-fisted 'Suckers.' " Whatever their background or occupation, the volunteers were united by a spirit of adventure, eagerly anticipating a "grand jubilee in the halls of the Montezumas." It was an army of democracy, and the citizen soldier became an honored symbol of the republic.

Many of the volunteers had military experience, in the War of 1812 or the Seminole wars in Florida, and a large number of them had spent time at West Point. One-third of the volunteer regiments were commanded by West Pointers, and well over a third of the field officers had had at least some West Point training.

Everywhere they went, the volunteers attracted crowds of well-wishers. Residents of the towns and farms along the Ohio and Mississippi rivers gathered on the riverbanks to shout their encouragement, waving flags and handkerchiefs, as the volunteers passed on their way down river to New Orleans. There, they camped on the Chalmette battlefield, where Andrew Jackson had humbled a proud British army only 31 years before. At what they called Camp Jackson, they awaited transportation by sea to the mouth of the Rio Grande.

*   *   *

The Civil War has customarily been regarded as America's first literate war, that is, the first war in which significant numbers of literate individuals served as soldiers. Although statistics are sketchy or nonexistent, a good case for possession of this distinction might be made for the Mexican War. Numbered among the volunteers were many men of education, including college graduates and products of the country's common-school systems. They were avid letterwriters, corresponding with their families and friends and often serving as special correspondents for their hometown newspapers. Following the hard-fought battle for the northern Mexican city of Monterrey in September 1846, the volume of letters that passed through the New Orleans post office from the men in Taylor's army doubled in number to more than 14,000 pieces.

Reading materials—books and newspapers—were also in heavy demand and short supply. That many of the soldiers were exceptionally well-read was evident from the literary and historical allusions that filled their letters and diaries. European travelers to the United States had observed that the Americans were a "reading people," and the volunteers confirmed this judgment. Soldiers carried books in their knapsacks, received books in the mail from their families (often asking for specific titles), and sought

out booksellers in the Mexican towns they occupied. Still, there were never enough books available to satisfy the demand. Newspapers were even more scarce. Some of the eastern metropolitan dailies established papers in the larger Mexican cities, the so-called "Anglo-Saxon press," but this effort did not meet the needs of the troops.

The volunteer system was at the heart of Ameica's vision of responsible republican government, the principal means of defense during times of national crisis. Although President Polk called for a modest increase in the size of the regular army and later authorized 10 additional regiments, he shared the popular bias against a large professional military force. A standing army, he declared, was "contrary to the genius of our free institutions, would impose heavy burdens on the people and be dangerous to public liberty." Reliance, he insisted, must be on "our citizen soldiers." From the beginning of the war, there was no love lost between the regulars and the volunteers. To the volunteers, the regular soldier was a "drilled automaton," while the regulars, resentful of all the attention given to the volunteers, viewed them as little better than an untrained and undisciplined rabble, useless as fighting men and ignorant of even the basic rules of survival in the field.

General Winfield Scott, who commanded large numbers of volunteers, complained that they knew nothing of camp discipline, cleanliness, sanitation, and proper diet. Scott and his fellow officers had reason for concern. More than 6,000 volunteers died from exposure and disease, principally dysentery and chronic diarrhea, about 10 times the number killed in action, though regulars hardly fared much better.

*   *   *

Although there were numerous examples of friendly relations between the soldiers and Mexican civilians, including instances of the U.S. Army's defense of Mexican towns against marauding Indians and bandits, breaches of discipline among the soldiers were not uncommon, especially during long periods of inactivity. Individual acts of violence against the lives and property of civilians, often retaliatory in nature, generally went unpunished. Only rarely did large bodies of men engage in such acts. Following the destruction by Mexican irregulars of a three-mile-long supply train bound for Taylor's army in which the teamsters were slaughtered, a passing group of volunteers, said to be Texas Rangers whose thirst for vengeance against Mexicans was widely feared, avenged the massacre by murdering up to 40 inhabitants of a nearby village.

More widely publicized and condemned was the murder by Arkansas cavalry, "wild and reckless fellows" known as Rackensackers, of 30 Mexican men, women, and children who had sought safety in a mountain cave following the murder of one of the Arkansas officers. Taylor was outraged, and the incident was reported in gory detail in the American press, arousing an immediate popular reaction. The massacre was denounced as behavior inconsistent with "one of the most enlightened and civilized nations of the globe." "Let us no longer complain of Mexican barbarity."

*   *   *

In spite of what regulars said about them, the volunteers proved their mettle as combat soldiers, fighting with courage and tenacity. Their role in each of the three areas of military operation was crucial to the ultimate success of American arms. Victory owed much to the superior organization and efficiency of the regulars and to the high quality of training offered by West Point, but in many respects the Mexican War was a volunteers' war.

Following his early victories at Palo Alto and Resaca de la Palma, Taylor moved his army into northern Mexico, his first target the "stronghold of northern Mexico," the fortified city of Monterrey. Anticipated by the volunteers with exhilaration, the battle for Monterrey in late September 1846 proved to be a costly struggle, marked by bloody, desperate street and house-to-house fighting before the city was secured. Taylor's campaign culminated the following February in the Battle of Buena Vista, fought in a narrow pass between mountain ranges south of the city of Saltillo against a larger force commanded by General Santa Anna. Except for about 200 dragoons and three batteries of artillery, Taylor's men were volunteers, all but a few facing enemy fire for the first time. It was another hard-fought engagement, one the volunteers were not sure they could win. Exhaustion turned to rejoicing when Santa Anna withdrew his army under cover of darkness and began a long retreat southward, his force diminished by heavy casualties and mounting desertions.

A second army, commanded by General Stephen Watts Kearny, moved westward from Missouri along the Santa Fe Trail, occupying New Mexico without a shot, and, in conjunction with naval forces, going on to take possession of California.

A third front was opened in March 1847, after months of planning that required the careful coordination of military and naval operations and the collection of vast amounts of ordnance and quartermaster stores. General Scott, in the greatest amphibious operation to that time, landed 9,000 men on the beach south of Veracruz in five hours without suffering a single casualty. In addition to regular troops transferred from Taylor's command, Scott's army included volunteer regiments from Pennsylvania, New York, South Carolina, Tennessee, and Illinois. By the end of March, Veracruz had fallen to the Americans, and Scott began his march inland toward Mexico City, on the route followed by Cortés in the 16th century. Santa Anna's army blocked his path in Cerro Gordo, a wild, mountainous region, but by unexpectedly following a treacherous mountain path and scaling peaks under fire, Scott's force flanked an apparently impregnable Mexican position, sending the enemy's soldiers into headlong retreat. After several sharp engagements in the vicinity of Mexico City—at Contreras, Churubusco, Molino del Rey, and Chapultepec—Scott occupied the Mexican capital in September 1847. With the occupation of Mexico City the fighting came to an end, except for sporadic guerrilla raids along the lines of supply.

The logistical problems faced by Polk in directing the war were enormous and unprecedented. Large numbers of troops had to be raised in a short time, trained and equipped, and moved quickly over long distances to the scenes of the fighting. That the problems were met was a tribute to Polk's single-minded dedication to what he conceived to be the responsibilities of presidential leadership in time of war.

*   *   *

Polk was the first president to give full definition to the role of commander in chief. "Polk gave the country its first demonstration of the *administrative* capacities of the presidency as a war agency," historian Leonard D. White has written. "He proved that a president could run a war." He not only placed the nation on a wartime footing almost overnight, but he also involved himself directly in all the countless details that sprang from prosecuting a war in a distant, and, to a large extent, unknown land. He took the initiative in securing war legislation and finance, made many of the tactical decisions that were conveyed to the armies by the War Department, appointed generals and drafted their instructions, and coordinated the work of the various bureaus and cabinet departments. Polk was, as one author has written, "the center on which all else depended." Later, dealing with his own crisis, Abraham Lincoln devoted careful study to Polk's management of the war.

Anticipating a short conflict, Polk undertook negotiations to end the war almost from the moment it began. The terms of the treaty that finally concluded the war were Polk's terms from the beginning. Signed in early February 1848 in a suburb of Mexico City, the Treaty of Guadalupe Hidalgo recognized the Rio Grande boundary and provided for the cession of New Mexico and California to the United States. The United States canceled its long-standing claims against Mexico and agreed to pay Mexico $15 million. The two countries further agreed to submit all future disputes to arbitration.

The Mexican War provided combat experience and valuable military lessons for many young officers who would later become leaders in the Civil War. But the war had consequences far beyond the battlefield. It touched the lives of Americans more intimately and with greater immediacy than any major event to that time. Coinciding with the "print explosion" of the mid-19th century, of which the penny press was one manifestation, the war was reported in more detail than any previous conflict. Fast, steam-powered presses, innovative techniques in news gathering, the employment of war correspondents for the first time, the use of the new magnetic telegraph, and the rapid proliferation of books and periodicals all combined to carry the war into the lives of Americans on an unprecedented scale.

* * *

The first news of the war was greeted by an outburst of enthusiasm from one end of the country to the other: public demonstrations, bonfires, and illuminations, war rallies from Massachusetts to Illinois. "A military ardor pervades all ranks," wrote Herman Melville from his New York home. "Nothing is talked of but the 'Halls of the Montezuma.'"

How to explain the outburst of public support and the sudden rush of volunteers to the colors? How to account for what one newspaper called "this sub-

lime spectacle of military preparations"? One explanation was found in America's commitment to a republican form of government. Where the people were the rulers, the security of the country in times of crisis was in the hands of its citizens.

* * *

There is no doubt that the war awakened a latent spirit of patriotism among Americans, but there were other, less lofty reasons for the rush of volunteers. It was a time when Americans were "reaching out" beyond their borders; the expansion of commerce, the increase in travel made possible by improvements in transportation, and the exploration by government-sponsored expeditions of remote areas in Africa, the Middle East, and South America all stimulated a romantic interest in other lands and other peoples. For the volunteers, the war offered a first exposure to a strange and ancient land they had only imagined before. "To revel among the intoxicating perfumes and flowery plains," exulted an Ohio volunteer, "to gaze upon the magnificent scenery and wonderful exhibitions of Aztec civilization . . . to plant the flag of our young republic upon the capital reared centuries ago above the ruins of Montezuma's palaces! What prospect more captivating to the youthful imagination?" Filled with the spirit of adventure, the volunteers shared their experiences with the folks back home in their letters, diaries, and the many published accounts of their campaigns, travel narratives in their own right.

The war entered the stream of American popular culture in a myriad of ways. It was celebrated in poetry and song, in paintings and lithographs, and in great "national dramas" performed on the stage in the nation's theaters. Music publishers were quick to exploit the popular interest, and the chronology of the war could be told in the titles they issued. Piano arrangements in sheet music form, embellished with imaginative engravings depicting the war's events, evoked the conflict in such pieces as *General Taylor's Encampment Quickstep* and in the "elegant pianistic effects" of Stephen Foster's *Santa Anna's Retreat from Buena Vista*.

The Mexican War was dramatized even before the facts were known, but authenticity of detail was never a concern for playwrights and producers who sought to reenact the war's events on the stage. Capacity audiences thrilled to such stage creations as *The Siege of Monterey, or, The Triumph of Rough and*

Ready, which was so successful in New York that it went on tour, giving people the opportunity (according to its advertisement) "to exult in the triumph of American arms."

Book publishers met the popular demand with a flood of romantic tales with Mexican War settings. Bound in bright yellow covers, illustrated with crude woodcuts, printed on rough paper in double columns, they became America's first popular paperbacks. With such titles as *The Mexican Spy, or, The Bride of Buena Vista*, they combined all the popular Gothic elements—romance, intrigue, mystery, and suspense. The stories they told were strikingly similar—chivalric American volunteers displaying generosity to the vanquished foe, rescuing *senoritas* from the clutches of cruel Mexican guerrillas or corrupt priests, capturing these ladies' hearts and not infrequently carrying them back to Kentucky or Illinois as war brides. Published in editions of as many as 100,000 copies, these books are almost impossible to find today. Passed around from hand to hand among soldiers as well as civilians, they were literally used up!

*   *   *

Not all the publications were such "catch-penny affairs." James Fenimore Cooper, disappointed that the navy did not play a greater role in the war, made up for it by writing a novel of the Mexican War at sea, *Jack Tier, or, The Florida Reef* (1848), in which he imagined encounters between the United States and Mexican navies. For Cooper, America had embarked on a mission to break the "crust" that enclosed Mexico in bigotry and ignorance, and to bring the "blessings of real liberty" to the Mexican people. From his Brooklyn editorial office, Walt Whitman wrote eloquently of the victories in Mexico, viewing the war in terms of America's great democratic mission to "elevate the *true* self-respect of the American people."

No single individual did as much to kindle the war-spirit as the prominent historian and chronicler of the 16th-century Spanish conquest of Mexico, William Hickling Prescott. It was an ironic distinction, for Prescott was a dedicated antislavery New England Whig, strongly opposed to what he termed this "mad and unprincipled" war. The immense popularity of his *History of the Conquest of Mexico* (1843), published just two and a half years before the war, turned public attention toward Mexico, familiarizing countless Americans with the titanic struggle between Cortés and Montezuma. Prescott deplored the "dare-devil war spirit" following the first battles in May 1846, but what he did not realize was that his own work had much to do with provoking that spirit. By describing "the past Conquest of Mexico" so vividly, it was said, Prescott had in fact "foretold the future one."

The war heightened the popularity of Prescott's *History*, and his publisher brought out new editions to meet the demand. Volunteers read and re-read it, and many of them carried copies of the book with them into Mexico. One Indiana volunteer was so captivated by Prescott's history that he joined the war hoping to relive some of its episodes. For the soldiers in Winfield Scott's army, the book served as a guidebook along the route to the Mexican capital.

In spite of his antiwar attitude, Prescott expressed an admiration for the nation's citizen soldiers. Without conceding that the war was either jut or necessary, he judged the American campaigns to be as brilliant as those of the great 16th-century Spaniard himself. To some, it was only logical that Prescott should become the historian of the Second Conquest of Mexico, as he had of the First, and a number of people, including General Scott, appealed to the historian to consider the task. Prescott was tempted but in the end rejected the proposal.

Prescott's attitude toward the war reflected the ambivalence of many of those who opposed the conflict. Members of the American Peace Society, for example, deplored the outburst of war spirit yet seemed more concerned with averting war with Great Britain over the Oregon country than with denouncing the war with Mexico. When the crisis with the British was settled amicably, a leader of the movement declared 1846 to be "an era in the Peace cause," in spite of the fact that the Mexican War was already under way. Others believed that the prestige of victory over Mexico would prevent Europeans from complaining that American peace advocates supported the outlawing of war only because their country was too weak to fight one.

*   *   *

Although many members of the Whig Party defended the war and took an active part in it, others charged the war with being unjust, immoral, and unnecessary and held President Polk and his Democratic Party responsible for provoking it. Very few, however, assumed the extreme position of Senator

Thomas Corwin of Ohio, who characterized the war as organized thievery and counseled the Mexicans to greet the volunteers "with bloody hands" and to welcome them "to hospitable graves." Whig officers in the field were furious, charging that Corwin's words bordered on treason, while Ohio volunteers burned the senator in effigy. Even while opposing "Mr. Polk's war," however, Whigs were advised that patriotism as well as the discipline of an ordered society demanded that every citizen support it. The fact that both the commanding generals, Scott and Taylor, were Whigs was not lost on the party.

Outspoken and uncompromising in their opposition to the Mexican War were the abolitionists, whose leader set the tone of their protest a few days after Polk sent his war message to Congress. The war, proclaimed William Lloyd Garrison, was one "of aggression, of invasion, of conquest, and rapine—marked by ruffianism, perfidy, and every other feature of national depravity." To the abolitionists, the war was waged solely to extend and perpetuate the institution of slavery, a mistaken assumption but one that confirmed the charge that a slave-power plot was afoot to strengthen the hated institution. Some abolitionists were unwilling to follow Garrison's lead. The editor of a Cincinnati antislavery paper announced that he would not print antiwar articles for fear they would endanger the safety of American soldiers in Mexico. There was strong feeling that the shrill condemnations by such men as Corwin and Garrison played a part in delaying the peace negotiations and prolonging the war.

*   *   *

Eighty-seven-year-old Albert Gallatin brought the perspective of five decades of public service, as a diplomat, fiscal expert, and presidential adviser, to bear on the Mexican War. His concern was two-sided. The founder, in 1842, of the American Ethnological Society, he had just published a scholarly study of Mexican and Central American antiquities. He recognized that the war would advance his own ethnological research, and to this end he maintained a correspondence with officers in the army, asking for information on the native peoples of New Mexico and Arizona and urging them to collect books and documents relating to Mexico's ancient civilization. At the same time, he was profoundly disturbed by the war's impact upon the integrity of America's republican government.

The people, Gallatin believed, were blinded by the "romantic successes" of their armies in Mexico; their minds were captured by an "enthusiastic and exclusive love of military glory." More important, they had forgotten the mission God had assigned them, the mission to improve the "state of the world" and to demonstrate that republican government was attended by the "highest standard of private and political virtue and morality." Instead, he argued, Americans had abandoned the lofty position of their fathers and had carried patriotism to excess.

*   *   *

Gallatin's statement had little effect on public opinion in spite of its sincerity and uplifting tone. Its publication coincided with the signing of the peace treaty; the war was over and Gallatin's views seemed no longer relevant. Of more importance in shaping popular perceptions of the war were those who saw the conflict in terms of the duties and responsibilities of citizens in a republic. While they agreed that war was alien to the true purpose of a republic, they also maintained that there were some wars that even republics had to fight. "In what way," asked New England reformer Nahum Capen, "could the evils of Mexico be reached, unless by the strong hand of war?" As the world's leading republic, the United States had a duty to rescue its benighted neighbor and see that justice be done its people.

Through all the talk of American superiority, of America's providential destiny, and of its republican mission, there ran this theme of regeneration, or renewal. While some scholars have doubted the sincerity of those who argued the reform character of the Mexican War, the belief that it was America's duty to redeem the Mexican people was too widespread to be dismissed as nothing more than an attempt to mask ulterior desires for power and gain. People from all walks of life, including the soldiers in Mexico, echoed the belief that it was their mission to bring Mexico into the 19th century. Critics of the war such as Prescott and Gallatin might scoff at the exaggerated rhetoric of the war's supporters, but they too shared the view that America's role in Mexico was a regenerative one.

General Scott gave official sanction to the theme of regeneration in his first proclamation to the Mexican nation, issued from Jalapa on May 11, 1847, three weeks after the bloody engagement at Cerro Gordo. The war, he declared, was an evil. Nations, however,

Mexico's War of 1847

As the specter of war loomed over Mexico during the spring of 1846, its leaders pondered the prospect of an armed conflict with the United States. The outlook was not promising. Only 25 years before, after a destructive eleven-year war to win its independence from Spain, the new nation had begun a long and largely unsuccessful struggle to achieve social, economic, and political stability. But apart from a widespread determination to preserve Mexico's honor and its territorial integrity, little unified the bankrupt and divided nation in the mid-1840s.

The lack of domestic solidarity was largely the result of Mexico's failure to establish a durable political arrangement. Since independence, the nation had experimented with an empire, a federal republic, and various forms of centralized rule, but none of these had lasted. By midcentury, most of the country's roughly seven million inhabitants were ill-assimilated Indians who performed manual labor, while anti-Spanish sentiment had long driven off many of Mexico's better-trained elites. To make matters worse, the nation had little industry, a poor transportation network, and almost no government revenue apart from import tariffs.

On the eve of the war, the Catholic church and the military (whose chief strongman was General Antonio López de Santa Anna) were firmly established as the country's most powerful institutions. Separate entities within the state, they had their own courts and privileges, and any effort by reformers to curb their power ignited political disputes, including one that pitted three powerful factions against one another during the 1840s.

Led by Valentín Gómez Farías, the radicals (or *puros*) wanted to eradicate all vestiges of traditionalism by limiting the Church's economic and political privileges and by establishing a volunteer civic militia to break the regular army's power. Enlisting the support of the lower classes, the radicals hoped to bring back the federal form of government (set forth in the 1824 constitution), believing that it would give Mexico the strength and unity to regain Texas.

Like the *puros*, the moderates, led by Manuel Gómez Pedraza, favored putting restraints on the regular army and the Church, though only gradually in the case of the latter. Wary of the lower classes, the *moderados* wanted only property owners to serve in the civic militias. While preferring a constitutional monarchy, in 1845 they supported efforts to reform the centralist constitution of 1843. In foreign affairs, they stood almost alone in hoping to reach an amicable accord with the United States on the Texas question.

For their part, conservatives such as Lucas Alamán sought to salvage those elements of the Spanish colonial state that had benefited them. They wanted a strong centralized government, preferably a monarchy, built upon an alliance between the church and the regular army, and only limited citizenship for the lower classes. Finding it impossible to resist the prowar atmosphere, they reluctantly took up the jingoistic banner against the United States.

The episode that best illuminates Mexico's crippling political divisiveness is the February 1847 "rebellion of the *polkos*." On January 11 of that year, then-vice president Gómez Farías, the acting chief executive, issued a decree authorizing the government to raise 15 million pesos by mortgaging or selling ecclesiastical property. Designed to finance the war against the United States, the law set off a furor. *Moderado* politicians, senior army chiefs, and high-ranking clerical leaders plotted to overthrow Farías, relying on civic militia battalions (known as the *polkos* because the polka had become the most popular dance of elite society) organized during the fall of 1846 by Mexico City's well-to-do. The revolt, which erupted just a few days before General Winfield Scott's expeditionary army landed in Veracruz, prevented the Mexican government from coming to the defense of the port city.

Eventual defeat in what Mexicans called the War of 1847 did not bring unity to the nation. A new generation of *puro* and *moderado* thinkers concluded that Mexico's main problem had been the failure to extirpate the Spanish colonial legacy, while conservatives argued that monarchy was the best means of restoring national well-being. Debate grew increasingly rancorous and turned to open conflict in 1854. Only in 1867, after overcoming yet another round of civil war and foreign intervention by Napoleon III, who in 1862 installed Maximilian of Hapsburg as emperor, did the *puros* manage to establish a new republic and greater national consensus.

—Pedro Santoni

PEDRO SANTONI is a professor of history at California State University, San Bernardino.

"have sacred duties to perform, from which they cannot swerve." Mexican republicanism had become the "sport of private ambition" and cried out for rescue. Scott admonished the Mexican people to throw off their old colonial habits and to "learn to be truly free—truly republican." It is doubtful whether Scott's proclamation reached many Mexicans, but it had a deep effect on the men in his army. When the troops moved into Puebla later in the summer, one of the Mexican residents noted that the soldiers "talk of nothing but fraternity between the two republics, and say they have only come to save the democratic principle."

*   *   *

When President Polk reviewed the results of the Mexican War in his annual message to Congress in December 1848, he found its meaning in the nation's demonstration that a democracy could successfully prosecute a foreign war "with all the vigor" normally associated with "more abitrary forms of government." Critics, he noted, had long charged republics with an inherent lack "of that unity, concentration of purpose, and vigor of execution" that characterized authoritarian governments. A popularly elected representative government with a volunteer army of citizen-soldiers had bested a military dictatorship. No more persuasive argument for the strength and superiority of the republican system, he felt, could be advanced.

*   *   *

Polk's view was widely shared. The United States was yet a young and fragile nation, and its people were sensitive to the fact that in the eyes of the world theirs was still an unproven experiment in popular government. Europeans had scoffed at America's national pretensions, its bluster and spread-eagle rhetoric, ridiculed its romantic faith in the popular voice, and magnified the weakness of its institutions. Their opinions had been confirmed by a host of travelers, including Charles Dickens, who had toured the country four years before the war and found the "model republic" wanting in almost every respect. As for waging an offensive war, it was said

that the country would surely collapse into disunity and paralysis at the very thought.

Americans responded with a defensiveness that bordered on paranoia. The Mexican War, they were convinced, would silence the scoffers, for they had shown the world that a people devoted to the "arts of peace" could vanquish a "military people, governed by military despots." The prestige of victory, moreover, would not be without its influence overseas. When in the very month the treaty of peace was signed, on February 22 (the symbolism of the date, George Washington's birthday, was not lost on the Americans), revolution broke out in France against the monarchy and in favor of constitutional government, the connection with the Mexican War seemed obvious. James Fenimore Cooper reflected popular opinion when he exulted that the guns that had filled "the valley of the Aztecs with their thunder" were heard "in echoes on the other side of the Atlantic."

The victorious conclusion of the Mexican War and its repercussions in Europe seemed to herald the dawn of a new and golden age for the "model republic"—golden in fact, for gold was discovered in California at the very moment California became part of the United States. Expansion to the Pacific Ocean in California and Oregon (the latter by an 1846 treaty with Great Britain) was celebrated as the fulfillment of the nation's manifest destiny. "The far-reaching, the boundless future," John L. O'Sullivan proudly proclaimed, "will be the era of American greatness."

Yet, for all the lofty rhetoric and soaring predictions, clouds had begun to gather in the bright morning skies of the republic (as one writer put it). Some Americans feared that the Mexican War would result in a militarism that was antithetical to the purposes of the republic. Others saw an even greater danger in the revival of the troublesome question of slavery's expansion into new territories. Probably most Americans felt that the clouds would quickly dispel. Mutual concession and compromise had settled such questions before, and would surely do so again. With the new prestige and strength gained from victory over Mexico, the republic appeared indestructible. As well attempt to dissolve the solar system, declared Polk's treasury secretary Robert J. Walker, as to sever the ties that "must forever bind together the American Union."

Representing Truth: The Myth and Legend of Sojourner Truth

Nell Irvin Painter

During the second quarter of the nineteenth century religious and social reformers sought to bring American conduct into closer accordance with their perception of the American creed. It was an era of experiment by those most smitten by their own American Dream. In the region of western New York State, in an area known as the Burned-Over District, a number of utopian forms of religious revivalism sprang up. This great spiritual awakening was signaled by the publication of *The Book of Mormon* in 1830, transcribed by the religious visionary Joseph Smith. The Mormons' struggle to establish eventually the state of Deseret testifies to the myth of religious freedom that then prevailed. Others launched spirited attempt to democratize the nation by challenging long-standing social mythologies pertaining to womens' rights. Oberlin College set aside gender myths by opening its doors to women in the 1830s, and in 1837 Mary Lyon founded Mount Holyoke as the country's first women's college. At the women's rights convention in Seneca Falls, New York, in 1848, cultural myths about true equality and freedom lay exposed for at least some to see. The abolitionist movement scrutinized at last some racial myths, the transparent fictions supportive of the Peculiar Institution.

The life of one individual in particular—Isabella Van Wagner, also known as Sojourner Truth—perhaps best personifies the interlocking complexities of such religious, feminist, and racial reform impulses. As represented in the work of Nell Irvin Painter, Edwards Professor of American History at Princeton University, Sojourner Truth's life, shared in correspondence and public documents with Frederick Douglass, William Lloyd Garrison, and Harriet Beecher Stowe, is essentially a case study of myth-breaking and, at the same time, myth-making. Layers of misunderstanding cloud the traditional stories—of both the multiple social mythologies that she challenged and a quite conscious self-made myth. To see and hear her was, by all accounts, and to use a nineteenth-century term, a most "affecting" experience. Her rhetorical skills carrying a "subtle power" became legendary even in her time. She not only assumed a new name but fashioned an identity and a forceful public persona as a national symbol of race and gender. She "sold the shadow to support the substance." She functioned, and continues to function as a national icon—in the manner of Betsy Ross and Parson Weems' George Washington. In the truest American tradition, she reinvented herself, in the process forcing the nation to do likewise.

In New York City on the first of June, 1843, a woman known as Isabella Van Wagner changed her name to Sojourner Truth and began an itinerant ministry. The date was momentous, for in 1843, June 1 was Pentecost, the Christian holiday that falls fifty days after Easter and commemorates the day when the Holy Spirit filled Jesus' disciples and gave them the power to preach to strangers. Pentecostals such as Sojourner Truth heed Luke's narration in the biblical book of Acts, in which the Holy Spirit made the disciples speak in tongues, in the foreign languages that let them teach people of all nations of the wonderful works of God. God said through the disciples—already this was mediated knowledge—that he would pour out his spirit upon all flesh, and men and daughters and servants would prophesy.

Born into slavery in New York State, in the Hudson River county of Ulster, about 1797, Isabella took up her ministry in obedience to the Pentecostal imperative that had divided her life between slavery and freedom sixteen years before. The power of the Holy Spirit had struck her first in 1827, when emancipation in New York State, Pentecost, and the attendant slave holiday of Pinkster had virtually coincided. Isabella underwent a cataclysmic religious experience and the Holy Spirit, the power within Pentecost, remained a crucial force throughout her life—a source of inspiration and a means of knowing. . . .

More than a century and a quarter after its publication, the *Narrative of Sojourner Truth* still has not found its niche in the literature of ex-slaves. Although Truth's images often figure as symbols of black womanhood, she is never discussed as a slave narrator and her account is rarely quarried for information on enslaved blacks in New York State. Compared with Douglass's three autobiographies—particularly the first, which has continually been republished in popular editions—Truth's *Narrative* until recently remained expensive and inaccessible.

Truth's strategy for publicizing her book and increasing its sales has served authors for centuries. Like authors then and now, Truth went on the lecture circuit after she published her book in 1850, speaking and selling copies to audiences who were intrigued by her personal appearance. Among the meetings she attended to sell her book was the 1851 woman's rights convention in Akron.

Personal appearances worked well in the market that Truth could reach personally, but her obscurity militated against her with people she could not address. To communicate with a broader range of potential buyers, she needed the endorsement of those better known than she. Although Garrison had introduced the first edition of her book in 1850, authenticating her standing as an ex-slave and attesting to the virtue of the purchase, in 1853 Truth seized the initiative when she realized that a profitable endorsement was within her reach. Joining the legions of authors and publishers seeking advantageous "puffs"—now called blurbs—Truth approached the world's best-selling author [Harriet Beecher Stowe] for a puff, which she received. It began:

> The following narrative may be relied upon as in all respects true & faithful, & it is in some points more remarkable & interesting than many narratives of the kind which have abounded in late years.
>
> It is the history of a mind of no common energy & power whose struggles with the darkness & ignorance of slavery have a peculiar interest. The truths of Christianity seem to have come to her almost by a separate revelation & seem to verify the beautiful words of scripture "I will bring the blind by a way that they knew not, I will make darkness light before them & crooked things straight."

There is no way of knowing whether Stowe's puff boosted Truth's sales, but it certainly began a discursive relationship between Sojourner Truth and Harriet Beecher Stowe that extended into the following decade.

* * *

The 1851 publication of *Uncle Tom's Cabin* as a serial in Gamaliel Bailey's moderate, antislavery Washington *National Era* had proved wildly successful, and when the book appeared in 1852, it became a sensation that transformed its author's career. Stowe had been writing since the mid-1830s, but the shocking revision of the Fugitivie Slave Act in the Compromise of 1850 galvanized her into writing the book that broke records throughout the world. The first year's sales of *Uncle Tom's Cabin* reached a phenomenal three hundred thousand, bringing Stowe ten thousand dollars in royalties, a fortune at the time. She built Oakholm, a huge Italianate Tudor mansion in Hartford, Connecticut, took trips to Europe, basked in adoration on both sides of the Atlantic, and turned her talents to the defense of her new friend, Lady Byron, and glorification of her native New England.

Uncle Tom's Cabin made Stowe a highly sought-after author. Her work appeared in the *Independent*, her brother Henry Ward Beecher's prestigious national religious newspaper, but soon she wrote less for the *Independent* and more for the even more sophisticated and less political *Atlantic Monthly*, where she was paid about two hundred dollars per article. In 1863, ten years after Sojourner Truth had come soliciting a blurb, Stowe reworked a short piece she had written in 1860 and published it in the *Atlantic Monthly* as "Sojourner Truth, the Libyan Sibyl."

Having adjusted her life-style to a prosperity that could be maintained only by a constant influx of additional funds, Stowe was writing quickly about a marketable subject. She had never been a radical abolitionist—and she was only a moderate advocate of woman's rights—but in the early 1860s material on the Negro was very much in demand. With the Emancipation Proclamation and the acceptance of black men into the Union army, northern newspapers and magazines were full of articles on blacks. Writing to the market, Stowe presented a tableau in which she and her family appeared as people of culture who appreciated Sojourner Truth as a primitive *objet d'art* and source of entertainment. In her use of the name *sibyl*, Stowe captured Truth's prophetic side. Above all, however, Stowe emphasized Truth's Africanness and otherness, rendering her speech in Negro dialect and praising her naïveté. Mining the vein that had produced her black characters in *Uncle Tom's Cabin*, Stowe made Truth into a quaint and innocent exotic who disdained feminism.

Stowe presents Truth as telling of becoming a Methodist in Ulster County in about 1827. The quote, in dialect, is framed by Stowe's comments, in standard English. Stowe quotes herself as asking: "But, Sojourner, had you never been told about Jesus Christ?" To which Truth answers:

> No, honey. I had n't heerd no preachin'—been to no meetin'. Nobody had n't told me. I'd kind o' heerd of Jesus, but thought he was like Gineral Lafayette, or some o' them. But one night there was a Methodist meetin' somewhere in our parts, an' I went; an' they got up an' begun for to tell der 'speriences: an' de fust one begun to speak. I started, 'cause he told about Jesus.... An' finally I said, "Why they all know him!" I was so happy! an' then they sung this hymn.

Stowe then adds, again in contrasting standard English: "(Here Sojourner sang, in a strange, cracked voice, but evidently with all her soul and might, mispronouncing the English, but seeming to derive as much elevation and comfort from bad English as from good)." After quoting Truth's hymn, "There Is a Holy City," Stowe explains that Truth "sang with the strong barbaric accent of the native African.... Sojourner, singing this hymn, seemed to impersonate the fervor of Ethiopia, wild, savage, hunted of all nations, but burning after God in her trojan heart."

In "Sojourner Truth, the Libyan Sibyl," Stowe made mistakes, some careless, some contrived: She wrote, for instance, that Truth had come from Africa, and, even though Truth was very much alive and active in Washington, D.C., at the time, that she was dead. (Truth did not die until 1883.) For all her misstatements, Stowe provided Truth with the identity that would cling to her until late in the nineteenth century.

A more obscure person who was still in the thick of the woman's rights and antislavery movements might well be chagrined by Stowe's commercialism, particularly if there was an element of rivalry. Stowe's article thus roused another woman writer with far stronger reform credentials, Frances Dana Gage, to write.

*   *   *

An Ohio radical, Frances Dana Gage (1808–1884) was known as a woman's rights woman whose writing appeared occasionally in the *Independent*. Largely self-educated, Gage contributed to feminist and agricultural newspapers in the 1850s and 1860s under the pen name Aunt Fanny and became a popular public speaker. She corresponded familiarly with Susan B. Anthony, with whom she toured in 1856. As an antislavery feminist, Gage was both a sharp critic of the patriarchal family and a folksy character who wrapped her critique of conventional society in the commonplaces of her role as wife and mother of eight. Although recognized as a talented speaker and writer within temperance, antislavery, and feminist circles, Gage never took the step up to the *Atlantic Monthly* or other widely read fashionable magazines. Throughout her life she remained with the religious and feminist press, and among her eleven books of fiction, those published for temperance organizations predominate.

Gage was unusual, though not unique, in focusing her woman's rights rhetoric on working-class women. From the 1850s through the 1870s, she constantly subverted antisuffrage argument by describing women who did taxing labor, such as a woman in rags who walked along a canal in Cincinnati with "half a cart load of old fence-rails set into a big sack that was strapped round her neck . . . half bent down to the earth with a burden that few men could have carried" and a woman in St. Louis who walked two miles "with a child six months old—a large fat boy on her left shoulder, while on her head she is holding some thirty, forty, or fifty pounds of flour. She walks with a firm step, and carries her burden with apparent ease." When antifeminists protested that equal rights would expose women to the rough-and-tumble of economic and political strife, Gage pointed to poor women who were already immersed in an acute struggle for existence, working as hard as men in thoroughly unpleasant circumstances but handicapped by their lack of civil rights and equal pay.

Gage had chaired the 1851 woman's rights convention in Akron where Truth had come to sell her newly published *Narrative*. She did not write an essay dedicated entirely to Truth immediately, but Gage recognized the attractiveness of Truth's persona and used her as the model for an October 1851 episode of a series she was publishing in Jane Swisshelm's *Pittsburgh Saturday Visiter*. In "Aunt Hanna's Quilt: Or the Record of the West. 'A Tale of the Apple Cellar,' " Gage drew the fictional word portrait of a fugitive slave whom she called Winna:

> She was black—black as November night itself—tall, straight and muscular. Her wool was sprinkled with grey, that showed her years and sorrows, and her countenance was strikingly interesting. Her features once must have been fine, and even yet beamed with more than ordinary intelligence; her language was a mixture of the African lingo and the manner of the whites among whom she lived.

Winna lamented that all her children had been lost to the slave trade: "I'se had thirteen of 'em. They are all gone—all gone, Miss, I don't know where's one [of them]."

In 1862 and 1863 Gage was in the South Carolina Sea Islands working with freed people in the "rehearsal for Reconstruction," and after her return to the North, she undertook an interstate tour to solicit support for freedmen's relief. Reading Stowe's article twelve years after the meeting in Akron, Gage may well have realized that she could produce a more riveting and true-to-life version of Sojourner Truth than Stowe's quaint little character.

Less than a month after the appearance of Stowe's "Libyan Sibyl," Gage published in the *Independent* the account of Truth that we recognize today. Gage quoted Sojourner Truth as saying that she had had thirteen children, all of whom had been sold away from her (although Truth had five children and said so in her *Narrative*). In this letter these famous lines appeared for the first time: "And ar'n't I a woman? Look at me. Look at my arm. . . . I have plowed and planted and gathered into barns, and no man could head me—and ar'n't I a woman?"

* * *

Stowe and Gage let many years intervene between meeting Truth and writing about her by name. But while Stowe drew Truth as a quaint, minstrel-like, nineteenth-century Negro, Gage made her into a tough-minded, feminist emblem by stressing Truth's strength and the clash of conventions of race and gender and by inventing the riveting refrain, "And ar'n't I a woman?" During the mid-nineteenth century Stowe's rendition of Truth captured American imaginations, and the phrase "Libya Sibyl" was endlessly reworked, even by Gage, who termed Truth the "Libyan Statue" in her letter to the *Independent*, and Olive Gilbert, who in a letter to Truth written in the 1870s spoke of Truth as the "American Sibyl."

Along with another phrase that had appeared in Stowe's piece—Truth's rhetorical and possibly apocryphal question to Douglass, "Frederick, is God dead?"—versions of the "Libyan Sibyl" personified Truth until the end of the nineteenth century. As an expression of enduring Christian faith, she became the authentic Negro woman, the native, the genius of spiritual inspiration uncorrupted by formal education. Toward the end of the century, however, Gage's verion of Truth began to overtake Stowe's, as woman suffragists advanced Gage's Truth.

Although Frances Titus had reprinted Gage's letter as well as Stowe's article in the 1878 edition of *The Narrative of Sojourner Truth*, the primary means of popularizing "And ar'n't I a woman?" was the publication of the *History of Woman Suffrage* in 1881. As for the antislavery movement, so for woman suffrage: those nineteenth-century Americans who were attuned to the power of the published record have profoundly influenced subsequent representations of the past. Nineteenth-century evangelicals outside the mainline denominations—who were far more likely to hear, comprehend, and appreciate Sojourner Truth in her own self-definition as a preacher—were less solicitous than reformers about preserving and publishing their records. Practically by default, the feminists and abolitionists who published copiously, fashioned the historic Sojourner Truth in their own image, the one created by the feminist Frances Dana Gage.

*   *   *

As the woman suffrage pioneers Susan B. Anthony and Elizabeth Cady Stanton were growing old in the late 1870s, they recognized a need to gather and publish the papers of the movement they had inspired in 1848 and organized in the succeeding thirty years. They wrote surviving activists to request documents, which they combined with newspaper reports and published in three volumes between 1881 and 1886. Stanton was living in Tenafly, in northern New Jersey, as she carried out most of the work; Anthony came from Rochester, New York, from time to time to visit and assist. Gage, who in the years since 1851 had moved from McConnellsville, Ohio, to St. Louis, was then living in Vineland, in southern New Jersey, a center of temperance and woman's rights enthusiasm. Having corresponded with Anthony and Stanton since the 1850s, Gage would have welcomed a request to contribute material for the *History of Woman Suffrage*. In 1879 she wrote that she was looking over her old papers and manuscripts.

The feminist press of the 1880s testifies to Gage's enduring reputation as an ardent feminist. Although in wretched health, she continued to contribute to women's newspapers. After Sojourner Truth's death in 1883, the Boston *Woman's Journal* reprinted Gage's report of Truth's Akron speech. Through letters to feminist gatherings and published utterances, Gage spoke for temperance and woman suffrage right up to her death in 1884. Stowe, in contrast, had turned away from reform entirely. From the early 1860s through the mid-1880s she was still writing a book a year, but she did not return to political themes. In her old age Stowe lived in Florida and became increasingly childlike, and her writing was of local color and quaint New England characters.

By the end of the century, Gage's Truth was doing feminist work for woman suffragists all around the country, though sometimes in turn-of-the-century fashion. A Memphis suffragist who imagined Truth as an "old negro mammy" nevertheless quoted Gage's report of the 1851 speech as a stick with which to beat antisuffragists, in this instance, the Reverend Thomas Dixon. No longer the symbol of Christian trust, the uncorrupted Negro, or African genius, Truth was now the embodiment of women's strength that Gage had crafted. Stowe's 1863 portrait of Truth, written by a best-selling author whose religious sensibility was stronger than her feminism, expressed Victorian sentimentality. Gage's 1863 portrait of Truth, written by a woman whose radicalism had kept her at the far margins of American letters during her lifetime, has worn—and sold—well during the twentieth century.

*   *   *

It may seem ironic that Sojourner Truth is known for words she did not say, but American history is full of symbols that do their work without a basis in life. As a black and feminist talisman rather than a text, Sojourner Truth is still selling. She remains more sign than lived existence, like Betsy Ross, Chief Seattle, and Mason ("Parson") Weems's George Washington, who are also best remembered for deeds they did not perform and words they did not utter. Like other invented greats, Truth is consumed as a signifier and beloved for what we need her to have said. It is no accident that other people writing well after the fact made up what we see as most meaningful about each of those greats.

Parson Weems, who was, incidentally, a book distributor, invented the story of young George Washington's chopping down a cherry tree and being unable to tell a lie about his deed. The story played a major role in Weems's biography of Washington, which was, of course, for sale. It is perhaps not so well known that the legend of Betsy Ross, the woman celebrated for sewing the first American flag, is also fiction. Elizabeth Griscom Ross Ashburn Claypoole was a seamstress who lived in Philadelphia when the Declaration of Independence was being drafted, but her tale is the invention of her grandson, William Canby, who made it all up in 1870. During the mid-1770s the house that the city of Philadelphia has designated a historical place, where the Betsy Ross doll is for sale for $19.95, was a tavern. The bones in her grave are unidentified. Canby's Betsy Ross fills the need for a Founding Mother among the parade of men who personify the birth of the United States of America.

The practice of inventing great people endures as in the legend of *Brother Eagle, Sister Sky*, a best-selling volume said to be an 1854 speech by wise old Chief Seattle, a Native American and environmental prophet. This book, which the Earth Day U.S.A. Committee sends out as a fund raiser, is the creation of a screenwriter from Texas named Ted Perry. He wrote the text in 1971 and is horrified that it has been attributed to Chief Seattle. As in the case of Sojourner Truth's "Ar'n't I a woman?" and Betsy Ross's American flag, what makes Chief Seattle's speech work in American culture has little to do with the historical person.

Today Americans who love Sojourner Truth cherish her for what they need her to have said and buy her images to invest in the idea of strong women, whether or not they are black. As in the nineteenth century, Americans consume Sojourner Truth as the embodiment of a meaning necessary for their own cultural formations, even though that meaning has changed radically since Harriet Beecher Stowe first presented it. The market for historical symbols is not limited to words, however, and Sojourner Truth images, now distributed mostly through outlets catering to feminists, have also sold briskly. This is as it was in the mid-nineteenth century.

As a person whose depiction in print depended upon the imagination of other people, Sojourner Truth was able to influence those representations only marginally. Although she never distanced herself from the texts through which Gilbert and Gage portrayed her, she attempted to correct Stowe's article within three months of its publication, protesting in a letter to the *Boston Commonwealth* that she was not African and that she never called people, "Honey." She sent the editor, James Redpath, six copies of her *Narrative*, suggesting that her correct history was to be found between its covers. She also asked readers to purchase her photograph, for she was in ill health and restricted to her home in Battle Creek, Michigan. "I am," she said, "living on my shadow."

V

Myths of the Civil War and Reconstruction

Even today the Civil War remains central to the American experience, the nation's defining moment, the greatest single event in national history. The War Between the States, or the War to Save the Union, has the greatest mythic stature. From the epic struggle emerges a gallery of heroic figures and memorable episodes—Lincoln and Lee, Shiloh and Gettysburg. As the novelist and poet Robert Penn Warren suggests, the Civil War marked the nation's "Homeric Age." The war quickly became the great synthesis of the American experience and an inexhaustible reservoir of American myth and symbol: "From the first, Americans had a strong tendency to think of their land as the Galahad among nations, and the Civil War, with its happy marriage of victory and virtue, has converted this tendency into an article of faith nearly as sacrosanct as the Declaration of Independence." Even during the war years themselves the epic struggle, wherein some 620,000 died, could have done no other than to influence the time with the contrary impulses of glory and tragedy. And the American imagination continues to cling to a mythic memory that composes the heroism of the conflict and its bearing on the two great issues of the nation's history up to that time: slavery and Union. Between 1862 and 1900, for instance, over 480 short stories and novels were published about the war and its effects. One scholar has counted 512 novels alone published on the subject between 1862 and 1948. Another measure of the war's impact is that of the two best-selling novels in the entire history of American fiction, *Uncle Tom's Cabin,* published in 1852, addresses the great issues that brought the war on, and *Gone With the Wind*, appearing in 1936, the cultural results of northern victory and southern defeat.

The nation's cultural focus on the Civil War is due especially to the era's principal figure—Abraham Lincoln. He produced a body of printed work—the most famous being his *Gettysburg Address*—totaling over two million words, more wordage than is found in either the Bible or the works of Shakespeare. They contain "words that remade America." With so much having been said both by and about Lincoln, makes it inevitable that myth should work to obscure the man, his message, and his times.

A proper view of the country's "Homeric Age" requires that the cultural tendency to over-dramatize the heroic elements of the civil conflict—what one literary critic has called the "patriotic gore" of the war years—be set aside. A proportioned understanding of the era must yield more than the past constructed of the crusade of the planters, the deep dedication of southern womanhood to sustain the region's rebellion, the legacy of the martyred Lincoln, and the mystique of the Christ-like Lee. The Civil War and its heritage are destined long to remain central to our national historical experience.

The Great Emancipator: Legacy and Legend. (*Courtesy, Library of Congress*)

Robert E. Lee: Marble Man.
(Courtesy, Library of Congress)

Grand Illusion: The Reality of War. *(Courtesy, Library of Congress)*

"Johnny Reb." *(Courtesy, Library of Congress)*

"Billy Yank." *(Courtesy, Library of Congress)*

Abraham Lincoln and the Self-Made Myth

Richard Hofstadter

Rather than attempt to destroy the immense body of myth that surrounds Abraham Lincoln, Richard Hofstadter, late De Witt Clinton Professor of American History at Columbia University, looks to the myth's origin, development, and final effect on its subject. Recognizing that elements of the myth are true, Professor Hofstadter finds that Lincoln himself was the "first author of the Lincoln legend" and then continued to be its chief exponent. The "self-made myth" propelled Lincoln's political ambition for the presidency. The effects of the myth's fulfillment on the sensitive Lincoln were tragic; instead of glory, "he had found only ashes and blood."

I happen, temporarily, to occupy this White House. I am a living witness that any one of your children may look to come here as my father's child has.
Abraham Lincoln to the 166th Ohio Regiment

His ambition was a little engine that knew no rest.
William H. Herndon

The Lincoln legend has come to have a hold on the American imagination that defies comparison with anything else in political mythology. Here is a drama in which a great man shoulders the torment and moral burdens of a blundering and sinful people, suffers for them, and redeems them with hallowed Christian virtues—"malice toward none and charity for all"—and is destroyed at the pitch of his success. The worldly-wise John Hay, who knew him about as well as he permitted himself to be known, called him "the greatest character since Christ," a comparison one cannot imagine being made of any other political figure of modern times.

If the Lincoln legend gathers strength from its similarity to the Christian theme of vicarious atonement and redemption, there is still another strain in American experience that it represents equally well. Although his métier was politics and not business,

Lincoln was a preeminent example of that self-help which Americans have always so admired. He was not, of course, the first eminent American politician who could claim humble origins, nor the first to exploit them. But few have been able to point to such a sudden ascent from relative obscurity to high eminence; none has maintained so completely while scaling the heights the aspect of extreme simplicity; and none has combined with the attainment of success and power such an intense awareness of humanity and moral responsibility. It was precisely in his attainments as a common man that Lincoln felt himself to be remarkable, and in this light that he interpreted to the world the significance of his career. Keenly aware of his role as the exemplar of the self-made man, he played the part with an intense and poignant consistency that gives his performance the quality of a high art. The first author of the Lincoln legend and the greatest of the Lincoln dramatists was Lincoln himself.

Lincoln's simplicity was very real. He called his wife "mother," received distinguished guests in shirtsleeves, and once during his presidency hailed a soldier out of the ranks with the cry: "Bub! Bub!" But he was also a complex man, easily complex enough to know the value of his own simplicity. With his morbid compulsion for honesty he was too modest to pose coarsely and blatantly as a Henry Clay or James G. Blaine might pose. (When an 1860 campaign document announced that he was a reader of Plutarch, he sat down at once to validate the claim by reading the *Lives*.) But he did develop a political personality by intensifying qualities he actually possessed.

Even during his early days in politics, when his speeches were full of conventional platform bombast, Lincoln seldom failed to strike the humble manner that was peculiarly his. "I was born and have ever remained," he said in his first extended campaign speech, "in the most humble walks of life. I have no popular relations or friends to recommend me." Thereafter he always sounded the theme. "I presume you all know who I am—I am humble Abraham Lincoln. . . . If elected I shall be thankful; if not it will be all the same." Opponents at times grew impatient with his self-derogation ("my poor, lean, lank face") and a Democratic journal once called him a Uriah Heep. But self-conscious as the device was, and coupled even as it was with a secret confidence that Hay called "intellectual arrogance," there was still no imposture in it. It corresponded to Lincoln's own image of himself, which placed him with the poor, the aged, and the forgotten. In a letter to Herndon that was certainly not meant to impress any constituency, Lincoln, near his thirty-ninth birthday, referred to "my old, withered, dry eyes."

There was always this pathos in his plainness, his lack of external grace. "He is," said one of Mrs. Lincoln's friends, "the *ungodliest* man you ever saw." His colleagues, however, recognized in this a possible political asset and transmuted it into one of the most successful of all political symbols—the hard-fisted rail-splitter. At a Republican meeting in 1860 John Hanks and another old pioneer appeared carrying fence rails labeled: "Two rails from a lot made by Abraham Lincoln and John Hanks in the Sangamon Bottom in the year 1830." And Lincoln, with his usual candor, confessed that he had no idea whether these were the same rails, but he was sure he had actually split rails every bit as good. The time was to come when little Tad could say: "Everybody in this world knows Pa used to split rails."

Humility belongs with mercy among the cardinal Christian virtues. "Blessed are the meek, for they shall inherit the earth." But the demands of Christianity and the success myth are incompatible. The competitive society out of which the success myth and the self-made man have grown may accept the Christian virtues in principle but can hardly observe them in practice. The motivating force in the mythology of success is ambition, which is closely akin to the cardinal Christian sin of pride. In a world that works through ambition and self-help, while inculcating an ethic that looks upon their results with disdain, how can an earnest man, a public figure living in a time of crisis, gratify his aspirations and yet remain morally whole? If he is, like Lincoln, a man of private religious intensity, the stage is set for high tragedy.

*　　*　　*

The clue to much that is vital in Lincoln's thought and character lies in the fact that he was thoroughly and completely the politician, by preference and by training. It is difficult to think of any man of comparable stature whose life was so fully absorbed into his political being. Lincoln plunged into politics almost at the beginning of his adult life and was never occupied in any other career except for a brief period when an unfavorable turn in the political situation forced him back to his law practice. His life was one of caucuses and conventions, party circulars and speeches, requests, recommendations, stratagems, schemes, and ambitions. "It was in the world of politics that he lived," wrote Herndon after his death. "Politics were his life, newspapers his food, and his great ambition his motive power."

Like his father, Lincoln was physically lazy even as a youth, but unlike him had an active forensic mind. When only fifteen he was often on stumps and fences making political speeches, from which his father had to haul him back to his chores. He was fond of listening to lawyers' arguments and occupying his mind with them. Herndon testifies that "he read specially for a special object and thought things useless unless they could be of utility, use, practice, etc." When Lincoln read he preferred to read aloud. Once when Herndon asked him about it he answered: "I catch the idea by two senses, for when I read aloud I *hear* what is read and I see it . . . and I remember it better, if I do not understand it better." These are the reading habits of a man who is preparing for the platform.

For a youth with such mental habits—and one who had no business talents in the narrower sense—the greatest opportunities on the Illinois prairies were in the ministry, law, or politics. Lincoln, who had read Paine and Volney, was too unorthodox in theology for the ministry, and law and politics it proved to be. But politics was first: at twenty-three, only seven months after coming to the little Illinois community of New Salem, he was running for office. Previously he had worked only at odd jobs as ferryman, surveyor, postmaster, storekeeper, rail-splitter, farm hand, and the like; and now, without any other preparation, he was looking for election to the state legislature. He was not chosen, but two years later, in 1834, Sangamon County sent him to the lower house. Not until his first term had almost ended was he sufficiently qualified as a lawyer to be admitted to the state bar.

From this time to the end of his life—except for the years between 1849 and 1854, when his political prospects were discouraging—Lincoln was busy either as officeholder or office-seeker. In the summer of 1860, for a friend who wanted to prepare a campaign biography, he wrote in the third person a short sketch of his political life up to that time: 1832—defeated in an attempt to be elected to the legislature; 1834—elected to the legislature "by the highest vote cast for any candidate"; 1836, 1838, 1840—re-elected; 1838 and 1840—chosen by his party as its candidate for Speaker of the Illinois House of Representatives, but not elected; 1840 and 1844—placed on Harrison and Clay electoral tickets "and spent much time and labor in both those canvasses"; 1846—elected to Congress; 1848—campaign worker for Zachary Taylor, speaking in Maryland and Massachusetts, and "canvassing quite fully his own district in Illinois, which was followed by a majority in the district of over 1500 for General Taylor"; 1852—placed on Winfield Scott's electoral ticket, "but owing to the hopelessness of the cause in Illinois he did less than in previous presidential canvasses"; 1854—". . . his profession had almost superseded the thought of politics in his mind, when the repeal of the Missouri Compromise aroused him as he had never been before"; 1856—"made over fifty speeches" in the campaign

for Frémont; prominently mentioned in the Republican national convention for the vice-presidential nomination. . . .

The rest of the story is familiar enough. . . .

*   *   *

As an economic thinker, Lincoln had a passion for the great average. Thoroughly middle-class in his ideas, he spoke for those millions of Americans who had begun their lives as hired workers—as farm hands, clerks, teachers, mechanics, flatboatmen, and rail-splitters—and had passed into the ranks of landed farmers, prosperous grocers, lawyers, merchants, physicians, and politicians. Theirs were the traditional ideals of the Protestant ethic: hard work, frugality, temperance, and a touch of ability applied long and hard enough would lift a man into the propertied or professional class and give him independence and respect if not wealth and prestige. Failure to rise in the economic scale was generally viewed as a fault in the individual, not in society. It was the outward sign of an inward lack of grace—of idleness, indulgence, waste, or incapacity.

This conception of the competitive world was by no means so inaccurate in Lincoln's day as it has long since become; neither was it so conservative as time has made it. It was the legitimate inheritance of Jacksonian democracy. It was the belief not only of those who had arrived but also of those who were pushing their way to the top. If it was intensely and at times inhumanly individualistic, it also defied aristocracy and class distinction. Lincoln's life was a dramatization of it in the sphere of politics as, say, Carnegie's was in business. His own rather conventional version of the self-help ideology is expressed with some charm in a letter written to his feckless stepbrother, John D. Johnston, in 1851:

> Your request for eighty dollars I do not think it best to comply with now. At the various times when I have helped you a little you have said to me, "We can get along very well now"; but in a very short time I find you in the same difficulty again. Now, this can only happen by some defect in your conduct. What that defect is, I think I know. You are not lazy, and still you are an idler. I doubt whether, since I saw you, you have done a good whole day's work in any one day. You do not very much dislike to work, and still you do not work much, merely because it does not seem to you that you could get much for it. This habit of uselessly wasting time is the whole difficulty.

Lincoln advised Johnston to leave his farm in charge of his family and go to work for wages.

> I now promise you, that for every dollar you will, between this and the first of May, get for your own labor . . . I will then give you one other dollar. . . . Now if you will do this, you will soon be out of debt, and, what is better, you will have a habit that will keep you from getting in debt again. . . . You have always been kind to me, and I do not mean to be unkind to you. On the contrary, if you will but follow my advice, you will find it worth more than eighty times eighty dollars to you.

Given the chance for the frugal, the industrious, and the able—for the Abraham Lincolns if not the John D. Johnstons—to assert themselves, society would never be divided along fixed lines. There would be no eternal mud-sill class. "There is no permanent class of hired laborers among us," Lincoln declared in a public address. "Twenty-five years ago I was a hired laborer. The hired laborer of yesterday labors on his own account today, and will hire others to labor for him tomorrow. Advancement—improvement in condition—is the order of things in a society of equals." For Lincoln the vital test of a democracy was economic—its ability to provide opportunities for social ascent to those born in its lower ranks. The belief in opportunity for the self-made man is the key to his entire career; it explains his public appeal; it is the core of his criticism of slavery.

There is a strong pro-labor strain in all of Lincoln's utterances from the beginning to the end of his career. Perhaps the most sweeping of his words, and certainly the least equivocal, were penned in 1847. "Inasmuch as most good things are produced by labor," be began,

> it follows that all such things of right belong to those whose labor has produced them. But it has so happened, in all ages of the world, that some have labored, and others have without labor enjoyed a large proportion of the fruits. This is wrong and should not continue. To secure to each laborer the whole product of his labor, or as nearly as possible, is a worthy object of any good government.

This reads like a passage from a socialist argument. But its context is significant; the statement was neither a preface to an attack upon private property nor an argument for redistributing the world's goods—it was part of a firm defense of the protective tariff!

In Lincoln's day, especially in the more primitive communities of his formative years, the laborer had not yet been fully separated from his tools. The rights of labor still were closely associated in the fashion of Locke and Jefferson with the right of the laborer to retain his own product; when men talked about the sacredness of labor, they were often talking in veiled terms about the right to own. These ideas, which belonged to the age of craftsmanship rather than industrialism, Lincoln carried into the modern industrial scene. The result is a quaint equivocation, worth observing carefully because it pictures the state of mind of a man living half in one economy and half in another and wishing to do justice to every interest. In 1860, when Lincoln was stumping about the country before the Republican convention, he turned up at New Haven, where shoemakers were on strike. The Democrats had charged Republican agitators with responsibility for the strike, and Lincoln met them head-on:

> . . . I am glad to see that a system of labor prevails in New England under which laborers can strike when they want to, where they are not obliged to work under all circumstances, and are not tied down and obliged to labor whether you pay them or not! I like the system which lets a man quit when he wants to, and wish it might prevail everywhere. One of the reasons why I am opposed to slavery is just here. What is the true condition of the laborer? I take it that it is best for all to leave each man free to acquire property as fast as he can. Some will get wealthy. I don't believe in a law to prevent a man from getting rich; it would do more harm than good. So while we do not propose any war upon capital, we do wish to allow the humblest man an equal chance to get rich with everybody else. When one starts poor, as most do in the race of life, free society is such that he knows he can better his condition; he knows that there is no fixed condition of labor for his whole life. . . . That is the true system.

If there was a flaw in all this, it was one that Lincoln was never forced to meet. Had he lived to seventy, he would have seen the generation brought up on self-help come into its own, build oppressive business corporations, and begin to close off those treasured opportunities for the little man. Further, he would have seen his own party become the jackal of the vested interests, placing the dollar far, far ahead of the man. He himself presided over the social revolution that destroyed the simple equalitarian order of the 1840's, corrupted what remained of its values, and caricatured its ideals. Booth's bullet, indeed, saved him from something worse than embroilment with the radicals over Reconstruction. It confined his life to the happier age that Lincoln understood—which unwittingly he helped to destroy—the age that gave sanction to the honest compromises of his thought.

A story about Abraham Lincoln's second trip to New Orleans when he was twenty-one holds an important place in the Lincoln legend. According to John Hanks, when Lincoln went with his companions to a slave market they saw a handsome mulatto girl being sold on the block, and "the iron entered his soul"; he swore that if he ever got a chance he would hit slavery "and hit it hard." The implication is clear: Lincoln was half abolitionist and the Emancipation Proclamation was a fulfillment of that young promise. But the authenticity of the tale is suspect among Lincoln scholars. John Hanks recalled it thirty-five years afterward as a personal witness, whereas, according to Lincoln, Hanks had not gone beyond St. Louis on the journey. Beveridge observes that Lincoln himself apparently never spoke of the alleged incident publicly or privately, and that for twenty years afterward he showed little concern over slavery. We know that he refused to denounce the Fugitive Slave Law, viciously unfair though it was, even to free Negroes charged as runaways. ("I confess I hate to see the poor creatures hunted down," he wrote to Speed, ". . . but I bite my lips and keep quiet.")

His later career as an opponent of slavery extension must be interpreted in the light of his earlier public indifference to the question. Always moderately hostile to the South's "peculiar institution," he quieted himself with the comfortable thought that it was destined very gradually to disappear. Only after the Kansas-Nebraska Act breathed political life into the slavery issue did he seize upon it as a subject for agitation; only then did he attack it openly. His attitude was based on justice tempered by expediency—or perhaps more accurately, expediency tempered by justice.

Lincoln was by birth a Southerner, a Kentuckian; both his parents were Virginians. His father had served on the slave patrol of Hardin County. The Lincoln family was one of thousands that in the early decades of the nineteenth century had moved from the Southern states, particularly Virginia, Kentucky, and Tennessee, into the Valley of Democracy, and peopled the southern parts of Ohio, Indiana, and Illinois.

During his boyhood days in Indiana and Illinois Lincoln lived in communities where slaves were rare or unknown, and the problem was not thrust upon him. The prevailing attitude toward Negroes in Illinois was intensely hostile. Severe laws against free Negroes and runaway slaves were in force when Lincoln went to the Springfield legislature, and there is no evidence of any popular movement to liberalize them. Lincoln's experiences with slavery on his journeys to New Orleans in 1828 and 1831 do not seem to have made an impression vivid enough to change his conduct. Always privately compassionate, in his public career and his legal practice he never made himself the advocate of unpopular reform movements.

While Lincoln was serving his second term in the Illinois legislature the slavery question was discussed throughout the country. Garrison had begun his agitation and petitions to abolish slavery in the District of Columbia had begun to pour in upon Congress. State legislatures began to express themselves upon the matter. The Illinois legislature turned the subject over to a joint committee, of which Lincoln and his Sangamon County colleague, Dan Stone, were members. At twenty-eight Lincoln thus had occasion to review the whole slavery question on both sides. The committee reported proslavery resolutions, presently adopted, which praised the beneficent effects of white civilization upon African natives, cited the wretchedness of emancipated Negroes as proof of the folly of freedom, and denounced abolitionists.

Lincoln voted against these resolutions. Six weeks later—the delay resulted from a desire to alienate no one from the cause that then stood closest to his heart, the removal of the state capital from Vandalia to Springfield—he and Stone embodied their own opinions in a resolution that was entered in the journal of the House and promptly forgotten. It read in part: "They [Lincoln and Stone] believe that the institution of slavery is founded on injustice and bad policy, but that the promulgation of abolition doctrines tends to increase rather than abate its evils." (Which means, the later Lincoln might have said, that slavery is wrong but that proposing to do away with it is also wrong because it makes slavery worse.) They went on to say that while the Constitution does not permit Congress to abolish slavery in the states, Congress can do so in the District of Columbia—*but* this power should not be exercised unless at "the request of the people of the District." This statement breathes the fire of an uncompromising insistence upon moderation. Let it be noted, however, that it did represent a point of view faintly to the left of prevailing opinion. Lincoln had gone on record as saying not merely that slavery was "bad policy" but even that it was unjust; but he had done so without jeopardizing his all-important project to transfer the state capital to Springfield.

In 1845, not long before he entered Congress, Lincoln again had occasion to express himself on slavery; this time in a carefully phrased private letter to a political supporter who happened to be an abolitionist.

> I hold it a paramount duty of us in the free States, due to the Union of the States, and perhaps to liberty itself (paradox though it may seem), to let the slavery of the other states alone; while, on the other hand, I hold it to be equally clear that we should never knowingly lend ourselves, directly or indirectly, to prevent that slavery from dying a natural death—to find new places for it to live in, when it can not longer exist in the old.

Throughout his political career he consistently held to this position.

After he had become a lame-duck Congressman, Lincoln introduced into Congress in January 1849 a resolution to instruct the Committee on the District of Columbia to report a bill abolishing slavery in the District. The bill provided that children born of slave mothers after January 1, 1850, should be freed and supported by their mothers' owners until of a certain age. District slaveholders who wanted to emancipate their slaves were to be compensated from the federal Treasury. Lincoln himself added a section requiring the municipal authorities of Washington and Georgetown to provide "active and efficient means" of arresting and restoring to their owners all fugitive slaves escaping into the District. (This was six years before he confessed that he hated "to see the poor creatures hunted down.") Years later, recalling this fugitive-slave provision, Wendell Phillips referred to Lincoln somewhat unfairly as "that slavehound from

Illinois." The bill itself, although not passed, gave rise to a spirited debate on the morality of slavery, in which Lincoln took no part.

* * *

When Lincoln returned to active politics the slavery issue had come to occupy the central position on the American scene. Stephen Douglas and some of his colleagues in Congress had secured the passage of the Kansas-Nebraska Act, which, by opening some new territory, formally at least, to slavery, repealed the part of the thirty-four-year-old Missouri Compromise that barred slavery from territory north of 36° 30'. The measure provoked a howl of opposition in the North and split Douglas's party. The Republican Party, built on opposition to the extension of slavery, began to emerge in small communities in the Northwest. Lincoln's ambitions and interests were aroused, and he proceeded to rehabilitate his political fortunes.

His strategy was simple and forceful. He carefully avoided issues like the tariff, internal improvements, the Know-Nothing mania, or prohibitionism, each of which would alienate important groups of voters. He took pains in all his speeches to stress that he was not an abolitionist and at the same time to stand on the sole program of opposing the extension of slavery. On October 4, 1854, at the age of forty-five, Lincoln *for the first time in his life* denounced slavery in public. In his speech delivered in the Hall of Representatives at Springfield (and later repeated at Peoria) he declared that he hated the current zeal for the spread of slavery: "I hate it because of the monstrous injustice of slavery itself." He went on to say that he had no prejudice against the people of the South. He appreciated their argument that it would be difficult to get rid of the institution "in any satisfactory way." "I surely will not blame them for not doing what I should not know how to do myself. If all earthly power were given me, I should not know what to do as to the existing institution. My first impulse would be to free all the slaves and send them to Liberia, to their own native land." But immediate colonization, he added, is manifestly impossible. The slaves might be freed and kept "among us as underlings." Would this really better their condition?

> What next? Free them, and make them politically and socially our equals. *My own feelings will not admit of this,*

and if mine would, we well know that those of the great mass of whites will not. Whether this feeling accords with justice and sound judgment is not the sole question, if indeed it is any part of it. A universal feeling, whether well or ill founded, cannot be safely disregarded.

And yet nothing could justify an attempt to carry slavery into territories now free, Lincoln emphasized. For slavery is unquestionably wrong. "The great mass of mankind," he said at Peoria, "consider slavery a great moral wrong. [This feeling] lies at the very foundation of their sense of justice, and it cannot be trifled with. . . . No statesman can safely disregard it." The last sentence was the key to Lincoln's growing radicalism. As a practical politician he was naturally very much concerned about those public sentiments which no statesman can safely disregard. It was impossible, he had learned, safely to disregard either the feeling that slavery is a moral wrong or the feeling—held by an even larger portion of the public—that Negroes must not be given political and social equality.

He had now struck the core of the Republican problem in the Northwest: how to find a formula to reconcile the two opposing points of view held by great numbers of white people in the North. Lincoln's success in 1860 was due in no small part to his ability to bridge the gap, a performance that entitles him to a place among the world's great political propagandists.

To comprehend Lincoln's strategy we must keep one salient fact in mind: the abolitionists and their humanitarian sympathizers in the nation at large and particularly in the Northwest, the seat of Lincoln's strength, although numerous enough to hold the balance of power, were far too few to make a successful political party. Most of the white people of the Northwest, moreover, were in fact not only not abolitionists, but actually—and here is the core of the matter—Negrophobes. They feared and detested the very thought of living side by side with large numbers of Negroes in their own states, to say nothing of competing with their labor. Hence the severe laws against free Negroes, for example in Lincoln's Illinois. Amid all the agitation in Kansas over making the territory a free state, the conduct of the majority of Republicans there was colored far more by self-interest than by moral principle. In their so-called Topeka Constitution the Kansas Republicans *forbade free Negroes even to come into the state*, and gave only

to whites and Indians the right to vote. It was not bondage that troubled them—it was the Negro, free or slave. Again and again the Republican press of the Northwest referred to the Republican Party as the "White Man's Party." The motto of the leading Republican paper of Missouri, Frank Blair's *Daily Missouri Democrat*, was "White Men for Missouri and Missouri for White Men." Nothing could be more devastating to the contention that the early Republican Party in the Northwest was built upon moral principle. At the party convention of 1860 a plank endorsing the Declaration of Independence was almost hissed down and was saved only by the threat of a bolt by the antislavery element.

If the Republicans were to succeed in the strategic Northwest, how were they to win the support of both Negrophobes and antislavery men? Merely to insist that slavery was an evil would sound like abolitionism and offend the Negrophobes. Yet pitching their opposition to slavery extension on too low a moral level might lose the valued support of the humanitarians. Lincoln, perhaps borrowing from the old free-soil ideology, had the right formula and exploited it. He first hinted at it in the Peoria speech:

> The whole nation is interested that the best use shall be made of these Territories. *We want them for homes of free white people. This they cannot be, to any considerable extent, if slavery shall be planted within them.* Slave States are places for poor white people to remove from, not to remove to. New free States are the places for poor people to go to, and better their condition. For this use the nation needs these Territories.

The full possibilities of this line first became clear in Lincoln's "lost" Bloomington speech, delivered at a Republican state convention in May 1856. There, according to the report of one of his colleagues at the Illinois bar, Lincoln warned that Douglas and his followers would frighten men away from the very idea of freedom with their incessant mouthing of the red-herring epithet: "Abolitionist!" "If that trick should succeed," he is reported to have said, "if free negroes should be made *things,* how long, think you, before they will begin to make *things* out of poor white men?"

Here was the answer to the Republican problem. Negrophobes and abolitionists alike could understand this threat; if freedom should be broken down they might themselves have to compete with the labor of slaves in the then free states—or might even be reduced to bondage along with the blacks! Here was an argument that could strike a responsive chord in the nervous system of every Northern man, farmer or worker, abolitionist or racist: *if a stop was not put somewhere upon the spread of slavery, the institution would become nation-wide.* Here, too, is the practical significance of the repeated statements Lincoln made in favor of labor at this time. Lincoln took the slavery question out of the realm of moral and legal dispute and, by dramatizing it in terms of free labor's self-interest, gave it a universal appeal. To please the abolitionists he kept saying that slavery was an evil thing; but for the material benefit of all Northern white men he opposed its further extension.

The importance of this argument becomes increasingly clear when it is realized that Lincoln used it in every one of his recorded speeches from 1854 until he became the President-elect. He once declared in Kansas that preventing slavery from becoming a nation-wide institution "is *the purpose* of this organization [the Republican Party]." The argument had a great allure too for the immigrants who were moving in such great numbers into the Northwest. Speaking at Alton, in the heart of a county where more than fifty percent of the population was foreign-born, Lincoln went out of his way to make it clear that he favored keeping the territories open not only for native Americans, "but as an outlet for *free white people* everywhere, the world over—in which Hans, and Baptiste, and Patrick, and all other men from all the world, may find new homes and better their condition in life."

During the debates with Douglas, Lincoln dwelt on the theme again and again, and added the charge that Douglas himself was involved in a Democratic "conspiracy . . . for the sole purpose of nationalizing slavery." Douglas and the Supreme Court (which a year before had handed down the Dred Scott decision) would soon have the American people "working in the traces that tend to make this one universal slave nation." Chief Justice Taney had declared that Congress did not have the constitutional power to exclude slavery from the territories. The next step, said Lincoln, would be

> another Supreme Court decision, declaring that the Constitution of the United States does not permit a *State* to exclude slavery from its limits. . . . We shall lie down pleasantly, dreaming that the people of Mis-

souri are on the verge of making their State free; and we shall awake to the reality instead, that the Supreme Court has made Illinois a slave State.

So also the theme of the "House Divided" speech:

> I do not expect the Union to be dissolved—I do not expect the House to fall—but I do expect it to cease to be divided. It will become all one thing or all the other. Either the opponents of slavery will arrest the further spread of it, and place it where the public mind shall rest in the belief that it is in the course of ultimate extinction; or its advocates will push it forward, till it shall become alike lawful in all the States, old as well as new, North as well as South.
>
> Have we no tendency to the latter condition?

The last sentence is invariably omitted when this passage is quoted, perhaps because from a literary standpoint it is anticlimactic. But in Lincoln's mind—and, one may guess, in the minds of those who heard him—it was not anticlimactic, but essential. Lincoln was *not* emphasizing the necessity for abolition of slavery in the near future; he was emphasizing the immediate "danger" that slavery would become a nation-wide American institution if its geographical spread were not severely restricted at once.

Once this "House Divided" speech had been made, Lincoln had to spend a great deal of time explaining it, proving that he was not an abolitionist. These efforts, together with his strategy of appealing to abolitionists and Negrophobes at once, involved him in embarrassing contradictions. In northern Illinois he spoke in one vein before abolition-minded audiences, but farther south, where settlers of Southern extraction were dominant, he spoke in another. It is instructive to compare what he said about the Negro in Chicago with what he said in Charleston.

Chicago, July 10, 1858:

> Let us discard all this quibbling about this man and the other man, this race and that race and the other race being inferior, and therefore they must be placed in an inferior position. Let us discard all these things and unite as one people throughout this land, until we shall once more stand up declaring that all men are created equal.

Charleston, September 18, 1858:

> I will say, then, that I am not, nor ever have been, in favor of bringing about in any way the social and political equality of the white and black races [ap-

plause]: that I am not, nor ever have been, in favor of making voters or jurors of negroes, nor of qualifying them to hold office, nor to intermarry with white people. . . .

And inasmuch as they cannot so live, while they do remain together there must be the position of superior and inferior, and I as much as any other man am in favor of having the superior position assigned to the white race.

It is not easy to decide whether the true Lincoln is the one who spoke in Chicago or the one who spoke in Charleston. Possibly the man devoutly believed each of the utterances at the time he delivered it; possibly his mind too was a house divided against itself. In any case it is easy to see in all this the behavior of a professional politician looking for votes.

Douglas did what he could to use Lincoln's inconsistency against him. At Galesburg, with his opponent sitting on the platform behind him, he proclaimed: "I would despise myself if I thought that I was procuring your votes by concealing my opinions, and by avowing one set of principles in one part of the state, and a different set in another." Confronted by Douglas with these clashing utterances from his Chicago and Charleston speeches, Lincoln replied: "I have not supposed and do not now suppose, that there is any conflict whatever between them."

But this was politics—the premium was on strategy, not intellectual consistency—and the effectiveness of Lincoln's campaign is beyond dispute. In the ensuing elections the Republican candidates carried a majority of the voters and elected their state officers for the first time. Douglas returned to the Senate only because the Democrats, who had skillfully gerrymandered the election districts, still held their majority in the state legislature. Lincoln had contributed greatly to welding old-line Whigs and antislavery men into an effective party, and his reputation was growing by leaps and bounds. What he had done was to pick out an issue—the alleged plan to extend slavery, the alleged danger that it would spread throughout the nation—which would turn attention from the disintegrating forces in the Republican Party to the great integrating force. He was keenly aware that the party was built out of extremely heterogeneous elements, frankly speaking of it in his "House Divided" speech as composed of "strange, discordant, and even hostile elements." In addition

to abolitionists and Negrophobes, it united high- and low-tariff men, hard- and soft-money men, former Whigs and former Democrats embittered by old political fights, Maine-law prohibitionists and German tipplers, Know-Nothings and immigrants. Lincoln's was the masterful diplomacy to hold such a coalition together, carry it into power, and with it win a war. . . .

Lincoln was shaken by the presidency. Back in Springfield, politics had been a sort of exhilarating game; but in the White House, politics was power, and power was responsibility. Never before had Lincoln held executive office. In public life he had always been an insignificant legislator whose votes were cast in concert with others and whose decisions in themselves had neither finality nor importance. As President he might consult others, but innumerable grave decisions were in the end his own, and with them came a burden of responsibility terrifying in its dimensions.

Lincoln's rage for personal success, his external and worldly ambition, was quieted when he entered the White House, and he was at last left alone to reckon with himself. To be confronted with the fruits of his victory only to find that it meant choosing between life and death for others was immensely sobering. That Lincoln should have shouldered the moral burden of the war was characteristic of the high seriousness into which he had grown since 1854; and it may be true, as Professor Charles W. Ramsdell suggested, that he was stricken by an awareness of his own part in whipping up the crisis. This would go far to explain the desperation with which he issued pardons and the charity that he wanted to extend to the conquered South at the war's close. In one of his rare moments of self-revelation he is reported to have said: "Now I don't know what the soul is, but whatever it is, I know that it can humble itself." The great prose of the presidential years came from a soul that had been humbled. Lincoln's utter lack of personal malice during these years, his humane detachment, his tragic sense of life, have no parallel in political history.

"Lincoln," said Herndon, "is a man of heart—aye, as gentle as a woman's and as tender. . . ." Lincoln was moved by the wounded and dying men, moved as no one in a place of power can afford to be. He had won high office by means sometimes rugged, but once there, he found he could not quite carry it off. For him it was impossible to drift into the habit-ual callousness of the sort of officialdom that sees men only as pawns to be shifted here and there and "expended" at the will of others. It was a symbolic thing that his office was so constantly open, that he made himself more accessible than any other chief executive in our history. "Men moving only in an official circle," he told Carpenter, "are apt to become merely official—not to say arbitrary—in their ideas, and are apter and apter with each passing day to forget that they only hold power in a representative capacity." Is it possible to recall anyone else in modern history who could exercise so much power and yet feel so slightly the private corruption that goes with it? Here, perhaps, is the best measure of Lincoln's personal eminence in the human calendar— that he was chastened and not intoxicated by power. It was almost apologetically that he remarked in response to a White House serenade after his re-election that "So long as I have been here, I have not willingly planted a thorn in any man's bosom."

There were many thorns planted in *his* bosom. The criticism was hard to bear (perhaps hardest of all that from the abolitionists, which he knew had truth in it). There was still in him a sensitivity that the years of knock-about politics had not killed, the remarkable depths of which are suddenly illumined by a casual sentence written during one of the crueler outbursts of the opposition press. Reassuring the apologetic actor James Hackett, who had unwittingly aroused a storm of hostile laughter by publishing a confidential letter, Lincoln added that he was quite used to it: "I have received a great deal of ridicule without much malice; and have received a great deal of kindness, not quite free from ridicule."

The presidency was not something that could be enjoyed. Remembering its barrenness for him, one can believe that the life of Lincoln's soul was almost entirely without consummation. Sandburg remarks that there were thirty-one rooms in the White House and that Lincoln was not at home in any of them. This was the house for which he had sacrificed so much!

As the months passed, a deathly weariness settled over him. Once when Noah Brooks suggested that he rest, he replied: "I suppose it is good for the body. But the tired part of me is *inside* and out of reach." There had always been a part of him, inside and out of reach, that had looked upon his ambition with detachment and wondered if the game was worth the candle. Now he could see the truth of what he had long dimly known and perhaps hopefully suppressed—that for a man of sensitivity and compassion to exercise great powers in a time of crisis is a grim and agonizing thing. Instead of glory, he once said, he had found only "ashes and blood." This was, for him, the end product of that success myth by which he had lived and for which he had been so persuasive a spokesman. He had had his ambitions and fulfilled them, and met heartache in his triumph.

Altars of Sacrifice:
Myth and Confederate Women

Drew Gilpin Faust

The plantation legend, that cherished, sunny stage piece of the antebellum period—the utopian world of the gentlemanly "massa," the gracious southern belle, the sinister overseer, and the ubiquitous happy Negro, the general romantic ambiance of the plantation itself in all its ceremonial detail—strongly conditioned both regional *and* national thinking and expectation regarding the Land of Cotton. Mythological heritage, moreover, assumed that this legendary sociology of the Old South sustained itself—at least ideologically—on into the great sectional conflict. It has been assumed that people behind Confederate lines, and especially the long-suffering women of the South, sustained their pride of region and status, displaying the same undaunted dedication to the southern way of life as the soldiery. On the home front women served the cause, as the cultural tradition said, "to the last shred of cloth, the last crust of bread," with notable patriotism and sacrifice. Perhaps no greater readjustment to this once fashionable historical imagery has come of late than to the place of women, both black and white, in what was once regarded as this romantic world of southern solidarity.

Drew Gilpin Faust, professor of history at the University of Pennsylvania, is one scholar critically responsible for revising the former image. Basing her research on correspondence, journals, memoirs, household accounts, and diaries, Professor Faust finds that beyond the fond remembrance of the plantation's mythic pillared world, southern women were far more than prim, asexual, duty-bound angels. While the South still was aggressively a region of traditional sex role ideology, with rather sharply prescribed gender boundaries, the Civil War broke the cake of custom and gender assumptions came to be challenged. Confederate women themselves fundamentally refashioned the Southern Lady. Beyond the demands of their traditional roles—which in effect forced women to sustain the courtly illusions associated with them, even while attending to the rigorous domestic needs of house and hearth—frustration and discontent pervaded the Confederacy as womens' already complex roles multiplied in the face of demanding war conditions. As the cause was coming to be lost, as the emotional and physical deprivation of women at home escalated, the foundation ideology of sacred female dedication started to lose its mythic meaning. Women began to desert the cause of useless sacrifice. In the end, without their crucial logistical and psychological support, the Confederate effort at large was subverted, to such a degree perhaps as to help explain why the South lost the Civil War.

It is the men, Hector tells Andromache in the sixth book of the *Iliad*, who "must see to the fighting." From ancient history to our own time, war has centered on men, for they have controlled and populated its battlefields. Even in our era of shifting gender definitions, perhaps the most assertive—and successful—defense of traditional roles has been the effort to bar women from combat. Yet war has often introduced women to unaccustomed responsibilities and unprecedented, even if temporary, enhancements of power. War has been a preeminently "gendering" activity, casting thought about sex differences into sharp relief as it has both underlined and realigned gender boundaries.

Like every war before and since, the American Civil War served as an occasion for both reassertion and reconsideration of gender assumptions. Early in the conflict, Louisianian Julia Le Grand observed that "we are leading the lives which women have led since Troy fell." Yet because the Civil War was fundamentally different from those that had preceded it, the place of women in that conflict stimulated especially significant examination and discussion of women's appropriate relationship to war—and thus to society in general. Often designated the first "modern" or total war because of the involvement of entire populations in its terrible work of death, the Civil War required an extraordinary level of female participation. This was a conflict in which the "home front" had a newly important role in generating mass armies and keeping them in the field. Particularly in the South, where human and material resources were stretched to the utmost, the conflict demanded the mobilization of women, not for battle, but for civilian support services such as nursing, textile and clothing production, munitions and government office work, slave management, and even agriculture. Yet white Southern women, unlike their men, were not conscripted by law. They had to be enlisted by persuasion. The resulting discourse about woman's place in Confederate society represented the rhetorical attempt to create a hegemonic ideology of female patriotism and sacrifice.

Articulate Southerners, male and female, crafted an exemplary narrative about the Confederate woman's Civil War, a story designed to ensure her loyalty and service. As in the tales of war enshrined in Western literature from Homer to Sir Walter Scott, its plot recounted woman's heroic self-sacrifice, casting it as indispensable to the moral, political, and military triumph of her men and her country. The historian John Keegan has compellingly described the way in which the "battle piece," the highly conventionalized and heroic account of combat, has shaped men's expectations and experiences of war. But women have been no less influenced by a genre of female "war stories," intended to socialize them through accounts of their foremothers' deeds. The conventional designation of all women as noncombatants inevitably enhances the wartime significance of gender as a social category, as well as a structure of self-definition. The focus of Confederate public discourse on a "classless" white woman reinforced the privileging of female identity. Usually cast in the homogeneous singular, the "woman" who shared with her sisters rich and poor the experience of sacrificing men to battle represented a useful rhetorical convention within a Confederate ideology struggling to minimize the class divisions that might threaten national survival. At the same time that Confederate discourse appealed to a new and recognizable commonality widely shared by white Southern women—whose husbands or sons were nearly three times as likely to die as were their Northern counterparts—it promoted the notion of an archetypal "Confederate woman" as a form of false consciousness obscuring social and economic differences among the new nation's female citizens. Ultimately, the focus of Confederate ideology on female self-abnegation and sacrifice as ends in themselves would alienate many women from that rendition of their interests, from the war, and in many cases, from the Confederacy itself. Ideology and its failures played a critical role in shaping the relationship of women to the Southern Cause and in defining Confederate viability. In recent years scholars have answered the historiographical perennial, "why the South lost the Civil War," by emphasizing deficiencies in Southern morale. Almost all such arguments stress the importance of class conflict, especially growing yeoman dissent, in undermining the Southern Cause. Yet with a white civilian population that was overwhelmingly female and that bore an unprecedented responsibility for the war's outcome, we must not ignore gender as a factor in explaining Confederate defeat.

To suggest that Southern women in any way subverted the Confederate effort is to challenge a more than century-old legend of female sacrifice. The story of Confederate women's unflinching loyalty originated during the war and first found official expression in legislative resolutions offered by Confederate leaders to mark the contributions of female citizens. The Confederate Congress established the model in a declaration of gratitude passed in April 1862; the gesture was replicated in proclamations like that of the Mississippi legislature in 1863 thanking the "mothers, wives, sisters and daughters of this State" for their "ardent devotion . . . unremitting labors and sacrifices." After Appomattox this hortatory narrative of female dedication was physically realized in monuments to wives and mothers of the Confederacy and incorporated into scholarly literature on women and the war as conventional historical truth. Even the titles of scholarly works, such as Mary Elizabeth Massey's *Bonnet Brigades*, published in 1966 as part of the Civil War centennial, or H. E. Sterkx's more recent *Partners in Rebellion: Alabama Women in the Civil War*, communicate the image of Southern women fighting alongside their men. The same vision had a century earlier inspired Henry Timrod, poet laureate of the Confederacy, to entitle his wartime ode to Confederate ladies "Two Armies." Praising women's contributions in caring for the sick, plying the "needle and the loom," and "by a thousand peaceful deeds" supplying "a struggling nation's needs," Timrod promised women equal glory with the war's military heroes.

> When Heaven shall blow the trump of peace,
> And bid this weary warfare cease,
> Their several missions nobly done,
> The triumph grasped, the freedom won,
> Both armies, from their toils at rest,
> Alike may claim the victor's crest.

The tenacity of such a rendition of Southern women's wartime role—its survival from Confederate myth into twentieth-century historiography—is less curious than at first it seems. Confederate versions originated so early in the conflict as to have been necessarily prescriptive rather than descriptive. This was not simply a story, but an ideology intended to direct Southern women, to outline appropriate behavior in the abruptly altered wartime situation. The flattery, the honorific nature of this discourse, was central to its rhetoric force. And the deference to women's importance ensured the survival of the narrative and its evolution into historical interpretation. Ironically, it fit neatly with an emergent twentieth-century feminist historiography eager to explore women's contributions to past events previously portrayed from an exclusively male point of view. Yet the passage of women's history beyond its earlier celebratory phase and the adoption of more critical and analytic approaches to female experience may enable us at last to see the story as the fiction it largely is, to explore its development, political origins, and rhetorical purposes and thus to understand how it shaped Confederate women's wartime lives.

*   *   *

With the outbreak of hostilities in early 1861 public discourse in the Confederacy quickly acknowledged that war had a special meaning for white females. The earliest discussions of the Confederate woman in newspapers and periodicals sought to engage her in the war effort by stressing the relevance of her accustomed spiritual role. The defense of moral order, conventionally allocated to females by nineteenth-century bourgeois ideology, took on increased importance as war's social disruptions threatened ethical and spiritual dislocations as well. "Can you imagine," asked the magazine *Southern Field and Fireside*, "what would be the moral condition of the Confederate army in six months" without women's influence? What but a woman "makes the Confederate soldier a gentleman of honor, courage, virtue and truth, instead of a cut-throat and vagabond?" "Great indeed," confirmed the *Augusta Weekly Constitutionalist* in July 1861, "is the task assigned to woman. Who can elevate its dignity? Not," the paper observed pointedly, "to make laws, not to lead armies, not to govern empires; but to form those by whom laws are made, armies led . . . to soften firmness into mercy, and chasten honor into refinement."

But many Southern women, especially those from the slave-owning classes most instrumental in bringing about secession, were to find that a meager and unsatisfactory allotment of responsibility. As one woman remarked while watching the men of her community march off to battle, "We who stay behind may find it harder than they who go. They will have new scenes and constant excitement to buoy them up and the consciousness of duty done." Another felt herself "like a pent-up volcano. I wish I had a field for my energies . . . now that there is . . . real tragedy, real romance and history weaving every day, I suffer, suffer, leading the life I do." Events once confined to books now seemed to be taking place all around them, and they were eager to act out their designated part. "The war is certainly ours as well as that of the men," one woman jealously proclaimed.

In the spring and summer of 1861, many articulate middle- and upper-class women sought active means of expressing their commitment, ones that placed less emphasis than had the *Augusta Constitutionalist* on what they might not do but instead drew them into the frenzy of military preparation. As recruits drilled and bivouacked, women found outlet for their energies sewing countless flags, uniforms, and even underwear for departing units; penning patriotic songs and verse; submitting dozens of designs for the national flag to the Confederate Congress; raising money as Ladies Gunboat Societies, forming more than a thousand relief associations across the new nation; and sponsoring dramatic performances to benefit soldiers, particularly tableaux representing historic and literary themes. "I feel quite important," one lady observed with some amazement after an evening of such scenes raised a substantial amount of money for Virginia troops.

That declaration of importance was in marked and self-conscious contrast to the feelings of purposelessness that appeared frequently in letters and diaries written by women of the master class. "Useless" was a dread epithet, repeatedly directed by Confederate women against themselves as they contemplated the very clear and honored role war offered men. "We young ladies are all so . . . useless," bewailed Sarah Wadley of Louisiana. "There are none so . . . useless as I," complained Amanda Chappelear of Virginia. "If only I could be of some use to our poor stricken country," wrote a young Louisiana girl to a friend in Tennessee, while Emma Holmes of Charleston sought escape from her "aimless existence." "What is the use of all these worthless women, in war times?" demanded Sarah Dawson. "I don't know how to be useful," another Virginia woman worried.

Some women translated these feelings into a related, yet more striking expression of discontent. Without directly challenging women's prescribed roles, they nevertheless longed for a magical personal deliverance from gender constraints by imagining themselves men. Some few actually disguised themselves and fought in the Confederate army, but far more widespread was the wish that preceded such dramatic and atypical action. "Would God I were a man," exclaimed Elizabeth Collier. "How I

wish I was a man!" seconded Emma Walton. "I do sometimes long to be a man," confessed Sallie Munford. Such speculation represented a recognition of discontent new to most Confederate women. Directed into the world of fantasy rather than toward any specific reform program, such desires affirmed the status quo, yet at the same time, they represented a potential threat to existing gender assumptions.

Without directly acknowledging such frustrations, Confederate public discussion of women's roles sought to deal with this incipient dissatisfaction by specifying active contributions women might make to the Southern Cause and by valorizing their passive waiting and sacrifice as highly purposeful. Confederate ideology construed women's suffering, not as an incidental by-product of men's wartime activities, but as an important and honored undertaking. In a popular Confederate novel aptly entitled *The Trials of a Soldier's Wife*, the heroine explained to her husband, "Woman can only show her devotion by suffering, and though I cannot struggle with you on the battle-field, in suffering as I have done, I feel it has been for our holy cause."

Public treatments of woman's patriotism soon broadened her accepted spiritual responsibilities to encompass wartime morale. "The time has come," Leila W. wrote in the *Southern Monthly* of October 1861, "when woman should direct into the right channel the greater power which she possesses in giving tone to public sentiment and morals, and shaping national character and national destiny." Moral service to God would now be paralleled by moral service to the state. Southern women, the *Mobile Evening News* concluded, held the "principal creation and direction" of Confederate public opinion "in their hands." The *Natchez Weekly Courier* assured the "Women of the South," that "the destinies of the Southern Confederacy" rested "in your control."

Women thus became acknowledged creators and custodians of public as well as domestic culture in the wartime South, exercising their power over communal sentiment in a variety of ways. They filled the pages of newspapers and periodicals with patriotic stories and verse and, perhaps even more important, composed many of the songs that served as the central medium of public wartime expression and constituted the most substantial publishing effort of the war. With the men preoccupied by military affairs, magazines such as the *Southern Literary Mes-*

senger eagerly sought contributions from women writers and struggled to evaluate the torrents of unsolicited poetry with which patriotic ladies flooded their offices.

But the escalating demand for troops after the bloody battle of Manassas in July 1861 offered women a new role to play. Here their patriotism and moral influence began to assume a more personal dimension, foreshadowing demands to be made of them as the conflict intensified. And this contribution involved women from a much wider social spectrum than had many of the earlier, largely middle- to upper-class efforts of ladies' societies and lady authors. Military manpower needs from the fall of 1861 onward required a rationalization of female sacrifice and a silencing of women's direct interest in protecting husbands and sons. The nineteenth-century creed of domesticity had long urged self-denial and service to others as central to woman's mission. But war necessitated significant alterations, even perversions, of this system of meaning; women's self-sacrifice for personally significant others—husbands, brothers, sons, family—was transformed into sacrifice *of* those individuals to an abstract and intangible "Cause."

The effective redefinition of women's sacrifice from an emphasis on protection of family to a requirement for relinquishment of family was problematic enough to occupy a significant portion of Confederate discourse on gender. Songs, plays, poems, even official presidential pronouncements sought to enlist women of all classes in the work of filling the ranks. One popular theme inverted *Lysistrata*, urging young women to bestow their favors only on men in uniform. In a much-reprinted song, a male songwriter assumed a female voice to proclaim, "I want to change my name." This fictionalized heroine was searching for a husband,

> But he must be a soldier
> A veteran from the wars,
> One who has fought for "Southern Rights"
> Beneath the Bars and Stars.

"None but the brave deserve the fair," a letter from "MANY LADIES" to the *Charleston Daily Courier* warned cowards and slackers in August 1861. Even Jefferson Davis addressed the question of ladies' appropriate marital choice, declaring the empty sleeve of the mutilated veteran preferable to the "muscular arm" of "him who staid at home and grew fat."

One song published early in the war acknowledged the conflict between woman's traditional role and the new demands on her. From "stately hall" to "cottage fair," every woman, rich or poor, was confronted by her own "stormy battle," raging within her breast.

> There Love, the true, the brave,
> The beautiful, the strong,
> Wrestles with Duty, gaunt and stern—
> Wrestles and struggles long.

But, like male songwriters who addressed that theme, the "Soldier's Wife" who had penned the lyrics was certain that women would win their own "heart victories" over themselves and in their "proudest triumphs" send their menfolk off to war. Stirring popular marches captured the very scene of parting, with men striding nobly into the horizon, while women just as nobly waved handkerchiefs and cheered their departure. "Go fight for us, we'll pray for you./Our mothers did so before us." Popular songs and poems urged women to abandon not just interest but also sentiment, repressing their feelings lest they weaken soldiers' necessary resolve. One graphic, even gruesome, ballad entitled "The Dead" protrayed a boy "oozing blood" on the battlefield as in his dying breath he insisted,

> Tell my sister and my mother
> Not to weep, but learn to smother
> Each sigh and loving tear.

A poem published in the *Richmond Record* in September 1863 elevated such repression of emotion into woman's highest duty. "The maid who binds her warrior's sash/ And smiling, all her pain dissembles," "The mother who conceals her grief" had "shed as sacred blood as e'er/ was poured upon the plain of battle." Not only was she to sacrifice husband, brother, or son, woman was to give up feeling as well. As a Virginia woman diarist remarked, "we must learn the lesson which so many have to endure—to struggle against our feelings." But "tis a hard struggle for me sometimes," she admitted.

Much of Confederate discourse negated the legitimacy of that emotional struggle by denying its reality altogether. Women, one newspaper proclaimed, had been offered a "glorious privilege" in the opportunity to contribute to the Cause by offering up their men. Any lingering resistance, the logic of the essay implied, should be overcome by the far greater—because transcendent—satisfaction of participation in the birth of a new nation.

Yet popular expressions often acknowledged women's doubts in an effort to dispel them. A newspaper poem. "I've Kissed Him and Let Him Go," was among the frankest of such treatments.

> There is some, I know, who feel a strange pride
>   In giving their country their all,
> Who count it a glory that boys from their side
>   In the strife are ready to fall,
> But I sitting here have no pride in my heart;
>   (God forgive that this should be so!)
> For the boy that I love the tears will still start.
>   Yet I've kissed him, and let him go.

Best was to feel right, so dedicated to the Cause that personal interest all but disappeared. Next best was to stifle lingering personal feeling. But the minimal requirement was to silence doubt and behave properly, even if right feeling proved unattainable.

There is considerable evidence that women of all social levels acted in accordance with these principles in the early months of conflict. Wartime gender prescriptions were so clear to a group of young ladies in Texas that they sent hoopskirts and bonnets to all the young men who remained at home. Other women comprehended the message well enough but, even early in the conflict, embraced it reluctantly. "Oh how I do hate to give him up," a Louisiana woman sighed, but "I suppose I have to be a martyr during this war."

And propelling men into the army was only the beginning. Once soldiers had enlisted, women were to help keep them in the ranks. The silencing of feeling and self-interest was to continue. "DON'T WRITE GLOOMY LETTERS," warned the *Huntsville Democrat*. Some women, noted an 1862 correspondent to the Georgia *Countryman*, seemed to be giving "up too easily. Some of them write very desponding letters to the soldiers. This is wrong. I am not surprised at their feeling badly; but they should not write gloomy letters," which would cause soldiers to "lose cofidence in themselves."

From the outset, the home front was acknowledged to exert significant control over military morale. And as the conflict wore on and desertions and disaffection increased, the connection became clearer. Women must do more than send their men to battle. When men deserted, women were to demonstrate that devotion to the Cause had primacy over personal commitments to husbands or sons. The *Richmond Enquirer* appealed directly "to the women to aid us in this crisis. None have so momentous an interest; and none, as we firmly believe, wield so much power. . . . They know those stragglers, one by one, and where they are to be found. They, the mothers and the sisters, may, if they will, be a conscript guard impossible to be evaded. They know whose furloughs are out, whose wounds are healed, who are lingering idly about . . . philandering and making love. . . . Will not the women help us, then?"

As the character of the war changed, so did public considerations of woman's place in it. Early discussions struggled to define some positive contribution women might make, some outlet for the patriotism that especially characterized women of the slave-owning classes. But the growing scale of the conflict transformed a rhetoric that tended to patronize women into one that implored them to make essential and increasing sacrifices for the Cause. As the Reverend R. W. Barnwell emphasized in an address to the Ladies Clothing Association of Charleston, "WITHOUT YOU, THIS WAR COULD NOT HAVE BEEN CARRIED ON, FOR THE GOVERNMENT WAS NOT PREPARED TO MEET ALL THAT WAS THROWN UPON IT." Beginning with the rising toll of battle deaths, the reality of the demands on women—the reality of war itself—intruded unremittingly not just on women's lives but on the stylized narrative created about them. Experience began to challenge the assumptions sustaining their early sacrifices.

From the perspective of 1865, the first months of the conflict would come to seem an age of innocence, a time, as one Virginia matron put it, "when we were playing at war." Stories of military history and romance began to pall in face of the unrelenting pressures of real war. In mid-1862 a Virginia girl answered in verse her cousin's inquiry, "If I had found enough romance in this War":

> Yes, wild and thrilling scenes have held
> A joyous sway upon my heart,
> But what a dread romance is this,
>   To fill in life so sad a part.
>
> Slighter changes oft have thrilled
> My Spirit's gay and gladening song.
> But this plaug'd [plagued], horrid, awful War
>   Has *proved* to *me romance too long.*

Much of the shift in women's perceptions of the war arose from the ever-expanding dimensions of required sacrifice. The need for military manpower was unrelenting, until by the end of the war, three-fourths of white Southern men of military age had served in the army and at least half of those soldiers had been wounded, captured, or killed, or had died of disease. This left almost every white woman in the South with a close relative injured, missing, or dead. But women had to sacrifice more than just their men. First luxuries, then necessities were to be relinquished for the Cause. "Fold away all your bright tinted dresses. . . . No more delicate gloves, no more laces," one poem urged. Women "take their diamonds from their breast/ And their rubies from the finger, oh!" a song proclaimed. A Virginia lady later reminisced that in the summer of 1861 she felt "intensely patriotic and self-sacrificing" when she resolved to give up ice creams and cakes. This, she remarked with some irony, "we called putting our tables on a war footing." By the next year, meat and grain had begun to disappear from many plates, and by 1864 one Confederate official informed Jefferson Davis that in Alabama, at least, civilian "deaths from starvation have absolutely occurred." In face of such realities, a Richmond periodical struggled to reassure the region's women and revalidate the notion of sacrifice:

> But e'en if you drop down unheeded,
> What matter? God's ways are the best:
> You have poured out your life where 'twas needed,
> And He will take care of the rest.

An initial conception of wartime self-denial as an enforced separation from loved ones and the absence of cakes and ice cream had been transformed even for the most privileged women of the South into the possibility of starvation for themselves and their families and the likelihood of death or injury for a husband or child.

For women of the slave-owning classes, the departure of husbands and sons and the continuing pressures of war took on additional significance. The burden of slave management, the designated responsibility of male planters and overseers before the conflict, now often devolved on women. The isolation of many plantation women in rural areas populated overwhelmingly by blacks exacerbated white women's dismay. Unsupervised slaves began to seem an insupportable threat. "I lay down at night," Addie Harris of Alabama complained, "& do not know what hour . . . my house may [be] broken open

& myself & children murdered. . . . My negroes very often get to fighting."

The slave system of the American South rested upon the realities of paternalistic domination—upon the power of white males over both women and black slaves. But the ideology of paternalism always presumed reciprocal obligations between the supposedly powerful and the powerless. Both the rhetoric and the practice of white gender relations had assigned political and social control to males in return for their assumption of the duty to maintain social order, to exert effective dominance over potentially rebellious bondsmen. Protecting white women from threats posed by the slave system upon which white male power rested was an inextricable part of planters' paternalistic responsibility. Yet when masters departed for military service, the Confederate government, as collective representation of slaveholders' power, failed to provide adequate means to control plantation slaves. Under such circumstances, many Confederate mistresses felt not only terrified but also abandoned and betrayed. Slave management was a duty for which most women believed themselves unsuited; they had not understood it to be in the domain allocated them by the paternalistic social order they had long accepted as natural and right. As one woman explained, she was simply not "a fit and proper person" to supervise bondsmen; another insisted she had not the "moral courage" to govern slaves. "The idea of a lady" exercising the required corporal dominance over slaves, Alice Palmer of South Carolina noted, "has always been repugnant to me."

The absence of white men accustomed to managing slaves and the disintegration of slavery under the pressures of growing black assertiveness thus placed an unanticipated and unwanted burden on plantation mistresses, most of whom had never questioned the moral or political legitimacy of the South's peculiar institution. But in the new war-born situation, Confederate women could not indulge in the luxury of considering slavery's merits "in the abstract," as its prewar defenders had urged, nor unthinkingly reap its material rewards. Slavery's meaning could not rest primarily in the detached realms of economics or politics, nor could white women any longer accept it as an unexamined personal convenience. The emotional and physical cost of the system to slaveholding white women had dramatically changed. Women now confronted all but overwhelming day-to-day responsibilities that they regarded as not rightfully theirs, as well as fears that often came to outweigh any tangible benefits they were receiving from the labor of increasingly recalcitrant and rebellious slaves.

The war's mounting death toll dictated the emergence of yet another dimension of female responsibility. While men at the front hurried their slain comrades into shallow graves, women at home endeavored to claim the bodies of dead relatives and to accord them proper ceremonies of burial. Woman's role was not simply to make sacrifices herself but also to celebrate and sanctify the martyrdom of others. In the Cofederacy mourning became a significant social, cultural, and spiritual duty. Through rituals of public grief, personal loss could be redefined as transcendent communal gain. Women's tears consecrated the deaths of their men, ensuring their immortality—in Southern memory as in the arms of God—and ratifying soldiers' individual martyrdom. Such deaths not only contributed to Confederate victory but also exemplified the sacred conception of Christian sacrifice with which the South had identified its nationalist effort. And in honoring men's supreme offering, women reminded themselves of the comparative insignificance of their own sacrifices. Loss of life of a beloved could not compare with loss of one's own; civilian anxiety and deprivation were as nothing in face of soldiers' contributions. "Even when a woman does her best," Kate Cumming observed of her efforts to nurse wounded soldiers, "it is a mite compared with what our men have to endure."

       *   *   *

As the emotional and physical deprivation of Southern white women escalated, the Confederate ideology of sacrifice began to lose its meaning and efficacy. Hardship and loss were no longer sacred, no longer to be celebrated, but instead came to seem causes for grievance. Late in 1862 an article in the *Children's Friend*, a religious periodical for boys and girls, found in what might earlier have been labeled a dedicated wartime "sacrifice" only deplorable "Oppression." "Many women," the paper reported, "especially in large cities, have to work hard, and receive very little for it. Many of them sew with their needles all day long, making garments for others, and get so little for it that they have neither food enough, nor clothes, nor fire to make their children comfortable and warm. There are many such now in

Richmond working hard, and almost for nothing." Southerners had defined the purpose of secession as the guarantee of personal independence and republican liberty to the citizens and households of the South. Yet the women of the Confederacy found themselves by the late years of the war presiding over the disintegration of those households and the destruction of that vaunted independence. Most white Southern women had long accepted female subordination as natural and just, but growing hardships and women's changed perception of their situation transformed subordination, understood as a justifiable structural reality, into oppression, defined as a relationship of illegitimate power.

The erosion of the sacredness of sacrifice was also evident in the changed attitudes toward death that appeared among Confederate civilians by the last months of the war. As one Virginia woman explained. "I hear now of acres of dead and . . . wounded with less sensibility than was at first occasioned by hearing of the loss of half a dozen men in a skirmish." This shift in perception was reflected in altered mourning customs. As Kate Stone explained in the spring of 1864, "People do not mourn their dead as they used to." Constance Cary was shocked by the seemingly cavalier and uncaring manner in which military hospitals treated the deceased, dropping six or seven coffins in "one yawning pit . . . hurriedly covered in, all that a grateful country could render in return for precious lives." The immediate and tangible needs of the living had become more pressing than any abstract notion of obligation to the dead.

The urgency of those needs yielded a sense of grievance that by 1863 became sufficiently compelling and widespread to erupt into bread riots in communities across the South. In Savannah, Georgia, Mobile, Alabama, High Point, North Carolina, Petersburg, Virginia, Milledgeville, Georgia, Columbus, Georgia, and in the capital city of Richmond itself, crowds of women banded together to seize bread and other provisions they believed their due. Their actions so controverted prevailing ideology about women that Confederate officials in Richmond requested the press not to report the disturbance at all, thus silencing this expression of female dissent. In the newspapers, at least, reality would not be permitted to subvert the woman's war story that editors had worked so assiduously to develop and propagate. A Savannah police court charged with disciplining that city's offenders similarly demonstrated the incompatibility of such female behavior with the accepted fiction about Southern women's wartime lives. "When women become rioters," the judge declared baldly, "they cease to be women." Yet in resorting to violence, these women were in a sense insisting on telling—and acting—their own war story. One Savannah rioter cared enough about the meaning of her narrative to print up and distribute cards explaining her participation in the disturbance. "Necessity has no law & poverty is the mother of invention. These shall be the principles on which we will stand. If fair words will not do, we will try to see what virtue there is in stones."

Upper-class women did not usually take to the streets, but they too expressed their objections to the prescriptions of wartime ideology. And, like their lower-class counterparts, they focused much of their protest on issues of consumption and deprivation. The combination of symbolism and instrumentalism in the bread riots was paralleled in the extravagance to which many Confederate ladies turned. In important ways, reckless indulgence represented resistance to the ideology of sacrifice. Mary Chesnut's husband James found her "dissipated" and repeatedly criticized her refusal to abandon parties and frivolity. In February 1864 the *Richmond Enquirer* declared the city to be a "carnival of unhallowed pleasure" and assailed the "shameful displays of indifference to national calamity." Richmond's preeminent hostess was reported to have spent more than thirty thousand dollars on food and entertainment during the last winter of the war. Even a council of Presbyterian elders in Alabama felt compelled in 1865 to "deplore the presence, and we fear, the growing prevalence of a spirit of gaity, especially among the female members of some of our congregations." And instead of resorting to riots, numbers of more respectable Richmond ladies subverted ideals of wartime sacrifice and female virtue by turning to shoplifting, which a Richmond paper reported to be "epidemick" in the city, especially among women of the better sort. Women, one observer noted in 1865, seemed to be "seeking nothing but their own pleasure while others are baring their bosoms to the storms of war."

The traditional narrative of war had come to seem meaningless to many women; the Confederacy offered them no acceptable terms in which to cast their experience. Women had consented to subordi-

nation and had embraced the attendant ideology of sacrifice as part of a larger scheme of paternalistic assumptions. But the system of reciprocity central to this understanding of social power had been violated by the wartime failure of white Southern males to provide the services and support understood as requisite to their dominance. And in a world in which Augusta Evans's independent and assertive Irene could become the war's most popular literary heroine, women would not assent indefinitely to the increasing sacrifice and self-denial the Civil War came to require. Although the fictional Irene was able to bear the tension between self-abnegation and self-realization in her own life, many Southern women found themselves unable or unwilling to construct their own experiences within a similar narrative. By the late years of the conflict, sacrifice no longer sufficed as a purpose. By early 1865, countless women of all classes had in effect deserted the ranks. Refusing to accept the economic deprivation further military struggle would have required, resisting additional military service by their husbands and sons, no longer consecrating the dead, but dancing while ambulances rolled by, Southern women undermined both objective and ideological foundations for the Confederate effort; they directly subverted the South's military and economic effectiveness as well as civilian morale. "I have said many a time," wrote Kate Cumming in her diary, "that, if we did not succeed, the women of the South would be responsible." In ways she did not even realize, Cumming was all too right. It seems not insignificant that in wording his statement of surrender, Robert E. Lee chose terms central to women's perceptions of themselves and the war. The Confederate effort, he stated at Appomattox, had become "useless sacrifice." Confederate ideology about women had been structured to keep those terms separated by interpreting sacrifice as a means of overcoming uselessness, by rendering sacrifice itself supremely purposeful. But the war story offered Confederate women at the outset of conflict had been internally flawed and contradictory and finally proved too much at odds with external circumstance; it was an ideology designated to silence, rather than address, the fundamental interests of women in preservation of self and family. As Julia Le Grand explained, it was an ideology that left women with "no language, but a cry," with no means of self-expression but subversion. In gradually refusing to accept this war story as relevant to their own ives, women undermined both the narrative presented to them and the Confederate cause itself. And without the logistical and ideological support of the home front, the Southern military effort was doomed to fail.

Historians have wondered in recent years why the Confederacy did not endure longer. In consider-able measure, I would suggest, it was because so many women did not want it to. The way in which their interests in the war were publicly defined—in a very real sense denied—gave women little reason to sustain the commitment modern war required. It may well have been because of its women that the South lost the Civil War.

Robert E. Lee: The Man and the Myth

Stephen W. Sears

Perhaps because Jefferson Davis, President of the Confederate States of America, offered limited appeal as a heroic figure—being in the words of one scholar, "a leader without legend"—the South and eventually the nation at large came to lavish their attention on Robert E. Lee. Particularly after the Civil War Lee gained mythical status, "the aristocrat as hero," as even the North came emotionally to concede him special standing in the American pantheon. Lee achieved, in peace, a national consensus that had eluded him in war. An illustrious lineage—he was the son of "Light Horse Harry" Lee, of Revolutionary War fame—had much to do with his cultural transition from man to mythic monument. The earlier Lee's close associations with George Washington allowed the luster of that legendary figure subsequently to accrue to his son's notable prestige. Lee indeed seemed a logical heir to Washington's personal glory, especially given his leadership of a valiant cause. Their quiet inner confidence, their embodiment of the ideal of Christian, gentleman, and soldier, rather perfectly suited both men.

Stephen W. Sears, Civil War historian and a former editor at *American Heritage*, examines some of the contours of Lee's mythic image. His was a legend that grew to maturity only after his death. His transformation was conditioned and abetted supplementally both by military colleagues and—in the tradition of Parson Weems— by men of the cloth. His rise to secular sanctity was largely at the expense of Lee's lieutenants—P.T.G. Beauregard, James Longstreet, and Jubal Early. Lee emerged triumphant in death and public memory as he seldom had been, or had wanted to be, in real life. The power of both regional and national remembrance has forced him to surrender to this fate. A mythic Midas touch on his historical reputation endures to this day.

In 1905, on a visit to Richmond, the noted man of letters Henry James was struck by the sight of the equestrian statue of Robert E. Lee high atop its pedestal overlooking Monument Avenue. There was about it, James thought, "a strange eloquence . . . a kind of melancholy nobleness." Something in the figure suggested "a quite sublime effort to ignore, to sit, as it were, superior and indifferent . . . so that the vast association of the futile for the moment drops away from it." Several decades later Lee's biographer Douglas Southall Freeman passed the Lee statue in

Richmond daily and invariably saluted it. "I shall not fail to do that as long as I live," Freeman said. Lee has that effect on people. For almost a century and a third, Americans, Northerners and Southerners, have been trying to get right with Robert E. Lee.

Such is the paradox of the man that today both those who consider General Lee a detriment to the Confederacy and those who consider him an undefiled military genius reach the same conclusion: The South would have been better off without him. The detractor says Lee squandered the South's slim resources of men and matériel, destroying any chance for ultimate Confederate victory; the admirer says that without Lee the Confederacy would have crumbled early, thus saving numerous Southern lives and much Southern suffering. It is at least safe to say that the course of the Civil War as we know it would have been very different without this one man.

Getting right with Lee has never been a simple task. Mary Chesnut, who observed him carefully during the war, wondered if anyone could really know him: "He looks so cold and quiet and grand." When Lee took command of the Army of Northern Virginia in 1862, writes Bruce Catton, "This gray man in gray rode his dappled gray horse into legend almost at once, and like all legendary figures he came before long to seem almost supernatural, a man of profound mystery." To the poet Stephen Vincent Benét, Lee was:

> A figure lost to flesh and blood and bones,
> Frozen into a legend out of life,
> A blank-verse statue— . . .
> For here was someone who lived all his life
> In the most fierce and open light of the sun
> And kept his heart a secret to the end
> From all the picklocks of biographers.

Benét called him "the marble man."

*   *   *

In the aftershock of Appomattox most Southerners were not immediately drawn to idolizing their generals. The war, after all, had been lost on the battlefields, and now there was nothing at all to celebrate except the end to the killing. To be sure, of all the South's generals Lee was even then the most respected, for back in the days when there had been victories to celebrate, most of them were his. In the years after the war, first in Richmond and then as president of little Washington College in Lexington, Lee was quietly honored by his fellow Virginians whenever they had the opportunity. At his death in Lexington in 1870 there was a modest military cortege and bells tolled and a battery from the Virginia Military Institute fired minute guns. The general's last words had been "Strike the tent," and that seemed to sound the proper final note for the old soldier's passing.

But of course that was not the end of it. The tent was never struck. Creating the mythic Robert E. Lee began only after his death, for in life he would never

have permitted it. In life Lee was not without ambition, nor was he self-effacing to the point of false modesty, and he harbored pride in what he had accomplished in the war. "There is nothing left me to do but to go and see General Grant," he had said on the day he surrendered his army at Appomattox, "and I would rather die a thousand deaths." But the process whereby he was canonized to secular sainthood would have triggered in him that icy anger that withered anyone at whom it was aimed. Those who created him the marble man, however, were out of his reach from beyond the grave. The marbling process, writes the historian C. Vann Woodward, "was the work of many hands, not all of them pious, the product of mixed motives, not all of them worthy."

In *The Marble Man: Robert E. Lee and His Image in American Society*, Thomas L. Connelly chronicles the rise of what he terms the Lee cult. Two initially rival Lee cliques, in Lexington and Richmond, coalesced and within a decade, by the end of the 1870s, were hard at work. Theirs was an all-Virginian operation—States' Rights energized the cult as well as the Confederacy—spearheaded by the former Army of Northern Virginia generals Jubal Early, William N. Pendleton, Fitzhugh Lee (General Lee's nephew), Lee's former staff members Walter Taylor and Charles Marshall, and J. William Jones, a Baptist minister. The cult's mission, Connelly writes, was to appropriate Robert E. Lee "as a balm to soothe defeat" and as the paladin of the lost cause. "To justify Lee was to justify the Southern cause."

*   *   *

Through speeches, articles, biographies, campaign narratives, and the editorship of the *Papers* of the Southern Historical Society, cult members seized control of Confederate historiography and turned it to their own purposes, which was the production of Lee hagiography. This veneration, explains the Lee biographer Marshall Fishwick, resulted in a St. George of Virginia, a remarkable phenomenon in white Southern Protestantism. To a beaten South, suffering under the lash of Reconstruction, this sainted Lee, so without blemish of character that his defense of the cause and his ultimate failure could only be examples of God's will, was truly a figure of worship.

Lee's elevation was necessarily accomplished at the expense of other Confederate generals, and here the mixed motives of the Lee cult became apparent.

Such rivals for military eminence as P. G. T. Beauregard and Joseph E. Johnston were systematically diminished in the pages of the Southern Historical Society *Papers*, which its editor, the Reverend Jones, turned into a showcase for General Lee and his Army of Northern Virginia. Even the heroic Stonewall Jackson, struck down at his moment of victory at Chancellorsville, was carefully reduced to simply Lee's lieutenant, his triumphs gained under the all-seeing direction of the general commanding. But these various demotions pale next to what Connelly terms the "crucifixion" of Lt. Gen. James Longstreet.

The assault on Longstreet was tied directly to the most difficult task the cult faced in its burnishing of Lee's military reputation: explaining the Battle of Gettysburg. Lee partisans would not admit that Gettysburg was an outright Confederate defeat—it was merely a check—yet there was no way they could transmute it into any semblance of a victory either. The greatest single battle of the war could not be reshaped into anything much better than a failure to achieve Lee's goals.

It could be reshaped into someone else's failure instead of Lee's, however, and Jubal Early took charge of that effort. Early was a grouchy, disagreeable sort with an undistinguished war record. He had actually been relieved of his last command, in the Shenandoah Valley, by Lee, who normally juggled subordinates without resorting to dismissal. Furthermore, at Gettysburg it was Early's failure to press an attack on July 1, the first day of the battle, that was widely regarded as a main reason the Federals retained their hold on Cemetery Ridge, from which they repelled the later Confederate attacks. By directing fire at Longstreet, Early was intent on diverting fire from himself.

*   *   *

Longstreet made an easy target. Not only had his second-day attack at Gettysburg failed (albeit narrowly), but in the years after the war he dared to criticize Lee's conduct of the battle. To compound his felony, during Reconstruction Longstreet embraced Republicanism. A barrage of articles on Gettysburg in the Southern Historical Society *Papers*, heavily freighted with innuendo and unsubstantiated charges, locked Longstreet into the scapegoat's role. Jubal Early put the matter with perfect clarity. "Either General Lee or General Longstreet was responsible for the remarkable delay that took place

in making the attack," Early wrote of the fighting on July 2. "I choose to believe that it was not General Lee." In that kind of contest Longstreet had no chance.

By the turn of the century the heroic, saintly Lee was no longer being seen merely as a Virginian or a Southerner but instead as a national hero. In a series of influential addresses and essays, Charles Francis Adams, Jr., grandson and great-grandson of Presidents, firmly ensconced Lee in this new role. Adams spoke of "the debt of gratitude this reunited country of ours—Union and Confederate, North and South—owes to Robert E. Lee of Virginia." Journalists linked Lee with Washington and Lincoln as the "first triumvirate of greatness." When the Hall of Fame was established at New York University in 1901, Lee was one of the first welcomed into the pantheon. Gamaliel Bradford's wide-selling 1912 biography was called simply *Lee the American*. A Southerner nicely summed up the enhanced stature of the foremost soldier of the Confederacy: "Whatever else we may have lost in that struggle, we gave the world Robert E. Lee."

While Lincoln remains unchallenged as the Civil War's most written-about figure, the volume of words expended on Lee, especially when Lee-related accounts of Gettysburg are included, holds second place. Heading the vast Lee literature is Douglas Southall Freeman's monumental four-volume biography, published in 1934 and 1935. With literary mastery and eminent scholarship Freeman firmly fixed greatness on Lee. In his hands Lee the general was certainly not above criticism, but it was never diminishing criticism. Freeman saw Lee's military failings as both few and proper. In Lee the man, Freeman found no contradictions, no secret self that was proof against the picklocks of biographers. "Robert Lee," he wrote, "was one of the small company of great men in whom there is no inconsistency to be explained, no enigma to be solved. What he seemed, he was—a wholly human gentleman, the essential elements of whose positive character were two and only two, simplicity and spirituality."

Thomas Connelly sees considerable irony in the hagiographical efforts of the Lee cult. The general's "military greatness alone would have assured his niche as a major national figure," he writes, without all the manipulation that went into creating the marble man. Perhaps in reaction to the image of the marble man, and certainly in challenge to it, historians in recent years (including especially Connelly) have sifted through everything Lee wrote and was quoted as saying to uncover the real man behind the improbable mask of the demigod. At the same time, Lee's military thought, his wartime strategy and tactics, have been plumbed anew in efforts to reinterpret his role in Confederate history. These efforts constitute one more attempt to get right with Robert E. Lee.

*   *   *

The Lee who emerges from these investigations is marked by more humanity and affected by more normal emotions than the demigod Lee. There can be little doubt, for example, that his youthful ambition to succeed and his awesome sense of duty were goaded by the cautionary tale of his father, Light-Horse Harry Lee, the Revolutionary War hero but a ne'er-do-well who deserted his family when Lee was just six years old. No doubt, too, the slack pace of promotion in the antebellum Army caused Lee frequently to question the worth of a career that brought him a colonelcy only after thirty-two years of service. Whether his marriage was less than a success, as has been argued, is not something that can be clearly settled at this distance, but it is clear that Lee complained about the seemingly endless separations from wife and family during his service in the old Army. And it is hardly surprising that amid the uncertainties of war he would fall back increasingly on the rationalization that God ruled all human affairs, the outcome of which were beyond earthly control.

At the same time, it must be said that Lee was hardly singular in his musings about the unfairness of life and in questioning his choice of the Army as a career. There cannot have been a single officer in the 1850s who expressed himself satisfied with his lot in that bureaucracy-ridden, glacier-paced antebellum army. The only surprise is that Lee did not resign to pursue a civilian career, as many others did. As for his religious fatalism, that too was common enough among Civil War generals. It was, after all, the duty of a field commander in wartime to organize and make efficient the mass killing of human beings, and anyone at all sensitive to the paradox of that was likely to seek reassurance that what he was doing was God's will.

*   *   *

Connelly offers the speculation that these various background pressures on Lee's psyche produced in him a repressed personality, turning him overly audacious and aggressive when in command on the battlefield. Lee's penchant for attack was in the end more than the Confederacy could afford, he writes; the Army of Northern Virginia "was bled to death by Lee's offensive tactics."

Such an explanation for Lee's military persona seems unduly complicated. In December 1862, watching a series of doomed Yankee attacks smash against his line at Fredericksburg, Lee remarked, "It is well that war is so terrible—we should grow too fond of it." That thought lends weight to an observation by Paul C. Nagel, the biographer of the Lees of Virginia. "At two points in his life," Nagel writes of the general, "he showed daring and imagination. These were on the battlefields of the Mexican War and the Civil War. But across the longer stretches of time, he seemed lethargic and inclined to stick with what was familiar and at hand." It was the opportunity for leadership and command in battle that raised Lee's consciousness and energized him; possibly his trust in himself did wane at other times, but never in war. It was this supreme confidence in his own generalship that enabled Lee to face down every general he met in the war but the last one, U. S. Grant, who possessed equal confidence in himself as a commander.

The corollary to this battlefield self-confidence is equally important to any understanding of Robert E. Lee the soldier: He invariably fought to *win*. Not every Civil War general fought that way. The Federals' Henry W. Halleck, for example, was primarily interested in gaining territory when in field command. General McClellan was notorious for fighting, when he did fight, so as not to lose. Joseph E. Johnston, when he opposed McClellan in Virginia and later Sherman in Georgia and the Carolinas, constantly retreated in order to avoid defeat. Lee's critics T. Harry Williams and the Englishman J. F. C. Fuller charge him with being both overly aggressive and strategically parochial, interested only in the Virginia theater of war. Williams terms him un-modern, "the last of the great old-fashioned generals." In fact Lee was neither parochial nor old-fashioned. He understood exactly where the South might win this war and what was required to win it, and he single-mindedly bent every effort to that victory. It was a decidedly modern concept.

Southerners might win the war through foreign intervention, as their forefathers had won the Revolution, or they might win on the battlefield and so force the North to the peace table. Militarily the best the Confederacy could hope from any Western victories was simply to arrest the Federal advance there and gain a stalemate. On the other hand, the Confederacy could win its independence at a stroke by winning victories, or just one great victory, in the East. The destruction of the Union's principal army and guardian of Washington, the Army of the Potomac, at a Sharpsburg or a Gettysburg or perhaps at Washington itself, offered the best chance to force the Lincoln administration to sue for peace. Even achieving a bloody stalemate against that army, as Lee nearly accomplished in the summer campaign of 1864, might go far toward gaining at least a negotiated peace and status quo antebellum—the South's return to the Union with its "rights" and its peculiar institution intact.

*   *   *

While Lee did not discount the possibility of British and French intervention, he was realistic in warning against relying on it. "We must make up our minds to fight our battles ourselves," he wrote in December 1861. "Expect to receive aid from no one. . . . The cry is too much for help." There was nothing at all parochial in his outlook. One of his staff recorded his observation that "since the whole duty of the nation would be war until independence should be secured, the whole nation should for the time be converted into an army, the producers to feed and the soldiers to fight." Toward this end Lee strongly endorsed a Confederacy-wide manpower draft, and the conscription bill that passed the Confederate Congress in Richmond in April 1862 was largely of his making.

That Lee frequently acted very aggressively in his strategy and often in his tactics is beyond dispute. That he often had no other practical choice is not always appreciated by those critics who, viewing Civil War battles through the lens of hindsight, rule them inherently indecisive because of the new weaponry and the old tactics of that day. It is true that Lee never gained the great war-winning battle, like Hannibal's Cannae, that he sought, but that result was not foreordained. In 1862 and 1863, before the two armies became locked in the trenches before Petersburg, Lee fought battles that were decided by chance or by fate or simply by human frailty.

*   *   *

He grasped the enormous advantage in war of holding the initiative, of forcing the enemy to march to his drum, especially so since his was always the smaller army. At every opportunity he aggressively seized the strategic initiative, as he did on taking field command for the first time in June 1862 during the Peninsula campaign.

In fighting McClellan for Richmond in the Seven Days' Battles, which opened in the last week of June, Lee adopted the offensive tactically as well as strategically. While his overall strategy was excellent, his tactics reflected his inexperience: his battle plans were too complicated, his staff work was poor, his orders were too demanding. The closest he came to a Cannae was at Glendale on June 30; Malvern Hill, the next day, was a disaster. Yet Lee had no real alternative to playing the role of aggressor in this week-long battle. To remain on the defensive was to allow McClellan to besiege Richmond, and to lose Richmond was a blow the Confederacy could not have survived, armchair generals to the contrary. In the event, Lee's offensive, flawed as it was, was relentless, and his opponent gave way before it. This was also McClellan's first experience of field command, and he broke under the strain. Lee took note of that lesson.

If Chancellorsville can be considered Lee's tactical masterpiece, his strategic masterpiece was the Second Manassas (Second Bull Run) campaign in August of 1862. In it, demonstrating an unerring sense of time as an element in warfare, he broke John Pope's army, one of the two arrayed against him, before the other one, under McClellan, could join it to overwhelm him. His margin in accomplishing this feat was a matter of only a few hours, but Lee was unruffled. When asked if he was not worried that his advance, under Stonewall Jackson, might be destroyed before he came up with the rest of the army, he replied calmly, "Not at all. I knew he could hold on till we came, and that we should be in position in time." Second Manassas, too, demonstrated how well he had learned the lessons of tactical command during the Seven Days. Now, as Robert Frost put it, "his dispositions for battle were beautiful. His two great divisions under Longstreet and Jackson were like pistols in his two hands, so perfectly could he handle them."

* * *

Lee's decision after the victory at Second Manassas to cross his country's northern frontier (as he called the Potomac) and march into Maryland toward Pennsylvania has been much debated. Was it intended as an invasion? A raid? What could he hope to gain by changing the Confederacy's overall posture from defensive to offensive? Lee's rationale was simple and straightforward: Crossing the Potomac was the only way to retain the initiative, and marching north offered the best way toward victory. General McClellan, he had learned, was once again his opponent, and he considered McClellan "an able general but a very timid one." Looking back on the campaign, Lee put the case with nice brevity: "I went into Maryland to give battle," and had all gone as intended, "I would have fought and crushed him."

Of course, all did not go as Lee intended, for chance intervened. A careless courier lost a copy of his campaign plan, and it was found by a Yankee soldier and brought to McClellan. The consequence was the Battle of Sharpsburg (or Antietam), on September 17. Sharpsburg was a battle Lee did not have to fight; so slow was McClellan to act on the lost order that Lee could have slipped back across the Potomac had he wished. Porter Alexander, an artillerist in Lee's army and a particularly astute observer, was blunt in calling it "the greatest military blunder that Gen. Lee ever made." However, Alexander offered the further observation that when General McClellan brought his greatly superior army to the banks of Antietam Creek, "he brought *himself* also." This was the actual reason Lee stood and fought there. He was certain he could beat the timid, cautious McClellan in any pitched battle, and indeed, he did out-general him that day and gain a narrow tactical victory, inflicting 20 percent more casualties than he suffered. Even at that, his army was too badly hurt to continue the campaign, and he had to fall back to Virginia. The profit of Sharpsburg was not worth the cost.

To say this is not to say that Lee was being overly aggressive in crossing the Potomac and marching north. With his army intact and rested and operating as he intended on ground of his own choosing, facing a general he was supremely confident he could beat, Robert E. Lee had every reason to believe he would win the showdown battle he sought. In these fall months of 1862 his troops and his lieutenants were in good form and good morale, and he was at the peak of his own powers, and when he insisted that without the mischance of the lost order he would have crushed McClellan, his opinion is worth respect.

* * *

The wounding of his army in Maryland forced Lee to surrender the strategic initiative for the first time since taking command, but thanks to the two generals who faced him next, this proved to be no disadvantage. "I fear they may continue to make these changes till they find some one whom I don't understand," Lee said when he learned of McClellan's dismissal after Sharpsburg. He need not have worried. He understood these two perfectly.

December saw McClellan's successor, Ambrose Burnside, hurl his army fruitlessly against the Army of Northern Virginia at Fredericksburg in the most senseless attack of the war. Longstreet remarked that so long as his ammunition held out and they kept coming, he would kill Yankee soldiers until there were none left in the North. Five months later, in May 1863, it was "Fighting Joe" Hooker's turn to challenge. Lee sarcastically referred to him as "Mr. F. J. Hooker" and once again took cruel advantage of the fact that his opponent was commanding an army in battle for the first time.

At Chancellorsville, Hooker lost his nerve and halted. "For once I lost confidence in Hooker," he admitted, "and that is all there is to it." Seizing the moment, Lee divided his forces in front of an army outnumbering him almost two to one and sent Stonewall Jackson on one of his patented flank marches. Jackson's attack sent the Yankees flying, Lee exerted pressure on all points of the line, and Hooker hastily admitted defeat and took his army back to its starting point. For Lee the great victory was marred by the mortal wounding of Jackson; with Jackson gone, he said, he had lost his right arm.

* * *

In opening the Gettysburg campaign a month after Chancellorsville, Lee was once again acting to hold the strategic initiative, and he was once again challenging a general, George G. Meade, who was commanding an army in battle for the first time. It was a familiar pattern, one that Lee had exploited with great success before, and it is not surprising that he would try it again.

In the first two days of the fighting at Gettysburg, Lee came tantalizingly close to winning his Cannae. His blood was up, as Longstreet put it, and he continued the offensive and so committed the deadly mistake of Pickett's Charge. That attack makes the best argument for critics of Lee's overaggressiveness, but the order for it came out of everything Lee was, everything that made him a great general; only this time he failed. "All this has been my fault—it is I that have lost the fight," he told Pickett's surviving soldiers. Still, so imposing was his reputation in that July of 1863 that General Meade was content with the battle's outcome and launched no counterattack and offered no pursuit when Lee retreated to Virginia. "Gettysburg," the historian Shelby Foote sums up, "was the price the South paid for having R. E. Lee."

The two bruised armies sparred inconclusively through the autumn as the war's focus shifted west, where Vicksburg had fallen and the Federals threatened to break through the Chattanooga gateway to the Deep South. Longstreet's corps was sent west as reinforcement, and Jefferson Davis proposed that Lee go west himself and take command there. He would do so if the president wished, Lee said, but he suggested it be a permanent change; the Western high command would never cordially support a visiting general. Of equal concern, who would command the Army of Northern Virginia in his stead? Jackson was dead and Longstreet was in the West, and Lee could suggest no one else competent for the post. Davis agreed, and Lee remained in the East. In the weakening Confederacy Lee's army was preeminent, and Lee was irreplaceable.

Lee's contest against Grant in the spring and summer of 1864, from the Wilderness and Spotsylvania to Cold Harbor and Petersburg, is in many respects as remarkable as anything in his Civil War record. With an army failing steadily and inevitably, against a general who was at last a true match, Lee countered every advance and repelled every charge and inflicted nearly twice the casualties he suffered. At Petersburg the two armies went to ground in a siege that lasted nine months. Here the Army of Northern Virginia was finally brought to bay by Grant, who was the sixth general to attempt it, yet at the same time the effort stalemated the Army of the Potomac, leaving the war in the East on dead center. The Confederacy's two Western generals, Joe Johnston and John B. Hood, could not achieve a comparable stalemate, however, and by the spring of 1865 Lee saw that final defeat was inevitable. "This is the people's war," he said at the time. "When they tire, I stop."

In February he had been appointed general in chief of all the Confederacy's armies, but by then there was little left for him to direct. In line with his earlier call for the entire Southern nation to mobilize for war, he advocated arming the slaves, which act would earn them their freedom. As regards black soldiers in Confederate gray, he said, "I think we could at least do as well with them as the enemy."

Lee felt duty-bound that spring to attempt one last campaign, and he managed to extricate his army from Petersburg and head it westward, hoping to join Joe Johnston in North Carolina and somehow carry on the fight. By the time he approached Appomattox Courthouse he had but eight thousand armed men left and knew he must meet General Grant and end it.

* * *

Gen. Porter Alexander urged Lee not to surrender but instead to let the men scatter to the hills to carry on a guerrilla war against the Yankee invaders. No, said Lee, that would mean ultimate ruin for the South; "a state of society would ensue from which it would take the country years to recover." To destroy what he had fought so hard to preserve would be senseless. "We have now simply to look the fact in the face that the Confederacy has failed." By his surrender, which initiated the surrender of the rest of the Confederacy's forces, Lee performed one of his most lasting services for the Confederate States of America.

When all is said and done, getting right with Robert E. Lee is a task that requires less analysis of his psyche and more analysis of his deeds. He was not by nature eloquent or introspective; even his personal farewell to his army at Appomattox was composed for him by one of his aides. "General Lee has done wonders—and no words wasted," the Charleston diarist Mary Chesnut said of him in 1865. For Henry James there was eloquence enough just in the figure of the man. In the few years left to him after the war, Lee never explained or justified in a memoir as did so many other generals. Among the major figures of the Civil War, he left the least words and the fewest inner thoughts for historians and biographers to pick over. It was Lee's actions that spoke volumes

If Douglas Freeman's Lee sometimes has the shadings of a mythic figure, he was surely right to dismiss the idea that there was anything enigmatic about his subject. Lee was simply a professional soldier who found his true calling in war, who, in Bruce Catton's phrase, "understood the processes of war as few men have ever done." Part of that understanding was a Midas's touch for crafting remarkable battlefield feats from limited resources.

*   *   *

Porter Alexander recorded a prophecy about Lee, made early in the war, before he had a record as a battlefield commander, that has been widely quoted. Alexander asked an aide to President Jefferson Davis if he thought Lee had audacity enough to lead a field army. "Lee is audacity personified," the man replied. "His name is audacity, and you need not be afraid of not seeing all of it that you will want to see." Lee's was an instinctive audacity for doing whatever was necessary for winning, and if it resulted in such repulses as Malvern Hill and Pickett's Charge, it was also responsible for the brillance of Chancellorsville and Second Manassas and a dozen other combats that extended the life of the Confederacy beyond all reasonable expectations. That singular accomplishment is the mark of the man.

The Words that Remade America: Lincoln and the Myths of Gettysburg

Garry Wills

The figure of Abraham Lincoln lends itself to mythmaking. Actual books exist on the subject: for example, *Myths After Lincoln* and *Abraham Lincoln: The Man Behind the Myths.* Myths abound concerning his birth, birthplace, and youth (reading by candlelight); frontier highjinks, notably earthy storytelling; lost love (the Ann Rutledge affair); aborted duels; law and politics, including the debates with Stephen Douglas and his rise to the presidency; his health; and myths of the war years. Lincoln's assassination remains a major myth industry, with no signs of abating.

Lincoln's words also have provided much mythic material, particularly his address at Gettysburg in November 1863, where he dedicated the memorial to the Union soldiers who had fallen in the great battle there the previous July. In this article Garry Wills, former Henry R. Luce Professor of American Culture and Public Policy at Northwestern University, centers on Lincoln's words as he remade the nation for the future. Legend has it that Lincoln did not take his speaking responsibility very seriously, that he practically delivered his remarks extemporaneously. The address was supposely penciled on a piece of cardboard during the train ride to Gettysburg (some say on the back of an envelope). Other myths have Lincoln dashing off the words the evening before; some suggest that he rather rudely wrote the text during the two-hour main peroration, delivered by Daniel Webster's friend and rhetorical heir, Edward Everett. In setting aside these myths, Wills points to Lincoln's long-standing love of the meaning and power of words—what could be accomplished through their economical use. Here at Gettysburg an opportunity was presented that deserved much more than just a few casually-chosen words, cavalierly scribbled on a piece of scrap paper. Lincoln understood this and welcomed the chance to speak, however briefly, and shaped his remarks very carefully. The key word among the 272 was *equality*, meaning equality for all, black and white. This was a national right not to be left to the states, for the nation had preceded the states' existence. This view is evidenced in the Declaration of Independence, the Constitutution (even though it does not specifically mention equality), and the Bill of Rights. According to Wills, "Lincoln not only presented the Declaration of Independence in a new light, as a matter of founding law, but put its central propositiion, equality, in a newly favored position." Lincoln had chosen this solemn occasion to exercise the power of words to accomplish nothing less than the refashioning of the country, including its stories about itself.

In the aftermath of the Battle of Gettysburg, both sides, leaving fifty thousand dead or wounded or missing behind them, had reason to maintain a large pattern of pretense—Lee pretending that he was not taking back to the South a broken cause, Meade that he would not let the broken pieces fall through his fingers. It would have been hard to predict that Gettysburg, out of all this muddle, these missed chances, all the senseless deaths, would become a symbol of national purpose, pride, and ideals. Abraham Lincoln transformed the ugly reality into something rich and strange—and he did it with 272 words. The power of words has rarely been given a more compelling demonstration. . . .

Lincoln knew the power of his rhetoric to define war aims. He was seeking occasions to use his words outside the normal round of proclamations and reports to Congress. His determination not only to be present but to speak is seen in the way he overrode staff scheduling for the trip to Gettysburg. Stanton had arranged for a 6:00 A.M. train to take him the hundred and twenty rail miles to the noontime affair. But Lincoln was familiar enough by now with military movements to appreciate what Clausewitz called "friction" in the disposal of forces—the margin for error that must always be built into planning. Lamon would have informed Lincoln about the potential for muddle on the nineteenth. State delegations, civil organizations, military bands and units, were planning to come by train and road, bringing at least ten thousand people to a town with poor resources for feeding and sheltering crowds (especially if the weather turned bad). So Lincoln countermanded Stanton's plan:

> I do not like this arrangement. I do not wish to so go that by the slightest accident we fail entirely, and, at the best, the whole to be a mere breathless running of the gauntlet. . . .

If Lincoln had not changed the schedule, he would very likely not have given his talk. Even on the day before, his trip to Gettysburg took six hours, with transfers in Baltimore and at Hanover Junction. Governor Curtin, starting from Harrisburg (thirty miles away) with six other governors as his guests, was embarrassed by breakdowns and delays that made them miss dinner at David Wills's house. They had gathered at 2:00 P.M., started at five, and arrived at eleven. Senator Alexander Ramsey, of Minnesota, was stranded, at 4:00 A.M. on the day of delivery, in Hanover Junction, with "no means of getting up to Gettysburg." Lincoln kept his resolution to leave a day early even when he realized that his wife was hysterical over one son's illness soon after the death of another son. The President had important business in Gettysburg.

* * *

For a man so determined to get there, Lincoln seems—in familiar accounts—to have been rather cavalier about preparing what he would say in Gettysburg. The silly but persistent myth is that he jotted his brief remarks on the back of an envelope. (Many details of the day are in fact still disputed, and no definitive account exists.) Better-attested reports have him considering them on the way to a photographer's shop in Washington, writing them on a piece of cardboard as the train took him on the hundred-and-twenty-mile trip, penciling them in David Will's house on the night before the dedication, writing them in that house on the morning of the day he had to deliver them, and even composing them in his head as Everett spoke, before Lincoln rose to follow him.

These recollections, recorded at various times after the speech had been given and won fame, reflect two concerns on the part of those speaking them. They reveal an understandable pride in participation at the historic occasion. It was not enough for those who treasured their day at Gettysburg to have heard Lincoln speak—a privilege they shared with ten to twenty thousand other people, and an experience that lasted no more than three minutes. They wanted to be intimate with the gestation of that extraordinary speech, watching the pen or pencil move under the inspiration of the moment.

That is the other emphasis in these accounts—that it *was* a product of the moment, struck off as Lincoln moved under destiny's guidance. Inspiration was shed on him in the presence of others. . . . Research, learning, the student's lamp—none of these were needed by Lincoln, whose unsummoned muse was prompting him, a democratic muse unacquainted with the library. Lightning struck, and each of our informants (or their sources) was there when it struck.

The trouble with these accounts is that the lightning strikes too often, as if it could not get the work done on its first attempt. It hits Lincoln on the train, in his room, at night, in the morning. If inspiration was treating him this way, he should have been short-circuited, not inspired, by the time he spoke.

These mythical accounts are badly out of character for Lincoln, who composed his speeches thoughtfully. His law partner, William Herndon, having observed Lincoln's careful preparation of cases, recorded that he was a slow writer, who liked to sort out his points and tighten his logic and his phrasing. That is the process vouched for in every other case of Lincoln's memorable public statements. It is impossible to imagine him leaving his Gettysburg speech to the last moment. He knew he would be busy on the train and at the site—important political guests were with him from his departure, and more joined him at Baltimore, full of talk about the war, elections, and policy. In Gettysburg he would be entertained at David Wills's house, with Everett and other important guests. State delegations would want a word with him. He hoped for a quick tour of the battle site (a hope fulfilled early on the nineteenth). He could not count on any time for the concentration he required when weighing his words. . . .

* * *

As a former Secretary of State, [Edward] Everett had many sources, in and outside government, for the information he had gathered so diligently. Lincoln no doubt watched closely how the audience responded to passages that absolved Meade of blame for letting Lee escape. The setting of the battle in a larger logic of campaigns had an immediacy for those on the scene which we cannot recover. Everett's familiarity with the details was flattering to the local audience, which nonetheless had things to learn from this shapely presentation of the whole three days' action. This was like a modern "docudrama" on television, telling the story of recent events on the basis of investigative reporting. We badly misread the evidence if we think Everett failed to work his customary magic. The best witnesses on the scene—Lincoln's personal secretaries, John Hay and John Nicolay, with their professional interest in good prose and good theater—praised Everett at the time and ever after. He received more attention in their biography's chapter on Gettysburg than did their own boss.

When Lincoln rose, it was with a sheet or two, from which he read. Lincoln's three minutes would ever after be obsessively contrasted with Everett's two hours in accounts of this day. It is even claimed

that Lincoln disconcerted the crowd with his abrupt performance, so that people did not know how to respond ("Was that *all?*"). Myth tells of a poor photographer making leisurely arrangements to take Lincoln's picture, expecting him to be standing for some time. But it is useful to look at the relevant part of the program:

Music. *by Birgfield's Band.*
Prayer. *by Rev. T.H. Stockton, D.D.*
Music. *by the Marine Band.*
ORATION. *by Hon. Edward Everett.*
Music. *Hymn composed by B. B. French.*
DEDICATORY REMARKS BY THE PRESIDENT OF THE UNITED STATES
Dirge. *sung by Choir selected for the occasion.*
Benediction. *by Rev. H.L. Baugher, D.D.*

There was only one "oration" announced or desired here. Though we call Lincoln's text *the* Gettysburg Address, that title clearly belongs to Everett. Lincoln's contribution, labeled "remarks," was intended to make the dedication formal (somewhat like ribbon-cutting at modern openings). Lincoln was not expected to speak at length, any more than Rev. T. H. Stockton was (though Stockton's prayer *is* four times the length of the President's remarks). A contrast of length with Everett's talk raises a false issue. Lincoln's text *is* startlingly brief for what it accomplished, but that would be equally true if Everett had spoken for a shorter time or had not spoken at all.

Nonetheless, the contrast was strong. Everett's voice was sweet and expertly modulated; Lincoln's was high to the point of shrillness, and his Kentucky accent offended some eastern sensibilities. But Lincoln derived an advantage from his high tenor voice—carrying power. If there is agreement on any one aspect of Lincoln's delivery, at Gettysburg or elsewhere, it is on his audibility. Modern impersonators of Lincoln, such as Walter Huston, Raymond Massey, Henry Fonda, and the various actors who give voice to Disneyland animations of the President, bring him before us as a baritone, which is considered a more manly or heroic voice—though both the Roosevelt Presidents of our century were tenors. What should not be forgotten is that Lincoln was himself an actor, an expert raconteur and mimic, and one who spent hours reading speeches out of Shakespeare to any willing (or sometimes unwilling) audience. He knew a good deal about rhythmic delivery and meaningful inflection. John Hay, who had submitted to many of those Shakespeare readings, gave high marks to his boss's performance at Gettysburg. He put in his diary at the time that "the President, in a fine, free way, with more grace than is his wont, said his half dozen words of consecration." Lincoln's text was polished, his delivery emphatic; he was interrupted by applause five times. Read in a slow, clear way to the farthest listeners, the speech would take about three minutes. It is quite true the audience did not take in all that happened in that short time—we are still trying to weigh the consequences of Lincoln's amazing performance. But the myth that Lincoln was disappointed in the result—that he told the unreliable Lamon that his speech, like a bad plow, "won't scour"—has no basis. He had done what he wanted to do, and Hay shared the pride his superior took in an important occasion put to good use.

* * *

At the least, Lincoln had far surpassed hope for words to disinfect the air of Gettysburg. His speech hovers far above the carnage. He lifts the battle to a level of abstraction that purges it of grosser matter—even "earth" is mentioned only as the thing from which the tested form of government shall not perish. The nightmare realities have been etherealized in the crucible of his language.

Lincoln was here to clear the infected atmosphere of American history itself, tainted with official sins and inherited guilt. He would cleanse the Constitution—not as William Lloyd Garrison had, by burning an instrument that countenanced slavery. He altered the document from within, by appeal from its letter to the spirit, subtly changing the recalcitrant stuff of that legal compromise, bringing it to its own indictment. By implicitly doing this, he performed one of the most daring acts of open-air sleight of hand ever witnessed by the unsuspecting. Everyone in that vast throng of thousands was having his or her intellectual pocket picked. The crowd departed with a new thing in its ideological luggage, the new Constitution Lincoln had substituted for the one they had brought there with them. They walked off from those curving graves on the hillside, under a changed sky, into a different America. Lincoln had revolutionized the Revolution, giving people a new past to live with that would change their future indefinitely.

Some people, looking on from a distance, saw that a giant (if benign) swindle had been performed.

The Chicago *Times* quoted the letter of the Constitution to Lincoln—noting its lack of reference to equality, its tolerance of slavery—and said that Lincoln was betraying the instrument he was on oath to defend, traducing the men who died for the letter of that fundamental law:

> It was to uphold this constitution, and the Union created by it, that our officers and soldiers gave their lives at Gettysburg. How dared he, then, standing on their graves, misstate the cause for which they died, and libel the statesmen who founded the government? They were men possessing too much self-respect to declare that negroes were their equals, or were entitled to equal privileges.

Heirs to this outrage still attack Lincoln for subverting the Constitution at Gettysburg—suicidally frank conservatives like M. E. Bradford and the late Willmoore Kendall. But most conservatives are understandably unwilling to challenge a statement now so hallowed, so literally sacrosanct, as Lincoln's clever assault on the constitutional past. They would rather hope or pretend, with some literary critics, that Lincoln's emotionally moving address had no discernible intellectual content, that, in the words of the literary critic James Hurt, "the sequence of ideas is commonplace to the point of banality, the ordinary coin of funereal oratory."

People like Kendall and the Chicago *Times* editors might have wished this were true, but they knew better. They recognized the audacity of Lincoln's undertaking. Kendall rightly says that Lincoln undertook a new founding of the nation, to correct things felt to be imperfect in the Founders' own achievement:

> Abraham Lincoln and, in considerable degree, the authors of the post-civil-war amendments, attempted a new act of founding, involving concretely a startling new interpretation of that principle of the founders which declares that "All men are created equal."

Edwin Meese and other "original intent" conservatives also want to go back before the Civil War amendments (particularly the Fourteenth) to the original Founders. Their job would be comparatively easy if they did not have to work against the values created by the Gettysburg Address. Its deceptively simple-sounding phrases appeal to Americans in ways that Lincoln had perfected in his debates over the Constitution during the 1850s. During that time Lincoln found the language, the imagery, the myths, that are given their best and briefest embodiment at Gettysburg. In order to penetrate the mystery of his "refounding," we must study all the elements of that stunning verbal coup. Without Lincoln's knowing it himself, all his prior literary, intellectual, and political labors had prepared him for the intellectual revolution contained in those 272 words.

*   *   *

Lincoln's speech is brief, one might argue, because it is silent on so much that one would expect to hear about. The Gettysburg Address does not mention Gettysburg. Or slavery. Or—more surprising—the Union. (Certainly not the South.) The other major message of 1863, the Emancipation Proclamation, is not mentioned, much less defended or vindicated. The "great task" mentioned in the address is not emancipation but the preservation of self-government. We assume today that self-government includes self-rule by blacks as well as whites; but at the time of his appearance at Gettysburg, Lincoln was not advocating even eventual suffrage for African-Americans. The Gettysburg Address, for all its artistry and eloquence, does not directly address the prickliest issues of its historical moment.

Lincoln was accused during his lifetime of clever evasions and key silences. He was especially indirect and hard to interpret on the subject of slavery. That puzzled his contemporaries, and has infuriated some later students of his attitude. Theodore Parker, the Boston preacher who was the idol of Lincoln's law partner, William Herndon, found Lincoln more clever than principled in his 1858 Senate race, when he debated Stephen Douglas. Parker initially supported William Seward for President in 1860, because he found Seward more forthright than Lincoln in his opposition to slavery. But Seward probably lost the Republican nomination *because* of that forthrightness. Lincoln was more cautious and circuitous. The reasons for his reserve before his nomination are clear enough—though that still leaves the omissions of the Gettysburg Address to be explained.

Lincoln's political base, the state of Illinois, runs down to a point (Cairo) farther south than all of what became West Virginia, and farther south than most of Kentucky and Virginia. The "Negrophobia" of Illinois led it to vote overwhelmingly in 1848, just ten years before the Lincoln-Douglas debates, to amend the state constitution so as to deny freed blacks all right of entry to the state. The average vote of the state

was 79 percent for exclusion, though southern and some central counties were probably more than 90 percent for it. Lincoln knew the racial geography of his own state well, and calibrated what he had to say about slavery according to his audience.

Lincoln knew it was useless to promote the abolitionist position in Illinois. He wanted to establish some common ground to hold together the elements of his fledgling Republican Party. Even as a lawyer Herndon said, he concentrated so fiercely on the main point to be established ("the nub") that he would concede almost any ancillary matter. Lincoln's accommodation to the prejudice of his time did not imply any agreement with the points he found it useless to dispute. One sees his attitude in the disarming concession he made to Horace Greeley, in order to get to the nub of their disagreement:

> I have just read yours of the 19th addressed to myself through the New-York Tribune. If there be in it any statements, or assumptions of fact, which I may know to be erroneous, I do not, now and here, controvert them. If there be in it any inferences which I may believe to be falsely drawn, I do not now and here, argue against them. If there be perceptible in it an impatient and dictatorial tone, I waive it in deference to an old friend, whose heart I have always supposed to be right.

Obviously, Lincoln did not agree with the aspersions that Greeley had cast, but this was not a matter he could usefully pursue "now and here." In the same way, Lincoln preferred agnosticism about blacks' intellectual inferiority to whites, and went along with the desire to keep them socially inferior. As George Fredrickson points out, agnosticism rather than *certainty* about blacks' intellectual disability was the liberal position of that time, and there was nothing Lincoln or anyone else could do about social mixing. Lincoln refused to let the matter of political equality get tangled up with such emotional and (for the time) unresolvable issues. What, for him, was the nub, the realizable minimum—which would be hard enough to establish in the first place?

At the very least, it was wrong to treat human beings as property. Lincoln reduced the slaveholders' position to absurdity by spelling out its consequences:

> If it is a sacred right for the people of Nebraska to take and hold slaves there, it is equally their sacred right to

buy them where they can buy them cheapest; and that undoubtedly will be on the coast of Africa . . . [where a slavetrader] buys them at the rate of about a red cotton handkerchief a head. This is very cheap.

Why do people not take advantage of this bargain? Because they will be hanged like pirates if they try. Yet if slaves are just one form of property like any other,

it is a great abridgement of the sacred right of self-government to hang men for engaging in this profitable trade!

Not only had the federal government, following international sentiment, outlawed the slave trade, but the domestic slave barterer was held in low esteem, even in the South:

You do not recognize him as a friend, or even as an honest man. Your children must not play with his. . . . Now why is this? You do not so treat the man who deals in corn, cattle or tobacco.

And what kind of *property* is "set free"? People do not "free" houses or their manufactures to fend for themselves. But there were almost half a million freed blacks in Lincoln's America:

How comes this vast amount of property to be running about without owners? We do not see free horses or free cattle running at large.

Lincoln said that in 1854, three years before Chief Justice Roger Taney declared, in the Dred Scott case, that slaves were movable property like any other chattel goods. The absurd had become law. No wonder Lincoln felt he had to fight for even minimal recognition of human rights.

If the black man owns himself and is not another person's property, then he has rights in the product of his labor:

I agree with Judge Douglas [the Negro] is not my equal in many respects—certainly not in color, perhaps not in moral or intellectual endowment. But in the right to eat the bread, without leave of anybody else, which his own hand earns, *he is my equal and the equal of Judge Douglas, and the equal of every living man.*

Lincoln, as often, was using a Bible text, and one with a sting in it. The *curse* of mankind in general, that "in the sweat of thy face shalt thou eat bread" (Genesis 3:19), is, at the least, a *right* for blacks.

Lincoln tried to use one prejudice against another. There was in Americans a prejudgment in

favor of anything biblical. There was also antimonarchical bias. Lincoln put the text about eating the bread of one's own sweat in an American context of antimonarchism.

That is the issue that will continue in this country when these poor tongues of Judge Douglas and myself shall be silent. It is the eternal struggle between these two principles—right and wrong—throughout the world. They are the two principles that have stood face to face from the beginning of time; and will ever continue to struggle. The one is the common right of humanity and the other the divine right of kings. It is the same principle in whatever shape it develops itself. It is the same spirit that says, "You work and toil and earn bread, and I'll eat it." [Loud applause.] No matter in what shape it comes, whether from the mouth of a king who seeks to bestride the people of his own nation and live by the fruit of their labor, or from one race of men as an apology for enslaving another race, it is the same tyrannical principle.

In at least these two ways, then, slavery is wrong. One cannot own human beings, and one should not be in the position of a king over human beings.

Lincoln knew how to sneak around the frontal defenses of prejudice and find a back way into agreement with bigots. This explains, at the level of tactics, the usefulness to Lincoln of the Declaration of Independence. That revered document was antimonarchical in the common perception, and on that score unchallengeable. But because it indicted King George III in terms of the equality of men, the Declaration committed Americans to claims even more at odds with slavery than with kingship—since kings do not necessarily claim to own their subjects. Put the claims of the Declaration as mildly as possible, and they still cannot be reconciled with slavery:

I, as well as Judge Douglas, am in favor of the race to which I belong having the [politically and socially] superior position. I have never said anything to the contrary, but I hold that notwithstanding all this, there is no reason in the world why the negro is not entitled to all the natural rights enumerated in the Declaration of Independence, the right to life, liberty and the pursuit of happiness. [Loud cheers.] I hold that he is as much entitled to these as the white man.

*   *   *

Lincoln's speech at Gettysburg worked several revolutions, beginning with one in literary style. Everett's talk was given at the last point in history when such a performance could be appreciated without reservation. It was made obsolete within a half hour of the time when it was spoken. Lincoln's remarks anticipated the shift to vernacular rhythms which Mark Twain would complete twenty years later. Hemingway claimed that all modern American novels are the offspring of *Huckleberry Finn*. It is no greater exaggeration to say that all modern political prose descends from the Gettysburg Address. . . .

[But] it would be wrong to think that Lincoln moved toward the plain style of the Gettysburg Address just by writing shorter, simpler sentences. Actually, that address ends with a very long sentence—eighty-two words, almost a third of the whole talk's length. So does the Second Inaugural Address, Lincoln's second most famous piece of eloquence: its final sentence runs to seventy-five words. Because of his early experiments, Lincoln's prose acquired a flexibility of structure, a rhythmic pacing, a variation in length of words and phrases and clauses and sentences, that make his sentences move "naturally," for all their density and scope. . . .

The spare quality of Lincoln's prose did not come naturally but was worked at. Lincoln not only read aloud, to think his ways into sounds, but also wrote as a way of ordering his thought. He had a keenness for analytical exercises. He was proud of the mastery he achieved over Euclid's Elements, which awed Herndon and others. He loved the study of grammar, which some think the most arid of subjects. Some claimed to remember his gift for spelling, a view that our manuscripts disprove. Spelling as he had to learn it (separate from etymology) is more arbitrary than logical. It was the logical side of language—the principles of order as these reflect patterns of thought or the external world—that appealed to him.

He was also, Herndon tells us, laboriously precise in his choice of words. He would have agreed with Mark Twain that the difference between the right word and the nearly right one is that between lightning and a lightning bug. He said, debating Douglas, that his foe confused a similarity of words with a similarity of things—as one might equate a horse chestnut with a chestnut horse.

As a speaker, Lincoln grasped Twain's later insight: "Few sinners are saved after the first twenty minutes of a sermon." The trick, of course, was not simply to be brief but to say a great deal in the fewest words. Lincoln justly boasted of his Second Inaugural's seven hundred words, "Lots of wisdom in that

document, I suspect." The same is even truer of the Gettysburg Address, which uses fewer than half that number of words. . . .

*   *   *

James McPherson has described Lincoln as a revolutionary in terms of the economic and other physical changes he effected, whether intentionally or not—a valid point that McPherson discusses sensibly. But Lincoln was a revolutionary in another sense as well—the one Willmoore Kendall denounced him for: he not only presented the Declaration of Independence in a new light, as a matter of founding law, but put its central proposition, equality, in a newly favored position as a principle of the Constitution (whereas, as the Chicago *Times* noticed, the Constitution never uses the word). What had been mere theory in the writings of James Wilson, Joseph Story, and Daniel Webster—that the nation preceded the states, in time and importance—now became a lived reality of the American tradition. The results of this were seen almost at once. Up to the Civil War "the United States" was invariably a plural noun: "The United States are a free country." After Gettysburg it became a singular: "The United States is a free country." This was a result of the whole mode of thinking that Lincoln expressed in his acts as well as his words, making union not a mystical hope but a constitutional reality. When, at the end of the address, he referred to government "of the people, by the people, for the people," he was not, like Theodore Parker, just praising popular government as a Transcendentalist's ideal. Rather, like Webster, he was saying that America was *a* people accepting as its great assignment what was addressed in the Declaration. This people was "conceived" in 1776, was "brought forth" as an entity whose birth was datable ("four score and seven years" before) and placeable ("on this continent"), and was capable of receiving a "new birth of freedom."

Thus Abraham Lincoln changed the way people thought about the Constitution. For a states'-rights advocate like Willmoore Kendall, for an "original intent" advocate like Edwin Meese, the politics of the United States has all been misdirected since that time. The Fourteenth Amendment was, in their view, ultimately bootlegged into the Bill of Rights. But as soon as it was ratified, the Amendment began doing harm, in the eyes of strict constructionists. . . .

As Kendall put it, Lincoln's use of the phrase

from the Declaration about all men being equal is an attempt "to wrench from it a single proposition and make that our supreme commitment."

> We should not allow [Lincoln]—not at least without some probing inquiry—to "steal" the game, that is, to accept his interpretation of the Declaration, its place in our history, and its meaning as "true," "correct," and "binding."

But, as Kendall himself admitted, the professors, the textbooks, the politicians, the press, *have* overwhelmingly accepted Lincoln's vision. The Gettysburg Address has become an authoritative expression of the American spirit—as authoritative as the Declaration itself, and perhaps even more influential, since it determines how we read the Declaration. For most people now, the Declaration means what Lincoln told us it means, as he did to correct the Constitution without overthrowing it. It is this correction of the spirit, this intellectual revolution, that makes attempts to go back beyond Lincoln to some earlier version so feckless. The proponents of states' rights may have arguments to advance, but they have lost their force, in the courts as well as in the popular mind. By accepting the Gettysburg Address, and its concept of a single people dedicated to a proposition, we have been changed. Because of it, we live in a different America.

The Southern Rape Myth Reconsidered

Diane Miller Sommerville

Despite or because of the South's defeat in the Civil War, the mythical version of the mannered and manorial plantation Old Regime became during the postwar period even more an assumption. Whether by pure nostalgia, illusion nourished by desire, or a regional need for some measure of collective cultural redemption to compensate for defeat and humiliation, blissful belief in the noble plantation regime before the war retained its emotional currency long after Appomattox. But the plantation myth, in Stephen Vincent Benét's words, was, after all, "the sick magnolias of the false romance." Behind the fragrant facade of plantation polite society resided a world of southern violence: general economic exploitation under the slave system, sometimes punctuated by whipping, branding, beating, and rape. Social mythology simultaneously caricatured black men as bestial sexual aggressors, and white women as celestial virgins. A great fear in the Old South, then, was black male sexual desire for white females. The white response to these anxieties, to any perceived indiscretion or outrage in this realm, was clear and often swift—legal codes clearly prescribing patterns of conduct between blacks and whites, males and females, and quick justice should these be violated. Lynching or the death penalty frequently resulted. The myth has prevailed that kangaroo court justice toward black men accused of raping white women typified both the Old and the New South. In challenging this assumption, while never denying the racial and gender mytholgies that sustained the belief, Diane Miller Sommerville of Princeton University discovers multiple mythologies. She finds that the antebellum South had been largely respectful at least of due process for blacks. Only during the New South era—supposedly an environment of slightly greater racial justice— was the southern rape complex most in evidence.

In Southhampton County, Virginia, the site of Nat Turner's 1831 revolt, another man of color was alleged to have committed an egregious act a few years earlier; in 1826 and 1827 Henry Hunt appeared before superior court accused of raping a white woman named Sydney Jordan. Hunt was a twenty-two-year-old laborer from St. Luke's parish and was described by his jailer as six feet tall, "straight and well made" with "a considerable share of effrontery." The latter attribute may have been prompted by Hunt's escape from jail. His flight from justice, however, was short-lived, as he was quickly apprehended. Hunt's defense rested on his assertion that his relations with Sydney Jordan were entirely consensual. In fact, Hunt claimed to have "long been in the habit of sexual intercourse" with Jordan. Furthermore, Hunt maintained that on the night of the alleged sexual assault not he but another free black man had bedded Jordan.

Hunt's protestations notwithstanding, the jury found him guilty of rape and sentenced him to hang. In an astonishing turn of events, a group of white citizens from Southampton County, including Hunt's jailer, the court clerk, and a member of the jury that had found him guilty, petitioned the governor and the executive council and asked that they extend clemency to the convicted rapist. Sydney Jordan, the petitioners explained, had committed perjury. Hunt averred throughout his defense that his and Jordan's relationship was based on mutual consent. Jordan denied this; in fact, she denied having met Henry Hunt prior to the night of the alleged assault. The crowning piece of evidence put forth in the petition defending Hunt was the statement that Jordan had given birth to a "black child" over a year after the alleged rape. The birth of a nonwhite child belied Jordan's assertion that she had not maintained intimate relations with black men and thus lent credibility to Hunt's account. Eventually Jordan acknowledged that the child's father was Nicholas Vick, the free black man whom Hunt claimed to have found in bed with Jordan on the night she claimed to have been raped by Hunt. With her lies unsalvageable, Jordan admitted having had "frequent criminal intercourse with . . . Henry Hunt" as well as with Nicholas Vick. The petitioners concluded that Henry Hunt was not guilty of the alleged sexual assault and pleaded that "humanity requires the interposition of the Executive council to rescue him from an undeserved doom." A sympathetic governor granted Hunt a pardon.

Seizing a pen instead of rope and fagot to deal with an accused black rapist seems irreconcilable with the image, largely the product of the postbellum period, of lawless, unrestrained southern lynch mobs bent on vigilante "justice" and retribution. Not only did this black man receive a trial, presumably attendant with certain procedural rights, but he also became the object of white citizens' sympathies and concern. The collective fear and anxiety about black sexual assault that loomed large in postbellum southern society seem conspicuously absent in the case of Henry Hunt. Moreover, his case is not isolated: over 250 cases of sexual assault by black males on white women or girls are reported in the records of twelve southern states from 1800 through 1865. Although

this study focuses primarily on Virginia and North Carolina, admittedly two of the northern-most slaveholding states, secondary sources as well as published primary sources, such as appellate decisions, reveal that similar occurrences were turning up throughout the slave South. In Virginia alone there are over 150 cases from 1800 through 1865 of African American men, free and slave, condemned to die for sexually assaulting white women or children. Nearly half of these condemned black rapists escaped their sentences of execution, suggesting that antebellum white southerners felt less compelled to exact death from a black man accused of sexually violating a white female than did postbellum white southerners. The argument here is that the rape trial of Henry Hunt, as well as those of dozens of other black southern males, demonstrates that antebellum white southerners were not nearly as consumed by fears of black men raping white women as their postbellum descendants were. As Eugene Genovese has written, the "titillating and violence-provoking theory of the superpotency of that black superpenis, while whispered about for several centuries, did not become an obsession in the South until after emancipation. . . ." The pervasive sexual and racial anxieties that galvanized scores of lynch mobs after the war failed to manifest themselves before emancipation. Why is it, then, that so much scholarship has perpetuated the notion that such fears were a constant throughout the history of the slaveholding South? . . .

A quick overview of southern statutes suggests that legislators considered sexual assault a heinous crime whether committed by black or white males. Eight slaveholding states at various times before the Civil War prescribed death for white rapists. Death sentences, however, seem to have been reserved for white rapists of children. The more prevalent punishment for white offenders was imprisonment. Of the southern states and territories that punished white rapists with prison, the terms ran the gamut from Georgia statutes, being the least harsh (from two to twenty years), to Alabama, Louisiana, and Mississippi statutes, which at one time or another sentenced white offenders to life imprisonment. Virginia prison registers reveal that the sentences of white men serving time for rape or attempted rape ranged from three to twenty years, although most averaged between ten and seventeen years.

The trend of rape statutes through the Civil War, nonetheless, was to lessen the punishment for convicted white rapists while retaining capital punishment for African Americans, free and slave. As an example, a Virginia law passed in 1847 called for convicted white rapists to serve from ten to twenty years in prison while prescribing the death penalty for black men. In most southern states by the beginning of the Civil War, racial disparity permeated sexual assault statutes. Rape statutes were equally discriminatory in defining the victims. Females of color, whether free or slave, assaulted by white men found virtually no redress from the judicial system. The widely held belief in the depraved and promiscuous nature of African American women coupled with a female slave's status as the property of a white man shielded rapists, whether black or white, from prosecution.

Though statutes expressly addressed race, issues of class or "respectability" are not mentioned in laws on rape. In applying these statutes to individual cases, judges, jurors, and community members nonetheless took it upon themselves to utilize juridical prerogative and frequently applied such standards to cases of sexual assault, as in the case of Sydney Jordan. Jordan was no doubt one of the Old South's "unruly women" portrayed in Victoria Bynum's recent study of the same name. Jordan, who was white but outside the circle of the genteel, defied rigid race and gender conventions by engaging in illicit sexual behavior with African American men. Because she did so and was caught at it, the protection bestowed upon her, presumably because of her whiteness, was withdrawn. In short, she had not behaved as a proper white woman should and was therefore not to be treated as one. Instead, the overseers of her community, white men who were probably her social betters, accused her of perjury and sought clemency for the black man whom she alleged had sexually violated her. Her race failed to shield her from assaults on her moral character.

Like Sydney Jordan twenty years later, Sarah Sands of Henry County, Virginia, claimed to have been raped by an African American man. She accused a slave named Jerry owned by Edward Osborne. Also like Jordan, Sands was reported to have kept company with black men. Jerry was tried in the local court in 1807, found guilty, and sentenced to be hanged. A petition to the governor penned by Jerry's legal counsel, Peachy R. Gilmer, purported to reflect the sentiments of others who attended the trial and argued for a reduction in sentence from execution to

transportation. Gilmer based his request on Sands's indiscreet sexual history and cited Sands's "very infamous character" and her status as another man's concubine. And if a questionable character weren't enough to erode Sands's credibility, the petition places in evidence the woman's size. Gilmer portrayed Sands as "large and strong enough to have made considerable resistance if she had been so disposed, yet there was by her own confession no mark of violence upon any part of her."

Undoubtedly Jerry's counsel presented this evidence at the 1807 trial, but the court remained unconvinced and rendered a guilty verdict. A number of the white residents of the community believed that the honor of such a deviant, debased woman was not worth the life of the rapist, and they took their case to the governor, who granted Jerry a reprieve.

A group of Virginians made a similar appeal in 1803 on behalf of Carter, a slave found guilty of raping a poor white woman who, like Jordan and Sands, had a reputation for consorting with African American men:

> Carter did commit the said offense—from the whole of the evidence your subscribers felt themselves bound by law to pass sentence of death upon the said Carter. Yet for reasons, hereinafter mentioned the court aforesaid are of the opinion that the said Carter is a proper object of mercy . . . [I]t appeared that the said Catherine Brinal was a woman of the worst fame, that her character was that of the most abandoned in as much as she (being a white woman) has three mulatto children, which by her own confession were begotten by different negro men; that the said Catherine has no visible means of support; that from report she had permitted the said Carter to have peaceable intercourse with her, before the time of his forcing her.

According to the petitioners, having previously consented to "peaceable" sexual relations with Carter, Catherine Brinal effectively lost her right to deny him sex at any future time. Brinal, and white women like her who flaunted prevailing social conventions about race and sex, risked the embarrassment of the public airing of their social histories. Carter cheated the executioner and was transported out of the state.

Consider also the case of Cato, a Florida slave accused in 1860 of raping Susan Leonard, a white woman whom twelve defense witnesses described as a "common prostitute." Nevertheless, the lower court judge instructed the jury that if they were satisfied that Cato had "carnal knowledge . . . against her will" they must find Cato guilty, which the jury ultimately did. On review, the Florida Supreme Court acknowledged its own role as judicial patriarch and balanced "the fact that a most foul offence" had been perpetrated against the consideration that the "life of a human being" was dependent on the outcome. Mindful of its commitment to oversee justice of accused slaves, the court boasted of the "crowning glory of our 'peculiar institution,' that whenever life is involved, the slave stands upon as safe ground as the master." The court was disturbed by the "abundant proof" that the alleged victim and her friend who testified for the state were "common prostitutes." Lacking corroborative testimony, the court refused to turn its back on Cato. Quoting the seventeenth-century English jurist Lord Chief Justice Matthew Hale, the court sympathized that "rape is an accusation easily to be made and hard to be proved and harder to be defended by the party accused. . . ." The high court vacated the execution decree and ordered a new trial.

Although not all cases led to reprieves or pardons of convicted African American rapists, the defense could be counted on to raise questions about the character of the female accuser. In the 1829 rape case of Lewis, a Virginia slave, two witnesses tarnished the reputation of the accuser, Amy [Amey] Baker, and her housemate, who had been an eyewitness to the assault, with accusations of debauchery and sexual impropriety. Five other witnesses, however, took the stand to defend the reputation of the two women. As Baker, who was forty-five years old, and her live-in companion, "old Mrs. [Drucilla] Kirkland," recounted, in the dark hours before daybreak on May 23 the accused came to Baker's house demanding to be let in. After the women refused to admit Lewis, he broke down the door. They claimed that Lewis brutally raped Amy Baker four times over a two-hour period while Mrs. Kirkland hid under the bed. Soon thereafter the accused dozed off, and the two women fled to the home of a neighbor, Burwell Coleman, whose son, Richard Coleman, returned with them to their house. Coleman groped blindly in the dark and found the intruder still lying on the bed clothed only from the waist up. After a brief struggle Coleman subdued the alleged rapist and demanded to know what had driven the slave to such unthinkable behavior. Lewis replied that he did not know but he reckoned he was drunk.

The court-appointed defense counsel surely faced a difficult task since the accused had been apprehended partially clad at the scene. Lewis's attorney, Alexander G. Knox, appears to have formulated a three-pronged strategy as revealed in the depositions of various witnesses. First, he challenged the women's ability to identify the accused by pointing out that the assault had taken place entirely in the dark. Upon cross-examination Baker flip-flopped a bit, at first claiming that there had been sufficient moonlight to identify the rapist but then contradicting herself somewhat by admitting that as dawn broke the light had not carried to her attacker. Despite the darkness, however, upon seeing the prisoner the next day she was confident that he had been her assailant.

The presence of an eyewitness was rare in a rape case since most rapists targeted unaccompanied females in desolate or distant locations, out of earshot of bystanders. The testimony of Mrs. Kirkland, then, must have been considered crucial in the prosecution's case. Nonetheless, discrediting Kirkland's testimony was the second prong in Knox's strategy to vindicate Lewis. At first glance, Mrs. Kirkland seems to have made a poor eyewitness to the crime since by her own admission she spent the entire assault hiding beneath a bed, presumably the very bed where the rape took place. She claimed, however, that at some point she emerged from her hiding place and "at the risque of her life" made up a light by which she was able to identify the assailant who was on top of Amy Baker. Knox, no doubt skeptical of this testimony (Baker had not mentioned Kirkland's putting on a light), then took another tack with Kirkland. He inquired about her marital and maternal status, thus insinuating her ignorance of coitus and therefore her unreliability in testifying that sexual intercourse had in fact taken place in her presence. This deft defense maneuvering placed Kirkland in an awkward position. If she admitted to having had intercourse outside of marriage, jurors would in all likelihood dismiss her testimony as unreliable due to the woman's bad character. If she denied having had intercourse, she lent weight to the defense claim that she may not have known intercourse if she saw it. Kirkland appears by her answer to have been piqued by Knox's intimation and replied rather indignantly that indeed she had neither married nor borne children but that she certainly "had seen such acts of [intercourse performed] and knows very well that the prisoner was in the act of enjoying Mrs. Baker."

The third prong of the defense strategy was to impugn the character of Amy Baker and her friend Drucilla Kirkland and, by implication, to question their veracity. One of only two witnesses who testified to Baker's dubious history was William Coleman, who claimed that he "had been to the house of Mrs. Baker for the purpose of unlawful intercourse with females and have known others to do so." Coleman reported that her neighbors were suspicious of Mrs. Baker. He did not consider her to be a "respectable woman" and would not believe her "as soon as he would a respectable woman." Alexander Pritchett, the second defense witness, did not admit to engaging in illicit sexual relations with women at the Baker house as did Coleman, but reported that on two occasions he had observed several Negro men on the premises, who were, by implication, up to no good.

The prosecution summoned five character witnesses to refute the accusations levied by Coleman and Pritchett about Baker and Kirkland. Their testimony variously described Baker as "industrious," "always correct," and of "good character." Samuel Farrar claimed never to have heard anyone speak ill of Amy Baker and discounted allegations that she consorted with black men, reasoning that had Baker "been in the habit of entertaining slaves" he would have heard about it.

Perhaps the sheer number of witnesses who testified to Amy Baker's good character provides a good reason to doubt that she "entertained" slaves—which, even if proven true, obviously does not prove that she lied about being sexually assaulted. But Knox's finding even one witness willing to admit in public to having had sexual intercourse with women at Baker's home is surprising. Given the likelihood of swift admonishment from family and community members, public acknowledgment of illicit sexual relations is astonishing. Such an admission by a white male was indeed aberrant and, in terms of evidence, was probably unnecessary; in most rape cases sufficient proof of a woman's bad character was gleaned from the hearsay testimony of people who had merely heard about the alleged victim's reputation through the neighborhood gossip network.

Quite possibly the most revealing evidence pertaining to Baker's status in the community is her own testimony. Her deposition is striking for its explicit, graphic details and bawdy language. Typically, depositions contained language that was carefully couched, especially any testimony relating to a sexual act, usually cryptically referred to as "it." Drucilla Kirkland, for instance, testified to the intruder's bellowing that he "was sent there for it and was told that there was a plenty of it there." Amy Baker's testimony defied such conventions. Her deposition reveals a complete lack of inhibition in retelling the details of the crime she alleged. She repeated verbatim what the accused had said upon entering the house. "He came for cunt and cunt he would have, that he had been told that there was a plenty of it there and he would have his satisfaction before he left." Nor did Baker choose to mince words when describing a brutal sexual assault. She testified that the prisoner penetrated her four times and during one instance he threw "her head over the bedstead and forced her legs over the prisoner's shoulders and used such violence in the penetration of the act as almost to have deprived her of her life."

Baker's choice of language in retelling her account of the assault, her decision not to mince words, suggests a conscious effort to forgo any pretense about her status in southern society. Nor did the court transcriber feel compelled to "clean up" her deposition. At the very least the evidence suggests that Baker lived on the margins of respectability in the eyes of this white community. The guilt or innocence of Lewis the slave at times seems to have taken a back seat to the contest over Amy Baker's reputation.

In the end, the court remained unswayed by allegations of Baker's past sexual improprieties and found Lewis guilty of rape. Possibly Lewis's admission that he had been drunk at the time of the alleged assault made the attack seem more plausible to the jury. Or perhaps the well-documented brutality of the assault ruled out Baker's compliance. These factors, combined with Lewis's capture at the scene, no doubt were crucial in the jury's decision to levy a guilty verdict and death sentence with no attendant recommendation for mercy. In contrast to cases cited previously in this study, this case demonstrates that not every incident of an accused black rapist led to reprieve. Considering the weight of the evidence against Lewis, however, what is surprising is not so much his conviction and subsequent hanging as the vigor with which his defense was conducted. And the typical form of an ambitious defense was an attack on the character of the white accuser.

Even white female children who claimed to have

been sexually assaulted by African American men found their lives probed for clues of past sexual indiscretion or immoral conduct. Few good things were said by anyone about the character and integrity of Rosanna Green, an eleven-year-old orphan servant girl who lived in Wythe County, Virginia, with the family of Peter Kincer. Neighbors, slaves, and of course Kincer himself, rallied in 1829 to defend Gabriel, a slave owned by Kincer, from Rosanna's charge of rape. Another Kincer slave testified to having heard reports that Green had "behaved badly with a black boy in the neighborhood." In addition, Green had a reputation for "telling stories" and "making mischief," which seriously jeopardized the credibility of her testimony. The court found Gabriel guilty, but extenuating circumstances led the court to recommend leniency.

By no means was sympathy for the slave universal. In a letter to the governor one Wythe County resident urged the executive to disregard pleas for leniency. Of Gabriel, the accused rapist, Alexander Smyth wrote: "I think it right to say, that I apprehend him a proper subject to be made an example, and that an example is required. It is not many years since a man suffered emasculation for an attempt on his mistress; and a few days since a youth received 120 lashes from his master for an attempt on a girl. This fellow seems to be 40, and is notorious as a thief." With the letter Smyth enclosed a newspaper clipping that conveyed sympathy for the orphan girl. "[H]ad her father been living, or, had she have had any natural protector, who had reaked [sic] the vengeance due to such an offence, in the blood of the perpetrator, we could never have consented to his punishment for the offence." In other words, male kin would have sought personal justice through revenge and not left the girl to be vilified in the local court. Likewise, one can infer that the author of the piece sensed class bias in the adjudication process. Had Rosanna Green not been a servant girl, the outcome might have been substantially different. In the end, Smyth's appeal went unheeded, and Gabriel was sold and transported out of Virginia.

Indeed, nonslaveholding whites at times openly displayed disgust at what some believed to be the blatant economic motives of a master's behavior in trying to exonerate his slave from the charge of rape. This is evident in the 1831 rape case of Dick, a slave belonging to Hamilton Rogers. Dick was charged with attempting to ravish Pleasant Cole, wife of Peter Cole, of Leesburg, Virginia. Mrs. Cole successfully fought off her attacker, struggling with him for about fifteen minutes before a friend, hearing her screams, frightened Dick off. Cole managed to scratch Dick's face, a fact entered as evidence by the prosecution. Cole boasted that she "kept him off by catching [Dick] by his privates."

Throughout the trial witnesses described Cole as a "woman of truth." One witness swore that he made some inquiries of her character "to do justice to the prisoner" and found everyone spoke "in the highest terms of her character." The jury found Dick guilty and ordered his execution. However, as a last resort, Dick's owner, Hamilton Rogers, and his defense counsel quickly fired off letters to the governor requesting a reduced sentence, a request made more difficult because the jury had made no recommendation for leniency. On Dick's behalf, attorney Burr W. Harrison and Hamilton Rogers, Dick's owner, cited mitigating circumstances, including Mrs. Cole's uncertainty about the identity of the perpetrator and discrepancies in the testimony of various prosecution witnesses. Harrison also cited Dick's age (which he did not state) and the fact that "no actual injury . . . [was] sustained by the object of his attempt." No mention is made of Mrs. Cole's character with the exception of a single unexplained reference to her "indiscretion." In addition to Harrison and Rogers, at least one other petitioner, who identified himself as "a member of the court who found him [Dick] guilty," concurred that mitigating circumstances, foremost being the very severe punishment, warranted mercy.

Other members of the community, probably friends of the Coles, got wind of the letter-writing campaign on Dick's behalf and put pen to their own angry grievances. The complainants accused Hamilton Rogers, Dick's master, of cronyism; he reportedly had persuaded a sheriff, a relative of his, to investigate the character of Mrs. Cole. To the delight of the petitioners the inquiry yielded only that she was a woman of "unblemished character." They were appalled at the naked self-interest of the slaveholder. Venting class discord, the petitioners pondered the future safety of the community if Dick were set free, especially for "females in the humble walks of life, who have not thrown around them the protection of wealth and influential friends," an obvious dig at Hamilton Rogers. These folks, who seem to have shared a greater identification with the "more humble walks of life" than with Rogers, observed that in this case the availability of legal protection ran along class lines. Pleasant Cole, decidedly not a member of the slaveholding class, lacked money and powerful friends but did have a good reputation and neighbors who were outraged not only at the greed of a slave-holder more interested in his pocketbook than in justice and community safety but also at the legal system's apparent favoritism to the rich. In an analysis of community, class, and crime in the Old South, Bertram Wyatt-Brown argues that non-elites chafed at the bias they observed in the judicial process. "When decisions seemed flagrantly generous toward those with powerful friends, money, and batteries of legal talent, feelings of class animosity could be aroused." No doubt aware that the case had created a political hornet's nest, which he was not eager to disturb, the governor denied Hamilton Roger's appeal, and the death sentence was allowed to stand. Dick was executed, and his owner had to settle for $400 in compensation from the state, no doubt less than the market value of the slave.

Class chafing is also observed in a letter to Virginia's governor following the 1846 trial of Anthony, a King George County slave. "Suppose for instance that she [the alleged victim] had . . . been of a rich family . . . you know he [the accused rapist] would never have gotten to gaol, but because she was poor she must suffer. . . ." The governor was unmoved by the plea and had Anthony transported out of the state.

The oft-cited 1825 North Carolina case of Jim and his alleged rape of a young white servant also reveals class divisions among southern whites. The numerous documents that this case generated permits a rare glimpse into what quite plausibly had been consensual sex between a poor white servant woman and a slave, which was tolerated until the resulting pregnancy forced the community to confront the "taboo" relationship.

Polly Lane, a white servant about eighteen years old and Jim, a slave, both worked in the home of Abraham Peppinger, an elderly man. Jim was one of several slaves owned by Peppinger. According to Polly Lane's testimony at Jim's subsequent trial, one morning in mid-August 1825 Jim overtook her, forced her to drink brandy, and then raped her several times. Because Jim had threatened her, she claimed she did not call out for help until well after dark. Another slave, Dick, after hearing the commo-

tion sneaked to where Polly and Jim were. Dick claimed that he had heard Jim implore Polly to quiet down and then heard Polly say "that if I am left in the fire I am now in I shall surely die." Dick then made himself known to the couple whereupon Polly accused Jim of assaulting her and implored Dick not to tell the Peppingers of the attack. She also confided to Dick that she was "big" and offered him a dollar to "get her something to destroy it." The inference to be made, of course, is that Polly and Jim had been having an affair, she became pregnant, then feigned the rape, perhaps realizing that the only way out of the embarrassing situation was to deny that consensual sexual relations had ever taken place with Jim. Several witnesses challenged her account, however, by testifying that they had seen Polly and Jim together intimately on numerous occasions.

Members of the jury, which convened in October and heard testimony, believed that the evidence weighed more heavily in favor of Polly Lane; they convicted Jim and set the date for his execution later that year, on December 23, despite suspicions that Polly was pregnant at the time of the trial, which she denied. As the execution date neared, Polly Lane was no longer able to conceal her pregnancy, which by this time had caused considerable excitement in the community. Had Jim, not Polly, told the truth? Had Polly been trying to conceal their relationship? Was she desperate to ward off ostracism from family and community, even at the cost of Jim's life? The white community was very divided and contentious in its response to these and other questions.

Six white male petitioners asked the governor to transport Jim out of the state or at least to grant him a reprieve until the birth of Polly Lane's child. Alexander Gray, a juror who had voted for conviction, defended the jury's guilty verdict in the face of weak evidence presented by the defense. While Gray acknowledged that "in that neighborhood a greater intimacy existed between the blacks and whites than is usual or considered decent," Jim's attorney failed to prove that Jim and Polly had an illicit sexual relationship. Though Gray continued to believe the correct verdict had been rendered, he nonetheless wanted to hedge his bets and requested the governor to postpone the execution. A second letter by Gray in March reveals an about-face; by that time Lane's advanced pregnancy had all but unravelled her tale, and Gray expressed outrage that she had knowingly perjured herself by denying consensual sex with Jim before the night of the alleged rape. "If this is the case and she knew it at the time [of the trial], no part of her testimony ought to be believed."

As the birth of Polly Lane's child approached, fewer and fewer of her supporters, such as Gray, remained in her camp. But as late as March 24 Jim's legal counsel, James Martin, feared that "many persons in the county . . . would execute this negro." Martin worried that the birth might be concealed in order to facilitate Jim's hanging. Martin's qualms appear not to have been unfounded, for when local officials attempted to serve bastardy papers on Polly Lane, she could not be located. On advice of those "anxious for the execution" of Jim she had hidden herself.

Polly Lane's mixed-race baby was born on April 7, thus strengthening Jim's claim that she was already pregnant in mid-August when she claimed to have been raped. Alexander Gray concluded his thoughts on the matter by writing the governor that the birth of Polly Lane's baby proved that "she must have knowingly and willingly sworn to a falsehood in saying . . . she was not pregnant [at the time of the trial. The] presumption naturally arises that the rest of it [her testimony] ought not be entitled to credit." Even in the face of strong material evidence, however, some members of the white community stubbornly refused to desert Polly Lane, choosing instead a different tack in arguing for Jim's execution. Doggedly denying that Polly Lane's baby was mulatto, John Smith denounced Jim's character as "one of the worst in my memory." Another letter writer reported that some residents of the county "are anxious for his execution not because they believe the conviction rightful but on account of general bad character." In other words, Jim's execution need not be sanctioned by Polly Lane's claim of sexual assault, which had been proved to be baseless. Jim was a troublemaker pure and simple, reason enough in and of itself to kill him. However, the governor's sympathies clearly rested with those who argued for Jim's release. Instead of being hanged, Jim was transported out of North Carolina.

Whether or not this protracted and bitter dispute among the white residents of Davidson County, North Carolina, was primarily caused by class prejudices is not certain. However, it is clear, because she was employed as a domestic servant, that Polly Lane was from a poor family. The Lane family's claim to honor is evidenced by its defiant attempt to shield Polly from probing community members bent on ascertaining the truth about very private and intimate matters. It is also conceivable that the Lanes saw themselves challenged by a propertied slaveholder, Abraham Peppinger, whose financial stake in saving Jim's life necessarily required that he challenge the integrity of their daughter and hence of the Lane family. Peppinger was wealthy enough to hire two of North Carolina's finest barristers, James Martin and John Motley Morehead, the latter of whom served two terms as governor in the 1840s. These two lawyers had developed a greater stake in procuring Jim's pardon because Abraham Peppinger promised to turn Jim over to the two should their efforts prove successful.

Ties of kinship and friendship, inextricably linked to class, also probably shaped the principals' sympathies and their responses to the unfolding events. John Smith, characterized by Bertram Wyatt-Brown as a "semiliterate member of the clan to which Polly Lane belonged," refused to sign a bastardy warrant against Polly Lane, yet magistrate Jesse Hargrave, himself the owner of twenty-eight slaves, did. Other motives vied for attention as well: humanitarianism (Peppinger's attachment to Jim; community members unwilling to see an innocent man, black or white, go to the gallows); financial interests (Peppinger's financial loss if Jim were executed; Jim's attorneys' prospect of acquiring Jim if his life were spared); and perceptions about gender and sexuality (proof of Polly Lane's compliance negated her claims of sexual assault).

As sectional tensions worsened and the political debate over slavery heated up in the years preceding the outbreak of war, one might expect to find a concomitant increase in anxiety about black sexual assault, especially since abolitionists had brought the issue of sexual assault of slave women to the forefront, making it a highly charged subject. By looking at the trends in transportation of convicted slaves out of the state during this time, one can indirectly gauge the pulse of the white community for any fears of black rapists. Governors were in no position to antagonize large pools of voters by pardoning or commuting sentences of convicted African American rapists if concerns over the "black-beast-rapist" were rampant.

In fact, transportation patterns by Virginia executives reveal that, as the Civil War approached, a convicted black sex offender was far more likely to be transported than hanged. Execution was the punishment of choice for slaves convicted of rape or attempted rape in the early part of the century. But as the Civil War approached and tensions heightened, state officials spared the lives of convicted slave rapists in a majority of cases.

The pattern, at least for antebellum Virginia, then, is one of greater leniency as the nineteenth century progressed. The irony here is that although the statutes for rape by black men of white women became harsher, implementation of the harsher penalties did not automatically follow. One can only speculate about the reasons. Perhaps as state executives became more concerned with fiscal savings, they increasingly utilized transportation of slave criminals, an option that allowed them to recover at least some of the compensation costs paid to the slaves' owners. The defensive posture struck by southerners in response to abolitionism may offer another explanation for the tendency to spare the lives of convicted black rapists. By showcasing their humanitarianism, elected officials may have hoped to demonstrate the benevolence and justice of slavery.

Whatever the motivation, the trend documented here appears to have been part of a larger tendency among authorities in Virginia to administer slave justice, even in these most serious cases, without resorting to capital punishment. Philip Schwarz's comprehensive account of slave crime in Virginia reflects similar patterns from the eighteenth century to the mid-nineteenth century. For example, the statistics he marshals on slaves executed or transported for murder from 1785 through 1829 also show a greater utilization of transportation as the decades wore on. Of the twenty-three Virginia slaves who were convicted of murder from 1785 through 1794, all twenty-three were executed. But from 1820 through 1829, a period in which eighty-three slaves were condemned to die for murder, sixty-one (73 percent) were actually hanged while twenty-two (27 percent) were transported out of Virginia. Similarly, Schwarz documents less reliance on execution of slaves convicted of conspiracy and insurrection. Of eleven slaves convicted for this crime from 1790 through 1799, one received corporal punishment and ten were executed. However, during the period 1830 through 1834, a time when the Nat Turner revolt had deeply aroused the Virginia countryside, eighty-nine slaves were tried for insurrection, of whom only

forty-five were convicted. Of these, one was pardoned, twenty-one transported, and twenty-three, or just about half, were executed. The trend toward saving convicted slave rapists from the gallows, then, appears to have been part of a larger tendency toward sparing the lives of all convicted slave criminals. Furthermore, there does not seem to have been any special onus attached to slave rapists that mandated special, harsher punishment.

If one accepts for the moment that the financial self-interest of the state, as well as that of the individual slaveholders, was the chief motive in sparing these slaves' lives, what then could have been the motivation for some whites in siding with free African American men accused of raping white women or girls? Official records yield two cases of attempted rape of young white girls by free black men in Virginia in 1833 only two years after the Nat Turner rebellion. Caleb Watts, a free black, met eleven-year-old Jane Barber one summer day at the local mill, and Watts offered to carry the girl's ground corn at least as far toward her home as he was going. At the place where the two were to part, according to Barber, the assault took place. By his own admission, Watts demanded some sort of compensation for his good deed. Barber replied that she was but a poor girl who had nothing to give but herself. "Give me yourself, then" Watts was said to have demanded. Barber cried out and apparently Watts choked the girl and wielded a knife in order to quiet her during the assault. Watts was indicted and tried for assault upon Jane Barber, and the jury found him guilty. Defense counsel then appealed the conviction on the inventive grounds that the victim was, at the time of the assault, under the age of twelve and thus had not yet attained puberty; therefore, Jane Barber was not a woman under the strict statutory definition of a woman. How then could Watts be guilty of raping a woman, reasoned his appeal. The Virginia high court found no merit in this argument and ordered that the death sentence be passed upon the prisoner.

As a last resort, Watts's attorney Edward Wood launched a feverish correspondence with the governor of Virginia. Wood wrote two letters himself and penned a preachy but emotional petition ostensibly signed by "almost every man of respectability" including one jury member. Although the sexual morality of the girl was never challenged directly, Wood did claim that she and her mother were of the "lowest order in society" and questioned the credibility of "a girl who has been raised with an aunt who has given birth to several bastard children."

The attorney for the Commonwealth, W. Thurman, who prosecuted the case in county court, also wrote to the governor claiming that he himself harbored doubts about the alleged victim and cited discrepancies in the testimony of some witnesses whom Thurman claimed possessed "prejudice against the defendant, and eagerness for his condemnation." He questioned the ability of the jury to have arrived at a fair and impartial decision given the "strong popular prejudice and excitement against the prisoner" that prevailed in the community. Although the light-skinned Caleb Watts did not have the unanimous support of the white community, he did seem to have the sympathy of several members of the local elite. Whether or not their patronage was sufficient to win a reprieve for Watts is not known, as no documentation of his ultimate fate has been found. Nonetheless, the case demonstrates that the white community was far from unified. Clearly, the alleged crime excited the community, and some citizens no doubt wished to see Watts hang. Still others, apparently not motivated by economic self-interest as a slaveholder might be, displayed great empathy for the free black man and his predicament, a man who "had borne a character of singular respectability for one of his own caste." Presumably his boosters were quite willing to sacrifice the reputation of an eleven-year-old white girl to save Caleb Watts's life.

Free black Tasco Thompson, a blacksmith from Frederick County, Virginia, was also found guilty in 1833 of the attempted rape of an eleven-year-old white girl, Mary Jane Stevens. However, the defense had presented mitigating circumstances that persuaded the jury foreman to recommend leniency. He cited

> the exceedingly disreputable character of the family of the said Stevens. . . . It was notorious that the mother had long entertained negroes, and that all her associations, with one or two exceptions were with blacks. . . . In a word she was below the level of the ordinary grade of free negroes. . . . There is no doubt that he [Thompson] repaired to the house of Mrs. Stevens in the belief that she would cheerfully submit to his embraces, as she doubtless had often done before, but finding her absent he probably supposed his embraces would be equally agreeable to her daughter. . . .

The sins of the mother are the sins of the daughter. Furthermore, the foreman argued, had Mrs. Stevens

been colored there would have been no case. The Stevenses "yielded their claims to the protection of the law by their voluntary associations with those whom the law distinguishes as their inferiors." In short, Mrs. Stevens acted "colored" and therefore should be treated as "colored." In the eyes of the foreman of the jury, because of her liaisons with black men, Mrs. Stevens had forfeited the privilege that her white skin might have accorded her, not only for herself but also for her daughter.

As these and numerous other cases demonstrate, judicial vindication for white females who claimed to be victims of sexual assault at the hands of black men in the Old South was neither axiomatic nor unconditional. White women who claimed to have been sexually violated by African American men sometimes actively sought redress from the courts. They may or may not have received it. A court or community's decision to extend support hinged on any number of factors, not the least of which was a white woman's compliance with socially acceptable behavior. Deviant conduct severely undercut a white woman's demand for protection in the Old South. Those white females, or their network of female kin, who failed to obey the established code of race and gender conventions may have found their road to protection strewn with obstacles. Race, then, was far from being the sole determining factor in the outcome of these cases.

As far as can be determined, most of the females claiming to have been sexually assaulted by African American males were not members of the planter class. The records reveal very few instances in which elite women and girls charged rape by a slave or free black man. If female members of the slaveholding class did levy accusations of rape or attempted rape against black men, mob action or plantation justice may have supplanted official authority in an endeavor to spare the women or girls the notoriety of a public trial. Such action, however, would run counter to slave owners' financial interest since masters did not receive compensation for the loss of slaves at the hands of de facto plantation executioners or lynching parties. In cases involving female family members, however, revenge and pride could well have overridden the concern for financial compensation.

Most complainants were poor white women or girls. They frequently lacked a male protector, either father or husband. Some were described by the courts as "weak-minded" or "idiots." Free black men and slaves seem to have assaulted poor white women and sometimes even to have gotten away with it, which indicates how marginal these women were to antebellum southern society. As Victoria Bynum has observed, poverty defeminized and thus further marginalized white women in the Old South. In strictly economic terms, poor white women in southern slave society were less valuable to elites than slaves were. And since slavery defined the status of most southern blacks, white racial solidarity across class lines was not necessary in the antebellum period; it became critical after emancipation, when African Americans, whose place in society was in constant flux, assumed unprecedented political positions and posed a threat to white elites.

Whites in the Old South appear not to have been so blinded by fear and anxiety of black male sexual assault as to deny the accused procedural rights. In confrontations between two marginalized groups in the South, poor white females and African American males, race proved not to be the sole factor shaping the outcome of the responses of white observers. Instead, any of a myriad of motives could have prevailed in the development and denouements of these violent sexual dramas. Masters motivated by economic self-interest repeatedly utilized the judicial system in last-ditch efforts to keep their valuable property from the gallows. In cases such as these, the slave's status as chattel worked effectively to save his life. By protecting their property, however, slaveholders turned their backs on women who shared their race but not their class.

More perplexing, perhaps, are the circumstances of free blacks who represented no such financial interest. Even so, community members, courts, and elected officials at times intervened to save the life of a convicted free black rapist. Motives here are less apparent but could include any combination of humanitarianism, personalism, misogyny, class prejudice, personal grievance, and fear of job competition.

The common denominator in sexual assault cases of both slave and free defendants, however, seems to be that white elites were animated by notions of class and gender that permitted them to hold poor white women and girls in such low regard that they would ally with African American men against the white female accusers. This does not mean that every black man charged with raping a white female could with certainty expect reprieve or pardon. In this context, it is instructive to answer the question, Under what circumstances would whites ever ally with an accused black rapist? And more important, What do such cases reveal about the nature of race and class relations in the Old South? Recently, Nell Irvin Painter issued a challenge to historians of the South to go "beyond lazy characterizations in the singular" and to recognize "the complex and contradictory nature of southern society." "Though southern history must take race very seriously," Painter continued, "southern history must not stop with race." If Professor Painter will permit the addendum, nor must southern historians use race as their starting point, a long-standing practice that has tended to mute the inherent contradictions of antebellum southern society. Was there far greater fluidity in race relations—and less in class relations—than historians heretofore have been willing to recognize? The recent scholarship of Martha Hodes and Victoria Bynum suggests as much. Peculiar cross-racial alliances such as the ones played out in these rape cases underscore the complex web of contested loyalties confronting antebellum southerners. Appreciation of fissures in the mind of white southerners along the fault lines of gender, race, and class may lead to a more complete understanding of how various groups within southern society configured in relation to each other. Simply stated, race represented only one of a number of competing interests and frequently gave way to those other interests, often at the expense of racial allegiances. . . .

Myths of Reconstruction

Eric Foner

Generations of American college students, at least those schooled prior to the 1960s, were rather comfortably conveyed the impression that Reconstruction had been an era of black rule (the "Africanization" of southern politics), resultant corruption, political subordination of southern whites, military despotism, and radical congressional control of Reconstruction policy. Offering a summary of new research findings, Columbia University professor Eric Foner demonstrates how almost every previous assumption regarding Reconstruction has been overturned. Black supremacy was a myth, the era was far more conservative than radical, and southern whites were not categorically disfranchised. Recent scholarship has formulated a new program of Reconstruction study, emphasizing social rather than political issues, noting the continuing relevance of Reconstruction issues to American society, and, most importantly, conceding the role of blacks as active agents in the profound changes of the time. The political, the economic, and particularly the humanitarian goals of Reconstruction of course failed of achievement. They necessarily remain a critical part of the nation's unfinished business.

No period in American history has undergone a more complete reevaluation since 1960 than Reconstruction. As with slavery, scholars began by dismantling a long-dominant one-dimensional view and then proceeded to create new and increasingly sophisticated interpretations. According to the portrait that originated with nineteenth-century opponents of black suffrage and achieved scholarly legitimacy early in this century, the turbulent years after the Civil War were a period of unrelieved sordidness in political and social life. Sabotaging Andrew Johnson's attempt to readmit the southern states to full participation in the Union immediately, Radical Republicans fastened black supremacy upon the defeated Confederacy. An orgy of corruption and misgovernment followed, presided over by unscrupulous carpetbaggers (northerners who ventured South to reap the spoils of office), scalawags (southern whites who cooperated with the new govern-

ments for personal gain), and ignorant and childlike freedmen who were incapable of responsibly exercising the political power that had been thrust upon them. After much needless suffering, the South's white communities banded together to overthrow these "black" governments and restore "home rule" (their euphemism for white supremacy).

Resting on the assumption that black suffrage was the gravest error of the entire Civil War period, this traditional interpretation survived for decades because it accorded with firmly entrenched American political and social realities—the disfranchisement and segregation of blacks, and the solid Democratic South. But the "Second Reconstruction"—the civil rights movement—inspired a new conception of the first among historians, and as with the study of slavery, a revisionist wave broke over the field in the 1960s. In rapid succession virtually every assumption of the old viewpoint was dismantled. Andrew Johnson, yesterday's high-minded defender of constitutional principles, was revealed as a racist politician too stubborn to compromise with his critics. By creating an impasse with Congress that Lincoln surely would have avoided, Johnson effectively destroyed his own presidency. Radical Republicans, acquitted of vindictive motives, emerged as idealists in the best nineteenth-century reform tradition. Their leaders, Charles Sumner and Thaddeus Stevens, had worked for black rights long before any conceivable political benefit could have flowed from such a commitment. Their Reconstruction policies were based on principle, not mere political advantage or personal gain. And rather than being the concern of a small band of extremists, the commitment to protecting the civil rights of the freedmen—the central issue dividing Congress and the president—enjoyed broad support within the Republican party.

At the same time, the period of "Black Reconstruction" after 1867 was portrayed as a time of extraordinary progress in the South. The rebuilding of war-shattered public institutions, the establishment of the region's first public school systems, the effort to construct an interracial political democracy on the ashes of slavery—all these were commendable achievements, not elements of the "tragic era" described by earlier historians.

The villains and heroes of the traditional morality play came in for revised treatment. Former slaves did enjoy a real measure of political power, but "black supremacy" never existed: outside of South Carolina blacks held only a small fraction of Reconstruction offices. Rather than unscrupulous adventurers, most carpetbaggers were former Union soldiers seeking economic opportunity in the postwar South. The scalawags were an amalgam of "Old Line" Whigs who had opposed secession in the first place and poorer whites who had long resented the planters' domination of the region's life and saw in Reconstruction a chance to recast southern society along more democratic lines. As for corruption, the malfeasance of Reconstruction governments was dwarfed by contemporary scandals in the North (this was the era of Boss Tweed, Crédit Mobilier, and the Whiskey Ring) and could hardly be blamed on the former slaves. Finally, the Ku Klux Klan, whose campaign of violence against black and white Republicans had been minimized or excused by earlier historians, was revealed as a terrorist organization

that beat and killed its political opponents to deprive blacks of their newly won rights.

By the end of the 1960s the old interpretation had been completely reversed. Most historians agreed that if Reconstruction was a "tragic" era, it was so because change did not go far enough; it fell short especially in the failure to distribute land to the former slaves and thereby provide an economic base for their newly acquired political rights. Indeed, by the 1970s this stress on the "conservative" character of Radical Reconstruction was a prevailing theme of many studies. The Civil War did not signal the eclipse of the old planter class and the coming to power of a new entrepreneurial elite, for example. Social histories of communities scattered across the South demonstrated that planters survived the war with their landholdings and social prestige more or less intact.

The denial of substantive change, however, failed to provide a compelling interpretation of an era whose participants believed themselves living through a social and political revolution. And the most recent work on Reconstruction, while fully cognizant of what was not accomplished, has tended to view the period as one of broad changes in southern and national life. In the first modern, comprehensive account of the period, Eric Foner portrays Reconstruction as part of a prolonged struggle over the new system of labor, racial, and political relations that would replace the South's peculiar institution. As in the study of slavery, moreover, some scholars of Reconstruction have sought to place this country's adjustment to emancipation in the broad context of international patterns of development, and to delineate what was and was not unique to the United States, but Reconstruction was; it stands as a dramatic experiment, the only instance in which blacks, within a few years of freedom, achieved universal manhood suffrage and exercised a real measure of political power.

Like recent studies of slavery and the Civil War, current writing on Reconstruction is informed by a recognition of the extent to which blacks themselves helped shape the contours of change. In a kaleidoscopic evocation of black response to the end of slavery, Leon Litwack has shown that freedmen sought to obtain the greatest possible autonomy in every area of their day-to-day lives. Institutions that had existed under slavery, such as the church and family, were strengthened, and new ones sprang into existence. The freedmen made remarkable efforts to locate loved ones from whom they had been separated under slavery. Many black women, preferring to devote more time to their families, refused to work any longer in the fields, thus contributing to the postwar "labor shortage." Continuing resistance to planters' efforts to tie black children to long periods of involuntary labor through court-ordered "apprenticeships" revealed that control over family life was a major preoccupation of the freedmen. Blacks withdrew almost entirely from white-controlled churches, establishing independent religious institutions of their own; and a diverse panoply of fraternal, benevolent, and mutual aid societies also sprang into existence. And though aided by northern reform societies and the federal government, the freedmen often took the initiative in establishing schools. Nor was black suffrage thrust upon an indifferent black population, for in 1865 and 1866 black conventions gathered throughout the South to demand civil equality and the right to vote.

As in every society that abolished slavery, emancipation was followed by a comprehensive struggle over the shaping of a new labor system to replace it. The conflict between former masters aiming to recreate a disciplined labor force and blacks seeking to carve out the greatest degree of economic autonomy profoundly affected economics, politics, and race relations in the Reconstruction South. Planters were convinced that their own survival and the region's prosperity depended upon their ability to resume production using disciplined gang labor, as under slavery. To this end, the governments established by President Johnson in 1865 established a comprehensive system of vagrancy laws, criminal penalties for breach of contract, and other measures known collectively as the "Black Codes" and designed to force the freedmen back to work on the plantations. As Dan T. Carter shows in a study of Presidential Reconstruction, the inability of the leaders of the white South's "self-Reconstruction" to accept the implications of emancipation aroused resentment in the North, fatally weakened support for the president's policies, and made Radical Reconstruction inevitable.

Out of the conflict on the plantations, new systems of labor emerged in the different regions of the South. Sharecropping came to dominate the cotton South. In this compromise between the blacks' desire for land and the planters' for labor discipline, each black family worked its own plot of land, dividing the crop with the landlord at the end of the year. In the rice-growing areas, with planters unable to attract the outside capital needed to repair wartime destruction and blacks clinging tenaciously to land they had occupied in 1865, the great plantations fell to pieces, and blacks were able to acquire title to small plots and take up self-sufficient farming. And in the sugar region, gang labor survived the end of slavery. In all cases, blacks' economic opportunities were limited by whites' control of credit and by the vagaries of a world market in which the price of agricultural goods suffered a prolonged decline. Nevertheless, the degree to which planters could control the day-to-day lives of their labor force was radically altered by the end of slavery.

The sweeping social changes that followed the Civil War were also reflected in the history of the white yeomanry. Wartime devastation set in motion a train of events that permanently altered these farmers' self-sufficient way of life. Plunged into poverty by the war, ravaged by war casualties, they saw their plight exacerbated by successive crop failures in the early Reconstruction years. In the face of this economic disaster, yeomen clung tenaciously to their farms. But needing to borrow money for the seed, implements, and livestock required to resume farming, many became mired in debt and were forced to abandon self-sufficient farming for the growing of cotton. A region in which a majority of white farmers had once owned their own land was increasingly trapped in a cycle of tenancy and cotton overproduction and became unable to feed itself.

The South's postwar economic transformation profoundly affected the course of Reconstruction politics. As the Black Codes illustrated, state governments could play a vital role in defining the property rights and restricting the bargaining power of planters and laborers. Not surprisingly, when Republicans came to power—largely on the basis of the black vote—they swept away measures designed to bolster plantation discipline and sought to enhance the status of sharecroppers by giving them a first claim on the growing crop. They also launched an ambitious program of aid to railroads, hoping to transform the region into a diversified, modernizing society with enhanced opportunities for white and black alike. But as Mark Summers has shown in an investigation of the program, railroad aid not only failed to achieve its economic aims but produced a sharp increase in taxes, thus exacerbating the economic plight of the yeomanry (attracted in some measure to Reconstruction in its early days by the promise of debtor relief) and preventing the Republican party from broadening its base of white support. Railroad aid also generated most of the corruption that undermined the legitimacy of the Reconstruction governments in the eyes of southern opponents and northern allies alike.

To blacks, however, Reconstruction represented the first time they had ever had a voice in public affairs, and the first time southern governments had even attempted to serve their interests. Recent studies of black politics have stressed both the ways black leaders tried to serve the needs of their constituents and the obstacles that impeded them from doing so effectively. The signal contribution of this new literature has been to reject the idea that Reconstruction politics was simply a matter of black and white. In a broad reevaluation of South Carolina politics, Thomas Holt has argued that many statewide leaders derived from the old Charleston free elite, whose conservative economic outlook rendered them unresponsive to the freedmen's desire for land; studies of Louisiana politics have reached similar conclusions. Free blacks, at the cutting edge of demands for civil and political equality during the Civil War and Reconstruction, failed to find ways of combatting the freedmen's economic plight.

At the local level, however, most black officeholders were former slaves. Although the arduous task of analyzing the local politics of Reconstruction has barely begun, it appears that men who had achieved some special status as slaves—such as ministers and artisans—formed the bulk of black officials. Their ranks were augmented by the little-studied "black carpetbaggers," who looked to the Reconstruction South for opportunities denied them in the North. The presence of sympathetic local officials often made a real difference in the day-to-day lives of the freedmen, ensuring that those accused of crimes would be tried before juries of their peers, and enforcing fairness in such prosaic aspects of local government as road repair, tax assessment, and poor relief. All in all, southern Reconstruction represented a remarkable moment in which the old white elite was stripped of its accustomed political power. It is hardly surprising that its opponents responded not only with criticism but with widespread violence, or that local Republican officials were often the first victims of the Klan and kindred groups.

Recent scholars, indeed, have not only emphasized the role of pervasive violence in the eventual overthrow of Reconstruction but have shown how the problem of law enforcement exposed growing resistance to the expanded federal powers generated by the Civil War. In the war's immediate aftermath Republicans altered the nature of federal–state relations, defining for the first time—in the Civil Rights Law of 1866 and the Fourteenth Amendment—a national citizenship and a national principle of equality before the law, and investing the federal government with the authority to enforce the civil rights of citizens against violations by the states. Then the Fifteenth Amendment prohibited states from infringing upon the right of suffrage for racial reasons, and the Enforcement Acts of 1870–71 gave the federal government the power to protect the civil and political rights of the former slaves against acts of violence.

These were profound changes in a federal system in which the states had traditionally determined and protected the rights of citizens. Yet Reconstruction failed to establish effective means for securing its lofty precepts. The burden of enforcing the new concept of equality before the law was placed upon the federal courts, and it was unrealistic to assume that the courts—even when supplemented on occasion by federal marshals and the army—could bear the major burden of putting down violence in the South. By the 1870s, moreover, many Republicans were retreating from both the racial egalitarianism and the broad definition of federal power spawned by the Civil War. As localism, laissez-faire, and racism—persistent themes of nineteenth-century American history—reasserted themselves, the federal government progressively abandoned efforts to enforce civil rights in the South.

Thus, a complex dialectic of continuity and change affected the ways Americans, black and white, responded to the nation's most profound period of crisis. By the end of the period, slavery was dead, the Union preserved, and both North and South transformed. The social structure populated by masters, slaves, and self-sufficient yeomen was evolving into a world of landlords, merchants, and sharecroppers, both black and white. Also fading into the past was Lincoln's America—a world dominated by the small shop and family farm—as a rapidly industrializing economy took hold in the North. Yet the aspiration galvanized by the Civil War for a society purged of racial injustice had yet to be fulfilled. The end of Reconstruction thrust former slaves into a no-man's-land between slavery and freedom that made a mockery of the ideal of equal citizenship. Scholars, indeed, have yet to assess fully the significance of Reconstruction's failure. That it was a catastrophe for black America is clear, but it also affected the entire structure of American politics, creating a solid Democratic South whose representatives increasingly aligned with northern conservatives to oppose every effort at social change.

It is hardly likely that recent writing represents the final word on slavery, the Civil War, or Reconstruction, for that era raised the decisive questions of America's national existence: the relations between local and national authority, the definition of citizenship, the meaning of equality and freedom. As long as these issues remain central to American life, scholars are certain to return to the Civil War period, bringing to bear the constantly evolving methods and concerns of the study of history.